Divide and Rule

Divide and Rule

Royal Women and Their Battles

Catherine Mayer

ONE PLACE. MANY STORIES

HQ
An imprint of HarperCollins*Publishers* Ltd
1 London Bridge Street
London SE1 9GF

www.harpercollins.co.uk

HarperCollins*Publishers*
Macken House, 39/40 Mayor Street Upper,
Dublin 1, D01 C9W8, Ireland

This edition 2026

1

First published in Great Britain by HQ,
an imprint of HarperCollins*Publishers* Ltd 2026

HB ISBN: 978-0-00-873017-8
TPB ISBN: 978-0-00-876909-3

This book is set in 10.3/15 pt. Meridien by Type-it AS, Norway

Printed and bound in the UK using 100% Renewable Electricity by CPI Group (UK) Ltd

For Andy, the king of my heart, and all my lovely dead. You know who you are.

Contents

About Names and
Biographical Games

There are many breaches of protocol within these pages. I rarely refer to royal women by their titles – which are liable to change through marriage or movement in the line of succession, sometimes along with either or both given or married names. To spare readers' confusion, I have opted to use the Christian names under which these women are most widely recognised.

The former Kate Middleton, for example, answered to Catherine as a child and has done so again since becoming Her Royal Highness the Princess of Wales, after more than a decade as HRH the Duchess of Cambridge. In this book, she mostly appears as Kate, an editorial decision made in an effort to distinguish her from a cornucopia of earlier Catherines in royal history, not all of whom maintained a consistent spelling from one signature to the next.

References to Queen Elizabeth can also be confusing, with two in the twentieth century alone. When Edward VIII abdicated, he became the Duke of Windsor. This elevated his brother and sister-in-law, formerly the Duke and Duchess of York, to King George VI and Queen Elizabeth. Once widowed, Elizabeth acquired a different label: Queen Mother. Many people still understand the phrase 'the queen' to apply to her daughter, Queen Elizabeth II. The numbering refers only to the Elizabeths who were so-called queens regnant – reigning queens – and the headcount is controversial in Scotland. Elizabeth Windsor, the second English queen regnant with that forename, was the first to preside over both countries, because Elizabeth Tudor predated the union of the thrones. In total, thanks to male primogeniture and the aversion to female leadership that underpinned it, there have been just eight English queens regnant, if we count the medieval monarch, Matilda, who was never crowned, and Lady Jane Grey, whose queenship lasted mere days and ended with her decapitation.

The woman in current possession of the title is not a queen regnant but a consort. She started life as Camilla Shand, came to prominence under her first married name, Camilla Parker Bowles, and on her second marriage, exchanged her double-barrel for a grander designation, HRH the Duchess of Cornwall. Though her new husband was the Prince of Wales, she never assumed the counterpart handle. Princess. Of. Wales. POW. The three words glowed with a dangerous energy, as likely to burn the wearer as burnish her; the property, even in death, of Camilla's predecessor, Diana. It fell to Kate to take on the mantle, the tenth woman to do so.

When (and if) William accedes, Kate is expected to be named queen consort and, like Camilla, to be known by the first of those words alone. Kings blithely raise their wives to queenship, whereas married queens regnant, perceiving the danger that their husbands might be seen as the real sovereigns, have tended to confer on them a lesser status than kingship. Most ranks open to royal women vibrate with the odd combination of disempowerment and privilege that is so often their lot. 'Princess' conjures up a delicate creature, while a duchess might be assumed, alliteratively and otherwise, to be difficult. I use a compound noun in this book for the specific form of patriarchy these women find themselves navigating: patrimonarchy.

Royals typically adopt their titles as surnames, but they also have family names. The current royal house rebranded during the First World War, when the family exchanged their embarrassingly Germanic trinity of Saxe-Coburg-Gotha for Windsor. A few days earlier, their Battenberg cousins had quietly translated themselves to Mountbattens. The marriage of the future Elizabeth II to Philip, a former prince of Greece and Denmark, combined these inventions into an ineffably British marque, Mountbatten-Windsor. Deleted from his dukedom and no longer a prince, their son, Andrew, now trails his hyphenated heredity behind a plain 'mister'.

For royalty, rank and respect go hand in hand. In the Netflix series, *With Love, Meghan*, the show's eponymous host objects to a friend calling her 'Meghan Markle'. 'It's Sussex now,' she says, quite correctly. It is not my intention in dispensing with honorifics to insult her or any other subjects of this book, or to imply a familiarity where there is none. While I have met a number of recent or current royals and have even progressed to first-name terms with a few of them, I would never mistake their weary acceptance of me hanging around in the course of research for the stirrings of friendship.

This might seem an obvious point, but it is also an important one. Royals rarely speak for themselves, instead tapping up proxies – confidantes, aides, reporters – to get their messages out. Some members of the royal press pack owe serial 'scoops' to this practice, in turn encouraging pundits to protect communication lines by showing partiality towards their sources, or even seeking to fight their battles for them. I remember participating in a BBC discussion programme after Harry published his memoir, *Spare*. 'I can't forgive him,' whinged another guest, the author of a brace of royal biographies. My exasperation trumped courtesy. 'It isn't your business to forgive him,' I shot back. 'You're supposed to be a *journalist*.'

Nobody is impartial, and one aim of this book is to examine the strains that mould and remould history, including the biases of historians and reporters. I am certainly not exempt. *Divide and Rule* offers a feminist analysis, and, as far as possible, transparency on this point and on sources. It is not always possible to name the people who spoke to me, but where I had concerns about what I was being told, or why, I have questioned those perspectives and balanced them with other testimonies.

My research has been informed not only by primary sources but a vast array and range of published material, historical and modern: books, academic papers, documents, articles, blogs, broadcast material, dramatisations and podcasts. The first draft of *Divide and Rule* staggered under the weight of nearly 700 endnotes. For ease of reading, I have pruned these to a minimum, instead indicating sources in the text except in instances such as academic studies involving multiple authorship or where a reference needed more detail than could easily be incorporated in brief. The bibliography lists books and other works cited in the text, loosely grouped by subject matter. I urge you to explore it. You may well find, as I did, that the more you read about these women and their times, the more you want to read.

Introduction

Choosing Not to Choose

Buckingham Palace stands gloomy against a black sky, just a few lights on and the flagpole bare. Outside its gates, we assemble quietly, not yet in numbers that constitute a crowd, though that is about to change. A little over an hour ago, a colleague woke me with news of a car crash in Paris and a princess badly injured. Across London, people are making their way to the places they associate with her. A hotel worker tells me she abandoned her night shift to be here. 'Where there's life, there's hope,' she murmurs. Within minutes, hope gutters and dies, confirmation of Diana's fate passing from one stranger to the next, shock giving way to grief and rage. The hotel worker points at the palace, her voice now clarion: 'They killed her.'

Over the following days, this accusation will gain currency, but few mean it literally. Anger centres on perceptions that the royal family hung Diana out to dry. Certainly, the Windsors contributed to Diana's vulnerability, but in researching this book, I finally grasped the nature of the most significant forces that placed her in the back of a speeding limousine. These were not the scenarios imagined by conspiracy theorists, but rather the reflexes of patriarchal systems, including the patrimonarchy, to defend their power structures and hierarchies.

Back in 1997, I remained dry-eyed. Now I wept for Diana and the damage such forces continue to inflict.

I also questioned the easy consensus that her death had posed an existential threat to the monarchy. No doubt the Windsors themselves believed that, but as crises go, this one went. Within less than a decade, Queen Elizabeth's missteps had been reframed as a sign of her authenticity, while Charles and Camilla charted their own course to redemption. Royal reporting returned to business as usual too, training its sights on individuals and only rarely scrutinising the institution. Yet everything about this strange hybrid of humans and machine should have held our attention: its longevity, its global reach, the good works and dubious dealings and scandals that left it mysteriously unscathed. As trust in most areas of public life plummeted, the monarchy defied gravity. By the final decade of Elizabeth's reign, her legacy appeared assured, the future of the Crown and her family secured. The younger cohort shone with promise, incomers Kate and Meghan hailed as superstars capable of revitalising the Windsor brand. Sentiment towards the royals reached new peaks of positivity.

Then, with astonishing speed, things fell apart.

As I write, the institution faces challenges more profound than anything the abdication or the 1990s served up, with royal ranks fractured and depleted, a former prince enmeshed in scandal, and the taint spreading. Support for the monarchy is dwindling even in the UK, particularly among the young and populations of colour, while overseas realms are heading for the exit. *Divide and Rule* takes a long view of how the monarchy reached this inflection point; the decisive roles women played in this history – and their critical importance to the institution's survival.

This last might seem counterintuitive, not least because of the current line of succession. Barring upsets, Charles will be succeeded by William, and William by his eldest child, George. Moreover, royal women are typically assumed to create crises rather than resolving them. In the last century alone, Wallis Simpson, Princess Margaret, Diana, Camilla and Meghan all stood accused of endangering the Crown for reasons connected to being female: their messy emotions and their ability to turn sober male heads with sexual wiles. As for women in general, you could be forgiven for assuming the vast majority of us do nothing noteworthy at all. According to historian Bettany Hughes, a mere 0.5 per cent of three and a half thousand years of recorded history bothers to chart the actions, achievements or even the existence of 51 per cent of the population.

Ruling women and their royal sisters are the exceptions to the rule, pinioned in the public gaze, misrepresented rather than ignored. Since the move to a constitutional monarchy, they have been routinely dismissed as inconsequential, yet make no mistake – their misfortune is yours too. Their prominence endows them with extraordinary influence, if not equivalent agency. Always scrutinised and forever judged, it is when they attempt to define themselves that things get really interesting. 'She won't go quietly. That's the problem,' declared Diana in her controversial BBC *Panorama* interview. Nor did she. More often princesses are damned as strumpets and schemers, or reduced to 'jointed doll(s) on which certain rags are hung', as *Wolf Hall* author, Hilary Mantel, described the phenomenon in her essay 'Royal Bodies'. Such caricatures not only affect them, often cruelly, but infect wider attitudes. Ideas are like air. We rarely notice that we are inhaling them, much less wonder where they came from, whom they benefit or whether the fumes might prove toxic. The ways in which royal women are instrumentalised and abused would have been prompt enough to write this book, but there is more.

Royalists and republicans alike routinely underestimate the continuing heft of the monarchy and the tremors its collapse could create. The following chapters will question this notion by demonstrating the far-reaching impact of royal women, past and present. *Divide and Rule* focuses on eight such women – Anne Boleyn, Elizabeth I, Victoria, Elizabeth II, Diana, Camilla, Kate and Meghan – each selected because of the yawning gulfs between the dominant views of them and the realities of who they really were or are; what their lives reveal of the mechanisms that seek to contain women, and for their stories, inspiring, enraging and moving by turn.

*

There is something else you will notice too: a series of eerie echoes.

Consider this member of the octet. A commoner raised to royalty, she has been the subject of duelling biographies, a heroine to some, a hate figure to others. Her adherents trumpeted her potential to refresh the monarchy. Her enemies disparaged her as an interloper: too dark, too ambitious, too difficult. Still the wedding went ahead – accounts differ on the number of ceremonies – but soon she was gone, her exit brutal.

As for the reasons, recollections may vary. Even now, complete strangers lose their heads while prosecuting the case for or against her, as if their own lives hung in the balance. Fans maintain that prejudice and plotting did for her. Critics hold her solely responsible for her own downfall. If you assume this to be a description of Meghan, you're not wrong – but here's the thing: the same details apply, word for word, to Anne Boleyn.

Another example: well connected at court, she met her future husband during his dalliance with her elder sister. He needed a wife to provide him with heirs but swiftly regretted his choice. Her magnetism drove him to jealous rages and still obscures the work she did in championing serious causes. She clashed with powerful people and feared being killed by them. Her untimely death translated her to eternity. This is Diana, yet every single element of the story again fits Boleyn.

Perhaps unsurprisingly, Diana believed in predestination, consulting a whole quackery of clairvoyants and mystics. If they foresaw her future, they failed to protect her from it, but her own prediction did come true. Before any hint of a romance with Charles, she assured friends she would marry him. 'It could be quite fun. It would be like Anne Boleyn or Guinevere,' she said. [1]

What if this apparent precognition were, in fact, pattern recognition? Boleyn and Tudor blood coursed through Diana's aristocratic veins. Perhaps she understood her privilege at cellular level, as a double-edged sword, sharp enough to sever a small neck with a single blow. Though cushioned from economic hardship, royalty inflicts a different form of precarity, especially for its female members.

A trick patriarchy pulls is to set women against each other, placing them at opposite ends of an infernal seesaw, where, for one to rise, the other must fall. The patrimonarchy is especially skilled at this game, aided and abetted by every form and iteration of media and culture. The contests can be real or confected, comparisons natural or forced. The six wives of Henry VIII are even now defined in opposition to one another, while Elizabeth I remains locked in combat with Mary, Queen of Scots; Diana still tangles with Camilla; and every female royal of modern times is measured against the Elizabeths or Victoria and, invariably, found wanting. That the battle pitching Meghan against Kate enmeshes millions across the globe speaks to an age backsliding on women's rights, roiled by culture wars and unprepared for the digital age.

Relationships sit at the heart of this book, among the royals themselves and between them and the media in its broadest sense. Boleyn's short life overlapped with and helped to drive the first truly mass medium: printing. Illuminated manuscripts reached a hundred or so readers at most and their production was slow and expensive. Printing presses, introduced to England by William Caxton in the late fifteenth century, enabled a speedier, cheaper distribution to much larger numbers of people. That, in turn, boosted literacy rates. Together these changes supercharged debates on inflammatory subjects from the role of women and the rights of monarchs to the religious reformation.

Boleyn's daughter, Elizabeth I, brilliantly harnessed all available media to overcome resistance to her rule, her court a fulcrum of creativity, culture deployed to buttress her power. Victoria's reign encompassed an exponential growth in journalism, the advent of still photography and the birth of film. Broadcast would expand and diversify during Elizabeth II's queenship, eventually reimagining her and her family as characters in a royal soap, and struggle, like other traditional media, to adjust as new technologies transformed the landscape. Diana died with old-style snappers snapping at her heels. Camilla's redemption offers a textbook case of media management, yet the techniques deployed are already out of date.

The Windsors seemed unprepared for the digital insurgency that has engulfed them. On Christmas morning 2023, they attended church near the Sandringham estate, all core royals present but for Harry and Meghan. Headline writers focused on Kate. She appeared 'radiant'. There would be no further confirmed sightings of her for eighty-eight days. This book will look at why conspiracists so swiftly filled the vacuum, each theory wilder than the next – and more importantly, what it means for the royals, indeed for all of us, that attempts to quell the frenzy by revealing her cancer diagnosis instead set new hares running.

Even after Kate's tentative return to royal duty, closely observed by cameras and spectators, sceptics queried whether she had really been there at all. Perhaps the footage had been deep-faked. Maybe the royals deployed a hologram. Meanwhile, government sources, experts and academics linked the spreading of disinformation about her to China, Russia and Iran.

That twist alone should give pause to anyone inclined to dismiss royal women as insignificant news about them merely fluff. The purpose of disinformation is to destabilise societies and governments. Polarisation serves a similar purpose, splintering movements and political parties and distracting people from the real dangers by sending them chasing after mirages or fighting among themselves. Think how avidly the press has reported tensions between royal women while for years barely interrogating the culture of impunity shielding Andrew.

The aftershocks of his association with the paedophile Jeffrey Epstein are shaking not only the monarchy but other arms of state. While this crisis of confidence should push institutions to be and do better, it also risks serving populist narratives that proclaim democracy too broken to mend.

So, a warning: if you come to *Divide and Rule* expecting me to champion Diana over Camilla, Meghan over Kate, Boleyn over any of Henry's other wives, pick a team or choose a side, you will be disappointed. No royal woman ever emerges from these battles victorious, but everyone experiences collateral damage from them.

There is an alternative. We could simply refuse to pit women against each other, looking behind constructed enmities and images to the far more compelling realities. That way, we all win.

Chapter 1

Anne Boleyn: Anne of a Thousand Faces

'HA'. The letters carved as a love knot into the first of eight quatrefoils across the fireplace read like an exclamation, while a modern eye might mistake the flowers and feathers and portcullises that follow for a stream of emojis. The sequence ends with an isolated H, as if a second outburst had been cut short. This isn't far from the truth. That lonc A, in the Tapestry Room of St James's Palace, is one of few remaining physical traces of Anne Boleyn, once, and for a thousand turbulent days, Queen of England.

The current title holder lives here now. When Charles III acceded to the throne, he and Camilla declined the opportunity to move up the road to Buckingham Palace, preferring to stay at the complex encompassing the Tudor mansion and the adjoining nineteenth-century Clarence House. On this particular evening, they throw open their doors to celebrate the Commonwealth diaspora, mixing and mingling with statesmen, politicians, tycoons and celebrities. As the King attempts a Samoan dance, *Strictly Come Dancing*'s Craig Revel Horwood and Motsi Mabuse watch but do not judge.

I have come to observe Camilla queening it as part of my research, yet my attention snags on that fireplace and an earlier story of a king who sought fulfilment in a second marriage. Henry VIII commissioned St James's Palace for Boleyn while still married to Katherine of Aragon. Perhaps his wife-to-be drew misplaced confidence from tangible signs of his devotion: her initials, emblems and heraldic beasts, a falcon and a leopard, inscribed into the fabric of the building.

Exactly how many such motifs once decorated this grand home nobody knows, but the Tudor monarch went big on most things: six spouses, endless wars, over sixty residences including those built or seized by him, and meals featuring more than twenty types of meat. It is unlikely that he would have stinted on tributes to Boleyn.

He love-bombed her with letters and gifts during their courtship, riding out at a joust in a tabard embroidered with a burning heart. To wed her, he sacrificed his closest adviser, Cardinal Thomas Wolsey, defied a pope, enraged his most powerful European rival and inflamed his own subjects. To ditch her, he agreed to florid allegations casting him as a cuckold to a string of men including her own brother. Convicted of high treason, Boleyn became the first English queen to suffer the death penalty. The level of interest these events generated and the sheer number of reminders the drama left in its wake made her near-complete erasure in the days after her execution on 19 May 1536, a mammoth task.

Household records held at another of Henry's bases, Hampton Court, include instructions to remove all of Boleyn's insignia. Workers duly scraped, painted and, with chilling practicality, remodelled Anne's leopard into a panther, the symbol of incoming queen, Jane Seymour. The two-year-old Elizabeth, now declared illegitimate, was banished from view.

Her mother's head and body were consigned to an improvised container in an unmarked grave in the Chapel of St Peter ad Vincula within the Tower of London, her portraits destroyed.

Written evidence of her existence met a similar fate but for papers stored beyond Henry's reach or considered beneath notice. A famous letter, purported to be written by Anne from the Tower, is probably a later forgery. However, Henry's habit of prosecuting wars and inflaming France against Spain boosted both the ranks of envoys at his court and the numbers of dispatches they sent – many of which, of course, described Anne and her impact on domestic politics and international relations. In addition, 'the Tudors were great record keepers,' historian Tracy Borman tells me. 'Domestic details . . . are just absolute gold dust for understanding how the court operated.' Even dull functionaries, if of rank, left footprints, and Boleyn's ranged more widely than most, from the rich trappings of her household to documents from her trial.

Despite this, Henry probably believed he had succeeded in expunging her from history. Tonight, watching the current king and consort rub shoulders with guests who routinely feature in power rankings, it occurs to me how badly he failed. His second wife never got to live at St James's Palace; in fact, she barely got to live at all, yet she is of greater consequence than anyone present, Charles and Camilla included. Half a millennium after she knelt for her executioner, she forever finds new incarnations in culture high and low, instantly recognisable despite the fact that no undisputed picture of her exists.

Whether as a catalyst, by design or both, she played a pivotal role in the birth of the Church of England and wider

Anglicanism, globally the third largest Christian communion, rerouting British history and expanding the powers of the monarchy. Her daughter became a great ruler, an icon in her own right. If that doesn't make Anne Boleyn the most influential of English queens, it's hard to see who takes that crown.

So how did Henry's efforts backfire so spectacularly?

*

Part of the answer relates to vacuums. Nature abhors them, rushing to fill any void with whatever comes to hand. The lack of reliable information about Boleyn, far from exiling her from public consciousness, makes her infinitely fascinating, endlessly interpretable. This might appear paradoxical given that the underreporting of female lives reinforces the misconception that women mean and matter less than men. In fact, while data gaps reliably diminish interest in whole segments of the population, the inverse effect can apply to individuals. Boleyn is a prime example. The outlines of her story are so dramatic that, irrespective of how you colour them in, the results will be eye-catching. Deprived of her own accounts of what she felt and feared, every imaginable possibility has been projected on to her. To counter these effects, historians and devoted fans truffle for buried facts or labour to clear the build-up of myths, raising her profile still further.

This chapter looks at the sources that did withstand Henry's cull and what they reveal not only about Anne but the furiously polarised responses their relationship provoked. First, though, since her name and story are eternally bracketed with his, a few thoughts about how lightly her husband gets to wear his history. David Starkey once lamented that the King had been 'absorbed by his wives'. But, added the historian-turned-controversialist, 'it's what you expect from feminised history, the fact that so many of the writers who write about this are women and so much of their audience is a female audience . . . Wives complicate the story of Henry.'

Like a stopped clock pointing to the correct time, Starkey was, of course, right: wives *do* complicate Henry's story – in useful ways. Historians miss or misapprehend the meaning of events if they consider only those figures who already hog the limelight.

Recently, I received a message from an American professor visiting Trinity College, Cambridge. Before she sat down to her first formal dinner in the grand dining hall, her hosts had explained that Trinity owed its existence to the advocacy of Henry's sixth queen, but Katharine Parr's portrait languished in an alcove. Henry, by contrast, manspread across the panelled wall in a famous likeness captured by Hans Holbein the Younger when king and codpiece were already supersized. The professor quoted the mnemonic that charts the fate of Henry's wives – *divorced, beheaded, died, divorced, beheaded, survived* – to ask why a man with such a terrible record of spousal abuse remained proudly on display. In the US, pictures and statues celebrating problematic figures have been relocated after protests. The UK, of course, has witnessed a similar trend. Critics of such actions claim it is wrong to judge earlier periods through a modern lens, yet it is equally unwise to accept, without question, versions of history formed over centuries by the political and cultural biases of each successive era.

This is not an argument for 'cancelling' Henry, but rather to query the way he occupies space. The 2023 film *Firebrand* offers an interesting example, with Jude Law playing him as the ruined carcass of a former golden boy, ulcerated legs leaking, his rage fuelled by paranoia and his own mortality. Damien Lewis gives a similarly multilayered performance of the King in *Wolf Hall*. However, the majority of Henries depicted across cultural forms and periods, whether in the prime of youth or as ageing chuckers of drumsticks, roister across our collective imaginations as avatars of power. While accurate in a formal sense – that Henry exercised and expanded the powers he inherited – he also often acted from weakness, both political and personal. The more we know about his queens, the better we can understand him too.

A settled era might not have tested England's most married monarch to and beyond his limits. Unluckily for Henry – and more so for his wives – he came to the throne as competing dynasties collided. Europe consisted of a ragtag mess of kingdoms, principalities, duchies and city states, all struggling for survival or supremacy amid an impulse towards consolidation and imperial expansion, threatened, to the East, by the Ottoman Empire.

Ideas and beliefs clashed too. Renaissance humanism asserted the possibility of a universal peace, but also invested individuals with agency, capable of interpreting scriptures or determining ethical behaviours with or without the intervention of clergy. This ratcheted up the pressure for reform within the Catholic church while galvanising breakaway movements. Religious conflicts consumed Europe and flare to this day.

Seventeen at his accession in 1509, Henry was the first of a trio of young bucks to lead the most significant royal houses of the region. Over the coming years he would sometimes ally, and more often lock antlers, with his rivals. Both had bigger pairs. In 1515, twenty-one-year-old Francis I ascended the French throne to rule over much of what is now modern France together with significant holdings elsewhere. Four years later, Charles of Hapsburg, still just nineteen and already overlord of the Low Countries and King of Spain, beat Henry and Francis in the contest to become Holy Roman Emperor, a position granting the titleholder sway over more than three hundred separate territories in central, eastern and southern Europe. It also made Charles, alongside the pope, the most prominent champion of Catholicism, a delicate position for a ruler whose subjects included ever larger numbers of reformers and schismatics. As challengers encroached on Hapsburg territory, he turned to allies from opposite sides of the emerging division between the Catholicism he espoused and followers of radicals such as Martin Luther.

Tricky alliances were the order of the day. Henry and Francis needed each other if they were to contain Charles's ambitions, but to say relations between France and England were complicated is to compress into a single phrase a history spanning the Norman conquest (1066 and all that), the Anarchy, the Hundred Years' War, and at least twelve other named conflicts. The English claimed the French throne as their own. The French meanwhile asserted title to the English Crown, also maintaining a centuries-old mutual support pact with Scotland against the English, the Auld Alliance. None of this deterred French kings from choosing to back English monarchs to further their own interests, or vice versa. Without France, there might not have been a Tudor dynasty. Henry's father, Henry VII, had relied on French assistance to end the Wars of the Roses and seize the English throne.

Once king, Henry senior appears to have become increasingly introverted. His son, by contrast, dazzled and peacocked, deploying personal magnetism as an instrument of foreign policy. His relationship with Francis could warm to the point of bromance or seethe with the anger of a scorned lover. In 1520, at an eighteen-day summit near Calais dubbed the Field of the Cloth of Gold because of its extravagant staging, the two sovereigns ended up wrestling at Henry's instigation. Francis bested him. It is possible that Boleyn watched this humiliation as a member of the French retinue, but nobody knows for certain.

*

On its muscular surface, this was a man's world. As a commoner and woman, Anne barely left a mark on it before Henry's passion for her made her indelible. Her date and place of birth are unknown, by some estimates as late as 1507, but more likely 1500 or 1501 at Blickling Hall in Norfolk. Her father, Thomas, inherited Hever Castle in 1505.

She had a sister, Mary, thought to be a couple of years older, and a younger brother, George. Their mother, Elizabeth, was an aristocrat whose brother, the third Duke of Norfolk, Thomas Howard, would help manoeuvre Anne into marriage with the King, only to throw her under the coach when Henry wanted rid of her, repeating the same trick five years later with another of his nieces, Catherine Howard. The Boleyn patriarch, Thomas, served as a courtier and a diplomat, using his links to foreign courts to secure placements for his children.

Sent abroad on the cusp of her teenaged years, Anne first alighted at the court of Margaret of Austria, Charles of Hapsburg's aunt, then ruling the Low Countries as his regent. Margaret's French-language motto gives a flavour of her indomitability and the love of puns that marked elevated societies of the time: *Fortune. Infortune. Fort Une*, luck [and] bad luck strengthen a person. Her new maid of honour swiftly earned her approval. 'I find her so bright and pleasant that I am more beholden to you for sending her to me than you are to me,' Margaret wrote to Thomas.

A shift in Tudor allegiance from the Hapsburgs to the French redeployed Anne to the service of Queen Claude, consort to Francis. There, Boleyn observed more strong women at work: the king's mother, Louise, and sister, Marguerite, who both acquired significant power despite so-called Salic laws that blocked women from ruling. Louise acted as regent when Francis led troops to war, and Marguerite conducted diplomacy on her brother's behalf, also writing texts on subjects from gender relations to religious reform. Her sharp political instincts eventually persuaded Francis to make her a duke, elevating her to notional manhood so she could join his advisory councils.

Several of Boleyn's biographers suggest that Henry granted her a similar honour, the Marquisate of Pembroke, though recent research contends that the patents of creation list her title not as Marquis but Marchioness.[2] As ever, no detail of her history is immune to challenge, but the bigger point is about power – and how the marginalisation of women damaged monarchies even as it protected patrimonarchy.

Female exclusion from the order of succession by law, or custom, made royal houses fragile by restricting the numbers of viable heirs and spares. Average life expectancy in sixteenth-century England stood at barely thirty, a statistic reflecting sky-high rates of infant death and maternal mortality. No king could feel secure about the future of his line unless he had sired and raised to adulthood more than one healthy son.

The birth of a princess, though a disappointment, fed a different market, for child bearers and chattel. A monarch seeking to extend his dominion had three choices: conquest, land purchase or strategic marriages. A new wife or well-placed son-in-law could open up valuable diplomatic and dynastic channels – and sometimes came with castles, or even countries. An engagement between the offspring of lofty lineages, whether it held or not, could temporarily shift the balance of power to the benefit of the families involved.

Even if Henry had not been married already, his determination to wed a woman without connections or dowry appeared foolhardy. The best way to appreciate how anomalous Boleyn's position was – and how exposed – is to look at a few edited highlights of the royal betrothals and marriages that shaped Tudor Europe. Many involved near-relatives, a convention that concentrated power and property and, in unintended consequence, passed on genetic traits such as prominent jaws and flaming hair.

The first Tudor monarch, Henry VII, as the founder of a new royal line, had some catching up to do. His union with Elizabeth of York helped reconcile Lancastrian and Yorkist factions but left him with a comparatively small taxable population and geographic base, just England, Wales, a part of Ireland seized by Anglo-Norman troops in the twelfth century, and Calais, all that remained of the Crown's once-extensive holdings in France.

Marital diplomacy appeared to offer solutions, but often disappointed. The marriage of Henry VII's elder daughter Margaret to the Stuart ruler, James IV, failed to keep peace between England and Scotland. The betrothal of his younger daughter, Mary, to Charles of Hapsburg fizzled. Once widowed, the old king mulled taking a new bride himself, Joanna of Naples. *Were her breasts adequate?* he asked the envoys he sent to inspect her. *Did she have hair on her upper lip?* Yes, they answered to the first question, no to the second, but her greatest attractions anyway lay in her familial links to Spain and the curvaceous Italian coastal region over which her first husband, who was also her nephew, had reigned.

In the end, exploratory talks foundered, but Henry VII continued to market his children. The wedding of his son and heir, Arthur, to Katherine of Aragon appeared to be a strategic triumph. Her parents, Ferdinand of Aragon and Isabella of Castile, presided over a chunk of Spain and territories as far afield as Italy, the Caribbean and Gulf of Mexico. Then Arthur died, leaving his brother Henry in line for the Tudor throne and consigning Katherine to a limbo made more uncomfortable by her father-in-law, who considered marrying her himself. In the last months of his life, the King pursued a new match for his son, with Charles's sister, Eleanor.

Charles, meanwhile, went on racking up fiancées, eventually amassing at least six, including a second Mary Tudor, niece of the original Mary Tudor and the only surviving child of Henry VIII and Katherine of Aragon – another of Charles's aunts. In infancy, Charles had also been contracted to Claude. One of Claude's daughters with Francis would join the list of Charles's fiancées before the Hapsburg emperor finally settled down with Isabella of Portugal, his first cousin, and stepdaughter to his sister Eleanor. After Claude died, Eleanor wed Francis.

Isabella brought Charles into closer concord with Portugal, itself an imperial power. Their son, the future Philip II of Spain, would become king consort of England through marriage to the second Mary Tudor, by then a reigning queen. After Mary's death, Philip considered her half-sister, Elizabeth I, as his next bride.

*

None of these royal splicings, not even the union between Joanna and her nephew, counted as incestuous, because they proceeded with papal dispensations. Canon law determined who could marry whom, banning consanguineous couplings (those between close relations) and those of affinity (pairs linked via family members, whether through holy matrimony or extramarital dalliances). However, the Church could and did issue exemptions to these rules, even as it annulled marriages on exactly the same grounds.

Boleyn's enemies told stories that, had they been true, snarled her relationship with Henry in skeins of affinity and consanguinity. Only one such tale is widely accepted by historians: that he made her sister Mary his mistress before falling for Anne. Mary too had sojourned at the French court. Later, gossip about her behaviour there cast her as a 'great and infamous whore' whose conquests stretched to Francis himself. The intended target of any mud that spattered her was, of course, Anne, whose enemies circulated similar slanders about her – and worse. A persistent rumour claimed she was Henry's daughter, the issue of a fling between him and the Boleyn matriarch, Elizabeth. This unlikely scenario may have prompted him to acknowledge his affair with Mary. Warned that marriage to Anne could be invalid and that any children of the union thus illegitimate because he had 'meddled both with the mother and the sister', the King is reported to have replied, 'Never with the mother.'

Hard evidence first puts Anne in the same room as Henry in 1522, at York Place, a setting at once fairytale and ominous. This was the lavish London home of Cardinal Wolsey, Henry's chief minister, Archbishop of York, Primate of England and papal legate. Within eight years, incensed by the barriers to jettisoning Katherine for Anne, Henry had stripped Wolsey of position and was drawing up plans to remodel the property for himself. Whatever he envisaged for it, history had messier ideas. York Place, renamed Whitehall Palace, would provide the venue for Henry's wedding to Anne and, eleven days after Boleyn's execution, to her successor, Jane Seymour. Here too, in 1547, Henry's reign of marital terror finally came to an end. His death also spared Anne's uncle, Thomas Howard, whose own death sentence would otherwise have been carried out in days. Just over a century later, Charles I benefited from no such reprieve. Guards led him from his bedchamber at Whitehall to a scaffold outside the banqueting hall. In 1698, the palace burned to the ground along with archives containing testimonies that helped to convict Anne. *Sic transit gloria mundi.*

On the prelapsarian evening in question, however, Wolsey still enjoyed Henry's favour, while the latter appeared settled with his first queen. All three sat down with other guests to dinner followed by a pageant in the courtly tradition. Originally tales told by medieval troubadours, courtly romances had by this stage diversified into masques, plays, poetry and other cultural forms, all of it freighted with messaging that continues to infuse and deform ideas of love. The heroes of these stories prized virginity even as they attempted to deflower virgins, besieging the objects of their devotion – sometimes literally – and regarding them as damaged goods if they surrendered. This particular masque saw eight women, embodying Beauty, Bounty, Constance, Kindness, Honour, Mercy, Perseverance and Pity, shower invaders with rosewater and sweetmeats from the towers of the *Château Vert*, a green castle specially constructed for the performance. Both Boleyn sisters took part, with Anne by some accounts playing Perseverance. It was a quality she seems to have possessed in abundance.

*

Listening to podcasts about the Tudors, I noticed that hosts often urge their guests to pick a side, champion a wife. While Henry's first two wives undoubtedly came to see each other as enemies, both are diminished by this framing. Here is what Katherine was not, despite frequent cultural depictions as such: a pious frump traded in for a racier model. Multilingual and highly educated, Katherine won public affection and the respect of those who knew her, including, for much of their married life, her husband. Her circle encompassed Dutch scholar Desiderius Erasmus, Thomas More and other leading thinkers. At her behest, the Spanish humanist Juan Luis Vives wrote a treatise advocating for universal education. While Vives believed that learned women more assiduously protected their virtue, his work encouraged families to invest in education for their female offspring.

Katherine's acute political instincts enabled her to sidestep court intrigues and negotiate Henry's temper. His paranoia may have intensified after a fall from his horse in early 1536, but there were earlier indications of a ruthless personality, including his decision within a year of accession to execute two of his father's closest henchmen, and a subsequent purge of anyone whose lineage or views might challenge his rule. One of More's *Epigrams*, perhaps inspired by Henry, whom he served as Lord Chancellor, warns against relying on royal goodwill: 'Often he roars in rage for no known reason,' More wrote, 'and suddenly the fun becomes fatal.'[3] Executed for treason after refusing to accept the legitimacy of Henry's second marriage and the new Church of England, More would be canonised as a Catholic saint four centuries after his death.

In happier days, Henry valued Katherine sufficiently to install her as his regent when he crossed the Channel to fight the French. In his absence, she successfully managed efforts to repel Scotland's opportunistic invasion and, after Flodden, sent Henry a trophy: the cloak of the slain Scottish monarch.

Their marriage, however, was never plain sailing. Her connections to the most powerful European dynasties failed to deliver the benefits Henry anticipated. The second half of

Katherine's promised dowry never materialised. Her direct line to Charles did not guarantee peace and sometimes proved a liability, all the more so when Henry initiated his Great Matter: the plan to discard her.

It is unlikely that he would have embarked on this course had their union produced a male heir. Their son, born to national celebrations, survived for just a few weeks. Only Mary lived to adulthood. As the years ticked by, and Katherine suffered multiple miscarriages and stillbirths, the King knew who to blame. After all, he had fathered a son with his long-term mistress Elizabeth 'Bessie' Blount.

Data analysis of Henry's reproductive history supports a different interpretation: that he possibly suffered from a disorder limiting the numbers of viable children he could sire with any one woman. Seventy per cent of his six queens' pregnancies ended in miscarriage or stillbirth, against a rate of 10 per cent among the wives of thirty-one members of his inner circle.[4] Injuries and indulgences are likely to have exacerbated any underlying condition. His suits of armour trace his arc from natural athlete to morbid obesity, which can damage fertility.

By the time Boleyn caught his eye, Katherine had likely entered menopause. Even so, Henry initially regarded the newcomer as merely mistress material, as his correspondence, lodged in the Vatican Library, makes clear. In what appears to be the earliest of seventeen undated letters from him to Anne, Henry begs her to end his 'great agony' and let him 'know expressly your whole mind as to the love between us two'. Such clarity is 'absolutely necessary . . . having been for above a whole year stricken with the dart of love, and not yet sure whether I shall fail of finding a place in your heart and affection, which last point has prevented me for some time past from calling you my mistress; because, if you only love me with an ordinary love, that name is not suitable for you, because it denotes a singular love which is far from common'. He then sets out his terms: 'I will take you for my only mistress, casting off all others besides you out of my thoughts and affections, and serve you only.'

There are several plausible explanations for Anne's rejection of this offer: piety, for example, or her understanding that women needed to protect what little social capital they possessed or that the game of courtly love rewarded only those maidens who remained out of reach. She had witnessed her suitor woo, win and discard her sister. Perhaps Anne already dreamed of snaring a king. Maybe she felt no attraction to her beau – or feared him. Without her letters, presumably destroyed on Henry's orders, we can only guess at her thinking. Still, if the missing half of the correspondence suddenly turned up, would we take her words at face value? Lovers tell pretty lies, and though first-person testimonies should carry more weight than the accounts of people who were neither present nor even born at the time of events described, that does not ensure their credibility.

The difficulty of trying to understand Boleyn is not only that her voice is almost entirely absent from the exercise, but that contemporary commentaries are nakedly partial, and accounts written throughout the Tudor century – many during the reign of her daughter, Elizabeth – violently polarised.

The dispatches of the imperial ambassador Eustace Chapuys, who charted the rise and fall of 'the concubine' in real time, flowed like bile from his pen, reflecting his Hapsburg master's loyalty to Katherine and Catholicism. Opposing factions in the reformation set the two main templates into which Boleyn has been squeezed ever since. Pick godliness as the reason she kept Henry at arms' length, and you have the Boleyn of George Wyatt's hagiographic *The Life of the Virtuous Christian and Renowned Queen Anne Boleigne*, written during Elizabeth I's reign, or Anne's characterisation in John Foxe's *The Acts and Monuments* as a Protestant martyr. Scabrous accounts by Catholic authors such as Nicholas Harpsfield's *A Treatise on the Pretended Divorce between Henry VIII and Catherine of Aragon* and Nicholas Sander's *The Rise and Growth of the Anglican Schism* damn her for ambition, promiscuity and witchcraft.

All of this makes Henry's letters the best source on the progression of their love affair, and a deeply problematic one at that. What they do reveal is their author, by turns vulnerable and aggressive, frantically punning and, despite some renown as a poet, clunking in his use of metaphors. He seems particularly entranced with the way in which the word 'hart', meaning deer, offers a soundalike for the organ most closely associated with love. In one missive, he writes that 'seeing my darling is absent, I can do no less than to send her some flesh, representing my name, which is hart flesh for Henry, prognosticating that hereafter, God willing, you may enjoy some of mine'. It is a grisly image and presumably came accompanied by the corpse of a stag. A separate billet-doux reads as if it arrived covered in bloody fingerprints: 'Written after the killing of a hart, at eleven of the clock, minding, with God's grace, tomorrow, mightily timely, to kill another, by the hand which, I trust, shortly shall be yours.' A third note, while less visceral, lacks romance: 'I send you, by the bearer of this, a buck killed late last night by my own hand, hoping that when you eat of it you may think of the hunter.'

Anne's absences from court increased his desire. 'The longer the days are, the more distant is the sun, and nevertheless the hotter; so it is with our love, for by absence we are kept a distance from one another, and yet it retains its fervour, at least on my side,' he declares. In what are likely later letters, his tone acquires greater intimacy. He addresses her as 'mine own sweetheart', complains that labouring over a book has given him a headache and wishes himself in her arms 'whose pretty dukkys [breasts] I trust shortly to kiss'. Technically, Anne might still count as a virgin, but their relationship appears to have become sexual, a dangerous turn of events for a woman playing the game of courtly love.

The letters include other presentiments of trouble too. When his beloved stays away too long for his liking, Henry upbraids her in a tone he might use to discipline a courtier. The headache he bemoans is metaphorical as well as literal. The book he mentions is probably *A Glass of the Truth*, published anonymously but thought to be part written by him. It asserted that the Holy See had exceeded its jurisdiction in waiving for him the divine prohibition against a man marrying his brother's widow, rendering his marriage to Katherine, and their daughter, illegitimate. It also warned against the dangers of female succession. The logic was clear: he owed it to his people to take a new wife and beget an unimpeachable male heir.

Until he met Anne, Henry had shown little sympathy for religious reform, accepting from Pope Leo X the title Defender of the Faith for his treatise *Assertio Septem Sacramentorum adversus Martinum Lutherum*, the Defence of the Seven Sacraments against Martin Luther. German-born Luther had published critiques of Catholic practices, most famously his *Disputatio pro declaratione virtutis indulgentiarum*, commonly known as the Ninety-five Theses and generally considered the real start of the reformation, which challenged the primacy of the papacy over temporal powers. Selling indulgences – offering absolution in return for payment – might be a money-spinner for the Church, but Luther saw true repentance as the only route to salvation. Henry's riposte insisted on the papacy's central role to European peace and unity. Luther responded with *Contra Henricum Regem Angliae*: Against Henry, King of England, a laugh-out-loud stream of invective against 'the fool-King'. Now Henry himself was feverishly mustering arguments against the pope's authority.

In courtly romances, knights wielded swords in pursuit of holy grails. In the name of love, Henry hacked away at foundations of his reign, his reputation, perhaps even his beliefs, struck out at friends and allies, and in going up against Charles and successive popes, made himself uncomfortably reliant on French support. Every time he slew a dragon, another stood in his path. Still, he pushed on, confident of securing twin prizes that would justify the toil and toll: his chosen queen and a settled succession. The air around the couple grew thick with smoke, not just from their smouldering passion but burning bridges.

*

What did the King see as he squinted through the haze? A clever woman, as educated as his queen, quick, charming, sometimes cutting, possibly mercurial and, towards Katherine, vindictive. Friends and enemies alike noted Anne's wit. Men noticed her in other ways. A sonnet by Thomas Wyatt, poet, courtier and grandfather of Boleyn's biographer George Wyatt, deployed the imagery that Henry had so comprehensively butchered to conjure up a strange and lovely spirit, a hind or doe, thought to be a representation of Anne. The hunter gives up the chase understanding she will always elude him, at once the property of an emperor and too independent to be constrained by anyone. 'There is written her fair neck round about / *Noli me tangere*, for Caesar's I am / And wild for to hold, though I seem tame.'[5]

The only surviving verified portrait of Boleyn is a carving on a 1534 commemorative coin that bears the initials A.R. and the inscription 'The Moost Happi'. Time and damage have eroded features crudely rendered in the first place. More familiar images, for example, a famous depiction of Anne in a pearl-studded chain from which a B is suspended – the first letter of the surname she had traded for noble titles before her marriage – are thought to date to her daughter's reign and may have been influenced by Elizabeth's own dark eyes and strong contours. Two sketches purporting to show Anne, both attributed to Holbein, resemble neither each other, nor these paintings. One captures a woman in a nightgown turning away from the artist to reveal a fairly substantial double chin. In another drawing, the sitter faces the opposite direction, jawline and nose conspicuously sharp.

Written descriptions are more contradictory still, apart from a few points of congruence around her divergence from the

Tudor ideal of pale skin and flaxen hair, and her preference for continental styles, including a crescent-shaped French hood in place of the clumsier English gable design. Lancelot de Carle, a French diplomat based in London during her queenship, called her beautiful. Wyatt's hind has a fair neck. Anne, contemplating her impending beheading, famously told the constable of the Tower, Sir William Kingston, 'I have a little neck.' Sander, determined to associate her with witchcraft, gives us a radically different view of this part of her body: 'There was a large wen under her chin,' he says, or – in alternative translation from the Latin – a swelling. 'Rather tall of stature, with black hair, and an oval face with a sallow complexion, as if troubled with jaundice . . . she had a projecting tooth under the upper lip.'

Is this the face that launched a king's courtship? Apparently so, for, says Sander, Anne was also 'handsome to look at [editor's note: *eh?*], with a pretty mouth [*despite the horizontal tooth*]'. He adds that she was 'amusing in her ways, playing well on the lute, and was a good dancer'. His book is also the original source for the sixth finger that supposedly disfigured her right hand.

If these details were accurate, Chapuys would surely have reported them with relish. Though he compared Henry's excitement at marrying Jane Seymour to 'the joy and pleasure a man feels in getting rid of a thin, old and vicious hack in the hope of getting soon a fine horse to ride', he perhaps intended this primarily as a comment on Anne's hot temper, for which he is a key source, rather than her appearance. Whatever his meaning, the phrase found echoes centuries later in descriptions of Camilla, widely reviled after Charles and Diana's separation and divorce as a 'horsey homewrecker', 'horse-faced' and 'horsey-looking'. 'She's very county, very horsey. Doesn't take a good picture,' an unnamed royal godparent mused of Camilla to the biographer Gyles Brandreth. 'Too like a horse herself. She must be an amazing screw.'

Study any heterosexual couple in which the woman is thought to be punching above her weight, and you will find similar responses. For centuries, Anne's denigrators have snickered about pleasuring techniques she supposedly imported from France, though she likely spent most of her time there cloistered away from the main court in the chaste ambit of Claude. The idea that the King might have been enthralled by Anne's intellect rarely troubles such interpretations, yet Henry's letters show her becoming his sounding board and informal adviser. Any veteran of a long-distance relationship will tell you that lengthy separations can forge a connection that, denied physical expression, discovers and builds on shared ideals and interests. Moreover, external opposition is a power-ful bonding agent. Henry and Anne found common cause in the Great Matter.

*

It helped that she really did bring scandalous knowledge back from France: a passionate engagement with the work of French humanists and reformers. In England, the nascent reforma-tion had triggered a series of injunctions against importing or owning heretical texts, but for the rest of her life, Anne continued, despite the dangers, to collect such books and explore related schools of thought.

Witnesses commented on her enthusiasm for more traditional devotional reading too. Three of her Books of Hours survive, illuminated texts designed for private prayer and contemplation, each containing annotations that speak to earthly as well as spiritual concerns. *'Le temps viendra,'* the time will come, *'Je* Anne Boleyn', she wrote in one. Into another, she sketched a verse in English: 'Remember me when you do pray / That hope doth lead from day to day.' Her third note, positioned below an illustration of the annunciation and evidently meant for Henry, reads: 'By daily proof you shall me find / To be to you both loving and kind.' Elsewhere in these pages, beneath an image of a bleeding Christ crowned with thorns, he has left a message for her: 'If you remember my love in your prayers as strongly as I adore you, I shall hardly be forgotten, for I am yours. Henry R. forever.'

Before assessing her pivotal role in the king's transformation from champion of Rome to its scourge, it is important to understand the role and importance of religion at that time. Although the term 'atheism' came into use during the latter half of the century, for most people, faith remained central to life, and how to live it. For the majority of believers, this meant following the spiritual and moral guidance and canonical laws of the Catholic church.

As the medieval period gave way to the renaissance, English dissenters known as Lollards criticised the Catholic hierarchy, arguing for a simpler and more open church. From the early sixteenth century, similar ideas animated newer reform movements across Europe, spreading fast and taking on different emphases depending on the dispositions of their founders and the cultures that embraced them. Lutheranism would find its most fertile ground in the German states, Scandinavia and the Baltics, while a French theologian called John Calvin, exiled to Switzerland, planted the roots of the evangelical branch that still bears his name. From the 1540s, Calvinism gained adherents in France, the Low Countries, Scotland and, after Edward VI's accession, England.

Dissent was dangerous. Anybody convicted of heresy – as determined by whichever authority currently held the upper hand – risked a terrible death. There are multiple documented instances of prisoners burning alive rather than recanting, preferring transient agony to eternal hellfire. Many of those condemned to die on different charges made similar calculations, confessing their sins and seeking absolution while they still had the chance. Anne and four men accused with her of treason and other damning crimes would maintain their innocence to the gallows.

A pair of words is often misused in discussing her downfall: 'divorce' and 'Protestant'. The church could not end marriages. It instead declared that some unions had never existed, annulling them on grounds such as non-consummation. The term 'Protestantism' derives from a 1529 'protestation' by followers of Luther. As Eric Ives, author of a seminal biography of Boleyn, warns his readers, applying this label to her is 'wholly inappropriate . . . During Anne's lifetime [there were] only two general positions in England – that the [Catholic] Church needed to be supported as it was, and that the Church as it was needed to be reformed – around which and between which most individuals ranged with varying levels of commitment.'

Key divisions centred on the extent of free will and paths to redemption. The Catholic Church insisted that charitable giving and other good works could deliver salvation. Luther viewed such acts as a matter of moral responsibility rather than tickets to heaven, with God's grace alone capable of cleansing sin. By that same logic, the distribution of Bibles and other religious texts in translation to local languages became a cornerstone of reform, widening access to general populations to enable personal accountability, while diminishing the gatekeeping powers of the priesthood. Luther also articulated an idea that Henry came to exploit, even as he attacked its author. 'The pope,' Luther wrote, 'should have no authority over the emperor, except to anoint and crown him at the altar, as a bishop anoints and crowns a king.'

Chapuys described Anne as 'more Lutheran than Luther himself', the most inflammatory slur available, but her library shows his jibe was wide of the mark. Her inclinations were towards French reformism. She did, however, show interest in a home-grown radical who at times chimed with Luther. Among her possessions were copies of William Tyndale's banned English translation of the New Testament, and his book, *The Obedience of a Christian Man and How Christian Rulers Ought to Govern*. In this tract, Tyndale, like Luther, depicted popes as an interruption to the divine chain of command between God and kings. Sovereigns should preside over their national churches.

Several sources claim that Anne contrived to bring *Obedience* to Henry's attention, a risky decision since Wolsey had by now declared Tyndale a heretic. George Wyatt spins a convoluted yarn about Anne lending the text to one of her gentlewomen whose lover borrows it, only for Wolsey to impound it. Anne then encourages Henry to retrieve the book, whereupon he alights on passages she has highlighted for him. A flourish added in later tellings has Henry declaring Tyndale's work 'is for me and all kings to read'. It is unlikely he would have done so had he known the identity of its author. An iconoclast, Tyndale stood not only in opposition to the papacy, but to reformists urging Henry to defy it, eventually nailing his colours to the mast with *The Practice of Prelates* which accused both sides of pursuing worldly interests. He reserved his greatest scorn for the man charged with pushing through the Great Matter: Wolsey, rendered in Tyndale's text as Wolf and Wolfsee.

Tyndale, soon to die a heretic's death himself, was kicking a man already down. After years of clever footwork, the cardinal had found himself wedged between a rock – Pope Clement, institutionally and theologically opposed to Henry's argument – and a hard place – a European power balance strongly skewed in favour of Katherine's nephew, Charles. Francis, the emperor's usual counterweight and the only ruler with sufficient clout to intercede with Clement on Henry's behalf, had suffered a run of extraordinary setbacks.

One pivotal moment came before any talk of annulment and remarriage, during the Italian wars between Charles and Francis. In 1525, the French king was captured at a battle outside the Lombardy city of Pavia and transferred to Charles's custody in Spain. After thirteen months in captivity, Francis secured his freedom by surrendering his Italian claims and sending Charles his heir and a second son as hostages. Despite the risk to his children, Francis's compliance proved fleeting. Determined to regain lost ground, he engineered a new military alliance, the League of Cognac, joining forces against the emperor with Northern Italian states and, fatefully, the pope.

Events did not go according to plan for anyone involved. Two years after Pavia, Hapsburg forces advanced on Rome in a show of force meant merely to chasten the pontiff. Instead, these troops mutinied over lack of pay and stormed the city. Clement fled to the Castel Sant'Angelo, remaining there at the emperor's mercy even as Wolsey and Henry's other representatives petitioned him for help.

Small wonder, then, that negotiations on the annulment stuttered and stalled. A flurry of correspondence between the French and English courts reveals two kings attempting to leverage each other's pain for their own ends. Anne also worked her personal relationships with the French royal house. Turf wars between the Boleyn family and allies and Wolsey complicated this picture. The wary dance between the cardinal and Anne provides rare glimpses of the latter's own writing. 'All the days of my life I am most bound of all creatures, next the king's grace, to love and serve your grace: of the which I beseech you never to doubt that never I shall vary from this thought as long as any breath is in my body,' she reassured Wolsey. Soon she was plotting to oust him.

First, though, came two false dawns, with Francis staging a fresh invasion of Italy, and Clement agreeing that an ecclesiastical court held in England could test the validity of Henry's first marriage. Any expectation of a breakthrough proved short-lived. Lorenzo Campeggio, the cardinal appointed by the Pope to try the case with Wolsey, waited six months before embarking on a circuitous journey to London, deploying further delaying tactics on arrival. English envoys sent in the opposite direction to plead with the pope initially found him too ill to grant them audiences and then, when he eventually met them, unreceptive. Finally, in the summer of 1529, Campeggio and Wolsey opened the legatine trial at Blackfriars, only for Katherine to use its platform to try to save her queenship and her marriage. At her first appearance, she accused the court of bias and called for the case to be determined in Rome, returning to the stand three days later to deliver a direct appeal to Henry. Then, she turned on her heel and left. Several versions of her speech exist. Accounts of her performance also vary, based on five separate eyewitness testimonies, each grinding a different axe. Whichever comes closest to the truth, Katherine succeeded in swaying public opinion in her favour.

Henry's suit rested, shakily, on a passage from Leviticus: 'If a man shall take his brother's wife, it is an unclean thing. He hath uncovered his brother's nakedness; they shall be childless.' There were obvious problems with this argument, not least Henry and Katherine's thirteen-year-old daughter, Mary. As Katherine is said to have reminded her husband, there had been additional live births too. Moreover, the Bible contradicts itself on exactly the point under scrutiny, with Deuteronomy actively urging marriages between widows and their brothers-in-law.

The court broached another grey area: the injunction in Leviticus would not necessarily apply to an unconsummated marriage, as Katherine swore hers to Arthur had been. To ward off such a line of argument, Henry's team assembled witnesses to insist that Arthur had deflowered Katherine, exiting the bridal bedchamber the morning after the wedding, schoolboy wit unsheathed, to demand 'a cup of ale, for I have been this night in the midst of Spain'.

None of this mattered. Charles had inflicted a fresh defeat on Francis's troops. After Campeggio adjourned proceedings for the summer, the Pope revoked the case to Rome, just as Katherine had requested. In early August, the French king and Hapsburg emperor signed a new treaty, the Peace of the Ladies, brokered by Francis's mother, Louise, and Charles's aunt, Margaret. The following February, the Pope conducted two coronation ceremonies for the ascendant Hapsburg, retroactively crowning him King of Spain and Holy Roman Emperor. Five months later, Charles's sister Eleanor sealed the Franco-imperial entente by marrying Francis, arriving at her new home with the bridegroom's sons, finally released from custody in Spain. As this event-filled year drew to a close, Wolsey died on the way to London to stand trial for privileging the papacy over loyalty to his monarch.

By now, Henry's case and much else besides had devolved to his chancellor and most influential adviser, Thomas Cromwell, who was pursuing a twin-track approach of attempting to sway Clement, while also contemplating contingencies in the event of the mission's failure. Katherine, banished from court, barred from seeing her daughter and burdened with a title she rejected – princess dowager – kept up the pressure from the other direction, begging the Pope to make a judgment not only in her favour, but swiftly. The lovers felt a sense of urgency too. Anne's window of fertility was limited. Barring a heavenly intervention, the King faced two options: endure the unsatisfactory status quo, or gamble on his chosen queen and a nursery full of heirs.

Though the latter option risked excommunication – exclusion from the Church with repercussions on earth as in heaven – Anne and Cromwell, allies at this juncture, urged Henry to take the plunge. Cromwell shared Boleyn's long-standing interest in religious reform and, with Archbishop of Canterbury Thomas Cranmer, was developing a vision for an English reformation more transformative than anything the King imagined or wanted. By instinct a religious conservative, Henry would revert to traditional Catholic practices later in his reign. What did excite him, though, was the prospect of sons, sex and C of E. Why shouldn't he helm his own church?

A fresh shift in international relations provided the impetus he needed. As Charles faced down challenges on separate flanks from German princes and Ottoman forces, Francis and Henry signed a treaty of mutual aid, pledging to defend each other against attacks from their frenemy.

*

In October 1532, Anne travelled with Henry, queen in all but name and glittering with jewels appropriated from Katherine, to a summit with Francis. The couple may have consummated their relationship during this trip. *Hall's Chronicle*, a contemporary history, claims they married the day they landed back in England. Their official nuptials, at Whitehall Palace in January 1533, remained secret for several months, not least because Henry still had a wife. That May, Archbishop Cranmer broke the logjam by declaring Henry's union with Katherine annulled and establishing, at least for the time being, the legitimacy of the baby that swelled Anne's belly. Clement, hoping Henry might yet be tempted back to Katherine and undiluted Catholicism, stayed his hand, dying before the

English parliament passed the 1534 Act of Supremacy, which installed Henry as head of the Church of England. Earlier that year, the Act of Succession had formalised, under English law, the annulment of Henry's first marriage, delegitimising Mary and requiring Henry's subjects to accept the new union as 'undoubted, true, sincere and perfect'. Two Suppression Acts followed, ramping up the practice of dissolving monasteries and other Catholic orders and siphoning off their wealth. Clement's successor Paul III finally excommunicated Henry in 1538.

These events defined not only Henry's reign, but those of his children and every ruler to come, including Charles I and his nemesis, Cromwell's great-great-nephew, Oliver Cromwell. Henry's immediate successor, his son Edward, would kick off a full Protestant reformation, only for Edward's half-sister, Mary, to earn the soubriquet 'bloody' by rolling back religious reforms with fire.

Here's another twist. In constituting himself head of the English church to fulfil his matrimonial desires, Henry complicated the marital plans of later kings. Each successive monarch heads the C of E and is expected to lead in deed as well as word. George IV tried to divorce his queen, Caroline of Brunswick, only to be thwarted when his government bowed to popular sentiment against the move. Edward VIII abdicated to marry divorcée Wallis Simpson. Charles and Camilla's wedding arrangements devolved into slapstick.

Circumstances denied Anne Boleyn a grand wedding, but Henry pulled out the stops for her coronation. She remains the only consort ever to assume St Edward's crown and to sit on St Edward's chair, both otherwise reserved for reigning monarchs. Though often interpreted as a sign of his love for her, Henry may well have been consumed by a different passion: the desire to quash rumblings about the legitimacy of her queen-ship and the child she carried. On the eve of the ceremony, as she processed from the Tower of London to Westminster Abbey, spectators failed to get on board with the project. According to the spiteful Chapuys, when crowds caught sight of the new royal monogram, that same intertwined H&A which decorates the fireplace at St James's Palace, they began to sound it out: *HA HA*, they mocked. *HA HA*.

Soon Anne's enemies had cause to laugh again. In September she gave birth to a girl, Elizabeth. So convinced had Henry been that this baby would be a boy that scribes drafted proclamations in advance. Now they tried to amend the mistake, changing 'prince' to 'princess', but limited space forced a compromise: 'princes'.

If celebrations appeared muted, so did Henry's response: they would have more children. Perhaps his equanimity should have served as a warning. For years, he had pursued Anne as a hunter might stalk a deer. Domesticated, she was losing her allure. It was not just that the chase was over. A mistress of the courtly game, Anne showed no sign of adjusting to the role of compliant consort. A damsel might command her swain to obey her, but woe betide the queen who gave orders to Henry. A dispatch sent by Chapuys just four days before she went into labour overflows with *Schadenfreude*. Henry is already showing interest in other women, prompting his pregnant spouse, 'full of jealousy, and not without cause' to use 'some words to the King at which he was displeased, and told her that she must shut her eyes, and endure as well as more worthy persons'.

She 'ought to know that it was in his power to humble her again in a moment more than he had exalted her'. The couple, Chapuys reports, has not spoken since. He welcomes this as a sign that Katherine might yet be recalled.

That ship had sailed. Henry's desire for sons trumped other concerns. Unfortunately for Anne, over the next two years, she, like Katherine, would endure false hopes and miscarriages. A failed pregnancy may have prevented her from accompanying her husband on his annual progress around the country in 1534. The following summer, she did join the tour, stopping with him at Wolf Hall, home to Jane Seymour. The first mention of Henry setting his sights on Jane appears in a letter from Chapuys a few months later.

Meanwhile, and to the bitter end, Anne maintained her hostility to Katherine and Mary, the latter demoted from princess to lady, and like her mother, steadfastly refusing to recognise Boleyn as queen. Anne responded by threatening, within the hearing of others, to kill the King's firstborn. There is no doubt that she behaved cruelly towards both women, but accusations that she planned to poison them appear baseless, so too the other charges soon to be levelled against her.

News of Katherine's death, probably from cancer, on 7 January 1536, prompted a show of unity from Henry and Anne. By now, Boleyn was once again pregnant. Perhaps she imagined herself secure with Katherine out of the picture and a longed-for heir on the way. She seems not to have realised that her predecessor, far from threatening her status, had secured it.

Now a cascade of events sealed Boleyn's downfall. She outlived Katherine by only nineteen weeks. Later that January,

Henry suffered his jousting accident, toppling from his horse in full armour and pulling the animal on top of him. Unconscious, by some accounts for several hours, he probably sustained a brain injury. His health was already deteriorating. Migraines, malarial fevers and leg ulcers increasingly soured his mood and the air around him.

Five days later, Katherine's funeral took place and Anne miscarried. 'The child had the appearance of a male about three months and a half old,' Chapuys reported. Other reports suggest the foetus had yet to reach the stage of development at which sex could be determined. Sander applied a different spin, accusing her, witch that she was, of birthing something inhuman, 'a shapeless mass of flesh'.

Anne attributed the loss to the shock of Henry's fall. He blamed it on marriage to her. 'I see,' Chapuys quotes him saying, 'that God will not give me male children.' This was pretty much the same rationale he had deployed to call doubt on the validity of his first union. Moreover, influential figures at court and in Europe, who had refused to accept its annulment, saw him, with Katherine's death, as a widower, free to remarry.

The Seymour family scented blood in the water. Adversaries with a range of gripes and grudges gathered in corners. The most consequential was Cromwell. Anne had tussled with her former ally for Henry's ear, notably over the dissolution of the monasteries. She argued that monies raised should be gifted to charitable causes. Cromwell looked to bolster Henry's position by channelling proceeds to state coffers and the King's key supporters.

England is dotted with symbols of Cromwell's pyrrhic victory. Years ago, I got to live and work as a researcher in one such, Mottisfont Abbey in Hampshire. An Augustinian order, resident since the thirteenth century, was evicted around the same time as Anne's trial, with the property passing to a member of her jury, William Sandys, Henry's lord chamberlain. Sandys would soon escort Boleyn to the block, attend Jane Seymour's wedding and funeral, and witness Cromwell lose his head for engineering the brief marriage between Henry and Anne of Cleves.

Nobody could afford to feel secure at Henry's court, but even by these standards, the coup against Boleyn was swift and brutal. Two commissions were set up without explanation at locations that turned out to match places named in allegations against her and her co-accused. Anne's father and maternal uncle would both be co-opted on to these. Next, writs were issued to summon parliament for no obvious reason, while Henry's privy council began to meet daily.

Unaware of these moves, Anne provided her enemies with the material they needed to set their plan in motion. The conversation began harmlessly enough, a piece of courtly banter between her and Henry Norris, her husband's groom of the stool, a position both elevated and as lavatorial at its title suggests – assisting the monarch with personal hygiene as well as statelier tasks. Boleyn teased Norris that he was dragging his heels over proposing to his paramour. Perhaps, she suggested, he harboured hopes of marrying Anne instead. As soon as she voiced the idea, she and Norris realised it could be construed as treason, defined by statute as 'compassing and imagining the king's death'. Immediately they backpedalled, with Norris seeking out Boleyn's chaplain to swear an oath to her good character, but to no avail. The story reached Cromwell.

During that same short run of days, Anne reprimanded a musician in her retinue, Mark Smeaton, for staring at her, only for him to reply in romantic and conspicuously overfamiliar terms that 'a look [from her] sufficed'. Arrested and interrogated, he confessed to adultery with her, presumably implicating Norris and others. That night, Henry ordered the postponement of a planned trip to Calais.

Boleyn must have known all was not well, but the next morning presided with her husband at a May Day joust, Henry relegated to spectating by his injuries. Those who did take to the field included Norris, Anne's brother, George, and possibly the courtiers William Brereton and Francis Weston. The event proceeded as usual until, without warning, Henry left the stands, summoning Norris and departing on horseback. Norris's journey ended at the Tower, soon to be joined by George Boleyn, Brereton, Weston and two suspects who would later be released, Thomas Wyatt, and a courtier called Richard Page. The following day, a barge carried the Queen to the same destination.

*

Anne's trial, for treason, adultery and incest with her brother, George, took place on 15 May in the oldest building in the complex, the King's Hall on the first floor of the White Tower, in front of a jury of twenty-six senior nobles, led by her uncle Thomas Howard.

Separate proceedings at Westminster Hall had already convicted Norris, Brereton, Weston and Smeaton of adultery and treason. Smeaton pled guilty. The others maintained their innocence. Thomas Boleyn, part of the commission that tried the men, must have known the outcome prejudiced his daughter's case.

Not that she stood a chance. Henry had probably already sent to Calais for a swordsman, part of the meticulous orders for her execution he set out for Kingston. He had been 'moved to pity', the King wrote, and thus would spare Anne from being burned at the stake. The sword was a further concession, more likely to slice cleanly through a neck than an axe, which often required several attempts. Moreover, Henry either believed the charges against Anne or would stop at nothing to rid himself of her. There is circumstantial evidence for the second interpretation.

A French diplomat described Henry rebuffing his new wife, Jane, when she offered him unsolicited advice: she should remember the fate of her predecessor before daring to 'meddle with his affairs'. Chapuys, no friend to Anne, doubted the case against her, observing that it rested 'on mere presumption or on very slight grounds, without legal proof or valid confession'. He also pointed out that Archbishop Cranmer had annulled Henry's marriage to Anne before her execution. There had therefore been no reason to kill her, 'since the executioner's sword and her own death were virtually to separate and divorce man and wife. But if such was their intention it strikes me that it would have been a far more decent and honest excuse to allege that she had been married to another man still alive'. Chapuys added, 'May God permit that this may be [Henry's] last folly.' It was not.

Reports of the trial, though of course varying in detail, coalesce around the clarity and concision of Boleyn's rebuttal of all charges. She had not been unfaithful with her brother or anyone else, nor had she hoped for the King's death or plotted the murders of Katherine and Mary or done any of the other things of which she stood accused.

George Boleyn made a compelling defendant too. The only supposed evidence of incest related to a single occasion when he and Anne had conferred in her bedchamber about the progress of the Great Matter. Asked to answer an allegation handed to him in writing to avoid its disclosure to the court, he instead read the question aloud. Did his wife, Jane, one of Anne's ladies-in-waiting, ever tell him that her mistress had complained about Henry as a lover, specifically that he possessed neither 'prowess nor force'? Already positioned as a cuckold by the process masterminded by Cromwell, Henry now carried the stigma of sexual inadequacy too.

*

Boats used to turn off the main course of the Thames to decant their prisoners at Traitor's Gate, but the waterway from the river to the Tower of London has long been bricked up, separating the bloody past from the civilised present. Today, on a visit to the Tower, I cannot but notice that one still flows into the other. Around the world, conflicts smoulder and flare like forest fires. The rich live on in their castles, the poor at their gates, gig-economy grooms of the stool but without any of the benefits of the original job. And wherever I look, Anne Boleyn stares back at me from posters and tourist tat, except of course that this is make-believe Anne: Anne of the B-pendant and Mona Lisa expression; Anne the unfathomable, inscrutable and endlessly recyclable; Anne of a thousand ways to keep women in their place. Anne of a thousand faces and none.

Researching and writing this book, I thought a lot about what history is and what it means. The lines between fact and fiction are often blurred. Historians frequently use novelistic techniques to bring dusty data to life, describing what people thought or felt, or how the sun shone through a window when no sources for these details exist. Similarly, historical fiction such as Philippa Gregory's 2001 blockbuster novel, *The Other Boleyn Girl*, and the films and play based on it, can more powerfully shape views of the past than any nonfiction, because such techniques make stories – and their characters – come alive.

Reading her book years ago, my sympathies, as the author intended, rested with the titular heroine, Mary Boleyn. Revisiting it for this project, I was struck by how clearly Sander's slanders echo down the centuries. Gregory's framing pits kind Mary against the ruthless Anne. The narrative would anyway be familiar: infused with courtly values; virtue rewarded; and a woman punished for her sexuality and her ambition.

A global bestseller, *The Other Boleyn Girl* has helped to perpetuate a caricature of Anne created by her enemies during the reformation. Does that matter? Should we send writers to the scaffold for taking liberties with history? If so, why not cancel Shakespeare for his ahistorical history plays or boycott *Wolf Hall*, more literary than *The Other Boleyn Girl* but also heavily drawing on Catholic sources? A couple of years ago, I watched a capacity audience in London cheer on Henry's queens as reimagined by the hit musical *Six*. Though intended as a feminist take – its moral is one of female solidarity – the Anne of *Six* ('the mystery, the one who changed history') is a creature drawn from anti-Boleyn mythology, a bubble-headed social climber. And what of the many portrayals that lean on Protestant sources: Boleyn as a saintly figure, a tragic heroine? Nor is bias the only force that distorts. French-Canadian actress Geneviève Bujold made such an appealing Boleyn in the 1969 film *Anne of a Thousand Days* that she popularised the notion that the real Anne spoke with a French accent (possible but unprovable) along with the more dubious claim of a confrontation in the Tower between Henry and his doomed wife.

These books and dramatisations all managed to trigger that quiet process of osmosis by which ideas seep through populations to reinvent themselves as accepted facts. Historical fiction routinely spreads ye olde fake news, plays with timelines, kills off inconvenient figures, sexes up the humdrum and leans on tropes.

For me, part of the problem lies in that phrase: 'historical fiction'. That is why, in discussion with Elizabeth Fremantle, the author of *Firebrand*, I suggest rebranding historical fiction as fictional history. Fremantle pauses, mulls and calls my idea 'interesting', sounding as if she means it. 'Novels,' she says, 'are anachronisms, stories, fairytales. I think we writers have to stand up and admit to that. I do my research, but sometimes I choose to set that aside if it is not serving the story I want to write.'

The more truthful a piece of fictional history feels – whether because it panders to our prejudices or holds a mirror up to humanity – the more easily we accept it as gospel, even though, as Fremantle warns, 'essentially any historical figure, once fictionalised, is nothing like the real person'. The problem with my proposed rebranding, of course, is that it implies there is such a thing as history free from fiction: established, immutable and entirely rooted in objective facts and physical proofs. As Boleyn and the other women featured in *Divide and Rule* demonstrate, all history is, to some degree or another, fictionalised, shaped in the telling by its fragmented sources and unreliable narrators.

*

On 17 May, George, Norris, Brereton, Weston and Smeaton took to the scaffold at Tower Hill. This would be their last chance to confess and repent any lies. The first four reiterated their innocence. Smeaton said that he deserved to die – a fate he may have felt his false testimony merited.

Anne awaited death in the same royal apartments that had accommodated her ahead of her coronation less than three years earlier – a mercy, but surely also a reminder of how far she had fallen, and how fast. William Kingston, her gaoler as constable of the Tower, noted her rapid-cycling moods, periods of calm giving way to terror and outbursts of gallows humour.

After he informed her that she was to be executed the following morning, she prayed until dawn, making a confession to Cranmer and receiving the sacrament. There would be no late-breaking admission of guilt, just a last, cruel twist: a postponement. Perhaps the swordsman had been delayed. Anne spent a second night in prayer, then got dressed, choosing an English gabled hood rather than the French style, and a gown cut low enough to avoid any impediment to the blade's clean sweep.

Kingston, his yeomen, her ladies, Sandys and other courtiers accompanied her on the short walk to a scaffold within the Tower walls. As she mounted the platform, she could not have anticipated that Henry planned to kill her memory too. Nor, it seems, did he realise that her parting speech, heard by crowds of spectators, would hand her a final victory, not because it was faithfully recorded, but for the opposite reason. Like Anne herself, there are multiple versions, all but one suggesting her innocence. She makes no confession, levels no accusations and for the King has only praise: 'A gentler nor more merciful prince was there never,' she says in the most widely quoted iteration. Lancelot de Carle's account, thought to be first hand, has her lauding Henry's 'great humanity' and begging 'compassion for those who judged me to die'.

We can never know the real Anne Boleyn, but the scene is familiar to millions of us alive today, engraved into history, reworked and reinvented for each successive age. Too vital to extinguish, this royal woman will not go quietly.

Chapter 2

Elizabeth I: The Heart and Stomach of a Queen

She sits astride her horse, clad in full armour, for as she often says, she is a prince. Or perhaps she rides side-saddle, a cuirass fastened over her gown, plumes atop her auburn hair. However she presents herself, and no matter her exact words, this will be her defining moment, her speech the most consequential ever delivered by an English sovereign. Elizabeth I has come to Tilbury on 9 August 1588, to rally troops massing against the first Spanish Armada. To stiffen their resolve and boost national morale, she must transcend her most conspicuous disadvantage.

Her father, Henry, led his forces into battle and asserted his virility in other ways too, jousting and wrestling and taking all those wives and siring children, though few survived. The boy-king and pair of sad queens who reigned between his death and Elizabeth's accession ended their fleeting terms in pain and disappointment. Elizabeth has easily outperformed them in achievement and longevity, already three decades on the throne, but she is still a member of the lesser sex. In under a month, she turns fifty-five, no longer fertile, if ever she was. Like her half-sister, England's first crowned queen regnant, she will not provide England with heirs. Unlike Mary I, she has not tried to do so. In vain, her councillors have pushed and cajoled her to take a consort. Often, she seemed to toy with the idea, only to reject numerous proposals including, early in her rule, from Mary's widower, the Spanish king now seeking to invade her country.

Imperilled and besieged, she must live with her choices. As if the occasion were not sufficiently charged, two of the men flanking her – Robert Dudley, first Earl of Leicester, and his stepson Robert Devereux, second Earl of Essex – are polarising figures, rumoured at different times, and despite the chaste image she cultivates, to be her lovers. She reins in her mount, waiting for silence, although surely not even a great monarch can subdue the wind. What matters is that the substance and sentiment of her speech carry, first from soldier to soldier, then recorded in letters and diaries, pamphlets and books, and thence into history.

'My loving people,' she begins. It is a confident phrase, especially combined with the intimacy of the first person, rather than the royal 'we'. Traitors might lurk in this crowd of armed men, but she has earned the affection of the military and her subjects. 'Let tyrants fear,' Elizabeth says. If necessary, she is 'resolved to lay down for my God, and for my kingdom, and for my people, my honour, and my blood even in the dust'. Then she utters the sentence that above all others will resonate through the ages: 'I know I have the body but of a weak and feeble woman, but I have the heart and stomach of a king and of a king of England too.'

A record of these words comes courtesy of Leonel Sharpe, then chaplain to Devereux, who included them in a letter sent thirty-five years after the event. A later version of the speech, embedded in a sermon, is clumsier: 'The enemy perhaps may challenge my sex for that I am a woman, so may I likewise charge their mould for that they are but men, whose breath is in their nostrils, and if God does not charge England with the sins of England, little do I fear their force.' A similar rendering can be found below a diptych at a Norfolk church. The image to which it relates, *Elizabeth at Tilbury*, is dated 1588, but might well have been painted in the early seventeenth century.[6] In the picture, the Queen, in a green-and-gold dress with a large ruff, looks readier for a ball than battle, except that she carries a sword.

A gifted wordsmith and orator with a command of nine languages, Elizabeth made public addresses throughout her reign, also putting her name to large numbers of orders, official letters and personal notes. Add to this her literary works as a translator and poet, the diaries and dispatches of courtiers and foreign emissaries, portraiture that captures her from youth to old age, and earthbound sources including household accounts and other bureaucratic records, and you have a life that, unlike her mother's, is abundantly documented.

Plenty can create its own problems. It took painstaking detective work to reveal the extent to which members of Elizabeth's inner circle composed or edited official communications on her behalf – and, not infrequently, in their own interests. Correspondence and speeches 'full of those resonant phrases we might otherwise believe to have come from her own pen turn out, when the provenance of the early drafts is checked, to have been ghostwritten,' cautions historian John Guy, whose research for his book *Elizabeth: The Forgotten Years* yielded this insight. That would hardly be an unusual shortcut for a busy monarch, but it might also point to a woman battling to assert herself in a system built by and for kings.

In the absence of a paper trail for the Tilbury tub-thumper, or reliable information about the circumstances of its production, its final form and authorship remain unproven. At a St James's Palace soirée, the current king's principal private secretary, Sir Clive Alderton, assured me that Elizabeth herself had written it and under that very roof, next to the fireplace on which her parents' initials entwine. Alderton might be right. It is also possible that Elizabeth made no speech at all.

William Camden's influential Latin-language *Annals of the Reign of Elizabeth I*, published in two parts in 1615 and 1625, describes her talking to soldiers at Tilbury. A translation of Camden's work into English formalised this interaction into a prepared address to the ranks. Sharpe and others gave us the rousing oratory to hang on the skeleton of that scene; and with that, it became central to her legend. It helps that we want to believe it, and in her.

*

The deeper we dive into Elizabeth's life story, the more obvious it becomes that the queen we think we know is a construct. That makes her the perfect subject for a book which aims to unpick mythmaking, yet I find myself strangely resistant to chipping away her layers – and there are many. Unlike her mother, Elizabeth chose to create or co-opt the identities that shroud her from view. Her face a white mask, wigs hard as helmets, her ornate dresses costumes rather than mere clothing, she transformed herself into a prince, a warrior and a trinity of courtly perfection: the Virgin Queen, immaculate mother to her peoples, the pacific Good Queen Bess and the Faerie Queene of Edmund Spenser's poem, also known as Gloriana. This use of imagery elevated her to gender-fluid divinity at a time when most countries around the world prohibited women from reigning.

'To promote a woman to bear rule, superiority, dominion, or empire above any realm, nation, or city, is repugnant to nature; contumely to God, a thing most contrary to his revealed will and approved ordinance; and finally, it is the subversion of good order, of all equity and justice,' wrote Scottish theologian John Knox. He based his judgement on one of the most famous stories ever told and retold against women: that Eve tempted Adam into tasting the forbidden fruit.

Though he assured Elizabeth that his animus was directed less at queens in general than Catholic queens, such views enjoyed widespread support. John Aylmer, Bishop of London, in a sermon delivered in Elizabeth's presence, denigrated the majority of her sex as 'fond, foolish, wanton flibbergibs . . . in every way doltified with the dregs of the devil's dunghill'.

Hostility to female rule meant that a queen ran a heightened risk of plots and insurrections against her. Moreover, she would be expected to combine her regal role with producing heirs, confined in a darkened room for the final six weeks of each pregnancy with limited expectations of emerging unscathed, either as a result of the birth or the machinations of opponents in her absence. Her consort might protect her or prove problematic, for the nation as well as his wife. If Mary Tudor's difficult reign underscored these fears, Mary, Queen of Scots, beset by rebellions and catastrophically undermined by two of her husbands, appeared to confirm them.

Not that a woman could reliably win over sceptics by effectively wielding power. Elizabeth's contemporary, Catherine de Medici, consort to Henry II of France, went on to act as regent or adviser to three of their sons. No French royal escaped censure during a period of bloody civil war between Catholics and Huguenots – followers of Protestant reformer John Calvin – but much of the abuse directed against de Medici reveals a separate wellspring of hostility: 'She unmans cocks, tearing off their crests and testicles, a virago holds sway over the French,' declared a pamphleteer.

Elizabeth, by contrast, attracted more cheers than jeers for long stretches of her reign. Foreign envoys to her court marvelled at these shows of public affection, aware that their own monarchs prompted quite different reactions. In afterlife, Elizabeth is more lionised than loathed. Yet her forty-four years on the throne were marked by the sorts of reversals and events that might have left her with a very different reputation. She could be cruel, repressive and capricious; she committed strategic errors, resented the increasing role of parliament and did not reliably return the love she expected from her subjects. Those same soldiers who gathered at Tilbury and engaged in the wider campaign against the Spanish waited in vain for wages they were due.

Ireland remembers her not as Good Queen Bess but a tyrant, far from the only country to do so. Expeditions by the notorious slaver John Hawkins, sponsored by Elizabeth, captured hundreds of West Africans to sell into bondage in the New World, returning to England laden with cargo. Hawkins' cousin and fellow slaver, Francis Drake, became the best known of the queen's privateers, licensed to raid and loot the ships of other nations, disrupting not only military threats against England but also international trade. By the time of her death, there was growing public disaffection with 'an old woman's government'.

Why, then, does her reputation ride so high? One answer – and this is the flipside of queenship – is that she stood out from the march of male monarchs. No king inspecting his troops, whether he gave a speech or not, could have captured the imagination as Elizabeth did. There is also her life span to consider – roughly thirty years longer than the average for the period, despite a bout of smallpox that nearly killed her. This gave her over four decades to embed herself in the national psyche. It helped too that her court fizzed with some of the greatest creative talents not only of that century but of all time. The roll-call of writers alone included Spenser, Philip Sidney, Christopher Marlowe and, of course, William Shakespeare.

It is also true that luck, an essential component of leadership, was often on her side. Her mariners weakened the Spaniards, but weather completed the rout. Her first two Stuart successors, far from overshadowing her, proved deeply unpopular, further burnishing her memory. Every subsequent century has found new ways to embroider her legend according to its own fixations. She took a dint in the early Victorian period for diverging from its feminine ideals, but by the close of the era, she was celebrated as Victoria's imperial forerunner. These days, Elizabeth shines brighter than ever, synonymous with a golden age. A 2025 YouGov poll ranked her the fourth most popular monarch behind only Elizabeth II, Victoria and George

VI, still enjoying a boost from his portrayal in *The King's Speech*. An earlier YouGov survey of the most popular historical figures of all time placed her in the top ten, just behind her mother Anne Boleyn, Jesus and Alexander Fleming.

There is another obvious influence at play. History is written by its victors. Elizabeth's accession anchored the English reformation triggered by her parents' marriage. Her reign confirmed her as a lodestar for Protestantism and a symbol too of an England ascendant. Add to these factors her public relations smarts and you begin to understand her iconic status.

Nor is that all. What if so many of us invest in Elizabeth because her multiple identities, in combination with a talent for ambiguity, mean she can be made to ventriloquise our own worldviews, whatever they might be? Sharpe shared the Tilbury speech in a letter protesting a proposed match between the future Charles I and a dreaded Spaniard and Catholic. Two years before the outbreak of the Second World War, the British film *Fire Over England* revisited Tilbury to show how the country and its plucky monarch might stand firm against enemies overseas. In 2017, as Theresa May attempted to strike a deal for the UK's departure from the European Union, arch Brexiteer Jacob Rees-Mogg wished the prime minister 'good luck and good fortune in her negotiations until she comes to true glory and is welcomed back to this House as a twenty-first century Gloriana'. Soon enough, he was accusing May of showing insufficient Elizabethan mettle against Johnny Foreigner.

To feminists and progressives, the mythic Elizabeth provides reassurance. Her mother, stepmothers, half-sister and other prominent women of the period lurched from one horror to the next, abused, attacked and instrumentalised. The lives of

Marys Tudor and Stuart are unbelievably depressing. Even Catherine de Medici suffered through a loveless marriage, drilling holes through the palace floor to watch her husband and his mistress going at it. In Elizabeth, history appears to allow us one woman who succeeded on her own terms.

It is a bonus if we ignore her problematic decisions and actions, embracing her instead as the warm, sexy Elizabeth embodied by the warm, sexy Helen Mirren in the TV series *Elizabeth I*, or the twinkly, wise Elizabeth as played by the twinkly, wise Judi Dench in the film *Shakespeare in Love*. These versions come closest to the Elizabeth in whom we yearn to believe: woman and queen, seizing life with both hands, proof that it is possible to beat the patriarchy and thrive.

That might be a stretch, but hers is a story richer and stranger than simple characterisations allow.

*

The precarity of Elizabeth's early years makes her accession something of a miracle. It is also key to understanding her success. Hardship shaped her as much as privilege. Not yet three when, at a single stroke, she lost her mother, her rank, comforts and fair-weather friends, Elizabeth grew up understanding the fragility of power and its lethality – as well as the downsides of marriage and maternity.

Her first stepmother, Jane Seymour, died twelve days after giving birth. Jane's replacement, Anne of Cleves, rejected by the decaying Henry for her supposed lack of physical appeal and hailed in popular culture as a buoyant survivor of the Bluebeard-king, appears to have manoeuvred after the failure of his next marriage to return as his queen, only to be rebuffed again.

Henry's fifth marriage was, by many measures, the most disturbing. As a child, Catherine Howard had been suborned into sexual activity by her music teacher before embarking on a liaison with her cousin Francis Dereham. When, at no more than seventeen, she married the King, Dereham's boasts and brawling triggered an investigation during which he identified the courtier Thomas Culpeper as Catherine's latest lover. Her lady-in-waiting, George Boleyn's widow, Lady Rochford, had helped to arrange her mistress's trysts. Dereham, Culpeper and Rochford all received death sentences. So too did Catherine, ferried along the river to the Tower of London, past the men's heads on spikes, and so weak by the time of her own execution that she had to be lifted onto the scaffold. Interred like Anne Boleyn somewhere beneath the floor of the Chapel of St Peter ad Vincula, she defied attempts to locate her remains during Victorian restoration works. Either Henry had ordered that she be buried in quicklime the more thoroughly to erase her, or her bones, soft with youth, simply dissolved.

Katharine Parr, the sixth and last spouse to Henry, ushered in a short period of comparative calm for his offspring, lavishing affection on them, interceding with their father to bring the fractured family closer together and helping to persuade him to restore his daughters to the royal line. She also encouraged Elizabeth's intellectual development. Keenly interested in religious reform, Katharine published a prayer book, the first literary work by an English woman under her own name. Later, she would rush to destroy the contents of her library, tipped off that her enemies had pushed Henry to agree her arrest. Books, as she knew, possessed the capacity for good and ill, vehicles for knowledge and potential death warrants.

It is hard to align this kind, cautious trailblazer with the impulsive and possibly abusive woman who embroiled Elizabeth in scandal. On Henry's death, Katharine invited the Princess, then thirteen, to live with her at her Chelsea manor. Unfortunately for Elizabeth, her stepmother extended hospitality to other parties too. Jane Grey – a direct descendant of the Tudor line – may have spent some time there. Grey's guardian certainly did. He was Thomas Seymour, uncle to the new king Edward VI – and secret husband of the newly widowed Parr.

The couple's hasty marriage and failure to seek royal assent are often interpreted as proofs of Katharine's passion for Seymour, thought to have been her lover before she caught Henry's attention. The musical *Six* is one of many cultural representations of Parr to construe her enforced separation from Seymour as a personal tragedy. Parr's greater misfortune lay in falling for Seymour in the first place. A seventeenth-century writer, Gregorio Leti, claimed that his first move on Edward's accession was to propose to Elizabeth, returning his attentions to Katharine only after the bigger catch turned him down. Leti is not a reliable source, but there is strong evidence that Seymour did target Elizabeth before or after Katharine's sudden death in September 1548. He may also have tilted at Mary Tudor.

Testimony from Elizabeth's governess, Kat Ashley, and cofferer (treasurer), Thomas Parry, about Seymour's behaviour during those nineteen months in Chelsea described him paying early morning visits to Parr's young houseguest, slapping her back and buttocks, making as if to get into bed with her, trying to kiss her and, at least once, arriving only in his nightshirt. Far from curbing this behaviour, Katharine reputedly joined in, tickling her stepdaughter and even holding her while Seymour cut Elizabeth's dress 'into a hundred pieces'. If Katharine persuaded herself that this was innocent horseplay, finding Elizabeth and Seymour 'all alone, he having her in his arms' apparently changed her mind. Elizabeth abruptly left the household, never to see Parr again. Days after giving birth, Katharine died. Seymour was free to remarry.

In letters between them, Elizabeth's feelings are opaque. Already, it seems that she understood that ambiguity could protect her. Seymour possessed no such subtlety. Jealous of his older brother, then governing England on behalf of the child monarch, he broke into the royal apartments, whether to kidnap the King or merely to gain his ear. The exploit cost two lives: a spaniel Seymour shot, and his own. Parliament condemned him to death through an act of attainder that cited conspiring to marry Elizabeth among thirty-three offences.

The affair left its mark on Elizabeth too. Long after Seymour's execution, rumours circulated about their relationship. One strand of gossip identified Edward de Vere, the seventeenth Earl of Oxford, as their child. (If the name rings bells, that is probably because a separate theory claims the Earl to be the true author of Shakespeare's works.) Any taint of impurity, never mind a baby out of wedlock, could consign an unmarried woman to a nunnery or social exile. Elizabeth, daughter to 'the great whore' Anne Boleyn, rendered illegitimate by the annulment of her parents' marriage, carried more baggage than most.

Already a longshot for the throne, the Seymour scandal appeared to put 'the little whore' entirely out of contention. The real loser would not be Elizabeth, however, but Jane Grey.

*

In early 1553, aged just fifteen, King Edward sickened, rallied, then began an irreversible decline. His privy councillors pressured him to name an heir. Unmarried and childless, he at first willed the Crown to his hypothetical issue, only surrendering to a crueller reality in later drafts. His 'Devise for the Succession' ruled out both half-sisters. Bastardised like Elizabeth, Mary's other defect was her devout Catholicism. Edward had overseen a raft of radical reforms to stamp out the old religion including an act of parliament that established the English-language *Book of Common Prayer*.

An additional consideration, or voice, surely influenced his final choice too: John Dudley, Duke of Northumberland. As the King entered his last months, Northumberland engineered the marriage of his son Guilford to Grey. The following month, the King, now sinking fast, anointed Jane his successor. To describe her term as lasting nine days, as many do, is to discount the period between Edward's death on 6 July and her formal procession to the Tower on the tenth, where she was proclaimed monarch and installed to await her coronation. Though that ceremony would never take place, Jane reigned until Mary seized power on 19 July, a total of fifteen days.

Numbers matter and so do labels. Popular culture, even its apparently women-friendly reaches – exemplified in this case by an Amazon Prime series that bills itself a feminist retelling of Jane's history – insists on referring to Grey as 'Lady Jane'. Yet she was born in wedlock of royal blood and called to the throne by Edward. Had things gone differently, we would know her as Queen Jane I, a religious reformer with a mind of her own, who demonstrated the last of these characteristics by refusing to make Guilford king alongside her.

Northumberland had underestimated her and, fatally, the women he thought he could brush aside. Mary neither submitted nor fled as he expected. Instead, she wrote to the privy council demanding allegiance, raised an army and marched on London accompanied by as many as ten thousand troops, cheering crowds and, in a moment of solidarity that would not last, Elizabeth.

Sequestered in the Tower, Jane transitioned from queen to traitor. She might yet have escaped with her life, because killing a sovereign, even a usurper, challenged the concept of monarchy as divinely ordained. It was the son of the poet Thomas Wyatt who forced Mary's hand. Thomas Wyatt the Younger, though Protestant, supported her accession but found it impossible to stomach her betrothal to Philip, Hapsburg heir to the throne of Spain, by now Europe's pre-eminent imperial power. Wyatt was far from alone in fearing their marriage would relegate England to a vassal state.

When Mary refused to look for a homegrown bridegroom, Wyatt and other nobles conceived a plot. They would depose Mary in favour of Elizabeth. The coup might have succeeded, but news of the conspiracy leaked, bouncing its leaders into premature action. Wyatt alone led troops to London. If he expected popular sentiment to swell their ranks, he realised his mistake soon enough, captured at the gates of the city, beheaded and quartered, some body parts burned, others boiled for display in a gibbet. Though Jane's father had been one of the plotters, Mary offered her a reprieve: embrace Catholicism and live. Jane refused. She saw Guilford's headless body from a window before herself submitting to the axe.

Elizabeth, suspected of complicity and forced to retrace her mother's route to the Tower, could easily have ended her days there as Boleyn had done. Jane's scaffold still stood, and, with Jane dead, Elizabeth represented the best hope and rallying point for Protestants. Moreover, though Catholics remained a majority in England at this stage, her popularity transcended confessional divisions. Bystanders applauded her on her way to prison. Nor was Mary certain of her loyalty. Elizabeth failed to offer a convincing explanation for her sudden decision, on the eve of Wyatt's rebellion, to leave her residence at Ashridge for a manor owned by one of his associates.

Transferred from the Tower on the eighteenth anniversary of her mother's execution, Elizabeth would spend the next eleven months under house arrest at Woodstock Manor, possibly for her own protection. She was already the target of Catholic assassins. History more often casts Mary as her pitiless gaoler and Elizabeth a heroine in the mould of courtly romances, palely loitering as she waits for deliverance. Two of the best-known chroniclers of the period, Raphael Holinshed and John Foxe, describe the lonely captive using her diamond ring to incise a verse into a pane of glass:

Much suspected by me,
Nothing proved can be,
Quoth Elizabeth prisoner.[7]

Like so many tales about her, it serves her legend whether true or not.

*

In the world beyond that unsubstantiated window, significant shifts were under way. Mary busily consolidated power and then shared some of it with her new consort, Philip.

European kingdoms and dynasties were still competing for supremacy, with the reformation adding heat and complexity to international relations. Mary looked to a future in which her children with Philip would affirm England as a Catholic nation, aligned with his kingdom of Spain, if not subsumed into its empire. In the shorter term, he sought English support for Spain's ongoing secular wars with France. On the face of it, the arrangement suited England too, with Spain acting as a bulwark against French aggression. Mary of Guise, scion of one of France's most powerful families, currently held Scotland's regency for her daughter, Mary, Queen of Scots.

Unfortunately for England's Mary, the Anglo-Spanish campaign inflicted high costs on her and her country: human, financial and, through the loss of Calais, the last English outpost in France. The outcome helped to feed the narrative that Philip dominated his wife and sublimated England's interests to Spain's. In fact, his powers as a consort were limited, by a special act, and through their marriage contract, from the start.

Look beyond the propaganda churned out against Mary by those opposed to female rule, Catholicism or both, and you might be surprised. Her persecution of Protestants, while undoubtedly brutal, was effective in its own terms, for a time stemming the growth of the new religion. Some eight hundred of its adherents fled the country during her reign, and around 280 burned. Elizabeth would initially appear more tolerant; she had no desire to 'make windows into men's souls' according to a letter written by her spymaster Francis Walsingham. Catholics could retain their beliefs and practices if they supported her queenship, and many did.

Others plotted, often from exile, sometimes with the assistance of foreign powers that also threatened invasions. After a flurry of assassination attempts, Elizabeth hardened her stance, backing Protestant insurgencies in other countries, eliminating Catholic challengers at home and putting to death seminary priests, many on the apparently secular grounds of treason. She would also demand for two plotters a punishment more severe than the standard traitors' death of hanging: drawing and quartering. They were revived after hanging to experience the removal of their genitalia and bowels.

Bloody Mary, bloodier Elizabeth. The last two Tudor monarchs had far more in common than English chroniclers have generally allowed. Mary's, however, was a short rule that ended in disappointment. Twice, she believed herself pregnant. On the first occasion, she made elaborate preparations for the birth, but something other than a baby swelled her belly: desperation and, probably, cancer. In her final hours, she reputedly agonised over her failure, murmuring, 'when I am dead and opened, you shall find Calais lying in my heart'. A word that did not pass her lips was 'Elizabeth'.

Mary's will, like Edward's, originally named the heirs she expected to produce. An updated version stipulated only that the crown should pass to her next in line. Close to death, she finally sent a message to Elizabeth via one of her ladies begging her to 'maintain the Catholic religion in England'. She died on 17 November 1558. Before the news could be confirmed, her former subjects were already celebrating the accession of a young woman who promised a fresh start.

*

History loops and repeats in the slipstream of unseen flows and forces. That can lead to confusion. Parallels in the lives and experiences of royal women do not reliably indicate similarities of character, but rather that these external pressures impact them in much the same ways. Moreover, monarchy projects majesty through pomp and form. The more ancient a ceremony is – or appears to be – the more effectively it asserts the legitimacy of the institution and its successive leaders. Thus it has always been, and so will it always be. That is why, on the eve of her coronation, Elizabeth returned to a place of personal pain, the Tower, a traditional staging post for monarchs on their way to being crowned. The next morning, she set out for Westminster.

The first sign that Elizabeth intended not merely to follow customs but to create them came just half a mile into the journey, at Gracechurch Street. There, her procession passed a tableau showcasing her lineage. Actors representing Henry VII and Elizabeth of York sat on the lowest of three stages, while above them, at the apex of the structure, a woman played the new queen herself. On the middle tier, a man costumed as her father sat companionably alongside a figure his real-life counterpart had tried to obliterate: Anne Boleyn.

'It is largely thanks to her daughter that the cult of Anne Boleyn starts,' says Tracy Borman, whose book *Anne Boleyn and Elizabeth I* identifies instances of Elizabeth memorialising her mother even when it was dangerous for her to do so. As a child, Elizabeth risked Henry's wrath to wear a necklace thought to have belonged to Anne to sit for a family portrait. On becoming queen, Borman explains, 'Elizabeth starts honouring her mother. She starts displaying her emblems. She talks about her. She appoints her Boleyn relatives to high positions.' Anne's falcon emblem and other devices decorated Elizabeth's palaces; she wore a ring enclosing portraits of herself and another woman, most likely Anne, and also adopted a motto – *semper eadem*: 'always the same' or 'as ever' – that Boleyn is thought to have used. These were bold moves given her mother's infamy.

What Elizabeth the Ambiguous never did was to criticise her father, even by implication. She neither challenged the dissolution of her parents' marriage, nor her mother's conviction. She left Boleyn's bones undisturbed. Henry, not Anne, entitled Elizabeth to sit on the throne, and throughout her reign she praised him rather than pulling him down. She was, says Borman, 'a master strategist', adept at modelling her intentions 'through actions more than words', something her twentieth century namesake, Elizabeth II, adapted to the gentler art of reigning without ruling.

On the day of her coronation, the first Elizabeth revealed something else about herself. She had survived Mary's queenship by appearing to conform, attending mass and expressing interest in deepening her engagement with Catholicism. Now she let her real inclinations show, telling the abbot and monks who met her at Westminster Abbey with lighted torches that she could see well enough without their help. This was not merely a statement of religious affiliation but one of independence. Key themes of her reign emerged at its dawn.

Mary had blazed a trail, but the path for queens regnant remained overgrown and thorny. The barriers were literal as well as cultural, political and psychological, with the geography of palaces mirroring the organisation of the court. A king hosted formal audiences and banquets in the public-facing series of rooms, collectively known as the presence chamber, but transacted much important business in his private or privy chamber (again, a suite of rooms). Often, he would continue to discuss weighty matters of state even after retreating to his inner sanctum, the bedchamber. To serve as a king's groom of the stool was to acquire all kinds of invaluable knowledge. A queen's ladies engaged with their sovereign in similarly personal ways but lacked the direct routes to translating intimacy to influence available to male courtiers. Nor could a queen so easily conduct private conversations with her advisers and emissaries. A man spending time alone with her inevitably attracted gossip, to her detriment more than his.

All monarchs endured intense levels of scrutiny because their wellbeing concerned the whole nation, their bodies its representation and guarantors. Unlike ordinary mortals, they had two such entities: a natural body, flesh and blood, and a notional body politic, repository of state powers. The death of the natural body threatened a crisis until the body politic safely transferred to its new host.

Queens suffered the same intrusive attention to their physical person as kings, but with an added dimension. Their reproductive capacity mattered to every subject and prospective consort.

The infant Elizabeth had been paraded naked to demonstrate her future marriageability. (All visible body parts were deemed present and in working order.) As an adult, she tolerated an obsessive focus on her menstrual cycle, hymen and health. Inevitably, her lack of children attracted speculation. The playwright Ben Jonson circulated the rumour that she 'had a membrana on her that made her uncapable of man'. Another theory speculated that she was not biologically female at all. In the twentieth century, this formalised into a potential diagnosis of complete androgen insensitivity syndrome (CAIS) with a research paper called 'Queen Elizabeth I: a case of testicular feminisation?' Anne Sebba's brilliant biography of Wallis Simpson, *That Woman*, wonders if Simpson's assertiveness, flat chest and childlessness might be a marker of the same condition. Yet intersex conditions are rare, unlike ideas about how 'real' women behave, and research suggests that psychological outcomes for women with or without CAIS are identical.

For Elizabeth, there was no safe ground between perceptions of being too masculine and presenting as overtly feminine. Women were thought too weak to rule, and any sign of infirmity – she suffered from insomnia, chronic headaches, stomach pains and decaying teeth – could tempt more plotters to try their luck.

Her concerns underpinned a daily routine of dressing and applying make-up that, in later years, could take her ladies more than two hours to complete. Elizabeth fiercely controlled her portraiture, ordering pictures destroyed if they fell short of her expectations. Laws backed and strengthened her hold on image-making, stipulating which versions of her face could be used and imposing penalties for flouting those rules. Mary had introduced a charter giving the Company of Stationers control over printing in England, an early attempt by royalty to regulate the media. Elizabeth forged a template for managing it. A famous portrait of her, painted shortly before or soon after her death in 1603, shows her radiant with health and majesty, every surface of her magnificent dress embroidered with symbols of wisdom, youth, virginity, prosperity and might and, in her right hand, a rainbow signifying peace. 'The thing that is still most powerful in royal comms and royal positioning is the picture,' says Paddy Harverson, who in the twenty-first century served as a royal communications secretary.

The care with which Elizabeth presented herself and curated her portraits sparked accusations of vanity, especially from those ill-disposed towards her. That does not explain why people who make a study of her continue to swallow the trope. A slew of biographies and scholarly papers apply the word 'vain' to her not once but multiple times. The term pops up in online searches as thick and fast as blisters on a smallpox sufferer. Here is a description of Elizabeth on Westminster Abbey's website: she was 'noted for her vanity and love of jewels'. A popular blog, *The Elizabeth Files*, repeats a common narrative, much of it derived from the dispatches of a French ambassador whose description of her decolletage has been distorted in translation to suggest she flashed her breasts. 'It is a sad fact,' says the blog post, 'that she became "mutton dressed as lamb" as she still dressed like a young woman, plastered her face in thick make-up, wore low necklines and bright-red wigs, and really became a laughing stock to visiting foreign ambassadors. As she aged and felt herself losing her grip on her male courtiers, she became bitter and jealous.'

The author, who concludes by professing admiration for the Queen despite these lapses, titles the piece 'Was Elizabeth a Jealous Old Hag?'

Critic and historian Kate Maltby asks a better question. Her *Guardian* article, 'Why is Elizabeth I, the most powerful woman in our history, always depicted as a grotesque?', deciphers a trend that uglies up actresses playing the later-stage queen. Maltby cites a run of Elizabeths from Glenda Jackson via Cate Blanchett to Anita Dobson, the last of whom appeared in a drama-documentary about the Armada 'streaked with white and red make-up' and resembling 'nothing so much as Heath Ledger's Joker, or perhaps his copycat grandmother'. Margot Robbie's Elizabeth postdates Maltby's piece but surely belongs in the same canon, her chalky make-up and bright-orange curls veer[ing] perilously close to Ronald McDonald cosplay,' according to a reviewer for *Slate*. Much of the publicity around Robbie's performance in the 2018 movie *Mary Queen of Scots* centred on the time it took to ravage her beautiful face with prosthetic smallpox.

Maltby's conclusion is that many such interpretations, even if notionally feminist, reflect a fear of older women. 'If we can't deny their political power, we'll deny their erotic power instead,' she writes, citing sexualised abuse directed at Hillary Clinton and Angela Merkel, respectively labelled a ball-breaker and 'unfuckable'.

Clinton, Merkel and the Tudor queen all responded to the intersections of ageism and sexism by donning protective clothing. Clinton and Merkel's trouser suits, symbols and signifiers of male leadership, are modern equivalents of Elizabeth's armour, jewel-encrusted robes and stiffened ruffs.

Merkel, Germany's first female chancellor and the country's first to be born in the communist GDR, resisted all outward alterations but one throughout her sixteen years at the pinnacle of politics. Those suits, near identical in boxy cut and numbering more than a hundred, ranged across such a broad palette that a graphic designer refashioned them into a Pantone chart. Childless, the politician nevertheless managed to recast herself as the only kind of older woman respected in patriarchal societies, acquiring the nickname 'Mutti': mummy. It was a trick Elizabeth had pulled four hundred years earlier. 'Though after my death you may have many stepdames,' the Queen told parliamentarians pushing her to marry, 'yet shall you never have any a more mother, then I mean to be unto you all.'

The consonances do not end there. Merkel grew up in an environment as fraught and surveilled as Henry's court – and this undoubtedly informed her adult life. Certainly, her early brushes with East Germany's secret police taught her the value of operating below the radar, even in the spotlight of high office. Criticised for indecision and inaction, the chancellor in fact possessed clarity and purpose, deliberately concealing these qualities to maintain combustible coalitions. The Tudor queen developed similar tactics. As historian Kate Williams writes in her book *Rival Queens*, 'Elizabeth had two refuges in times of great political import: ambiguity and refusal to decide.'

*

The foreigner who landed on English soil in 1568 would test those tactics to the full. Seven years earlier, the widowed Queen of Scots had returned to a country she barely knew despite reigning over it in name since she was six days old. When she married the heir to the throne of France, her in-laws envisaged the union as a route to absorbing not only Scotland but also England into their empire. Her husband's sudden death left Mary adrift. The new king, just ten, named his mother, Catherine de Medici, governor. De Medici immediately set about building closer ties with Elizabeth, whom she hoped to persuade to marry him or another of her remaining sons.

The homeland to which Mary returned required force and clever footwork to govern. Her subjects were embracing a strand of Calvinism, propagated by John Knox, that was suspicious of earthly power. Nobles enriched by lands acquired during the dissolution of the monasteries opposed any return to Catholicism.

Knox was among many voices urging Mary to mitigate her twin disadvantages of sex and religion by finding herself a Protestant consort. Elizabeth offered marital advice too – and also dangled an incentive. If Mary selected a spouse with her approval, she would name her heir to the English throne. Their back-and-forth continued until Elizabeth made a wildly inappropriate suggestion: Robert Dudley, her favourite and suspected lover. If that were not bad enough, she proposed that he and Mary live at her court. There would have been three of them in the marriage.

In other circumstances, Mary might have taken more time to evaluate the options. Scotland, however, was a tinderbox, and she faced another danger too: coerced wedlock. As Kate Williams observes, 'men kidnapping and raping women . . . was not uncommon. Heiresses were often at risk of being abducted.

In such cases, the rapist would be allowed, even encouraged, to marry the girl.'

Luckily, or so Mary believed, Henry Darnley offered a solution, English-born scion of the Scottish aristocracy, Catholic but flexible in his beliefs, he possessed the face of an angel and the blood of at least three royal houses. He also turned out to be a monster. As Mary awaited the birth of their child, armed men burst into her chamber, held a gun to her stomach, and stabbed her private secretary fifty-seven times. Darnley had sanctioned the plot, possibly hoping to make his wife miscarry. Their child, James, born three months later, pushed him further down the line of succession.

Recuperating after her difficult labour, Mary consulted with courtiers: how to contain Darnley? Annulling their marriage would delegitimise their child. Perhaps her spouse could be intimidated into better behaviour. At least one of those courtiers, the Earl of Bothwell, planned a more permanent solution. Somehow Darnley and a servant escaped the blast Bothwell engineered, only to be strangled. Their bodies were found in the orchard amid a strange harvest: a dagger, a rope and a chair.

Mary might have ridden out accusations of complicity had she not swiftly married Bothwell. Yet he quite possibly forced her to acquiesce by kidnapping and raping her. Hers is a story of violence and subjugation but also of courage and resilience. Intelligent and determined, she in many respects resembled the woman who would prove her undoing. Forced to abdicate in favour of her son and imprisoned in the remote fortress of Lochleven, Mary twice outwitted her captors to escape. Successful in her second bid, she immediately set about raising an army.

Only after defeat in battle did she decide to throw herself on Elizabeth's mercy. Both women would suffer the consequences as long as they lived. In death they remain locked in false opposition, Elizabeth denied her humanity, Mary her capacity for reason, their story twisted to confirm a central theme of the patrimonarchy: that there can be no true sisterhood within its ranks.

*

Fictionalised accounts of Mary's near two decades of English captivity and eventual beheading on Elizabeth's orders often imagine a pivotal encounter between the two queens. In fact, though they corresponded frequently, they never met. Elizabeth showed flashes of sympathy for Mary's predicament, but there was no upside to helping her regain her throne. James, a Protestant, made a preferable neighbour to his Catholic mother. Nor did it seem wise to let the refugee settle in France, in case she used her exile to revive her claim to the English crown. In years to come, Elizabeth's influential minister, William Cecil would urge Mary's execution, but that required a compelling case. Condemning her to die without sufficient grounds would surely unite the whole of Catholic Europe against England and Elizabeth. For now, the only viable option mirrored the Tudor queen's own instincts – equivocation and delay.

Darnley's murder provided the mechanism for implementing this strategy. Three hearings made a show of investigating Mary's role in these events. The slow process, held under English laws and with the participation of Mary's enemies, overrode her sovereign status and denied her access to damning evidence against her. The so-called casket letters, correspondence purporting to be between her and Bothwell and almost certainly doctored if not forged, proved sufficient to prevent a not-guilty verdict, but not to send her to the gallows. Mary could be held indefinitely pending further inquiries.

Much of her ensuing captivity passed in relative comfort under the relaxed watch of the Earl of Shrewsbury. Meanwhile, the world turned, its rotations giving her fresh hope only to dash it again. At the same time, Elizabeth faced down seemingly endless attempts on her life and rule. Months after she successfully quelled the Rising of the Northern Earls, Pope Pius V not only excommunicated her but incited Catholic subjects to depose and kill her. Though laws drafted in response criminalised any attempts to question Elizabeth's queenship, conspiracies against her multiplied. Mary featured in many as a replacement queen.

Such plots were not the only danger to Elizabeth. The assassination of the Dutch protestant leader, William of Orange, drove home how effective a lone-wolf attack could be. Cecil responded to the news by drawing up a bond of association whose signatories undertook to defend Elizabeth or, if she should die, to avenge her and, in a move that chipped away at the primacy of bloodlines, agree her successor. The bond affected Mary's status too, by making any person involved in a conspiracy against the sovereign jointly liable for it whether they knew about it or not. Henceforth, all plots centred on Mary would condemn her as a traitor.

More blows followed. Mary's son turned down her proposal that they rule Scotland jointly. With his eyes fixed on the prize of becoming Elizabeth's heir, he had, for some while, been negotiating with the English queen and her ministers and had no interest in aiding a mother he barely knew and who he believed may have sanctioned his father's killing. Weeks later, after fifteen years of house arrest, Mary lost many of her remaining privileges, deprived of all but a few attendants, transferred to more spartan accommodations and placed under the charge of a veteran statesman, Ralph Sadler, once a member of Thomas Cromwell's household. Reports of Sadler's leniency towards Mary led to his removal from the role. Her last gaoler, Amias Paulet, a Puritan with a fierce hatred of Catholicism, showed no such kindness.

Mary soon began corresponding with a fresh set of conspirators, including Shrewsbury's former page, Anthony Babington, writing in cipher and smuggling her notes in waterproof casings inside beer barrels. This evidence would have been sufficient under the bond of association to convict her, but Francis Walsingham instructed his cryptographer to add to one message a damning coda urging the plotters to hurry. The outcome of Mary's trial, at Fotheringhay Castle, was never in doubt. Not so Elizabeth's response to the verdict.

This time, her denial and deferral were born not of tactical considerations but turmoil. The daughter of the first queen to die on the scaffold, she recoiled from the idea of sending her cousin and sister sovereign to the same fate. Elizabeth also feared that subjecting a king or queen regnant to temporal laws eroded the office – and Charles I's downfall would prove the point. Plus, executing women did not always go down well, and Mary's death might prompt revulsion among Protestants as well as bolstering the Catholic cause. For months, Elizabeth prevaricated, then signed a warrant only to ask that it be stayed, casting around for ways to avoid being spattered with Mary's blood. A letter to Paulet, apparently sent at Elizabeth's behest, inquires why he has not yet 'found out some way to shorten the life' of his prisoner. Paulet gave the suggestion short shrift. 'God forbid,' he replied, 'that I should make so foul a shipwreck of my conscience.'

On 8 February 1587, ministers cut short the agonies of both women and Mary's life, carrying out the order before Elizabeth could intervene. As she prepared for the block, Mary shed her outer garments to reveal a petticoat and bodice the scarlet of Catholic martyrdom. Despite a show of dignity, hers was a messy end. The executioner missed his target with the first blow, slicing open Mary's skull, then sawed and hacked to finish the job. Some reports claim that when he tried to pick up her head to display it to onlookers, it rolled away, leaving him holding her wig. Her lapdog, drenched in blood, cowered under her skirts.

*

Philip II's decision a year later to invade England is often construed as an act of vengeance, but Elizabeth had long provoked her one-time brother-in-law and suitor. John Hawkins and Francis Drake constantly disrupted and looted Spanish shipping, while England bolstered Dutch Protestants in their efforts to throw off Hapsburg rule.

'Neither men nor war defined her reign.' This summary of Elizabeth's achievement appears at the end of the movie *Firebrand*, yet the Anglo-Spanish War outlasted her, overlapping and intersecting with Ireland's Nine Years' War against English rule. Also, the idea that the Elizabethan age represents a matriarchal interruption to the patriarchal continuum is mistaken. True, her mother, stepmothers, half-sister and other significant women, from Catherine de Medici to Elizabeth's mirror and mortification, the Queen of Scots, impacted Elizabeth's life and thus the era that bears her name. Yet these relationships formed within the crucible and context of male supremacy and man-made conflicts. Moreover, Elizabeth's choice to remain single, though sparing her the tensions between monarchical power and wifely submission, yoked her through gossip to battalions of men.

It does not help that ambiguity and delay proved so intrinsic to her approach to marriage that historians struggle to determine how seriously she took most of her suitors. Elizabeth's reinvention as the Virgin Queen, a move late in her reign that repositioned her childlessness as a superpower, also carried downsides, intensifying scrutiny of her body for evermore. Was she really virginal or, as scandalmongers claimed, a woman of prodigious sexual appetites? Apparently, we still yearn to know.

Queenship thrust her into constant interactions with men. Even now, women risk their dealings with male colleagues being misconstrued as liaisons. For Elizabeth, past scandals combined with the factionalism of court to enmesh many of her working relationships in feverish speculation.

In 1584, Mary wrote a letter from house arrest listing some of the ripest rumours in circulation. Elizabeth had supposedly 'slept with [Dudley] an infinite number of times with all the familiarity and licence as between man and wife' and also 'disported' herself with courtiers and suitors. For unspecified reasons, she was 'not like other women' and could indulge her appetites without fear of pregnancy. The inventory continued: Elizabeth could frequently be volatile and cruel, flying into rages with her ladies, breaking the finger of one and cutting another with a knife at the dinner table.

Elizabeth fed the rumour mill herself, giving Dudley quarters near to hers and, when she feared she might be dying from smallpox, naming him as her preferred regent. These details speak to her reliance on him but fall short of proving the sexual intimacy claimed in Mary's letter. Her ladies surrounded her and a select few routinely shared her bed for warmth and security. She and Dudley could have found other opportunities for lovemaking – they often rode out alone – but when Elizabeth imagined herself near death and in urgent need of confession, she reportedly professed herself innocent of sin. This does not exclude the possibility that the relationship extended to what might be termed heavy petting. Divine judgement and the potential earthly repercussions of sex outside wedlock deterred couples from full intercourse, but this by no means ensured total abstinence. The more important point is that Elizabeth loved Dudley, leaned on him, trusted him and bestowed substantial powers, positions and presents on him.

Elizabeth's co-option of courtly language, etiquettes and imagery added to the confusion, but what choice did she have? The sole template for a reigning queen, sketched by her immediate predecessor, was of no use. Unmarried and aged just twenty-five at her accession, Elizabeth forged a new approach. Rather than ignore the expectations of women, she harnessed and subverted them. She would be the courtly ideal, preternaturally powerful and eternally unavailable, flirting for England, dancing and bantering, touching and teasing and marking out her favourites with affectionate nicknames. Dudley became her 'Sweet Robin' and her 'Eyes'; her Lord Chancellor, Christopher Hatton, her 'Lids', while Walter Raleigh's expeditions earned him the label 'Water'. Even Walsingham, William Cecil and Cecil's son, Robert, who succeeded him as principal secretary, found themselves suborned into the game, Walsingham dubbed 'Moor' for his dark complexion, the elder Cecil Elizabeth's 'Spirit' and Robert, who suffered from scoliosis, her 'Elf' or 'Pygmy'. Communications between the Queen and her counsellors mined the floweriest forms of courtly romance. In a typically overwrought message to her, Hatton declared 'Passion overcometh me. I can write no more. Love me; for I love you.'

Between such courtly effusions and court gossip, we are left with two irreconcilable ideas of Elizabeth: a goddess, chased but chaste, and a born slattern, biologically abnormal and constitutionally corrupt. Both notions are patriarchal constructs and neither fits the available evidence. Writers often attempt to square the circle by depicting the Tudor monarch as a woman sacrificing her personal desires to duty – 'the lonely Queen' as per the subtitle of a 1954 biography. 'The hardest thing to govern,' sighs Mirren's TV Elizabeth, 'is the heart.' While such interpretations better accord with the known facts of Elizabeth's life, they also echo another patriarchal meme foisted on women in positions of power, especially those without children. Men are allowed to have it all: happiness and success. Women are assumed to trade one for the other.

Elizabeth's closest relationships were problematic, her queenship fraught and, like anyone who survives to middle age or beyond, she carried the scars of grief and disappointment. As she entered her final years, her melancholy became sufficiently palpable for observers to comment on it. Children might have brought her a modicum of contentment or given her peace of mind by securing a peaceful transition, but they could also have posed existential threats beyond the perils of childbirth. Family ties counted for little in the teeth of ambition. One's heir might seize power or, like Mary's son, James, installed as Scotland's king at thirteen months of age, be used as a puppet. Elizabeth was acutely aware of such risks. 'Princes cannot like their own children,' she told a Scottish emissary. 'Think you that I could love my own winding-sheet?'

As for love and companionship, who can say whether Elizabeth would have found more joy in life if she had taken a husband? What is clear is that her refusal to do so protected her from the fate of many royal women, locked in loveless, bloodless unions, or abusive ones. Eight years into her reign, she instructed her ministers to rebuff, in robust terms, parliamentarians urging her to marry: 'I will never be by violence constrained to do anything.' She would consider the matter at her own leisure and according to circumstances – and without pesky parliamentary interference. 'For it is monstrous that the feet should direct the head.' Take that, parliamentary democracy.

Marriage might have clipped her wings. Marriageability, however, gave her the means to keep friends close and enemies closer. She exploited the interest of suitors to the full, stringing along foreign royals including the Protestant Erik, King of Sweden, and a clutch of Catholics, from Philip and his Hapsburg nephew Charles, Archduke of Austria, to their French rivals. For decades, she allowed de Medici to believe she might be tempted into marriage with one of her sons, first Charles, then Henry, and finally the youngest, Francis, the Duke of Anjou. Despite a twenty-one-year age gap between them, negotiations proceeded further than with any previous suits. Dubbed by Elizabeth her 'Frog', Anjou developed a genuine rapport with her. Even so, he probably never stood a chance. His Catholicism counted against him, influential courtiers opposed the match, and her heart apparently lay elsewhere.

A famous painting, labelled *Queen Elizabeth dances the Volta with Robert Dudley, Earl of Leicester,* appears to show the monarch ignoring Anjou as she and Dudley participate in a dance damned in a contemporary account as 'lewd . . . full of scandalous, beastly gestures and immodest movements. The volta is also responsible for the misfortune that innumerable murders and miscarriages are brought about by it.' The male dancer lifts his red-haired partner by the crotch, while another man, possibly Anjou, turns his head away. The identities of the figures have been disputed but if the woman is Elizabeth, the artist who painted her will have done so without her agreement, and probably after her death. This was not an image she would have wished to share. Though it testified to her continuing vigour – she would have been in her late forties at the time of Anjou's courtship - it reveals the centrality of her relationship with Dudley.

They had crossed paths as children and coincided again in the Tower. Dudley's father, the Duke of Northumberland, and elder brother, Guilford, husband to Queen Jane, lost their heads in the attempt to supplant Mary Tudor. Robert survived Mary's rule, rushing to Elizabeth's side at her accession. She appointed him her master of horse, responsible for royal travels and entertainments, and he would swiftly rise to greater heights, joining her privy council, later created Earl of Leicester and Baron of Denbigh, gifted the stately home Kenilworth and sent to command English forces in the Netherlands. Such benefits flowed to the end of Dudley's life despite passionate arguments that regularly drove the pair apart.

As Dudley's star rose, his wife, Amy Robsart, stayed away from court, inevitably prompting speculation – all the more so after whispers that she had 'a malady in her breast'. Might this be a cover story concocted in advance of poisoning her? When Robsart turned up dead at the bottom of a staircase, it was not much of a stretch to conclude that Dudley had murdered her, possibly with his queen's connivance. But if Robsart's fall really was engineered to clear the way for Dudley to marry Elizabeth, it had the opposite effect. The coroner's investigation proved inconclusive. On the day she died, Robsart had issued a highly unusual instruction for a woman of her status, insisting that every member of her household leave her alone for the day. This jarring detail lends itself to two obvious interpretations: either that Robsart made an assignation to meet someone who killed her, or that she planned to end her own life. Then again, perhaps she just tripped.

Almost a quarter of a century later, a pamphlet, popularly known as *Leicester's Commonwealth*, put the blame squarely on Dudley. The tract, though published abroad, circulated widely in England. Almost certainly the work of Catholic propagandists, it constituted an attack not only on Dudley but the Queen herself. Her government's attempts to suppress the publication boosted its popularity, a lesson in media management that sometimes still eludes royal spin doctors.

Whether or not Elizabeth ever seriously contemplated making Dudley her consort, he certainly hoped for this outcome and remained unmarried, and therefore without an heir, for the best part of two decades after Robsart's death. In a final, desperate push, he splashed out a king's ransom on elaborate entertainments at Kenilworth, including pageants glorifying Elizabeth and matrimony. The nineteen-day extravaganza landed like a damp squib. Three years after this disappointment, he secretly married Lettice Knollys, a noted beauty, granddaughter of Anne Boleyn's sister Mary, and mother of five children including Robert Devereux.

Elizabeth erupted in fury when she found out. She never forgave Knollys but soon restored relations with Dudley, though they would fall out and reconcile again. He had regained favour by the time he petitioned her to make the trip to Tilbury. Their appearance there together would mark the pinnacle of his influence – and his last hurrah.

The following month, health failing, he set out for the spa town of Buxton. On the way, he sent a message to Elizabeth, thanking her for sending him medicine. He did not complete the journey. Brought news of his death, the Queen locked herself in her rooms, refusing food and drink for days, her grief overriding any care for duty or reputation, just as her feelings for the living man had sometimes done. Eventually, Cecil ordered that the doors be forced.

Lest you still wonder whether Elizabeth and Dudley loved each other in a full sense of the word, with a depth and understanding formed over decades, know this: after Elizabeth died, a casket next to her bed surrendered a forlorn scrap of vellum, his note about the medicine she had sent, labelled by her 'His Last Letter'. The smallest mementos from the lives of our beloved dead become our most treasured possessions, the containers that hold them, reliquaries.

*

Dudley's stepson Robert Devereux, the Earl of Essex, would also rise and glow under Elizabeth's auspices, but this was no romance. Neither does the relationship merit its other common characterisation, of a spinster in thrall to a charming chancer. Lytton Strachey's 1928 *Elizabeth and Essex* provides a vivid template for this particular misinterpretation. Sarah Gristwood, who has written widely on the period, described Strachey's book to me as 'wonderfully ludicrous'. Both words apply. A leading light of the Bloomsbury group, Strachey blended Freudian analysis with a grippingly novelistic approach.

Routinely flunking the question 'how would he know?', he landed on a different set of truths about Elizabeth: the gulf between her mythology and her person. 'Under the serried complexities of her raiment – the huge hoop, the stiff ruff, the swollen sleeves, the powdered pearls, the spreading, gilded gauzes – the form of the woman vanished, and men saw instead an image – magnificent, portentous, self-created – an image of regality, which yet, by a miracle, was actually alive.' The author continued: 'Posterity has suffered by a similar deceit of vision. The great queen of its imagination, the lion-hearted heroine, who flung back the insolence of Spain and crushed the tyranny of Rome with splendid unhesitating gestures, no more resembles the queen of fact than the clothed Elizabeth the naked one.'

Elizabeth had transformed herself into a deity, but gods and goddesses do not grow old. Through a Freudian lens, Elizabeth's refusal to accept defeat looks like denial, while her flirtatious exchanges with Devereux and his great rival, Raleigh, read as the delusions of a Norma Desmond. Yet to have these young bloods dance attendance on her served one of Elizabeth's key purposes, transfiguring her and, in combination with her theatrical presentation, distracting the eye. Contemporary accounts describe her cutting a vital figure in their company. She 'was so beautiful to my old sight as ever I saw her,' enthused a veteran courtier after watching Elizabeth flirt and dance with Devereux, more than three decades her junior. In 1603, the Venetian ambassador to London, Giovanni Scaramelli, reported that Elizabeth, by now sixty-nine, appeared in fine fettle, her jewels, which he described in enthusiastic detail, evidently performing much the same function as ornamental men. Beneath the glister, Elizabeth's body natural was, in fact, failing.

With age had come loss, her most important ministers and mainstays, Dudley, Hatton, William Cecil, all dead. The ranks of women who counselled as well as cared for her had worn thin as gossamer too, Kat Ashley and others all gone. Their replacements kept getting into scrapes and scandals, not the image a vestal queen wished to project. The rising generation of male courtiers lacked judgement and dedication, their courtly rhetoric diverging ever further from their true sentiments, their eyes fixed on the transition that soon must come.

The toll of keeping up appearances in combination with these bereavements helps to explain the missteps of her final years. Even Elizabeth's sober-sided Elf, Robert Cecil, played a double game, forming a covert alliance with her most likely successor, James. Elizabeth's refusal to confirm the Scottish king as her heir raised the risk that he might have to fight off other challengers including Isabella, the Infanta of Spain.

Devereux would claim to be protecting England against Isabella – a Hapsburg and Catholic – when he finally signed his own death warrant. His real reason lay closer to home. Much as he hated the Spanish, Devereux loved himself more. Considering his record of flouting and infuriating the Queen, the question is not why he fell but how he lasted as long as he did. This is the soil in which the notion of Elizabeth as a fond and foolish old woman is rooted. Yet other explanations seem at least as credible: her grief for Dudley, Devereux's utility as a prop to her image and his skills as a manipulator. He prided himself on his softening-up technique, describing it as *saepe cadendo*, the Latin term for the erosion by water of stone, a constant drip-drip-drip of demands, tantrums and love bombs. Familial links to Dudley will also have provided him with some ongoing protection. His military service fighting Spanish forces in the Netherlands gave a braggart bragging rights. Thus equipped, he proceeded to test Elizabeth's patience to destruction.

An early act of insubordination came after the first Armada, when he joined Drake on an ill-conceived foray to attack what was left of Philip's fleet despite Elizabeth's orders to remain at court. Soon Devereux provoked her again, secretly marrying the widow of the poet Philip Sidney, and shortly afterwards impregnating one of Elizabeth's maids of honour. Later, he would be linked to a married countess and yet more of the Queen's ladies – and still Elizabeth forgave him. By contrast, Raleigh's unlicensed marriage to lady-in-waiting Bess Throckmorton landed him and his bride in the Tower.

Devereux's ambition and thin skin made him dangerous. He engineered the execution of Roderigo Lopez, a Portuguese-Jewish physician-in-chief to the Queen, whose real crime may have been to let slip that he had treated Devereux for syphilis. Devereux continually clashed with Elizabeth, challenging her approach to military matters, appointments and money, but still she promoted and favoured him. One day, furious that she ignored his recommendation for a new lord deputy for Ireland, Devereux publicly turned his back on her. When she responded to the lèse-majesté by cuffing him across the head, he made to draw his sword. Bundled from the chamber, Devereux was reported to have called the Queen 'as crooked in her disposition as in her carcass'.

Even after this display, she gave him another chance. Again, he squandered it. Dispatched to Ireland in 1599 to put down a rebellion, Devereux instead made a truce, hurrying back to London in defiance of Elizabeth's orders to remain in post. He arrived without warning, travel stained and consumed with the import of his mission, barging into her private rooms – only to surprise Gloriana in her unvarnished state, without wig, make-up or distracting finery. It was a transgression she would not forgive.

A subsequent investigation found him guilty of dereliction of duty. Stripped of the positions and titles Elizabeth had gifted him and banished from court, in February 1601, he marched on London, warning that scheming ministers were lining up Isabella as Elizabeth's successor. He assumed supporters would flock to his cause. They did not. Outnumbered, he surrendered. Ten days later, news of his beheading at the Tower reached Elizabeth as she played the virginal. She is said to have paused, listened in silence, then picked up the melody where she left off.

*

In the end, time rather than men eroded Elizabeth's grip – that and great cultural and social shifts. Over the years, she had tangled with her parliament, making concessions under duress rather than by choice. Her instincts tended towards absolutism over democracy, to asserting her will rather than seeking consent. This approach proved increasingly inflammatory as the tax burden on her subjects ballooned. The Spanish and Irish conflicts and English support for French Huguenots depleted state coffers. Monopolies granted by the Queen jacked up food prices to unsustainable levels even before a series of devastating crop failures. The brutal repression of protests against hunger and poverty sparked more unrest and resentment.

Against this turbulent backdrop, her so-called 'golden speech' to parliament the same year as Devereux's execution looks more like gilt – surface, not substance. It worked, however. Politicians wept, understanding this as her farewell appearance. Her words – assuming that she wrote them – are still taken at face value, the Queen of Spin yet again reinforcing her own legend: 'Though God hath raised me high, yet this I account the glory of my crown, that I have reigned with your loves,' she said, claiming, in echo of Tilbury, uninflected popularity and to return her subjects' devotion in full. 'Though you have had, and may have, many mightier and wiser princes sitting in this seat, yet you never had, nor shall have, any that will love you better.'

*

She returned to the task again in January 1603, using a final letter to James to anticipate and rebut negative interpretations of her decisions to defend Dutch and French Protestants. She had done these things not to make war, but peace.

Elizabeth tried to protect herself in a more intimate way too. The corpses of monarchs were traditionally prepared for burial much as traitors met their deaths, slit open and their organs and bowels removed. Once embalmed and wrapped in cerecloth, the bodies could better endure prolonged mourning rituals and a state funeral. She gave explicit instructions forbidding such a procedure. Most accounts agree that her orders were obeyed. Did Elizabeth fear her remains would yield secrets that punctured her image as the Virgin Queen? The resulting information vacuum has been filled with theories – that she bore the marks of childbirth, for example, or was, biologically, a king.

What her body could not have revealed was the force of character that for so long sustained it. Elizabeth had the heart and stomach of a queen. As death approached, fighter that she was, she refused to lie down. For days, she remained propped upright. Once forced to her bed, still she lingered. Her privy councillors clustered around her, not to comfort but to pressurise. She must name her heir. For centuries, history described her capitulation: Elizabeth, beyond speech, endorsing James by raising a hand to an invisible crown on her head.

That appears to have been propaganda. In 2023, researchers at the British Library examining the manuscript of a key source, William Camden's *Annals*, discovered amendments made after James assumed the throne. These cast him in a more favourable light and added the deathbed scene. History was rewritten, Elizabeth in all probability misrepresented.

The night she died, bells rang out and bonfires flickered. In that moment and for the first years of the Stuart period, you might have thought her done and dusted.

Gloriana had other plans.

Chapter 3

Victoria: Queen of Contradictions

We enter along a Tudor cloister, then whisk through the centuries, ignoring women in wimples and men in breeches. Today's destination is the age of industrial and imperial expansion. Here, in an annex of Hampton Court Palace, off limits to visitors, curator Polly Putnam is preparing to show me Queen Victoria's underwear.

Curators interpret history through objects, and Putnam believes the monarch's smalls – and Victoria's chemise is *tiny*, as she was – tell a story at odds with majority views. The prospect of a new and unexpected glimpse of the Queen is especially intriguing because so many Victorias already jostle for attention. Her life has been richly documented, not just in later assessments, but myriad contemporary sources too. Agnes Strickland, whose works include a famous twelve-volume *Lives of the Queens of England from the Norman Conquest*, produced a slimmer offering in 1840, *Queen Victoria from her Birth to her Bridal*. The first biography of the young sovereign incensed its subject, who scribbled notes all over her copy and sent the author a slew of corrections. Strickland never again risked writing about Victoria, but hundreds of biographers have rushed in where Agnes feared to tread.

The print media, unshackled at the start of Victoria's reign from punitive taxes, flourished and diversified into the strands of journalism familiar today. There were periodicals and broadsheets; lifestyle columns offering advice for house and heart; current affairs reports; political commentaries, and low-quality, high-drama half-penny papers circulated at dusk, which gave the Victorians their own phrase for fake news: 'evening wheezes'.

Royals proved good fodder for many of these evolving types of publication, and it helped that punters could see what they looked like. Victoria was the first English monarch captured in photographs, originally for family albums, then *cartes de visites* – illustrated business cards – official and press portraits, and later still, with the rise of amateur photography, by members of the public. She frequently handed out signed pictures of herself as presents. In 1896, she joined the ranks of the earliest royals on celluloid, filmed at Balmoral with Russia's ill-fated Tsar Nicholas and Tsarina Alexandra, the latter one of her forty-two grandchildren.

The Queen did not just feature in the burgeoning media. She consumed and commented on it, conveying opinions – many and firm – in letters to officials, family, friends and servants that ranged in content from matters of state to advice on regulating bodily functions. Every day, she wrote thousands of words, sending messages even if the recipients lived under the same palatial roofs, and sometimes, if annoyed, when sitting next to them. She kept diaries too, from the age of thirteen, becoming the first bestselling royal memoirist (if not the last) by putting out two books of edited highlights, *Leaves from the Journal of Our Life in the Highlands*, and its sequel, *More Leaves from the Journal of a Life in the Highlands*. In later years, she studied Urdu and filled notebooks in the language.

Though her children censored her archive after her death, troves of her first-person jottings survive. Researchers, used to teasing out the inner lives of kings and queens from the slenderest of clues, face no such problem with Victoria. We know a good deal about what she thought and felt, said and did.

You might expect this wealth of evidence to combine into a settled picture of Britain's second-longest serving monarch. Paradoxically, it seems to have had the opposite effect, as if Victoria's complexity were too great a puzzle for history to resolve, and so she must be broken into manageable pieces. Some shards fit together; others might be assumed to stand in contradiction to each other.

If a single Victoria queens it over alternative versions, she is the We-Are-Not-Amused, straitlaced matriarch, who lumbered an entire era with a reputation for sexual prudery. Uptight Victoria sometimes merges with Sad Victoria, the black-clad, self-described 'Widow of Windsor', perpetually grieving her beloved Prince Albert. The vast majority of photographs reinforce her dour reputation. Surely this was a face that never cracked a grin; a mouth that knew only to follow gravity? You can see why courtiers, realising that the Queen didn't know what lesbianism was, feared to explain it to her.

Except that the story about why only homosexual men were targeted by criminal law is a myth, just as it is untrue that Victorians swathed furniture legs in case these sparked lustful thoughts. Their queen may never have declared 'We are not amused' – the multiple origin stories for the line offer no hard proof. Caricatures have more staying power than characters. This is the reason Putnam has brought me to the Hampton Court storerooms. She puts on white gloves, as if to serve tea to a royal, selects a box from Dexion shelving piled high with similar boxes, and opens it to reveal a black bodice that Victoria wore in the first flush of mourning.

'People always insist that she gave up on her appearance, but she didn't,' Putnam says, admiring a design that combines shades and textures of black, chenille, beading, fringes, miniature buttons and crape (a different material to crepe). 'She wore this same sort of thing until the day she died. It was her uniform.' As a widow myself, I understand the temptation to ward off well-intentioned *how-are-you*s by telegraphing the answer, but Putnam suspects that, for Victoria, a practice originally rooted in grief became a public relations strategy.

'This is the age of black-and-white photography, and her image is constant, which is really blimming clever, because if you think about what's going on – at the beginning of her reign European empires keep falling, then there's the Crimean War, technology is coming in at a rate of knots . . .' The curator trails off as she unwraps another bodice. Tailored to the older Queen's broader girth, it adheres to the same standards of elegance and attention to detail. Putnam points to another of its features. 'She always has pockets.'

We have yet to see Victoria's chemise, and already my sense of the sovereign is expanding, just as she did. She appreciated the importance of pockets. More significantly, she appears to have understood the challenges to her power, many of them, of course, gendered. She was not the first to do so, but the template she devised broke from that of her most obvious potential role model. In the TV drama series, *Victoria*, the newly crowned heroine studies a portrait of Elizabeth I and attends a costume ball dressed in her likeness. Though Victoria did consciously adopt elements of Elizabeth's virginal iconography at the start of her reign, as a viewer, I also took these plot devices to signal stronger affinities. My subsequent research turned up nothing to support that notion, along with a letter that appears to counter it: 'I have no sympathy with my great Predecessor,' Victoria wrote, 'descended as I am from her rival queen [Mary, Queen of Scots], whom she so cruelly sacrificed.'

The series' author, Daisy Goodwin, tells me that she in fact conceived the sequences to illuminate Elizabeth and Victoria's contrasting approaches to queenship. 'We forget how astonishing it was for a young woman to be the most powerful person in the country, at a point when women didn't have rights,' says Goodwin, adding that to manage this in tandem with marriage and children was more extraordinary still. 'To me, Elizabeth was a man in drag, whereas Victoria owned her femininity.'

The Tudor queen reimagined her body politic into a form of kingship-plus, not weakened by her sex but enhanced by it. Once widowed, Victoria inverted this approach, never departing from black apart from touches of white or, occasionally, a tartan throw, and always presenting herself in line with conventions of womanhood. She had come to the throne as industrialisation gave fresh definition to the ancient idea that women and men inhabit separate spheres, private and public. While the poor were likely to work from childhood and irrespective of gender, the emergent middle classes relegated women to the unpaid labour of domesticity.

A swathe of popular culture helped to enforce this social and economic order by promoting blissful visions of family life. English poet Coventry Patmore scored a runaway best-seller with his epic (and epically dull) poem about wifely virtue, *The Angel in the House*; Isabella Beeton in her *Book of Household Management* articulated the reproductive and societal expectations placed on women: 'A mother's responsibilities are the greatest that a woman can have, for with her rests not only the care for the daily needs of food, clothing and the like of her children, but, what is even more important, their moral training.'

In case sugared pills proved insufficient to maintain the status quo, laws enforced it, excluding every woman from voting and married women from owning property or their bodies. A husband – physically and intellectually superior to his wife and free from the hysteria that might grip her at any moment – was allowed to beat or rape her and, if refused sex, could demand that their marital contract be annulled, keeping any wealth she had brought to the union.

All of this presented Victoria with a dilemma. She needed to inspire confidence in her authority without triggering the hostility incurred by women who encroached on the public sphere. It probably helped that she herself internalised that hostility. 'I am every day more convinced that we women, if we are to be good women, feminine and amiable and domestic, are not fitted to reign,' she confided to her journal. 'At least it is *contre gré* [against their will] that they drive themselves to the work which it entails. However, this cannot now be helped, and it is the duty of everyone to fulfil all that they are called upon to do in whatever situation they may be.'

She responded to her internal conflict instinctively, con-structing a facsimile of middle-class life and embedding her queenship at the centre of what, at distance, could be mistaken for the domestic ideal.

Widowhood stripped her of some of this protective sheen, but only because she embraced the mores of mourning – helpfully set out in the manual *Manners and Rules of Good Society, or, Solecisms to be Avoided by a Member of the Aristocracy* – with a ferocity that defied all convention. Her court drained of colour apart from black and, eventually, the grey or violet 'half-mourning' she grudgingly permitted others. Custom dictated that normal life should resume two years after a bereavement. The date came and went, and still she shrouded herself in widow's weeds.

Otherwise, nothing about her outfits would have drawn criticism. If anything, they appeared hyper-traditional, emphasising the classical female silhouette of the period: pronounced bust, sloping shoulders and nipped-in waist. Nonetheless, concealed beneath the funereal crape lurked a surprise. When Putnam removes the lid of a third box, peeling back layers of tissue paper, I cannot immediately make sense of the garment lying before us, of fine linen and beautifully constructed, the ruched skirts so abbreviated that for a moment I think them folded. This is one of Victoria's full-length chemises, from early in her reign. Finally, I appreciate how petite she really was, hovering around the 5ft mark.

Women at court wore such shifts as their foundational garment, adding a petticoat, 'then stays – a corset – and then you'd have more petticoats,' Putnam says. 'You never put your stays next to your skin, except in men's fantasy.' Well-heeled women viewed these items of clothing as indispensable even during pregnancy, elevating the risk of miscarriage and uterine displacement. And yet, Putnam tells me, Victoria, supposed queen of convention, 'decided she couldn't be arsed to wear corsets any more after Albert died'.

Some historians view this turn of events as proof that the grief-stricken monarch gave up on self-care. That might have been true during her initial period of seclusion, and she was never one to follow doctor's orders. However, the style and verve of Victoria's bodices make her decision look more like liberation. Before you dismiss this as the confirmation bias of a twenty-first-century feminist, consider the many aspects of Victoria's life that support this interpretation: her difficult early years, which isolated her and pitted her against the authority of her mother and her mother's comptroller, forced her to develop all the backbone she needed and more. In adulthood, she asserted herself vigorously and jealously guarded her power. Only during her marriage did she struggle to do this. She acceded to the throne at eighteen, wed at twenty. Albert supported her but also undermined her, becoming not just a consort but de facto king and she let him, desperate for his approval and worn down by pregnancies, nine in total. His death crushed and freed her. It was not until she reigned alone that she fully grew into her royal role. In private, she indulged her interests and appetites, following new pursuits and old and by no means insensible to male attention. Over the four decades that remained to her, she would form close relationships across class and racial divides with younger men who, believe it or not, made her smile.

*

Before rummaging in more detail through Victoria's personal life, we should consider, as Putnam did, her outer layers. It might seem tautological to say that she was and is famous. Born royal and catapulted into contention for the throne by the absence of viable alternatives, Victoria had no choice in the matter. Yet she eclipses all but a few other sovereigns when it comes to name recognition. Until *Bridgerton*, Queen Charlotte would barely have raised a flicker in the UK, never mind further afield, apart from the brief spell when journalists searching for new angles on Meghan resurfaced the theory that the Georgian queen might have been mixed race. Anne, the last Stuart monarch and final queen regnant before Victoria, has also been pulled from relative obscurity through the power of drama, the butt of the joke in *The Favourite*.

Victoria, by contrast, commands a global profile, if a fragmented one – and most Britons like what they think they know, naming her along with two other women, Elizabeths I and II, among their all-time greatest sovereigns in a 2012 poll. To many of her compatriots, Victoria represents an era of unabashed pride in social and technological progress at home and imperial rule abroad.

That she presided over a society which denied fundamental rights to other women only adds to her legend. She wasn't much of a sister, but how strong she must have been. British dramatisations of her life tend to be overwhelmingly sympathetic. She is the dignified heroine of 1930s box office hits, *Victoria the Great* and *Sixty Glorious Years*; a teen queen overcoming the challenges of accession and marriage in the 2009 movie *Young Victoria* and Goodwin's three series of *Victoria* (2016–2019); and a mature monarch finding solace in relationships with subordinates in 1997's *Mrs Brown* and 2017's *Victoria and Abdul*.

It will not have harmed Victoria's status as a national treasure to have twice been played by two of the actresses who merit the same label. Anna Neagle, among Britain's most popular early movie stars, took on the role in the first brace of movies, and Judi Dench, who endowed Elizabeth I with humour and humanity in *Shakespeare in Love*, in the last pair.

Victoria's is a pervasive presence in British towns and cities. Buildings and streets are named after her; sculptures and monuments abound, most erected during her golden and diamond jubilees. Their profusion is noteworthy because a 2022 survey found that just 17 per cent of public statues in the UK depict named women. Victoria bucks this trend and another – her representations in stone and metal outnumber not only those of all other historical women but of every other sovereign before or since, male or female.

You will find her staring out across the remnants of empire too, commemorated in the realms and dependencies and former colonies despite attempts over more than a century to exorcise her. Proclaimed Empress of India in 1877, she was still on the throne eighteen years later when Indian nationalists tarred her statue in the city then known as Bombay, now Mumbai, hanging sandals round its marble neck in an added gesture of disrespect. That India remained under British rule for more than five decades after the incident was in significant part due to a relationship between the Empress-Queen and a country which mirrored her marriage to Albert: passionate and problematic.

She stood for a nation and institution that subjugated and

abused India, leached its wealth and seized its treasures. None of this deterred her from romanticising its people and culture, importing them to her court and co-opting them into her orientalist, imperial iconography. Her fascination did not go unreciprocated. 'As a female monarch,' writes historian Miles Taylor in his book *Empress*, 'she represented justice and charity [within India]. She was a beacon of beneficence in ways in which British bureaucracy in India could never be.'

Victoria's death, rather than prompting a harder-nosed look at her legacy, unleashed a further spate of mythologising. When India's viceroy Lord Curzon unveiled plans for a tribute in Calcutta, now Kolkata, other regions set about devising competing projects. Curzon's fundraising efforts nevertheless yielded huge sums, enough to build the vast Victoria Memorial Hall. Back in London, the new king, Edward VII, failed to coax Britons to shell out enough cash to pay for a mere statue of his mum outside Buckingham Palace. Colonial powers ended up underwriting a third of its cost, a backstory rarely mentioned by the news teams that, in this century, routinely wield microphones in front of it.

How did Victoria's popularity in India coexist with deep anger against British rule? 'Indians saw a woman of power and weight, and they were used to that,' explains Anita Anand, journalist, author and co-host of *Empire*, one of the world's leading podcasts in terms of listenership and sheer, bloody brilliance. 'You have a mother goddess, who represents power foremost and maternalism second. People would be furious with the British Empire and the Raj, but even proto revolutionaries would think that, if they could just get to Victoria, she'd set it all right, she'd sort it out.'

This misconception lingered. Anand provides a startling example of the loyalty the Queen could still inspire almost two decades after her death: 'In the prelude to the terrible massacre at Amritsar in 1919, the mob starts attacking a statue of Victoria and it is other Indians who make a ring around it, saying, "You will not touch her. We don't do that to her." They fight to keep her statue safe.'

Despite such reflexes, totems of British rule did fall, whether to summary justice or the gentler processes of relocation and renaming, a pattern echoed in other countries and still ongoing. Quebec separatists dynamited Victoria's statue in 1963. On Canada Day in 2021, protestors in Winnipeg toppled bronzes of her and Elizabeth II to highlight the abuse of some 150 thousand First Nations, children forcibly sent to schools intended to 'assimilate' them into white populations, a practice that dated to Victoria's reign and lasted into the second half of the twentieth century. In 2015, persons unknown decapitated her memorial in Nairobi. A local resident applauded the action, telling the *Africa News* that Kenyans 'do not want every time to be reminded of the kind of slavery, colonialism and all that kind of attachment with this kind of mistreatment. We did suffer a lot at the hands of colonialists.'

As dogs mark their territory, so empires demonstrate owner-ship in visible ways. After the British took control of Hong Kong, they christened the capital 'Queenstown', then 'City of Victoria', plonking a figure of the Queen at its heart. The statue, removed during the Japanese occupation and reinstated with the return of British rule, had been splattered with paint, dinged with a hammer and demoted from its original position by the time the island came under Chinese authority. It now sits in a park

named, like several other landmarks, Victoria, but if the Queen
has not been forgotten, she has also not been forgiven.

*

Director Xie Jin's film, *The Opium War*, released in 1997 to
mark Hong Kong's handover to China, presents a very different
Victoria to her incarnations back home. Icy and imperious,
she urges her ministers to tougher action against the Qing
dynasty, which is trying to stem the narcotics business. 'It's
not the opium issue, nor the issue of the lives and properties
of a few merchants,' she tells them. 'It's not even a matter of
the dignity of our British flag and royalty. If all nations follow
China's example and reject free trade, the British Empire will
no longer exist within a year. This is the reason for us to use
force. We must teach them a lesson on free trade.'

By the end of her reign, the British Empire stretched across
nearly a quarter of the world, yet Victoria had visited none of
her dominions, though she longed to travel to India and was
thwarted from doing so. Even Ireland, fully subsumed into
the United Kingdom and closer to Windsor than her Balmoral
home, got to see her in the flesh just four times. Her first trip
came during the latter stages of the Great Famine, after potato
blight ravaged the crop on which the majority of the population
depended. As the Irish starved, exports of other food crops
to England continued. By the time potato yields improved,
a million of the Queen's subjects had died, and an estimated
two million more had emigrated.

You might expect her to be met with torches and pitch-
forks – or worse. Her son Alfred survived an assassination

attempt by a Fenian during a later visit to Australia, while the sixth of seven attempts on her life would be carried out in London by Arthur O'Connor, a teenager intending to force her at gunpoint to sign a release order for Irish republican prisoners. Instead, she noted a different kind of warmth. 'Drove along the road above the Strawberry Beds, where the view overlooking a valley, is so very fine, round by Castle Knot, quite a small village, with such wretched cabins, but everywhere & from every individual, the same friendly greeting,' Victoria wrote in her journal. 'They often call out "God spare you", or "God speed you", & shriek instead of cheering. One sees such beautiful women & children, the latter, ever so ragged, & always barefooted. They have such fine dark eyes & hair. Equally remarkable are the beggars, or very poor people, all, in the most dreadful tatters, also the boys who run along by the carriages. – We dined at ½ p. 8 at the Castle in Dublin, with the Ld Lieut:, & were ready dressed for the Drawingroom. There were, I should say between 2 & 3000 people, who passed by, & 1600 Ladies were presented. The dresses were very fresh & handsome, & there were some very good looking people.'

In 1900, Maud Gonne, a republican, suffragette and actress, whose best-known, if least, accomplishment was to serve as muse to the poet W.B. Yeats, determined to stir up a rougher reception for Victoria's fourth and final foray to the country. By now, Prime Minister Gladstone's attempts to introduce Home Rule had foundered, its champion Charles Stewart Parnell was dead, and sectarian tensions were rising, pitting Catholic nationalists against Protestant unionists.

'Queen, return to your own land; you will find no more Irishmen ready to wear the red shame of your livery,' wrote

Gonne in a column for the *United Irishman* entitled 'The Famine Queen'. Police raided the newspaper and incinerated copies of the issue, but the title of Gonne's denunciation burned itself into Ireland's collective memory. Anand wonders if the label, still in currency today, is entirely deserved. 'She was a constitutional monarch, not a despot. She answered to a government and a parliamentary system. She donated money.' Anand pauses. 'But is that all she could have done?'

There it is again: the ambiguity that makes Victoria so fascinating. Her relationship with the British Empire offers the best way to understand her, Anand suggests, not because it was straightforward, but precisely because it was not.

'It formed and informed her, and Victoria would have regarded it as one of the richest parts of her reign. To ignore how she often was inconsistent in her attitudes to empire is also to ignore the humanity of the woman. People aren't binary, they're complicated, and you can see that through the lens of empire more clearly than in any other areas of her life. Her responses could be completely contradictory.'

*

That opinions of Victoria vary sharply across the world is hardly surprising. That she was deeply unpopular in Britain for great chunks of her reign may startle those educated – an elastic term – under the British school system. It isn't just about how we see her, but how we view history. Though recent work to plug gaps and address biases in syllabuses is feeding through to younger generations, the rest of us seem likely to have acquired an understanding of the past that is simultaneously disjointed and narrow. To test this proposition, I launched an unscientific survey across six social media platforms: had anyone schooled in the UK up to the age of sixteen been taught about either the English Revolution (or any part of the series of events also known as the Wars of the Three Kingdoms and the English Civil War), or the so-called Glorious Revolution four decades later? Of hundreds of respondents, a large majority, including prominent historian Rebecca Rideal, replied that their courses had covered neither. The only homegrown revolution that just about everybody had studied was not, in fact, a revolution at all: the industrial revolution.

Though US-born, I completed the bulk of my schooling in England. Our history teachers fleetingly touched on Charles I's sticky end before vaulting over the Interregnum to the Restoration, presenting the return of the monarchy as a cause for celebration. They completely ignored the inglorious upheaval, backed by Dutch troops, that deposed Catholic James II and replaced him with his Protestant daughter Mary and her husband, William of Orange.

An eleven-year republic seems like a curious omission for any history syllabus in a country still so engaged with its royalty that it suspends regular TV programming for state events. The Bill of Rights agreed by William and Mary redrew the relationship between Parliament and sovereign. It also blocked Catholics from taking the throne. All these arrangements persist today, with yet more power passing during Victoria's reign from Crown to people in the three Reform Acts that enfranchised millions more male voters, a development I recall our teachers presenting less as the result of Chartism and other social and political movements, riots and unrest, than the product of natural, unprompted progress.

In fact, republicanism reached a high-water mark a little past the halfway point of Victoria's sixty-three-years-and-seven-months rule, with the founding of some ninety anti-monarchy clubs plus another fifty societies that explored such views.[8] If you charted her popularity from beginning to end of her reign, it would resemble a crooked smile.

The upturned corner of Victoria's accession marks a surge not so much of devotion – the young Queen was an unknown quantity – but hope that she represented a new beginning. A run of hapless Hanoverians had left the monarchy in bad odour, though the reign of her grandfather, George III, started well enough. Conscientious and serious, he married Sophia Charlotte of Mecklenburg-Strelitz, aka Queen Charlotte, and soon produced a whole nursery of heirs. Ultimately, though, he would be remembered for turbulences abroad and at home, revolution in France and its aftermath which embroiled the UK in a cycle of wars, the loss of America and the bouts of mental illness that installed his eldest son, another George, as regent.

A carouser whose debts swelled along with his belly, the future George IV married his mistress but later declared the union invalid to wed his cousin, Caroline of Brunswick, then attempted to divorce her. By the time he acceded, aged fifty-seven and dependent on alcohol and laudanum, he was in the habit of outsourcing many of the responsibilities of kingship to government – a healthy precedent, if unintentionally so, for a monarchy seeking to survive a revolutionary era.

His brother, William IV, would have done well to maintain it. Enthroned at sixty-four, he succeeded in wooing back a little public support for the Crown but also attracted mudslinging, including of the literal kind, during a series of tussles with parliamentarians. In dismissing Prime Minister Lord Melbourne, he became the last monarch to override the will of parliament. When he died after just seven years on the throne, Melbourne, long since back in office, headed straight to Kensington Palace for an audience with the new queen. He would be her first mentor and the focus of gossip that attended all her close friendships with men.

*

Until that moment, Victoria had lived an existence she later described as 'melancholy'. Her widowed mother, Victoire, a German princess and Duchess of Kent through marriage to the fourth son of George III, leaned heavily on a mentor of her own. Sir John Conroy's official position of comptroller gave him authority over staff, but he lorded it over everyone at Kensington Palace and, with the backing of the Duchess, inflicted a set of stringent rules on her daughter. Under the regime, dubbed the 'Kensington system', Victoria experienced the strange fate of royalty, at once privileged and deprived. Constantly observed and denied the companionship of all but a few other children, she was forbidden to do so much as descend a staircase unsupervised. Conroy forced her to share a bedroom with Victoire and required her to fill out a daily behaviour log. This she did, with the dedication to journalling she would display throughout her life. Aged twelve, she judged herself 'naughty and vulgar'; by the age of thirteen, she had progressed to 'VERY VERY VERY VERY HORRIBLY NAUGHTY!!!!!', a phrase she underlined four times.

Historians have advanced theories about why her mother enabled Conroy's bullying – perhaps they were lovers (plausible); maybe he was Victoria's father (unlikely). What seems clear is that Conroy and Victoire intended to mould Victoria into docile dependency in order to preside as joint powers behind her throne. Their strategy backfired spectacularly.

Victoria described her accession in curiously unemotional terms. This was, after all, simultaneously a family bereavement, an emancipation and a fresh form of confinement. Never again would she be a private individual. Her diary entry is nonetheless revealing. She writes that, woken with the news of her uncle's death, she descended, in her bathrobe, to talk to the lord chamberlain and the Archbishop of Canterbury, then dressed, took breakfast, received Melbourne alone 'as I shall always do with all my ministers' – in other words, without her mother or Conroy present – began making appointments to her court, and held her first privy council and a run of individual meetings. Again, she emphasises that she carried out these duties alone. *Sit on that and spin, Conroy.* Afterwards, she ate a solitary dinner in her room, conducted yet more meetings, including a second with Melbourne, and trotted off to bed, stopping to say goodnight to her mother and her governess, Baroness Lehzen, who had been a rare source of comfort during the Kensington years. On the magnitude of the task ahead, Victoria sounds more resigned than excited: 'Since it has pleased Providence to place me in this station, I shall do my utmost to fulfil my duty towards my country,' she wrote. 'I am very young & perhaps in many, though not in all things, inexperienced. But I am sure that very few have more really good will & more real desire to do what is fit & right, than I have.'

Her first days and months in the job foreshadowed patterns that repeated throughout her reign. People underestimated her, and often regretted that error. Her strengths and weaknesses manifested in equal measure – and as you might expect of this queen of contradictions, they were often the same qualities. Her susceptibility to attractive men, in the first instance Melbourne – or 'Lord M' as she swiftly nicknamed him – is clear from the outset. The conversation was 'very comfortable . . . Each time I see him I feel more confidence in him; I find him very kind in his manner too,' she writes of their second meeting on the day of her accession. Soon, the journals are peppered with doting mentions and detail a routine that often includes multiple appointments with him per day, a heavy burden of time for a serving prime minister. Her obvious partiality, coupled with the iron will that saw Victoria block Conroy's ambitions and exile her mother to the far end of the new royal residence, Buckingham Palace, combined like nitroglycerine and celite: explosively.

Her diary entry for 2 February 1839 once more sang Melbourne's praises, but also laid bare her capacity for bearing a grudge. Her target was Lady Flora Hastings, originally appointed during the Kensington system, and still a member of the duchess's household. Victoria had concluded, on the basis of 'how exceedingly suspicious her figure looked' that Hastings, a single woman, was pregnant, and Conroy, 'the Monster and demon Incarnate', responsible. Melbourne counselled the Queen to 'be quiet and watch' before taking action. In another foretaste of things to come, Victoria ignored good advice, instead commanding that Hastings undergo an intimate medical examination. Her powerful family demanded an apology, and when stonewalled, went public, providing a newspaper with a letter in which Hastings detailed her humiliation.

What followed will feel familiar to anyone who has tracked the media wars between the Waleses and Sussexes. Supporters of the opposing sides fought it out in the press, aided by anonymous sources, with each party coming to represent a wider set of values than the narrative warranted. Victoria's critics conflated her fondness for her prime minister with support for his party, the Whigs. The Hastings clan were prominent Tories. Though both parties had roots in the English civil war, respectively the Roundheads and Cavaliers, later developing into the Liberal and Conservative parties, neither, at the time, fit the progressive versus traditionalist categories those associations suggest.

'The Queen's unpopularity reached an extraordinary height,' wrote Lytton Strachey, whose biography of Victoria is as colourful as his portrait of Elizabeth I, if more factually grounded. 'More than once,' he adds, 'she was publicly insulted. "Mrs. Melbourne" was shouted at her when she appeared at her balcony; and, at Ascot, she was hissed by [Tories] the Duchess of Montrose and Lady Sarah Ingestre as she passed.'

As if things were not bad enough for the novice sovereign, Melbourne tendered his resignation. When Sir Robert Peel, preparing to form a new government, proposed that Victoria's ladies of the bedchamber, all drawn from Whig circles, be switched, as per custom, for followers of his Tory party, Victoria refused, sparking a constitutional crisis on top of the Hastings mess. Peel refused to take office without his monarch's full support, leaving a reluctant Melbourne no choice but to return as her prime minister. Within months, Flora Hastings died from the cancer that had caused her abdomen to balloon in the first place.

'I was very young then, and perhaps I should act differently if it was all to be done again,' Victoria confided a lifetime later to her last private secretary, Arthur Bigge. That might be easier to believe if her most pronounced characteristic were not the impulse to double down in the face of criticism. Only a handful of people ever dared to stand in the path of the royal bulldozer. The most prominent of these was Prince Albert.

*

When the people you love die, there is a temptation to sanitise their memory. You want the world to remember them at their best. This impulse seems to express itself most powerfully in the survivors of difficult relationships, as if they can only make sense of history by rewriting it. The more I learned about Victoria and Albert, the more her prodigious grief and prolonged drive to memorialise her husband conformed to this pattern.

They met at seventeen, aware that their elders were keen for them to make a dynastic marriage. Victoria remained unconvinced and resisted a quick decision after her accession. She was not worried that her mother and Albert's father were siblings – inbreeding was commonplace among aristocrats – but she treasured her independence after the Kensington years. Indeed, Victoria 'dreaded the thought of marrying' and had swiftly come to appreciate the joys of 'having my own way', she told Melbourne. No Elizabeth Tudor, she fully intended to tie the knot eventually, just not yet. In the meantime, she revelled in male company – Melbourne's own, of course, and she also developed a crush on a fellow royal, the Grand Duke Alexander of Russia, 'an amiable and dear young man'. By contrast, she remembered Albert from their original encounter as stodgy, taciturn and not nearly as fun as his brother, Ernest. In fact, though nobody ever accused Albert of being the life and soul of a party, he was suffering from diarrhoea throughout his first visit to England.

By his second meeting with Victoria, in October 1839, Albert's stomach had settled, and hers, in the aftermath of the Bedchamber Crisis and Flora Hastings's death, churned. If she were in doubt that the shine had already come off her reign, an incident on the date her Saxe-Coburg cousins were due at Windsor made the position clear: 'Got up at ½ p.10 and saw to my astonishment that a stone or rather 2 stones had been thrown at my dressing room window and 2 glasses broke; the stone was found under the window; in the little blue room next the audience room another window broken and the stone found in the room; in the new strong room another window broke, and in one of the lodging rooms next to this, another broke and the stone found in the middle of the room.'

This may not have been a propitious start to the day, but the same journal entry records her rapturous response to Albert that evening, transformed in the three years since she last saw him. She found him and his brother 'grown and changed, and embellished. It was with some emotion that I beheld Albert—who is <u>beautiful</u> . . . handsome and pleasing.' In less than a week, Victoria proposed. She had to do the asking, because her rank trumped his male prerogative. Once married, she expected this status quo to continue, as

Melbourne, in an earlier conversation, insisted it would. The Prime Minister's response to the engagement revealed how hollow that assurance had been. 'I think it is a very good thing,' he wrote in his congratulatory note to Victoria, 'and you'll be much more comfortable; for a woman cannot stand alone for long, in whatever position she is.'

Thus Victoria and Albert's twenty-one-year union began as it is remembered, on a series of false premises. Popular culture claims theirs as 'the greatest royal love story of all', but if the phrase holds any truth, that is only because so many royal marriages prove disastrous. The wedding did, however, boost the monarchy. The scale of the 1840 ceremony was a gamble. The Queen's subjects were in the habit of booing her and grumped at the prospect of her bridegroom – yet another German – drawing on the public purse. Wealth inequality was yawning, with public provision for the poor, first written into law under Elizabeth I, wholly inadequate to the needs of populations cramming into city slums or dispossessed from rural smallholdings. Workhouses were designed not as places of refuge but correction, and poverty demonised as a choice. Politics, like monarchy, is full of echoes.

Another constant is British susceptibility to royal weddings. The pageantry – twelve bridesmaids carried Victoria's train, while Albert arrived with a squadron of cavalry – worked its magic. A lengthy report, syndicated to multiple newspapers, referred to 'this auspicious day . . . a universal and joyous holiday', exclaiming over the enthusiasm and size of the crowds and declaring the event a moment of national unity.

Behind closed doors, the couple were hammering out their own unification process. Victoria's description of their wedding night is rapturous. 'He clasped me in his arms, and we kissed each other again and again! His beauty, his sweetness and gentleness, – really how can I ever be thankful enough to have such a <u>Husband</u>! . . . At 20 m. p.10 we both went to bed; (<u>of course</u> in <u>one</u> bed), to lie by his side, and in his arms, and on his dear bosom, and be called by names of tenderness, I have never yet heard used to me before – was bliss beyond belief! Oh! this was the happiest day of my life! – May God help me to do my duty as I ought and be worthy of such blessings!'

How did this ardent queen gain – and retain – her reputation as a prude, then? Part of the answer is that Albert came close to meriting the description. His parents' divorce – his father, himself far from faithful, accused Albert's mother of an adulterous affair – left their son with a revulsion towards infidelity. His own low-watt sexuality presumably made it easier to practice what he preached. Melbourne was by no means the only person to notice the Prince Consort's 'indifference about ladies', while Albert himself complained that Victoria's conjugal passion exceeded his. In this respect, it was Albert, not Victoria, who set the tone for their marriage and the era.

Another factor was, and is, fear of female agency. When women flex their rights, dinosaurs roar. Victoria's lifetime, as ours, saw technologically driven social change outpace laws and attitudes. It helps keep women in their place if the most prominent are misrepresented in ways that diminish them. An asexual, anti-sex Victoria becomes a madonna – her nine conceptions immaculate and dutiful – and a figure of fun. She may have been powerful, but you don't have to take her seriously. This caricature of the Queen and her times also overlooks the practical and political basis for encouraging abstinence. The act of sex could be hazardous. Over a fifth of Georgian Londoners had contracted syphilis, 'the pox', by the age of thirty-five, and many more suffered from other sexually transmitted infections, including 'the clap', gonorrhoea.[9] These diseases were rampant by the time Victoria took the throne, literally weakening Britain's armed forces and inspiring a trio of infamous bills that she, as monarch, assented. It takes two to tango, but the Contagious Diseases Acts targeted women alone. Any suspected prostitute could be arrested, subjected to the same sort of invasive examination endured by Flora Hastings and, if found to be a carrier, detained in a prison-like hospital.

Virtuous wives who lay back and thought of England risked catching venereal diseases from their husbands, and this was not the only danger lurking in the marital bed. Methods of birth control were rudimentary. Coughing after copulating failed to prevent conception as reliably as its proponents claimed; early condoms, fashioned from linen, fish bladders or sheep guts, proved scarcely more effective. Unsurprisingly, 40 per cent of women in Victorian Britain gave birth to at least seven children, 15 per cent to ten or more. In that sense, the Queen found herself fully in tune with her female subjects, producing her eldest daughter, Vicky, nine months after marriage and pregnant again a blink of an eye later. By 1857, when she birthed her last child, Beatrice, the Queen had sustained a ventral hernia and a prolapsed uterus.

At least she did not die. While health outcomes for the poor were generally far worse than for their wealthy counterparts, women rich enough to pay doctors to supervise their confinements suffered higher maternal mortality rates than those who relied on cheaper midwives. Doctors carried and transmitted infectious diseases picked up from living patients and the corpses they dissected; their experience of delivering babies was often limited, and they tended to resist the use of drugs. The idea that a mother's birth pangs assisted her baby to prepare for life outside the womb derived not from medical science but religious belief. God punished Adam merely by expelling him from the Garden of Eden. The Almighty laid an additional curse on Eve, decreeing that she and every female descended from her should expiate the original sin by suffering agonies expelling their babies into a harsh and woman-hating world.

Here, as with her abandonment of corsets, Victoria defied tradition, insisting on chloroform for the births of her last two children and helping to make this standard practice for other women. Her mothering diverged in other and more profound ways from the ideal she supposedly embodied. In reality, she loathed the entire process and was not always keen on its end product either. Vicky, her favourite child, received frank and frequent letters from her mother. 'I think much more of our being like a cow or a dog at such moments [of childbirth] when our poor nature becomes so very animal and unecstatic,' Victoria remarked in one of her discursive missives. In another, she observed that 'an ugly baby is a very nasty object – and the prettiest is frightful when undressed. Until about 4 months; in short as long as they have their big body and little limbs and that terrible froglike action.' Nor did she reliably appreciate her offspring once they passed the amphibian phase. She drew them beautifully and with an eye that suggested she really saw and loved them. None, however, escaped her criticism. Her heir, Bertie, became her most regular target. His 'systematic idleness, laziness, disregard of everything,' she lamented, 'is enough to break one's heart'.

If a maternal instinct is often missing from her correspondence and diaries, we should cut her a little slack. Victoria's first four children were born in a period of less than four years. She had discovered the joys of love and sex, and instead of being able to enjoy these novel experiences, found herself either pregnant or recovering from pregnancy. Moreover, Albert, who initially appeared to accept playing second fiddle to his wife, used each pregnancy to annex more of her royal responsibilities – and to chip away at her confidence.

*

Before they married and during his first months as prince consort, Albert deferred to her. He asked to choose his own staff. She did it for him. He suggested a honeymoon. She replied, 'My dear Albert, you have not at all understood the matter. You forget, my dearest Love, that I am the Sovereign, and that business can stop and wait for nothing. Parliament is sitting and something occurs almost every day for which I am required, and it is quite impossible for me to absent from London.' She makes clear that duty is not the only factor in her decision. 'This is also my wish in every way.' Marriage is an exciting prospect, but it is evident that she is also revelling in being queen.

Historian and journalist Neal Ascherson, writing for the *New York Review* about a newly published collection of Victoria's letters more than a century after she wrote them, singles out this response to attack her. 'This is how a girl of twenty wrote to the young man she was about to marry. The candour is stunning. Some have found it disarming, but perhaps they also forget that Victoria remained the sovereign for no less than sixty-four years, in much the same frame of mind. These letters, covering the first part of her reign up to the death of the Prince Consort, produce a chilling effect. The imperiousness of fat-cheeked little Vic soon loses its charm. By 1862, she looks more like a little tyrant.'

Right up to the present day, Victoria's critics are apt to represent so-called Victorian values more consistently than the Queen ever did, viewing her through a fog of false assumptions about female capacities and capabilities. Just because Victoria emerged from the Kensington system assuming that everyone was trying to block and thwart her didn't mean they weren't truly out to get her. None of this is to say that the multiple and intersecting challenges of her upbringing and role, patriarchy and patrimonarchy, exonerate her from charges that she sometimes behaved badly or irrationally. To understand her is by no means to love her, but rather to see beyond the cardboard cutout versions to her true human complexity. 'She was like the weather,' Daisy Goodwin tells me, when we meet to discuss the author's portrayals of Victoria for television and in a novel. 'You can see that from the way she writes, but what she wasn't, ever, was cold.'

Goodwin's choice of imagery briefly distracts me from our immediate topic of discussion. In researching my 2015 biography of the then Prince of Wales, I noticed that members of Charles's inner circle often deployed meteorological metaphors to describe his rapid-cycling emotions, just as his first wife had done: 'It was hot and cold, hot and cold,' Diana said of him in an interview taped for her own biographer, Andrew Morton.

'You never knew what mood it was going to be, up and down, up and down.'

Royals are expected, if not fully to extinguish their feelings, then to master them. The patrimonarchy derives many of its values from a stiff-upper-lipped, buttoned-down form of masculinity. While the current King has struggled to mimic this model, Albert icily embodied it. 'His way of giving orders and reproofs was rather too like a master of a house scolding servants to be pleasant for those who were bound to listen in silence,' one of Victoria's maids of honour recalled.

A royal woman who shows emotion is doubly damned, failing her institution and triggering the hysterical women trope. It is conspicuous just how many modern authors apply an infantilising and gendered label to Victoria's arguments with Albert: 'temper tantrums'. Victoria's paternal grandfather also gave the men of her own time another way to gaslight her: doctors warned Albert that her moods might presage a descent into the madness that afflicted George III.

The Queen addressed her consort as 'master'. He patronised her as 'my child'. As a young girl, she had been made to keep a behaviour book. Albert revived the practice for his adult wife. He would then study her testimonies, doling out praise if she followed his lead – 'I can give you a very good certificate this time' – and more often issuing sharp reprimands. 'I try my best to be patient,' he complained, 'but I feel the dreadful waste of most precious time, and of energies which should be turned to the use of others.' Another of his letters depicts a scene in which he walks away from an argument: 'You have again lost your self-control quite unnecessarily,' he begins, chiding her that she followed him 'from room to room'. In Albert's version of events, Victoria is 'completely unreasonable', a phrase applied to her not by the Prince Consort but A.N. Wilson, describing the couple's rows in his biography of the Queen.

Even so, Wilson has joined a growing band of historians and biographers who are reassessing this famous relationship in the light of a form of abuse only defined in UK law in 2015: coercive control. As listed on the website of Women's Aid, an organisation that successfully campaigned for it to be made a criminal offence, signs of a coercive partner include 'monitoring you; isolating you from friends and family; taking control over aspects of your everyday life, such as where you can go, who you can see, what you can wear and when you can sleep; repeatedly putting you down, such as saying you're worthless; and humiliating, degrading or dehumanising you'.

Albert checked all those boxes. He dismissed Victoria's former governess, Lehzen, and lied to the distressed queen, telling her that the baroness had asked to return to Germany. He offered to assist Victoria with the work of government when she fell pregnant with their first child, then used the opportunity to embed himself in the system. He convinced his wife that his abilities far excelled her own. He curtailed her love of partying – she disliked exercise but adored dancing – increasingly secluding her within the domestic sphere, in remote homes he selected on the Isle of Wight and Scotland. Their growing brood represented to him not merely family or the future of the British monarchy and empire; this industrial quantity of children could secure the succession and therefore the survival of other European monarchies.

Wilson has likened Albert to Rob Titchener, a character in the BBC Radio Four soap opera, *The Archers*, whose abuse and rape of his wife provokes her to stab him. Eye-catching though the comparison is, it might risk an overcorrection. Victoria and Albert's relationship should never have been held up as an example of marital bliss, but perhaps it was more curate's egg than unmitigated catastrophe. The dynamic between them, seen within the context of the time and peculiar place they occupied, is deeply uncomfortable, but it is neither exceptional nor especially extreme. Her journal testifies to periods of joy, though of course sharper moments could have been self-censored by their author or removed by her children after her death.

Whatever the case, her love and grief were real, if complicated, and Albert's outward-facing legacy too is a mixed bag. He promoted science and academic excellence, championed some forms of social progress and, of course, masterminded the 1851 Great Exhibition, itself a blend of the good, the bad and the absolutely bonkers. Charles Dickens, originally a member of the advisory committee for the six-month long event, thought it so jingoistic that he proposed a counterpart: 'Exhibition of England's Sins and Negligences'.

Visitors to the purpose-built Crystal Palace could admire the Koh-i-Noor diamond, seized, along with the Punjab, by the British. Other exhibits included newfangled gas fittings, a perfume fountain, a pulpit with inbuilt ear trumpets for the pious hard-of-hearing, a bed that turfed out its occupants if they overslept and, displayed in a section showcasing advances in medicine, a hollow walking stick for doctors, filled with the ingredients and accoutrements for administering an enema.[10]

*

Medical science failed Albert. The royal website still lists his cause of death, in December 1861, aged forty-two, as typhoid, though more recent theories suggest that his long history of digestive problems might indicate Crohn's disease, ulcerative colitis or stomach cancer. Victoria, already rewriting her strained relationship with her mother who had died earlier that year, diagnosed another cause. Albert first showed symptoms of fever after walking in the rain with their eldest son to remonstrate with him about his liaison with an actress. Victoria would never forgive Bertie for what she saw as two deaths: Albert's and her own. 'My life as a happy one is ended! The world is gone for me!' Victoria wrote to her uncle, King Leopold I of Belgium. The letter also shows the extent to which marriage had remoulded her from monarch to angel in the house. 'Our pure, happy, quiet, domestic life alone enabled me to bear my much-disliked position,' she said.

Already, there were signs of her impulse to sanctify Albert. She commissioned written works, paintings and public memorials including, in Kensington Gardens, a canopied bronze prince on a plinth bedecked with Greek friezes, allegorical figures and representations of the four continents her empire bestrode. In their homes, servants daily laid out fresh clothes for him as if, at any moment, he might return. 'His purity was too great, his aspiration too high for this poor, miserable world!' she told Leopold.

Whether it was love that elevated her husband in her eyes, his erosion of her self-esteem or a combination thereof, the spectre of royalling without Albert compounded Victoria's despair. He had shouldered the lion's share of a workload far more voluminous than any faced by a modern royal, 'to assent to and sign countless formal documents . . . which any clerk could sign as well,' as economist Walter Bagehot put it. In addition, and far more importantly, a sovereign, as defined by Bagehot in his famous book, *The English Constitution*, published six years after Albert's death, had 'three rights – the right to be consulted, the right to encourage, the right to warn'.

When political conflicts arise, 'the greatest wisdom of a constitutional king would show itself in well-considered inaction,' Bagehot added. He meant this as a caution against royals taking party political sides, but overlooked the damage Victoria's inaction was at that very moment inflicting on the institution. The monarchy, having ceded most of its executive powers to parliamentary democracy, was now expected to justify its existence in a different way, by providing a focus of national pride, identity and unity. Instead, Victoria ignored the ceremonial and crowd-pleasing aspects of the role, retreating from public view.

Her subjects grew restive and the press sharply critical. Just three years after Albert died, a protestor hung a sign on Buckingham Palace's railings, declaring 'these commanding premises to be let or sold in consequence of the late occupant's declining business'. An editorial in the *Saturday Review* warned that 'the power which is derived from affection or from loyalty needs a life of almost unintermitted publicity to sustain it'. Such provocations, together with the urgings of family and ministers, spurred Victoria to fleeting appearances, but she also authored or planted a riposte in *The Times*: 'There are other and higher duties than those of mere representation which are now thrown upon the Queen, alone and unassisted . . . To call upon her to undergo, in addition, the fatigue of those mere State ceremonies which can be equally well performed by other members of her family is to ask her to run the risk of entirely disabling herself for the discharge of those other duties which cannot be neglected without serious injury to the public interests.'

Once again, she withdrew, remaining largely in the shadows until Bertie himself contracted typhoid. His illness revived sympathy for her and the monarchy as quickly as it had dissipated. When, finally, Victoria re-emerged after more than a decade to attend a service of celebration for Bertie's recovery, cheering crowds lined her route to St Paul's Cathedral. Almost thirty years remained to her reign. She would seal her future reputation as a great queen – and endanger it.

*

Here is another thing about grief: the initial paroxysms, though agonising, are also a form of validation. The pain you feel proves how well and deeply you loved. Its dulling leaves room for doubt, perhaps even guilt. A woman who has come to believe herself unworthy, and at times resented the person who did most to deepen her insecurities, might find this stage particularly challenging. Certainly, Victoria hinted at this phenomenon in her correspondence. Around the same time the 'For Sale' notice appeared on Buckingham Palace, she expressed shame and confusion over the realisation that, despite assertions to the contrary, she was not yet ready to follow Albert to the grave.

She ate insatiably and messily, ploughing her way through six-course meals and washing them down with beer, as she had always done. Eighteen months into widowhood, a brush with mortality forced her to recognise that she also hungered for life itself. Her carriage overturned on a rough road across the Balmoral estate and John Brown, a ghillie whom Albert had rated highly, rescued her and the other occupants. Brown would go on to protect his queen on many occasions, including tackling the teenager who brandished a gun at her in the name of Irish republicanism.

Victoria's children, who came to loathe Brown, unwittingly brought him and their mother together. Noting that pony rides at Balmoral cheered her more than any other activity, they proposed that Brown join her household in England. On the third anniversary of Albert's loss, the ghillie arrived at Osborne House, her Isle of Wight bolthole, and never again left her side until his own premature death.

We cannot know the nature of the attachment that developed between the Queen and her strapping manservant, a full foot taller and seven years younger than she, because no sooner had she herself died than her family and courtiers began destroying the relevant sections of her journals, along with any letters and papers on the topic. She had been pressurised into abandoning her attempt at a biography of Brown, and no drafts of this survive either. When a Balmoral employee blackmailed Bertie, now reigning as Edward VII, over a separate trove of Victoria's correspondence, the royal doctor, Sir James Reid, helped retrieve and shred those letters too. Brown's diaries suffered the same fate. What these censors could not do was excise Brown from Victoria's published Scottish memoirs, as peppered with mentions of him as her early journals had been with references to Melbourne. They also failed to anticipate how eagerly popular culture fills a vacuum or that evidence of Victoria's love for Brown would emerge via Reid's own archive.

Gossip had started the moment Brown became a fixture in her household, sparking the sorts of whispers endured by Elizabeth I, of a secret morganatic marriage and even an illegitimate baby, with at least some of these stories spread by staff disgruntled at the Scot's rapid rise and alcohol-fuelled bullying. His informality offended them too. Lady Elizabeth Longford's 1964 biography of the Queen quotes Brown reproving her, as he fastens her bonnet: 'Hoots, then wumman. Can ye no hold yerr head up?'

Julia Baird, while researching her book on Victoria, discovered in Reid's diary evidence of greater intimacy. 'Opening the door to Victoria's room at Windsor Castle, he saw her flirting with John Brown as she "walked a little",' Baird writes. 'Brown says to her, lifting his kilt, "Oh, I thought it was here?" She responds, lifting up her dress, "No, it is here."' That vignette, together with the fact that Brown always slept in an adjoining room to her, took solo trips with her to Glas-allt-Shiel, a lodge at Balmoral, acquired the moniker 'the Queen's stallion' in counterpart to her nickname 'Mrs Brown', and was said by a close family friend to enjoy 'every conjugal privilege', imply a sexual component to the relationship. Why then do so many leading biographers and historians believe their connection to have been platonic? The casting of the film *Mrs Brown* helped fix this interpretation in twenty-first-century imaginations. There is chemistry but no spark between Judi Dench, then in her early sixties, twenty years older than Victoria would have been at the time of these events, and Billy Connolly, more bluff than buff as Brown.

Given the frequency with which women in the public eye are assumed to sleep with every man who enters their orbit, it pains me to admit that queen and servant might, after all, have done the deed. However, the continuing majority insistence on their innocence (exceptions are Tom Cullen's 1969 book, *The Empress Brown*, and Fern Riddell's 2025 *Victoria's Secret*) appears no less rooted in cultural bias than any assumptions to the contrary.

Longford objected that if Victoria and Brown's relationship were physical, someone would have seen the two of them canoodling. Baird later turned up evidence of exactly such a sighting. Baird's own argument is that Victoria made no effort to conceal her feelings for Brown, and 'surely she would have been less defiant if they were full-blown lovers'. Ironically, Baird's excellent biography reveals Victoria as a woman just as prone to flout convention for herself as enforce it for others. More telling is the widespread, reflexive idea that Victoria would not have desired Brown. Beyond the obvious element of snobbery embedded in this reaction, the idea of a sexless queen is a figment taught us and transmitted through popular culture, and perhaps easier to accept than her multifaceted reality. Also, as already outlined with Elizabeth I, there are many ways to have sex, and in the absence of safe methods of birth control and disease prevention, our ancestors knew them all.

Brown's sudden death, after seventeen years of constant companionship, hit her hard. She compared it, artlessly, to the loss of Albert, confiding to her private secretary, Sir Henry Ponsonby, that she had 'sustained one of those shocks like in [18]61 when every link has been shaken & torn.'

More poignant still was another secret Baird discovered in Reid's archive. Victoria had given the doctor detailed instructions for her burial, in a white gown, surrounded by mementos of Albert, her children – and Brown. The doctor should place Brown's 'mother's wedding ring on her finger, his portrait and hair in her hand, [and] his handkerchief covering her body' and 'wrap her hand in gauze after placing Brown's hair in it'. Reid was then to lay flowers on top of the gauze to prevent her family and other mourners from seeing, and understanding, her last wishes.

*

Two other men loomed large in Victoria's life, both, by the standards of royal circles, notably lowborn: Prime Minister Benjamin Disraeli, and Abdul Karim, who, like John Brown, rose from the ranks of her household to become the Queen's companion.

Disraeli described his ascent to the highest office in politics as having 'climbed to the top of the greasy pole'. He first reached those heights during the decade the sovereign hid from public view, served her twice in the role and was defeated the same number of times by William Gladstone, leader of the Liberal party forged from an alliance of Whigs and disaffected Tories. Disraeli led the Conservatives, descended from a Tory faction that had argued for maintaining the Corn Laws, the trade tariffs which exacerbated the Irish famine and drove up food prices across Victoria's queendom. A convert to Anglicanism in childhood, he remains Britain's only premier of Jewish heritage to date, and the most flamboyant too, a dandy and novelist with a turn of phrase as rich as his clothing.

Impartiality and faith in democracy would never be Victoria's strong suits. When another of her favoured prime ministers lost an election, she bemoaned 'a defect in our famed constitution to have to part with an admirable Government . . . for no question of any importance or any particular reason, merely on account of the number of votes'. Nor did she make any secret of her violent preference for Disraeli over Gladstone. An anecdote about the two politicians, though probably apocryphal, gets to the reason Victoria loved one and loathed the other. A woman – in different versions of the story, either Victoria herself, Lady Randolph Churchill or an anonymous society lady – invited to dine with them on consecutive nights, comes away from her evening with Gladstone convinced that he is the cleverest man in England. After dinner with Disraeli, she believes herself to be the cleverest woman in England.

Disraeli's upbeat imperialism more closely matched Victoria's own instincts than Gladstone's zeal for social reform, and despite her early crush on the Whig Melbourne, she usually inclined to the Tories. However, the key factor in her relationships with these, and other men, was not politics, but how they made her feel.

Gladstone patronised Victoria. She was by now reaching the zenith of her queenship, vigorously exercising her rights to be consulted, encourage and warn, and frequently at odds with him on foreign policy and the future of Ireland. He opened cabinet meetings with a contemptuous run-through of her latest advice before intoning, 'And now, gentlemen, to business.' His rival, by contrast, tapped into the traditions of courtly love that had provided a crucial framework for Elizabeth I's interactions with advisers and allies. Disraeli acknowledged Victoria's femininity while using imagery that elevated her to a sphere of natural authority, conjuring compliments and borrowing one directly from Gloriana: Victoria was his 'Faerie Queen' as Elizabeth had been Edmund Spenser's. Another title Disraeli gave Victoria pleased her greatly too: Empress of India. As he lay dying, he batted away the idea of a visit from her. 'No, it is better not,' he joked. 'She would only ask me to take a message to Albert.'

Gladstone and the Queen never came close to the understanding implied by that affectionate jest and, since both were blessed (or cursed) with longevity, they had to endure each other on and off for a quarter of a century. Happily for Victoria, her golden jubilee fell between Gladstone's third term as prime minister and his fourth and final stint. He retired a few years before her diamond jubilee.

The celebrations in 1887 to mark her fiftieth year on the throne introduced the monarch to the last of her intimate companions. Two of her Indian subjects, Abdul Karim and Mohammed Buksh, found themselves plucked from jobs back home, respectively as a prison clerk and head of household to a British general, and shipped to England to wait tables for the Queen. Intended as exotic eye candy, the candidates for this dubious honour were selected for their height and good looks. Buksh missed both parts of the brief, a late replacement for an ailing compatriot.

The early stages of Shrabani Basu's compelling book, *Victoria and Abdul,* and the film based on it – inevitably starring Judi Dench – come across as comedy. The British might rule India, but that did not mean they knew or cared to know much about it. Their invention of the word 'Hindustani' was a symptom of this, lumping Urdu and Hindi together, and overlooking the cultural and religious differences bundled with the languages.

The Queen alone seemed concerned that her new staff members could find it difficult to adjust, and ahead of her annual summer visit to Balmoral ordered warmer tartan versions of the orientalist costumes confected for the duo. She also specified thirty-six pairs of gloves for them. A note scrawled across this list by a British member of her household stated that these items had been 'requested by Hindoos'. Karim and Buksh were Muslim.

Soon enough, the story reveals itself as more of a tragedy, theirs and hers, as well as a repeating motif and consequence of imperialism. All three, if for different reasons, experienced the loneliness of difference and the ache of prejudice. Karim and Buksh suffered more, of course, and in significant part because of Victoria.

They were not the first imports to Victoria's court, and few transplants thrived. Duleep Singh, deposed in childhood as Maharajah of the Sikh Empire and deprived of the famous Koh-i-Noor diamond, was made her ward. As an adult, running short of money, he rebelled against this arrangement, demanding the return of the gem and the Punjab and dying at fifty-five without regaining either. His wife, abandoned by him, succumbed to alcoholism. Their three daughters, raised as socialites, developed better uses for their talents, most prominent among them Sophia Duleep Singh, a leading campaigner for women's suffrage.

Buksh, who bore his changed circumstances with good grace, suffered the death of a young child and died himself after twelve years at court. He never showed any jealousy for Karim, even as his colleague rose and flourished – and perhaps he was right. Though Victoria's friendship conferred wealth and status on Karim, it ultimately destroyed him. To her, it brought joy but also conflict and criticism. Bertie even threatened to have her declared insane.

Karim found his way to the Queen's heart through her stomach, initiating her into the delights of curry by cooking a chicken dish, daal and pilau with spices he had brought to England. She enjoyed the taste so much that she asked her kitchens to produce curries every day. He caught her attention in other ways too: with a delicacy of touch when she needed assistance; a precision and elegance in service; and, once his English improved, he told her about India.

As he acquired her language, so she would learn his, shifting the power dynamics to become his eager pupil. In short order, Victoria's teacher or 'Munshi' began to fill the vacuum John Brown had left, as her sounding board, adviser and confidant. Phrases that he taught her in Urdu – 'You will miss the Munshi very much when he is gone' and 'hold me tight' – suggest a degree of flirtation but, within the context of the other information available, no more. Like Brown, Karim jumped in rank, but he sprang further, to fully-fledged courtier, with his own staff, honours, orders and a new title: India secretary. He and Rafiuddin Ahmad, a scholar, informed her support for Muslim minority rights in India. If Victoria's household had found the Scot's advancement hard to take, Karim's triggered their basest instincts.

Plots and rebellions proliferated. Agents in India investigated Karim's background in the hopes of discrediting him. Key members of the Queen's staff threatened to resign. Dr Reid warned her that the spectre of George III had returned to stalk her. 'There are people in high places . . . who say to me that the only charitable explanation that can be given is that Your Majesty is not sane, and that the time will come when to save your Majesty's memory and reputation it will be necessary for me to come forward and say so.' Reid added that Bertie 'has quite made up his mind to come forward if necessary, because quite apart from all the consequences to the Queen, it affects *himself* most vitally . . . because it affects the throne'.

Victoria responded to the bullying as she had done since her youth, with renewed determination, granting Karim tracts of land in India and making provisions in her will to try to protect his future when she was no longer there to look out for him. Henry Ponsonby had foreseen this: 'The advance of the Black Brigade is a serious nuisance,' her private secretary wrote to Reid. Opposition could 'intensify [Victoria's] desire to advance [Karim] further'. Ponsonby called this phenomenon 'progression by antagonism', and here again clear echoes of Victoria are visible in the current king. Throughout his life, Charles has leapt to defend members of his inner circle when they come under fire.

Karim was deserving of some of the criticism he attracted. The Queen's favour went to his head. Increasingly grandiose, he planted stories about himself in the press. When his brother-in-law stole one of Victoria's brooches, Karim explained away his behaviour as Indian tradition. The country, he said, operated on a system of finders keepers. Even so, nothing excuses the treatment meted out to him, and nothing explains it either, apart from racism and its regular accomplices, snobbery and fear. Things came to a head with Victoria's death in January 1901. She had specified that Karim should walk in her funeral procession. For the last time, her family did as she wished.

The next morning, Edward VII dispatched the newly minted Queen Alexandra, her sister-in-law Beatrice and a company of guards to rouse Karim, his wife and nephew from their beds at Frogmore Cottage on the Windsor estate. The delegation demanded that Karim hand over every letter or keepsake from Victoria. In an act of deliberate humiliation, they then proceeded to burn the correspondence in front of him. The King had also sent orders that the Karims pack their bags for India. Victoria's Munshi would die there eight years later, aged forty-six, a broken man.

Until Basu painstakingly gathered the charred fragments of his story, Karim had been all but forgotten. By contrast, a strange postscript saw Frogmore Cottage gain its own media profile. Given by Elizabeth II to her grandson Harry and his wife Meghan and stripped from them by King Charles in 2023, it features in the Netflix documentary about the couple and provides the backdrop for one of their most serious allegations, that Meghan's suicidal ideation was brushed aside by members of the royal household. You might think that the bonfire of Victoria's letters to Karim on the lawn of the Sussexes' home warranted a mention in discussions of racism within the royal family, but I have yet to see any programme, podcast, book or feature that makes the link. Censorship works, and absences shape our views just as much as information does.

*

'It is like a roof being off a house to think of an England queenless,' mused Arthur Benson, essayist and author of the lyrics of *Land of Hope and Glory*, written for the coronation of Edward VII and Alexandra. In reigning for so long, Victoria is defined not by the turbulences she weathered, but the idea that, because she survived them, the threats were not existential. She has come to stand for solidity.

Yet this same phenomenon also proved deeply unsettling to anyone who outlived her. People struggled to imagine a world without Victoria, simply because so few of them had experienced such a world. That empires and countries, including hers, felt increasingly fragile added to their disquiet. 'Since the passing of Victoria the Great, there had been an accumulating uneasiness in the national life,' wrote H.G. Wells on the eve of the First World War. 'It was as if some compact and dignified paperweight had been lifted from people's ideas, and as if at once they had begun to blow about anyhow.'

In truth, Victoria, like the Elizabeths, left a mixed legacy for the Crown, including problems of succession. Elizabeth Tudor had no direct heir as a result of her choices in swerving marriage and maternity. Victoria and Elizabeth Windsor lived to such ripe old ages that their sons came to the throne with limited time to stabilise or reform the institution.

And what of Victoria's contribution to female emancipation? Inevitably, she held positions on the topic that anybody else would have found mutually exclusive. In correspondence with Gladstone, she expressed her 'strongest aversion for the so-called & most erroneous "Rights of Woman"' and in the same year, 1870, wrote to Prince Albert's biographer Theodore Martin that 'The Queen is most anxious to enlist every one who can speak or write to join in checking this mad, wicked folly of "Women's Rights", with all its attendant horrors, on which her poor feeble sex is bent, forgetting every sense of womanly feeling and propriety.' The issue of women's suffrage had been gaining momentum, with a bill about to be debated – and soundly defeated – in parliament.

At the same time, Victoria's own experiences of marriage and childbirth led her to understand that the dream of perfect domestic bliss was just that, a fantasy, even if it was one she devoted much energy to promoting. Mary Ponsonby, feminist wife of the sovereign's private secretary, Sir Henry, persuaded Victoria to donate to the Society for the Promotion of the Employment of Women and then to become its patron. The Queen also gave money to the prison reformer, Elizabeth Fry, and praised Florence Nightingale as 'a remarkable person, having studied both Medicine and Surgery and having practised at hospitals at Paris & in Germany'.

Whatever Victoria believed, her accession created, as H.G. Wells later said, 'a stir of emancipation' and 'a wave of feminine partisanship throughout the country'. Representation matters, and here was a woman in charge. In the early part of her reign, just seven percent of middle- and upper-class women had paid employment, mostly as governesses. By its end, women were elbowing their way out of the domestic sphere into tradition-ally male areas, Millicent Fawcett had united activist groups under the umbrella of the National Union of Women's Suffrage Societies, and Emmeline Pankhurst would soon form the breaka-way Women's Social and Political Union, joined by Sophia Duleep Singh. The Maharajah's daughter regularly sold copies of *The Suffragette* newspaper at the gates of Hampton Court Palace.

During her final decades, Victoria's popularity arced upwards and stayed there, like the corners of her mouth in a photograph she approved for publication against the wishes of her daughters. They thought her expression inappropriate, for the Queen is not merely smiling in the picture but grinning at the Jubilee crowds. Victoria may not have been amused at their obvious devotion, but she was certainly delighted by it.

Chapter 4

Elizabeth II: Family Values

On 6 September 2022, photographer Jane Barlow arrived at Balmoral to discover her host on genial form. 'I got a lot of smiles,' said Barlow later. This was by no means guaranteed. Her Majesty, unlike her great-great-grandmother Victoria, found smiling, literally, tiresome. 'Her face really aches at the end of a long day,' her mistress of the robes once confided.

It takes determination to maintain a fixed expression. The Queen had two main modes: benign or solemn. Neither offered a reliable guide to her feelings. Criticised earlier in her reign for emoting too little, her unreadability had by now proved its worth many times over. A core function of the head of state – and arguably the only purpose of a constitutional monarchy – is to unify. A virgin screen, her subjects projected their idea of her on to that seeming neutrality, and perceiving no gap between their values and hers, hailed her quiet wisdom. Though Elizabeth's popularity, like Victoria's, ebbed in her middle years before climbing to its final high, she established herself as Britain's favourite sovereign, leaving her father and her Tudor namesake to vie with Victoria for second place. Family members might feud or fall, but she remained immaculate.

It is a curious twist that a culture uncomfortable with women in leadership prizes female monarchs. 'Famous have been the reigns of our queens,' intoned Prime Minister Winston Churchill in his 1952 speech eulogising George VI and ushering in his daughter. 'Some of the greatest periods in our history have unfolded under their sceptre.' Might there be deeper reasons for the phenomenon, or does it simply reflect the calibre of the queens in question? Their backbones strong, their lives long, Victoria and the two Elizabeths deceived contemporaries into believing them near immortal.

Barlow's photographs offer a case study. There had been disquieting rumours, yet the images show the second Elizabeth appearing to wear the passage of her ninety-six years lightly – a little stooped, leaning on a cane, but otherwise immutable, the famous helmet of hair impervious to the seasons, clothes unruffled by fashion trends. As ever – *semper eadem* – she carries a handbag, its contents as unknowable as her thoughts. *See*, people said, peering at their smiling queen, *she's doing OK*.

As Barlow worked, snapper and sovereign made small talk about the stormy weather. Within minutes, ill winds would blow in a brand-new British prime minister, the fifteenth of Elizabeth's reign. A pinch-me moment for any politician, to the Queen such interactions were routine. Monarch of thirty-two nations at her accession, and by the end of it still the crowned head of the United Kingdom and fourteen overseas realms, Elizabeth had been welcoming premiers and waving others on their way for more than seven decades.

The intervals between these occasions were narrowing, however. Earlier that morning, Elizabeth had accepted the resignation of Boris Johnson, forced out after only three years, the same abbreviated term as his predecessor, Theresa May, but a lengthier run than the second stint of May's forerunner, David Cameron. Both Cameron and May had fallen victim to a hard right emboldened rather than placated by the UK's referendum on the European Union. Johnson, who campaigned for Brexit under the slogan 'take back control', exercised none of it in office. Fined by police for breaking his own Covid rules, he presided over a chaotic administration that saw alcohol-sodden parties splatter the Downing Street wallpaper. Though a new low for British politics, this by no means marked its nadir.

The Queen was about to ask Liz Truss to form a government. Barlow took a picture of the pair together before leaving them to their private conversation. Truss would subsequently reveal that Elizabeth exercised exactly the constitutional rights of a monarch defined by Walter Bagehot – to be consulted, to encourage and to warn – heartening the politician with promises of another meeting soon and offering a piece of succinct advice: 'pace yourself'.[11] Truss failed to listen. Within weeks, she had triggered an economic meltdown, which, in turn, forced her resignation. Her forty-nine-day tenure is the shortest of any prime minister in UK history.

Although political ineptitude added to the turbulence, the fact that such flawed figures came to power in the first place was as much a symptom of dysfunction as its root cause. Across the world, a lurch towards populism was undermining the political mainstream. This made Elizabeth's death, so soon after the prime ministerial meet-'n'-greet, all the more unsettling. Many of us looked again at Barlow's photographs, this time noticing the monarch's two bodies: the transferable body politic, and her finite, failing natural body. One of Elizabeth's hands looks bruised, possibly from a cannula; her smile masks a long-distance gaze familiar to anyone who has tended to the dying.

Accounts of her final days would reveal that she not only continued to work through this period but pursued private enthusiasms, earlier that week closeting herself several times with John Warren, her racing and bloodstock adviser, and calling him a few hours after Truss left to celebrate the victory of her horse at Goodwood.[12] The next morning – her penultimate – she spoke to officials, confirming her remote attendance at a privy council session scheduled for that evening; the cancellation of that meeting and the sight of family members scrambling to reach Balmoral gave a first indication of what was to come.

Even then, and despite her age, news of the Queen's death hit people in ways they did not expect. As the political classes of every stripe jostled to pay their respects, the contrast between their bloviations and her reticence underscored the truth of an old saying: *you don't know what you've got until it's gone.* Only the very old had ever experienced a universe without her. The grief felt by millions was real. They – we – were not just mourning the woman but our own mortality, other losses, and the end of the second Elizabethan age with its seeming promises of peace and probity.

Commentators wheeled in front of television cameras to assess her significance – and I was one, contracted to ITV News for ten days and nights of obsequies – struggled despite all that airtime to do more than skate over the surface. Here was someone who had not merely witnessed history but made it, for Elizabeth was no mere figurehead. She navigated social and technological transformations, resisting some, promoting others, impacting attitudes as well as outcomes.

There were more amorphous contributions too. She had become a cultural lodestone; an embodiment of words and concepts such as 'England' and 'patriotism' and perhaps, as such, a bulwark against attempts to attach them, like the St George's Cross, to the radicalism now gaining purchase in the UK. That did not mean we could be sure where she stood on these or any other issues. Not even Sir John Major, whose premiership during one of the most turbulent periods of her reign forged a strong relationship between him and 'the Firm', seems willing to hazard a guess. 'Prime ministers who've seen the Queen at close quarters, often for many years, would not be able to tell you with any certainty what her party-political views are,' he told me in 2014.

Revisiting Barlow's photoshoot for a third time, I noticed a fresh detail: a painting behind Truss depicting Victoria on horseback, John Brown holding the bridle. Research for this book had thoroughly challenged my pre-existing views of the nineteenth-century monarch. Might Elizabeth serve up similar surprises? Minutely documented despite the official secrecy that still shrouds her, she can be discovered through posed portraits, candid snaps, audio, film and TV footage. At time of writing, the 1969 fly-on-the-wall documentary, *The Royal Family*, withdrawn decades ago, is back in blurry bootleg form on YouTube. She has been interpreted by at least fifteen actresses. Her first full-length biography, *The Story of Princess Elizabeth*, gives a detailed account of her life – up to the age of four. Published under the pseudonym Anne Ring, it was written by Beryl Poignand, a former governess to her mother, who approved the project. Through the years, Elizabeth would inspire many more books, from the serious to the seriously niche. There were histories, assessments and memoirs from people who knew her well – an ex-governess, Marion Crawford; her dresser Angela Kelly – and at least a few who talked up their intimacy.

Some of the most revealing material charts the only relationships entirely unaffected by her position: her husband learned to walk two paces behind her, her children to address her formally, but dogs and horses appreciated her because of the appreciation she showed them. A 2018 monograph profiles every one of her corgis and dorgis (a dachshund-corgi cross). Horses captivated her from her earliest years. Crawford's unauthorised biography described her first encounter with the Princess. She found Elizabeth pretending her bed was a carriage: 'I mostly go once or twice round the park before I go to sleep,' the child explained. This dedication to all things equine not only endured but produced champions four-legged and two. Elizabeth's daughter, Anne, and a granddaughter, Zara Tindall, are both Olympic equestrians.

I have read about Elizabeth exhaustively and written about her extensively, met staffers and intimates and nearly every member of her immediate family, including her mother, who visited my first British school. Fresh from America, I inflicted a recorder solo on a strange apparition who wore a giant hat indoors. As I squeaked to the end of *Greensleeves*, this person – I had only the vaguest idea who she was – swivelled that hat towards the exit.

In adulthood, I observed the royals in their natural habitat: palaces and public engagements. Occasionally, we interacted.

I spent time with Charles and eventually Camilla, and others, not always for work. Margaret and I were regulars at a restaurant in London's West End. Diana had some of the same friends in the entertainment industry. Anne and I built a Lego car together during an evening celebrating women in engineering, not that she would remember. Whatever your attitudes towards royalty, any encounters with the species are likely to make more of an impression on you than them. In this case, it sealed my impression that if you had to be stuck in a lift with a born Windsor, Anne would be the one to choose, as she can be both entertaining and resourceful.

Nobody ever thought that of Andrew – which made him surprisingly accessible to a journalist interested in the institution to which he belonged. I interviewed him twice, travelled with him, sat with him and Edward at awards ceremonies where they were VIP guests, and separately crossed paths with his ex-wife and daughters and some of the Queen's other grandchildren.

A handful of occasions brought me into direct contact with the monarch herself. There was a small lunch featuring an inquisitive Prince Philip and a few other guests, including *Wallace & Gromit* creator, Nick Park. Invitations to the 2009 Mexican state banquet forced my husband, Andy, to the rentals department at Moss Bross and me to repurpose a gold silk dress I wore for our wedding, only to realise how far we both strayed from the upper-crust aesthetic. Men who attend grand dinners regularly not only own their own white tie kit but look comfortable in it; the women array themselves in weird gowns with inbuilt sashes accessorised with family tiaras and dog hair.

'And what do you do?' This was the Queen to Andy. 'I'm in a band,' he replied. 'How int-er-esting,' she replied. After an abortive attempt to explain his particular brand of music to her ('pounding drums, analytical lyrics, screaming feedback'), he switched to what he imagined to be safer ground, telling her how much he had enjoyed the moment at the end of the meal when the doors opened to admit bagpipers. 'Oh,' she said, 'one can have quite enough of the bagpipes. They play outside my window every morning.'

Though the conversation took place at a state occasion, it counted, by royal convention, as private. Andy did not realise this and some years later, repeated her remarks to Mark Ellen, a broadcaster and music journalist. With Andy's permission, Mark ran the story as a brief item in *The Word* magazine, where it was spotted by someone from the *Evening Standard*. The first I learned of this sequence of events was when a palace official rang me to remonstrate. Her Majesty was not amused. The *Standard*, citing Andy as a source, gave the story a front-page splash. The role of queen's piper, 'one of the greatest accolades in the bagpiping community', might be endangered. 'This is a tradition that started with Queen Victoria and has been carrying on happily ever since,' a Palace spokesman said.

Despite this, other invitations followed: to a household meal, one of Elizabeth's birthday celebrations, two palace garden parties and farewell drinks for a departing aide. Over the course of these events, I began to imagine that I had the measure of her. But was I right?

*

To get to the nub of who Elizabeth was and what she meant, it is essential to clarify who and what she was not – a ruler. By the time she came to the throne, the monarchy occupied a constitutional position which, though deeply enmeshed with the rest of the apparatus of state, retained few powers of decision-making. The job grants its occupants the three rights defined by Bagehot and entrusts to them a range of duties, some clearly defined, others more flexible.

The most basic is to put in the hours. Visibility is not just a byproduct of royalty but its purpose, hence the queenly joke attributed to Elizabeth or her great-great-grandmother: 'I have to be seen to be believed.' Elizabeth doubted that she was its author: 'It sounds more like Queen Victoria,' she told her biographer and Philip's, Gyles Brandreth.

Perhaps, but Victoria tested public patience by hiding away. Elizabeth remained on show almost to her last breath. Close to a third of people in England, Wales and Scotland claimed to have encountered her at one time or another in the flesh, according to a poll late in her reign. She also achieved a balance that eluded her ancestor: doing enough to avoid the suggestions of shirking that clung to Victoria while mostly avoiding accusations of overreach. Twice, circumstances forced her to choose between possible prime ministers. Both times, she followed the advice of political grandees – who happened to direct her away from the edgier Richard Austin ('Rab') Butler and towards more establishment candidates. In 1957, the beneficiary, Harold Macmillan, proved an uncontroversial choice. The appointment in 1963 of aristocrat Alec Douglas-Home smelled like the stitch-up it was, by a Tory faction, not Elizabeth, though she approved. Changes in party rules saved her from having to make such decisions again, even if an electoral stalemate in 2010, when neither Labour nor the Conservatives secured a majority, nearly dragged her back into the selection process.

Her political and diplomatic skills burnished the soft powers of the throne. Her approval ratings expanded her influence. Politicians follow public opinion as often as they lead it, and few saw political advantage in going up against her. On the contrary, in multiple instances over many years, ministers sought to demonstrate their closeness to Elizabeth and reverence for the institution. Each time lawmakers agreed new arrangements for financing the royals, whether the Queen's move in 1992 to paying income tax or, twenty years later, a shift in the family's funding model, the outcome proved advantageous to the royals, giving the appearance of more transparency but too complex to be easily decoded. Only occasionally did decisions run counter to Elizabeth's wishes. Though she understood the volte-face on the government paying all the costs of repairs from the Windsor fire (more on the *annus horribilis* shortly), the decommissioning of the royal yacht *Britannia* distressed her.

If warned that attitudes to the monarchy risked souring, her priorities were clear, as she said in a 1997 speech: 'I know that, despite the huge constitutional difference between a hereditary monarchy and an elected government, in reality the gulf is not so wide,' she said. 'Each, in its different way, exists only with the support and consent of the people.' Public opinion about the royals might be hard to decipher, 'but read it we must'.

She became both the antithesis and apotheosis of celebrity culture, unwilling to bend to its dictates and all the more iconic for that. 'I want to be as famous as the Queen of England,' said

Andy Warhol. One of his silk-screen images of her resides in the royal collection.

In bearing three sons and a daughter, each of whom produced two children, Elizabeth fulfilled the traditional demand on royal women: propagating the line. She enjoyed far less success in showcasing her resulting family as an ideal.

As the titular head of the Church of England and pillars of the state from justice to the military, she appeared to stand against change. That perception is not unfounded. This book illuminates the ways in which royalty can serve as a brake on progress, its women presented as paragons or pariahs, its foundational principles rooted in inequality. However, the institution survives not by resisting alteration but by managing it through a process of slow adaptation. This combination – visible continuity and constant shifts so subtle as to be imperceptible to outsiders – allows the monarchy to remain in step with its subjects and in turn enables those subjects to cope with the inevitability of change. This, at any rate, is the theory top aides told me animated Elizabeth's approach to her role. They cited the vast transformations during her reign and comparative lack of traction of fascist movements in the UK throughout this period to argue that it proved effective, and they could be correct.

As the dominions she inherited grappled with new ways of being, doing and thinking – and reduced in number – her own adjustments generally went unnoticed. Waymarks vanished, grounds shifted, deference faded, trust decayed and, throughout this tumult, there she stood, not merely a symbol of constancy and restraint, but their personification. Hers was a long game. She rarely reversed decisions or fell for the lure of shiny, new ways of doing things. Most of her missteps flowed from the same qualities.

The symbol and guarantor of the Empire, she also participated in its dismantling, presiding as former colonies transitioned to new relationships with the Crown or into republics, some, but not all, joining a voluntary association headed by her, the Commonwealth. This was a new role that she defined in the doing of it, not a hereditary one, though Charles got the nod to succeed her.

By instinct and influence, she encouraged the ideal encapsulated in the slogan of opponents of Scottish independence, 'better together'. Her kingdom remained united, though fractured, after Scotland's 2014 referendum. Two years later, Buckingham Palace complained about the *Sun*'s banner headline, 'QUEEN BACKS BREXIT', forcing the newspaper to publish a lengthy retraction. A 2025 book by *The Times*' former royal correspondent, Valentine Low, alleges that she in fact held the opposite view. My own research suggests she harboured specific and personal concerns about the prospect of the UK leaving the European Union. Brexit would not only curtail the free movement of people but of horses. Ahead of the vote, experts and specialist media warned of severe consequences for equine industries. Nor were they wrong. Costs in the UK have trebled in areas such as the import of animals and participation in international competitions, while the sector is struggling with shortages of grooms, instructors and essential supplies, from veterinary drugs to saddles.

The outcome of the vote demonstrated the limits of her influence but not its extent. Though she could not keep Britain in Europe, might she have helped maintain the national identity that positions the UK as a defender of democracy through international cooperation? Was she, in the words of former tabloid editor Piers Morgan, 'the ultimate antidote to a world gone nuts'? Or might she, through her attempts to protect her son Andrew, have added to the madness? These questions acquire a fresh urgency with each passing day.

*

Until the short-lived Fixed-term Parliaments Act, introduced in 2011, a sovereign alone could dissolve parliament, at the request of the prime minister. The law's repeal in 2022 did not explicitly return that power to the Crown, leaving this most sensitive of roles to convention rather than statute.

Nobody expected that the baby born in a Mayfair town-house on 21 April 1926 would go on to exercise that prerogative on no fewer than fifteen occasions – twice in one year during a period of economic volatility – or to assent both the Fixed-term Parliaments Act and its repeal. Though her father Bertie, the Duke of York, was the second son of George V, placing Princess Elizabeth Alexandra Mary Windsor third in line of succession, she would surely lose that position to a brother or once her uncle, the future Edward VIII, married and produced children of his own.

As a result, 'Lilibet' enjoyed the upsides of royal status without the obvious disadvantages. Her mother, the Duchess of York, Elizabeth, née Bowes-Lyon, had an appetite for fun, interrupting such rudimentary schooling as she and little sister Margaret received to take them on outings. Only later would the elder princess receive private tutoring in constitutional history. There would be no brothers, no further sisters either. 'We four,' Bertie called his family unit, cosily. Yet if the Yorks' thick-carpeted existence shielded them from a world still reeling from the First World War and a devastating influenza pandemic only to slide towards the Great Depression, the risks to royalty had risen.

Eight European countries rid themselves of their monarchs in the first half of the twentieth century: Portugal, Germany, Austria, Hungary, Russia, Albania, Italy and Romania. In 1922, Constantine I was forced, for a second and final time, to surrender the throne of Greece. Four decades later, after a civil war and a military coup, his grandson Constantine II suffered the same fate. The junta finally abolished the Greek monarchy in 1973.

The house of Windsor, spared these tides, suffered an existential crisis of its own with the accession of Edward in 1936, followed after only 326 days in office by a shock announcement: 'I have found it impossible to carry the heavy burden of responsibility and to discharge my duties as king as I would wish to do without the help and support of the woman I love,' he said, before heading off as Duke of Windsor to wed the non-negotiable Wallis Simpson. His abdication thrust Bertie, renamed George VI, onto the hot seat just as tensions ratcheted up across Europe and Asia. He would be pinioned there throughout the Second World War, a period his eldest child and heir apparent recalled as 'terrible and glorious'.

The Blitz, a nightly aerial assault by the German Luftwaffe from September 1940 to May 1941, destroyed more than a million homes and killed at least twenty thousand residents of the capital alone. Nine of those bombs hit Buckingham Palace. The

King remained in London, touring the scenes of destruction. The initial walkabouts were not an unalloyed success. His consort initially drew jeers for thinking to boost morale by dressing up, not down, picking her way through the rubble in the fancy millinery that I remember from her visit to my school. Soon, however, their efforts paid off, understood and accepted as a mark of solidarity. Time – and myth-making – eventually perfected them into the exemplars of resistance portrayed in the 2010 movie *The King's Speech*, while she would separately carve out a place in public affections as the Queen Mother, merry widow of Windsor, fond of pink gin and a flutter on the horses.

An accidental monarch, George tended to submit to the advice of his ministers and aides, especially the formidable Alan 'Tommy' Lascelles, his last private secretary and his daughter's first. The pattern would influence her understanding of the sovereign's role and its boundaries, and George owes some of his own popularity to this reflex. In an age of dictators, he appeared shoulder to shoulder with his prime minister and out among his people. More significant is the allied victory, which still sits at the heart of Britain's view of itself. And – because every hero needs a villain to show them in their best light – he and his queen are also boosted by an interpretation of history that positions the Duke and Duchess of Windsor as the only royals on the wrong side of it.

That Edward and Wallis had fascist associations is not in doubt. In pre-war days, the couple visited Hitler at the Führer's expense. Churchill recommended the Duke's deployment as governor of the Bahamas during the war to stop him from becoming 'a centre of intrigue'. The former king nonetheless appears, wittingly or not, to have featured in a Nazi plot to reinstate him on the throne. Seen through the prism of Edward's known weaknesses and his wife's ill repute, the story swiftly acquired a predictable cast. The scheming, oversexualised duchess must be primarily to blame. The FBI certainly believed so.

An informant claimed that she had two-timed her future husband with the German ambassador to London in the run-up to the abdication. A memo warned that she was now passing information to the Germans via this ex-lover. Yet Edward's political susceptibilities were evident before Wallis arrived on the scene. A fellow guest at a 1933 gathering reported that 'the Prince of Wales was quite pro-Hitler and said it was no business of ours to interfere in Germany's internal affairs either re Jews or anything else, and added that the dictators are very popular these days, and that we might want one in England before long'. A home movie from the same period shows Princesses Elizabeth and Margaret receiving instruction from their uncle on performing the Nazi salute. There is a woman in the film too, the first to raise her arm. It is their mother.

Eight decades later, the Palace would decry the *Sun*'s decision to publish stills from the seventeen-second clip – accompanied by the banner headline 'THEIR ROYAL HEILNESSES' – as 'disappointing'. A source told the BBC: 'This is a family playing and momentarily referencing a gesture many would have seen from contemporary newsreels. No one at that time had any sense how it would evolve.'

That last point is, in a phrase John Major once used to describe *The Crown*, 'a barrel-load of nonsense'. As a parliamentary backbencher, Churchill correctly warned that Hitler favoured force over democracy. Many other voices sounded the alarm too. The royals, however, supported appeasement. When Prime Minister Neville Chamberlain returned to England after signing the Munich Agreement, famously declaring 'peace for our time', George and Elizabeth invited him onto the balcony of Buckingham Palace to mark the moment. A year later, Nazi forces invaded Poland and Britain entered the war. Even then, the Queen Consort remained obdurate, writing to Chamberlain to tell him, 'You were right.'

It is hard to test the narrative that sees Edward and Wallis as royal outliers in their sympathies and instincts. Tight restrictions on archival material relating to the family hampers efforts to assess the extent to which any other members favoured doing deals with Germany or supported fascism. Historian Karina Urbach has suggested that quite a few of the Windsors' German cousins 'were infatuated with Hitler'. A source of that infatuation and his appeal for at least some British royals, she said, was that they mistook Nazism for a movement that would protect royalty against communism.

*

Lilibet grew up primed to be cautious. Unbridled passions could batter a family, flatten cities, cost kingdoms. Even as a small child, her inscrutability drew comment. 'She has the serenest outlook on life,' observed biographer-governess Poignand, but that was probably a misreading. Research and my limited contact with her suggest not that the troubles of the world flowed off her, but rather that she endured tempests without flinching.

Evacuated to Windsor Castle during the Blitz, she addressed the nation for the first time in a radio broadcast. 'Thousands of you in this country have had to leave your homes and be separated from your fathers and mothers,' she said in that high voice. 'My sister Margaret Rose and I feel so much for you, as we know from experience what it means to be away from those you love most of all.' The dislocations and disruptions of war, which ripped most Britons from ordinary life, gave the princesses a taste of it. They dug for victory, as others did, if in the grounds of their castle. At eighteen, when in other circumstances she might have been filling her dance card, Elizabeth was wielding a monkey wrench, signed up to the women's Auxiliary Territorial Service against her father's wishes, and learning to maintain and drive heavy army vehicles. Margaret joined the Sea Rangers.

Peace returned the sisters to their gilded cage, but first there were two thrilling nights of anonymity. On 8 May 1945, they crept out of Buckingham Palace to celebrate Victory in Europe Day, positioning themselves just in time to cheer their own parents emerging onto the famous balcony with Churchill. Years later, Elizabeth would admit to 'having cheated slightly by sending a message into the house to say we were waiting outside'. That August, she and Margaret repeated the caper as the nation celebrated Japan's surrender.

While the war broadened Elizabeth's experiences and skill sets, it added to the catalogue of upheavals that marked the childhood of her future consort. A baby when his uncle, Constantine I, lost his throne, Prince Philip of Greece and Denmark grew up itinerant and mostly without parental oversight. His father, stripped of Greek citizenship and exiled, moved with his family to France, but any attempts at maintaining a united household quickly faltered. Philip's mother, Princess Alice of Battenberg, diagnosed schizophrenic, vainly protested her incarceration in a Swiss sanatorium, as well she might. Sigmund Freud, who consulted on her case, naturally assumed her problems to be hormonal rather than the result of trauma, and recommended blasting her ovaries with high-intensity X-rays. Once released, she established an order of nuns on the island of Tinos, only to be chased out of Greece again by the military coup. Philip's four sisters all married into the German nobility. One died in a 1937 plane crash with her husband and children. The spouse of another became a high-ranking SS officer. Philip's father settled in the south of France, living in hotel rooms and keeping company with a French actress. He succumbed to a heart attack in 1944.

Left to bounce between temporary berths – schools and scattered relatives – Philip developed a self-sufficiency that, while impressive, made few allowances for those of a more sensitive disposition. His mentor, Kurt Hahn, a German-Jewish educationalist, whose Schule Schloss Salem the Prince attended, helped to mould some of his most admirable qualities but did nothing to soften his hard edges. A prominent critic of Nazism, Hahn soon left Germany for Scotland, establishing Gordonstoun, a new school, in one of its more remote reaches. Philip arrived there a year later, thriving under its sink-or-swim regimen of physical exercise combined with a belief in the value of public service. In addition to academic subjects, boys were drilled in manual and practical skills and undertook shifts with the local lifeboats and fire brigade. Asked how his approach could benefit an introverted child, Hahn replied: 'By providing circumstances which turn him inside out.' And an extrovert? 'By turning him outside in.'

It is hard to know where on this spectrum Philip or Elizabeth would have fallen had they come of age in peacetime. Members of their so-called silent generation learned to keep calm and carry on, but fate had a nasty trick up its sleeve for all of them. Moulded by two wars into natural, small-c conservatives, this cohort would be bombarded by transformations sparked or speeded by those conflicts.

There were other legacies. Neither Elizabeth nor Philip had any tolerance for extravagance. They shuddered at her mother's spendthrift ways and recoiled from their eldest son's indulgences, though seem to have operated more elastic standards for Andrew. In 2003, a reporter managed to get a job as a footman at Buckingham Palace. He described the couple breakfasting on cereal decanted into Tupperware while they listened to an old Roberts radio.

The prompts of their wartime experiences reinforced the royal diktat of maintaining a brave face, whatever the circumstances. Only once was Elizabeth caught on camera crying, and then palace sources suggested that a chill wind might have been responsible. It was December 1997, and the Queen, face crumpled, saluted the royal yacht *Britannia*, about to be decommissioned after forty-four years of service.

She remained dry eyed after Diana's death, at least in public and possibly in private too. When the news reached Balmoral, Elizabeth though 'just feet away' from Charles in adjoining bedrooms did not go to him, nor he to her, according to biographer Penny Junor.

In Peter Morgan's 2006 movie *The Queen*, Helen Mirren's Elizabeth weeps alone on a Balmoral hillside, then sees a stag, and, hearing the noise of approaching hunters, shoos it away. The real-life Philip might have taken issue with any number of details in this scene – for example, the idea of his fastidious wife, an enthusiast for hunting, blowing her nose on one of her famous headscarves or trying to save a deer – but instead, he chose to rebut the tears. 'She doesn't cry,' he told Gyles Brandreth. 'They just make it up . . . You can have feelings without blubbing.'

*

You can also have a long and, by most standards, successful marriage without the frills and furbelows that romantic fiction deems essential. Elizabeth and Philip always resisted attempts to retrofit their relationship to a Hollywood script. They were especially irritated by a meet-cute moment Marion Crawford included in her controversial biography, in which Princess Elizabeth, on a visit to Dartmouth naval college, is struck by cupid's arrow while watching 'a fair-haired boy, rather like a Viking' leaping over the nets on a tennis court. 'How good he is, Crawfie! How high he can jump!'

'We'd met before,' Philip growled at Brandreth, 'but that doesn't suit the way they want to tell the story.' Elizabeth provided her own stilted account to an author who was preparing a souvenir book on their wedding. 'I was thirteen years of age, and he was eighteen and a cadet . . . He joined the navy at the outbreak of war, and I only saw him very occasionally.' Nor was she always certain that Philip was The One. She did develop a crush on him, but other young men caught her eye. Several remained lifelong friends, notably Henry Herbert, Lord Porchester. His grandfather, the fifth Earl of Carnarvon, had sponsored the discovery of Tutankhamun's tomb; his father competed as an amateur jockey and bred horses. 'Porchie' would inherit the earldom, interests and family seat, Highclere Castle, the location for *Downton Abbey*, going on to spend much of his life as Elizabeth's racing manager and closest male confidant. Rumours of an affair clung to them, but not as tenaciously as the gossip surrounding Philip.

After graduating from Dartmouth in 1940, the Prince went straight into active service, acquitting himself with distinction. Mentioned in dispatches for his role operating searchlights aboard the HMS *Valiant* during the Battle of Cape Matapan, he was later credited with saving another ship during the invasion of Sicily. As a Luftwaffe bomber targeted the vessel at night, Philip came up with a ruse to trick the pilot into thinking he had scored a hit by launching a raft ablaze with flare and smoke floats. Aboard a third ship, the HMS *Whelp*, as part of the British Pacific Fleet in the closing phases of the war, he served alongside Mike Parker, his future equerry. Parker alluded to 'armfuls of girls' during this period, then qualified the description in a second interview: 'There was no one special.'

It was after the war, while based at the Petty Officer School in Corsham – a market town later known as the site of Andrew and Camilla Parker Bowles' last marital residence – that Philip paid court to Elizabeth, making frequent visits to the Windsor residences including a six-week idyll at Balmoral. The relationship blossomed too fast for her protective father, and nowhere near speedily enough to please Philip's interventionist uncle,

Louis 'Dickie' Mountbatten. Born Prince Louis of Battenberg, Mountbatten avidly pursued dynastic advancement, first via Philip, and decades later in his efforts to matchmake his great-nephew Prince Charles to his granddaughter Amanda Knatchbull. All the while, he collected a jangle of posts and titles for himself, a rear admiralship, a peerage, viceroy and Governor-General of India, first sea lord and chief of the defence staff, an earldom and a baronetcy.

Elizabeth, a great-great-grandchild of Victoria like Philip, was related to her beau twice over – his third cousin and second cousin once removed. Intermarriage entailed risks including, for Victoria's descendants, a genetic mutation expressed in men as a rare form of haemophilia. Yet the couple viewed their shared heritage as a plus, appreciating their mutual understanding of what was expected of them. There were differences too, of course. Philip, baptised in the Greek Orthodox Church, continued to make its sign of the cross and pursue interfaith dialogue after his admission to the Church of England. Elizabeth's Anglican faith, though devout, was uncomplicated, incurious and intensely private.

Her impulse to concealment ran deep and wide. Funny, and an accurate mimic, she revealed that side of herself only to trusted friends and family. Philip, though shying as she did from the mushy stuff of emotions, was more open, his brain-mouth connection running at high and unfettered speeds. In 1969, with inflation and unemployment in the UK at postwar highs, he complained in an interview that the monarchy lacked funds. 'We had a small yacht that we've had to sell, and I shall probably have to give up polo fairly soon . . . Inevitably if nothing happens, we may have to move into smaller premises,' he said. Around the same time, he persuaded his family to participate in the behind-the-scenes documentary, *Royal Family*. Elizabeth and Anne, sceptics about the project from the start, united after its first and only broadcast to ensure the film was withdrawn. As Bagehot observed, royalty does not necessarily benefit from greater exposure, though the eminent Victorian couched his warning in flattering terms: 'We must not let daylight in upon magic.'

At first glance, you could see Philip as proof of Bagehot's observation. As my husband and I queued in the receiving line for the Mexican state banquet behind a clutch of the country's diplomats, the Prince spotted my husband, Andy, fair-skinned and, at the time, a bottle blonde: 'Thank heavens!' he exclaimed. 'One of us!' Philip told Malala Yousafzai, targeted by Taliban assassins for advocating girls' right to education, that children 'go to school because their parents don't want them in the house'; he warned a British student against lingering in China lest he become 'slitty-eyed'; he joked to an aboriginal Australian about 'throwing spears'. And on he went, spouting sexist and racist comments like they were going out of fashion. Sadly, they were not. Far from criticising his outbursts, many in the media celebrated him for them.

The blurb for a book of his collected sayings, *Prince Philip: Wise Words and Golden Gaffes*, distils this attitude: 'Irascible, controversial, outspoken, forthright and funny; the Gaffer, the Prince of Political Incorrectness, the Duke of Hazard, Phil the Greek. Whatever you call him – and he doesn't give a damn – you've got to love him!'

That, say people who knew them well, perfectly encapsulates Elizabeth's feelings. He sometimes drove her mad, gave her cause for jealousy through his friendships with other women, created problems as well as resolving them, but she adored him. Nor, despite his roving eye, did she lose confidence or bend herself out of shape seeking his approval. Always her own person, she became stronger through their union rather than diminished by it.

At lunch with the couple, I witnessed a little of their dynamics – and how fearsome she could be. Within minutes, she ticked me off for asking a British equestrian to what age she hoped to continue competing – Elizabeth deemed the question too personal – then pursed her lips when her dogs converged on me under the table, licking the salt from my legs and growling when I recoiled. It was a summer's day, and I had ignored the palace convention that women should wear tights. Turns out there might have been good reasons to do so, for protection rather than decorum.

Philip did not escape her censure either. The Queen twice reproved him for speaking to me across the table rather than confining his attention to his immediate neighbours. Later, over drinks, he sought me out again. *How did I spend my free time?* he asked. I mentioned wreck-diving off the British coast. 'Why the bloody hell would you want to do that?' he boomed. I replied with a question. As the first president of BSAC, the British Sub-Aqua Club, surely he should know?

*

What neither he nor Elizabeth anticipated in their early days of courtship and marriage was the hostility he would generate. Philip carried a taint his Windsor cousins did their best to obscure: all those continental genes; no actual Greek lineage but Danish, Russian and, of course, a lot of German in the mix. 'He comes to take "for better or for worse" / England's fat Queen and England's fatter purse,' ran a verse about Prince Albert. Philip prompted similar reactions. His future mother-in-law nicknamed him 'the Hun'. Courtiers deemed him 'rough, ill-mannered, uneducated' and warned that he quite possibly lacked the capacity to remain faithful.

Elizabeth, though not to be dissuaded, did agree to delay a formal engagement until she turned twenty-one, first embarking on a lengthy royal tour of South Africa with her parents and sister. In Cape Town, on that significant birthday, she gave a radio address that perfectly foreshadowed her queenship:

'There is a motto which has been borne by many of my ancestors, a noble motto, "I serve". [The original motto is in German, *ich dien*.] Those words were an inspiration to many bygone heirs to the throne when they made their knightly dedication as they came to manhood,' she said, then immediately acknowledged that courtly tradition excluded her sex from this tradition: 'I cannot do quite as they did.'

However, she had at her disposal a method of mass communication not available to earlier royals. 'I can make my solemn act of dedication with a whole empire listening. I should like to make that dedication now. It is very simple. I declare before you all that my whole life whether it be long or short shall be devoted to your service and the service of our great imperial family to which we all belong.'

This was no empty promise. Just as the fresh-faced princess had put duty before romance by coming to South Africa, the demands of her 'great imperial family' would almost always trump the concerns and desires of actual family. That included Margaret, who during this trip fell in love with a married equerry, Group Captain Peter Townsend, and would eventually be manoeuvred by her sister into abandoning the relationship for the greater good.

Philip chafed at some of Elizabeth's decisions but shared her priorities. With the wedding date set for 20 November 1947, he underwent a naturalisation process, ditched his Greek and Danish princedom, and took the Mountbatten surname. Created HRH the Duke of Edinburgh on the eve of the ceremony, he would not regain his original rank until his wife made him Prince of the United Kingdom of Great Britain and Northern Ireland a decade later.

The Crown interprets that promotion as part of a pattern that saw Elizabeth reward or mollify family members by handing them orders and honours, but her husband had in fact turned down earlier offers of preferment. The titles he regretted surrendering were those he had not yet attained, in the naval hierarchy. In the first years of their marriage, he commanded his own ship out of Malta. Elizabeth spent as much time on the island as she could, but her father's declining health forced her to deputise for him with increasing frequency. In February 1952, she and Philip embarked on a state visit to Kenya, still a Crown colony. Within days of their arrival, the King died in his sleep.

Elizabeth greeted the news with calm – whether equanimity or its drear cousin, resignation – grief too, but if there were tears, nobody recorded them. She flew home to a strange reception, the public in mourning but also excited at the prospect of the twenty-five-year-old monarch. Her prime minister on the other hand, and despite his speech about great queens, secretly doubted her readiness. 'She is only a child,' Churchill exclaimed to his private secretary.

Within weeks, she had won over Churchill. He delighted in how serious and studious she was, how open to his advice. Unfortunately for Philip, Churchill's guidance led her to a decision he could not stomach. It was partly Mountbatten's fault. Soon after the King died, Dickie made an ill-timed boast: the house of Mountbatten now reigned, he crowed. His words united older royals with Lascelles and Churchill in their determination to thwart this scenario. Elizabeth duly issued a proclamation confirming that her family would continue to be known as the Windsors. Her consort – a word never formally appended to any of his titles – raged. He was, he said, 'the only man in the country not allowed to give his name to his children. I'm nothing but a bloody amoeba.' In 1960, she introduced an intricate compromise, the creation of the hyphenate 'Mountbatten-Windsor' to be used by Elizabeth and Philip's line excepting 'those with the style of Royal Highness and the title of Prince/Princess, or female descendants who marry', who were restricted to deploying the double-barrelled option in limited circumstances, for example, on marriage certificates.

Both Philip and Elizabeth made concessions, but his alone are routinely construed as heroic. An 'alpha male' – another label applied to him with tedious frequency – is expected to dominate, not defer. 'In getting married she didn't sacrifice anything. [Philip's] life changed completely. He gave up everything,' Mountbatten's son-in-law, John Knatchbull, Baron Brabourne, told Brandreth.

A quick flick through Philip's obituaries gives a sense of how pervasive the trope is: 'How Prince Philip gave up a career for life with the Queen' (BBC); 'Philip gave up his crown, country and career to be with Elizabeth' (ABC); 'Huge sacrifices Prince Philip made to support the Queen as he ended his promising career' (*OK!*); 'While known for outrageous statements many saw as bigoted, Prince Philip made personal sacrifices to support the Queen' (*Al Jazeera*).

*

You would be hard put to find sympathy for any of the women who sublimated their ambitions to marry into the family. Sophie Rhys-Jones co-founded RJH Public Relations before her marriage to the Queen's youngest son and hoped to combine her job with royal life. She resigned after a *News of the World* journalist, Mazher Mahmood, posing as a sheikh, lured her into indiscretions about her in-laws and offers of access to them. That was a stupid mistake on her part. The question is whether journalists would have praised her if she had given up her business proactively, in the name of love. Media responses to Meghan and Harry's engagement suggest that many of them consider a prince a greater prize than a career.

Queens regnant must square a different circle, popular only if they embrace their gender; considered credible only if they transcend it. Elizabeth I managed to do both. Victoria showcased domesticity, and Elizabeth II pulled off a similar sleight of hand, but with an additional twist for a more demotic era, presenting as middle class and not so much unfashionable as outside of fashion. Her housewifely image suggested relatability, but, like Elizabeth Tudor's costumes or a pair of tights worn in the presence of corgis, acted as a shield. She did not look like one of the richest women in the world or someone exploiting her sway over your taxes. It was brilliantly effective but also ensured that she was, and remains in some quarters, underestimated.

One person who read her wrong was the Labour politician, Tony Benn. No fan of hereditary privilege – the monarchy, he wrote, 'helps to prop up all the privilege and patronage that corrupts our society' – Benn renounced the peerage that automatically fell to him on the death of his aristocratic father so he could continue sitting as an MP. Four years later, appointed postmaster general, he plotted to axe the Queen's head from a run of stamps commemorating the Battle of Britain. After an apparently cordial audience during which he laid out the proposal for the headless stamps, he left the palace convinced he had her agreement, only for the project to be halted in its tracks. Benn blamed aides for the about-turn, but Elizabeth herself had objected, flexing her influence without direct confrontation.

I thought about this skirmish when, decades later, the Bank of England decided to redesign the five-pound note, replacing an image of prison and social reformer Elizabeth Fry with Churchill. At the time, Fry was the only woman among distinguished figures from history celebrated on the reverse of English paper money. The prospect of an all-male line-up prompted author and activist Caroline Criado-Perez to push for the bank to improve female representation. The bank was persuaded, choosing Jane Austen for a new ten-pound note. Appreciation for Criado-Perez's efforts was not unanimous, however. She and assorted backers of her proposal, me included, received death threats.

In the midst of the noise, it was easy to overlook the significance of the woman on the front of every banknote. In this respect, the debate mirrored discussions around the pitiful numbers of public statues celebrating women. Criado-Perez soon turned her attention to that issue too, successfully agitating for a statue of suffragist Millicent Fawcett to join the eleven bronzes of men on Parliament Square. The unveiling felt simultaneously momentous and depressing; a sign that activism can work but also proof of how far there is to go. The addition of one statue, however prominent, did little to move the dial in terms of redressing the gender imbalance, which in fact was at risk of widening. Internal documents prepared by Hull City Council, amid debates over decolonising history, listed figures whose statues could be considered too controversial to retain. Queen Victoria featured, yet remove monuments to her and whole towns, maybe even cities, would be left without any female statuary at all.

In 2024, the Bank of England issued the first note that replaced Elizabeth with her son. Barring unforeseen developments, and despite a change in the law that finally ditched male primogeniture in the royal succession, every new design is likely to feature a male monarch for decades to come. Who knows when – or if – there will be another queen regnant.

Feminism has a habit of discounting Elizabeth II, focusing on the accident of birth that delivered her to prominence. Yet her presence made a difference from the outset, her accession coinciding not with a moment of progress for women but retrenchment: a push to rebuild the structures the Second

World War had weakened – gender norms included. When men go off to fight for kings and countries, women move into the labour force and prove their worth. Briefly, they reap rewards including a wider acceptance of the revolutionary idea that they are as capable as men. The end of the First World War saw the long campaign for suffrage finally bear fruit, with a tranche of women given the right to vote and stand for election. Even so – and despite the subsequent extension of the franchise to all females of voting age – only thirty-seven women won Westminster seats during the initial decades of eligibility. The Second World War provided another jolt to the system. The 1945 general election ushered in twenty-four female MPs, a record tally for a single intake.

However, as veterans returned home, they again began elbowing women out of sectors traditionally dominated by men. While the newly created National Health Service, production lines and service sectors created some alternative berths, female workers enjoyed neither the pay nor the protections afforded to their male counterparts. Meanwhile, corporations aggressively marketed a vision of happy domesticity that could only be perfected through the acquisition of white goods and women's return to the kitchen.

In 1966, as a rising generation of feminists challenged these inequities, the Queen paid oblique tribute to their forerunners in her annual Christmas broadcast: 'It is difficult to realise that it was less than fifty years ago that women in Britain were first given the vote, but parliament was first asked to grant this one hundred years ago. Yet, in spite of these disabilities, it has been women who have breathed gentleness and care into the harsh progress of mankind.'

She may not have seen herself as part of this narrative. Brandreth suggests that 'her achievement was not to set a tone or define a time, not to effect change or influence events' but to reassure. In his view, she 'made no particular impact' on issues including 'the sexual revolution that came with the advent of oral contraception [and] the rise of feminism'.

Something similar is often said of Margaret Thatcher, the UK's – and Elizabeth's – first female prime minister. In either case, it is wide of the mark. True, both women harboured suspicions of the f-word – feminism – and would never have applied it to themselves. Their presentation, the hats, hairdos, twinsets and handbags functioned well as protective colouring because it was authentic. Both were unlikely domestic goddesses. Thatcher, a keen if idiosyncratic cook, liked to treat dinner party guests to a starter of tinned consommé whisked with cream cheese and a pinch of curry powder. She insisted on whipping up dinner for her husband, Dennis, every night, sometimes chivvying members of her cabinet into joining them.

Visitors to Balmoral were amazed to witness Elizabeth revelling in housewifely duties. A glimpse of this phenomenon, captured in the documentary *Royal Family*, shows Philip and Anne incinerating meat on a barbeque while Elizabeth prepares accompanying dishes. Viewers are not privy to the Queen's oddest quirk, however. Time and time again, she set about the washing-up, even though, as a lady-in-waiting confided to a bemused guest, the dishes would be put through the dishwasher after the monarch's ministrations.

While these similarities did not create a rapport between the Queen and Thatcher, neither was their relationship fraught in the way popular legend suggests. Many assessments are shot through with the same biases identified elsewhere in this book, such as a sexualised response more revealing of the male gaze than of either Elizabeth or the Prime Minister. Ben Pimlott, one of the Queen's most respected biographers, refers to 'a flirtatious frisson' between the sovereign and Thatcher's Labour predecessor, Sir James Callaghan, on the basis that the politician 'would compliment [her] on her clothes and she would respond with banter'. Maybe, but women greeted with unsolicited remarks about their appearance often deflect with humour. A lot of comments about Thatcher are downright creepy. Her long-term press secretary Sir Bernard Ingham enthused that his boss possessed 'a film star's attractiveness', while French president François Mitterrand described her as having 'the eyes of Caligula but the mouth of Marilyn Monroe'.

That same male perspective also assumes women to be natural rivals. The frictions between Elizabeth and Thatcher, however, stemmed not from biological alignment but ideological differences. In 1976, an injudicious briefing to the *Sunday Times* from Elizabeth's aide, Michael Shea, laid bare some of their dividing lines: 'In an unprecedented disclosure of the monarch's political views, it was said that the Queen considers the Prime Minister's approach often to be uncaring, confrontational and socially divisive,' announced the newspaper's front-page exclusive, which identified points of contention including South Africa (Commonwealth countries were calling for sanctions against apartheid; Thatcher was resisting) and the aggression deployed to crush the miner's strike. The piece continued: 'The Queen fears that the whole thrust of the

Thatcher government's policies threatens to undermine the consensus in British politics which she thinks has served the country well since the Second World War.'

The Palace issued denials, Shea resigned soon afterwards, and it is unclear how accurately, or otherwise, he had transmitted Elizabeth's views. There is evidence, however, for some of her concerns. Thatcher herself said of the Queen, who as monarch never participated in elections, that she was 'the kind of woman who could vote SDP' – the centrist party formed in 1981 as Labour tacked to the left.

On a personal level, they got on well enough. After Thatcher left office, sitting in the House of Lords as Baroness Thatcher of Grantham, the Queen granted her two of the highest honours in her gift and also attended her eightieth birthday. At Thatcher's funeral seven years later, I watched Elizabeth maintain her usual impassivity yet appear somehow reduced, as if bowed by the weight of her own stubborn longevity and the loneliness of serial loss.

Security around St Paul's Cathedral had been tightened, not only to protect the Queen but in anticipation of protests. These did not materialise, but Thatcher continues to divide her compatriots and feminism – who can forget her declaration 'I owe nothing to women's lib'? Yet few would argue that women's lib owes nothing to her. She blazed a trail even as she repudiated the idea of helping others to do so and introduced policies that widened inequalities.

Elizabeth too felt no affinity for the women's movement and, like Thatcher, expanded notions of what women could do and be. Of course, her powers were inherited and circumscribed, but she spent seventy years at the helm of a global institution and brand. Dignitaries bowed to her; peers and MPs assembled to hear her read out the legislative programme of each new parliament. Her face gazed down from the walls of offices and from all those stamps and coins and banknotes.

Both women established templates for operating in male-dominated environments. They also provided high-profile examples of working motherhood. The postwar period had seen a matrimonial surge, followed by a baby boom, with most women marrying at twenty-one and starting families as fast as possible. Only 35 per cent of mothers held jobs outside the home. Elizabeth and Thatcher were not merely mothers who worked; they did so with an air of brisk efficiency and the support of their husbands. 'I can trust my husband not to fall asleep on a public platform,' said Thatcher of her spouse, 'and he usually claps in the right places.'

*

'All too often, I fear, Prince Philip has had to listen to me speaking.' This was the Queen marking her golden wedding. 'Frequently we have discussed my intended speech beforehand and, as you will imagine, his views have been expressed in a forthright manner. He is someone who doesn't take easily to compliments but he has, quite simply, been my strength and stay all these years.'

Harry characterised Philip's support in more colourful terms: 'Regardless of whether my grandfather seems to be doing his own thing, sort of wandering off like a fish down the river, the fact that he's there – personally, I don't think that she could do it without him.'

Some of Philip's wanderings were the subject of whispers; others occurred in plain sight. 'Queen Sees Philip off on Long Tour' ran a headline in the *New York Times* in 1959. In other circumstances, the US press might not have thought such an expedition newsworthy, even though, as the newspaper reported, it would be 'his third round-the-world trip in five years'. However, his last perambulations had given rise to so much press speculation over the state of the royal marriage that Buckingham Palace put out a statement: 'It is quite untrue that there is any rift between the Queen and the Duke.' Elizabeth swiftly underlined that message. When the couple reunited ahead of a joint state visit to Portugal, he found her and her entourage wearing false beards, mimicking the real one he had grown. Nothing says a relationship is on track like the ability to make each other laugh. Well, nothing other than a well-chosen gift. On their return to the UK, she announced Philip's new rank of prince.

He continued to be linked to other women, but there would be no kiss-and-tells. Gyles Brandreth, in his book about Philip, quoted from an interview conducted with fellow biographer Sarah Bradford: 'There is no doubt in my mind at all. The Duke of Edinburgh has had affairs – yes, full blown affairs, and more than one.' Bradford later disputed the quote. In his biography of Elizabeth, Brandreth quotes Philip's friend Sacha, Duchess of Abercorn, denying that she and the royal had consummated their 'passionate friendship', adding that Philip 'needs a playmate and someone to share his intellectual pursuits'. For many decades, that role was filled by Lady Penny Romsey, the wife of Mountbatten's eldest grandson, Norton Knatchbull.[13] The pursuit she and Philip shared was carriage-driving, a sport he took up when he became too old for polo and in which, according to Elizabeth's adviser on equestrian matters, John Warren, he 'excelled'.

'Prince Philip was a great horseman in his own right,' said Warren. This provided Philip and Elizabeth with a mutual interest and their closest friends outside of marriage. In *The Crown*, these relationships spark jealousy, each suspecting the other of straying. 'Porchie is a friend and yes, there are those who would have preferred me to marry him,' the fictionalised queen tells her dramatised husband. 'Indeed, marriage with him might have been easier, might have even worked better than ours. But to everyone's regret and frustration the only person I have ever loved is you, and can you honestly look me in the eye and say the same?'

The real couple slept separately, a fact made evident in 1982 when Elizabeth awoke to find a stranger in her Buckingham Palace bedroom. Accounts of the incident vary, but all align on her sangfroid in dealing with the intruder. She seems to have regarded Philip's flirtations with similar equanimity. Theirs was a partnership of equals, says a source, trusting enough for each of them to pursue independent interests and friendships.

Philip's backing was not always helpful. He reinforced her instinct to observe standard protocols after Diana died. He also persuaded William and Harry to walk with him behind their mother's coffin, an experience that scarred both boys. However, Elizabeth was able to lean on him when a heart attack felled Porchie. She was still mourning Porchie when, in February 2002, Margaret succumbed to a stroke. Seven weeks later, the Queen Mother died too. Elizabeth grieved but also, insiders say, she grew. Her mother disapproved of any change to conventions set in the previous reign. Now Elizabeth had nobody looking over her shoulder.

The Queen Mother lived to 101. Philip appeared hale enough to equal her span but had no desire to do so. 'I can't imagine anything worse,' he told Brandreth. 'I'm already falling to pieces as it is.' At ninety-six, he retired from royal duties and went to live at Wood Farm on the Sandringham Estate. Anyone unfamiliar with his and Elizabeth's modus vivendi might have mistaken this for an estrangement, especially when the Queen asked her page to call Philip 'and find out if he's still alive – I haven't seen him for six months.' Then came the pandemic and the couple 'bubbled' together harmoniously. Restrictions against the spread of Covid were still in place when Philip died in April 2021. Only thirty mourners were permitted to attend his funeral. Elizabeth made sure that Penny Romsey was among them.

*

Elizabeth and Philip sustained their marriage for over seventy-three years. Three of their four children divorced their first spouses. Those marital failures along with other turbulences and scandals in the lives of the quartet raise questions about the elder Windsors' parenting. Might Philip Larkin's most famous observation apply to Britain's most prominent family? Stroll through Queen Square in London and you will find these words Larkin wrote about his monarch incised into a paving stone:

In times when nothing stood
But worsened or grew strange
There was one constant good.
She did not change.

One of the better tributes composed for the 1977 silver jubilee, this is nevertheless not Larkin's most popular poem. Many Britons can quote the opening lines of *This Be the Verse* from memory: 'They fuck you up, your mum and dad.' A later couplet reads as if written with the royals in mind. 'But they were fucked up in their turn / By fools in old-style hats and coats.'[14]

Charles, Anne, Andrew and Edward were born in distinct batches a decade apart, the first pair in 1948 and 1950, the spare and the spare's spare in 1960 and 1964. The elder children received the kind of regimented upbringing Larkin's fools in old-style hats and coats would approve; the second set were indulged.

Elizabeth faced an unusual set of hurdles in raising her family. Planet Windsor is not conducive to producing well-balanced individuals. A royal child might be starved of emotional sustenance and served dinner on Sèvres porcelain, assured that he ranks higher than commoners yet expected to bow to his mother. The patrimonarchy, far from reliably appreciating Elizabeth's efforts to parent while keeping up her day job, not infrequently radiated disapproval. An aide grumbled to a journalist that 'If she'd spent less time reading those idiotic red boxes – to what effect, one asks – and taken being a wife and mother more seriously, it would have been far better. Yes, she can handle prime ministers very well, but can she handle her eldest son – and which is the more important?'

Charles and Anne belonged to the postwar demographic bulge driven by homecomings and the absences these reunions revealed. As Lady Anne Glenconner, friend and lady-in-waiting to Margaret, wrote in her memoir, her contemporaries 'all longed for big families, feeling it was nature's way of replacing a lost generation'.

That did not mean this cohort cosseted their children. Some new parents had been broken by their recent experiences, others hardened by them. As for familial separations, the whole population had come to expect them. Royal and naval duties regularly took Elizabeth and Philip away, singly or together, for prolonged periods. The fact that Elizabeth travelled for six weeks when Charles was barely one would seem unworthy of comment but for her decision, on her return, to spend four days catching up on admin and going to the races before reuniting with her child. After her coronation, both she and Philip departed on a tour of the Commonwealth for a full six months. When *Britannia* finally docked back in England, an excited Charles mistakenly joined the line of dignitaries waiting to greet them. 'Not you, dear,' said his mother.

In an inversion of gendered expectations, she devolved decisions about their children to Philip. While Anne thrived under his bracing regimen, the sensitive Charles struggled, wounded by his father's criticism and exiled at eight years old to the first of a run of boarding schools that would include Gordonstoun like his father before him.

By the time Andrew and Edward appeared, Elizabeth embraced motherhood with the same enthusiasm she showed for other domestic activities. The affection she lavished on her second son in particular attracted attention. Gossip columnist

Nigel Dempster floated the idea that Porchie could be Andrew's father. Tim Knatchbull, one of Dickie Mountbatten's grandchildren and Edward's contemporary, provided a more evidence-based explanation for the change in parenting style when he spoke to me in 2014. He remembered the Queen and her consort of that period as 'hip, savvy, intelligent, forward-looking . . . interested in young people, interested in the revolutions going on across Europe, the cultural revolutions, the social revolutions and rather in sympathy with them . . . They adopted some of the new ideas of the swinging sixties, including new ideas of parenting, which is that you spend masses of time with your kid.'

He experienced Elizabeth's maternal impulse at first hand. In 1979, the Provisional IRA bombed his grandfather's boat during a family outing off the coast of Ireland, killing Mountbatten himself, Knatchbull's twin brother Nicholas, grandmother Doreen, and a teenaged crew member Paul Maxwell. Tim's parents, Baron Brabourne and Mountbatten's daughter Patricia, were hospitalised for five weeks. Wounded by shrapnel, he travelled with his sister Amanda to convalesce at Balmoral, finding the Queen in 'almost unstoppable mothering mode'.

Charles did not see much of that side of her. This book will touch on some of the ways in which his early years affected his adult relationships, in particular with Diana and Camilla. He has tended to see those impacts as negative, yet the emotional austerity of his upbringing may also have helped to mitigate the sense of entitlement that can come with growing up on Planet Windsor. Prone to neediness more often than arrogance, he tried as Prince of Wales to create meaning from a position Edwards VII and VIII devoted to frivolling. The interventionism for which he drew criticism – including from his father – arose from that quest and in many ways conformed to Philip's Kurt Hahn-influenced philosophy of community engagement.

His sister, meanwhile, has always seemed to cope, managing the transition of a tricky first marriage to former army officer and Olympic equestrian Captain Mark Phillips into an amicable parental and professional partnership, while finding happiness with her second husband, former naval officer and equerry Commander Timothy Laurence. Her professional resumé would be impressive in any context. For a royal, it is exceptional. In 1976, already bedecked with gold and silver medals from other competitions, Anne became the first Windsor to compete in the Olympics, going on to develop her own equestrian businesses, all the while performing royal duties.

As a young woman, Anne's apparent lack of concern for Fleet Street's opinion earned snippy write-ups. 'I didn't match up to the public's idea of a fairy princess in the first place,' she told the *Sunday Times* magazine, obviously unbothered. She ploughed her own furrow in other ways too. Though styled Princess Royal, she rejected HRH designations for her son, Peter, and daughter, Zara. 'It was probably easier for them, and I think most people would argue that there are downsides to having titles,' she remarked to *Vanity Fair*. The decision allowed them to pursue careers without the restrictions working royalty imposes. Zara is herself a world-class equestrian, winner of an Olympic silver medal and a gold in the World Equestrian Games.

In her mid-seventies, and despite the demands of her commercial activities, Anne still undertakes more royal engagements than any other Windsor. After a head-butt from a horse hospitalised her with concussion, she remarked that retirement 'isn't really written in' to being royal. Nobody should be surprised by her steeliness. Half a century earlier, a would-be kidnapper forced her car to a halt, then shot her driver, her personal protection officer, a journalist who attempted to intervene and the first policeman on the scene, though all survived. She slammed the car door against her assailant only for him to yank it open again, tearing her dress. 'That was his most dangerous moment,' she quipped afterwards. 'I really lost my rag.'

She even kept her head in the midst of Edward's 1987 *Grand Knockout Tournament*. Earlier that year, he had given up on training with the Royal Marines, deciding instead that he could ace a career in television. This was his proof of concept, a mashup of courtly jousts and a TV show called *It's a Knockout*, itself descended from the European *Jeux Sans Frontières*. In an opening sequence, comedian Rowan Atkinson promised viewers that the games would be remembered for their 'grandeur, glory and overwhelming silliness'. Only the last of these phrases applied. Andrew, his wife Sarah Ferguson aka 'Fergie', Edward and celebrity participants made fools of themselves, while Anne calmly steered her team to a seven-point victory.

Edward flounced out of the closing press conference when journalists failed to praise his efforts. His subsequent adventures in TV would, like many *Grand Knockout Tournament* competitors, end up covered in mud. Eighteen million UK viewers and 400 million worldwide witnessed this royal nightmare. It was nothing compared to what was to come.

The Queen had been tested by external circumstances throughout her reign, whether the fallout from Britain's poorly judged military intervention in the Suez Crisis or the economic decline and industrial unrest of the seventies, but her constitutional status also limited the extent to which she could be blamed for them. The monarchy, as the nation's premier totem of class, might nevertheless have served as a lightning conductor for public anger as the economy tanked. Yet although the Sex Pistols' single 'God Save the Queen' with its oft-quoted line 'There is no future / In England's dreaming' soundtracked Elizabeth's silver jubilee, so too did the music of street parties to celebrate her twenty-five years on the throne.

England continued to dream, often of her. So embedded did she become in national consciousness that royalists and republicans alike experienced visitations. A 1972 book, *Dreams about HM The Queen and Other Members of the Royal Family*, charted the phenomenon, possibly inspiring the Sex Pistols' lyric and giving the Pet Shop Boys a lyrical hook for their song 'Dreaming of the Queen'. Invariably, in these visions, the monarch was in control and her subjects were not, often finding themselves drinking tea with her despite having forgotten to put on their trousers.

None of the scenarios imagined the Queen herself giving offence. Perhaps that reflects her real-life record. Before her misreading of the public mood in the wake of Diana's death, there were only two other prominent stumbles, both similar in nature. In 1966, a hundred and sixteen children and twenty-eight adults died when a mountain of coal waste at the edge of the Welsh town of Aberfan suddenly gave way, burying a school. On the advice of aides, Elizabeth stayed away to avoid impeding rescue work. In 1988, after a bomb downed a jet over the Scottish town of Lockerbie, the Queen failed to attend funerals for the victims. 'Broken-hearted Britain watching TV needed to see their equally grieving monarch,' wrote columnist Jean Rook. Elizabeth and Philip eventually visited Lockerbie for a memorial service. By then, the monarchy was in worsening odour for different reasons.

The previous year had started badly for the Windsors and continued to deteriorate. In January 1992, newspapers published paparazzi shots of Sarah Ferguson on holiday with another man; she and Andrew separated in March. Anne and Mark Phillips divorced the following month. Then came the serialisation of Andrew Morton's bombshell biography, *Diana: Her True Story*, followed by the publication of more photos of Sarah, this time with a different lover. Mere days later, revelations of a taped conversation between Diana and her intimate friend James Gilbey set off a new flurry of headlines. In November, Windsor Castle caught fire. Ceilings collapsed and rooms were gutted. The fire coincided with the fortieth anniversary of the Queen's accession. '1992 is not a year on which I shall look back with undiluted pleasure,' she said at a banquet in her honour. 'In the words of one of my more sympathetic correspondents, it has turned out to be an *annus horribilis*.' Nor was it yet done. In December, John Major announced that Charles and Diana were to separate.

One family member ended the year on something of a high note, despite personal turmoil. The Windsor Castle fire showcased a public version of Andrew that, with the benefit of hindsight, seems incredible – because it was. He had been there when the flames took hold, organised a human chain and helped to rescue artworks that would otherwise have been destroyed or damaged. This was the Andrew who had once been the darling of the press. 'Is it his cheerful charm, his naturalness, his exploits as a helicopter pilot in the Falklands, or his roguish reputation with beautiful girls, or a combination of these that go to make Andrew the most charismatic of the young royals?' wondered the authors of an early biography. 'His arrival on the scene has given a new meaning to the initials HRH. With Andrew they stand for His Royal Heartthrob.'

In fact, the princely naval career had plateaued after the Falklands; higher ranks demand a capacity for strategic thinking. He would stay in the navy until he retired, still only forty-one. That left the palace with a familiar problem. In her younger years, Margaret had done a decent enough job of filling in for her sister on state occasions, but there was not enough work to keep her occupied. Soon, she became a byword for aristocratic excess, part of a crowd that partied on Mustique and sometimes commandeered a corner table at the London restaurant I mentioned earlier. One night, my husband and I arrived there for the final sitting, just as she and her companions, all young men, were finishing up. Once they were safely off the premises, the maître d' brought over her mineral water for us to inspect – apparently, she liked to bring her own supplies. 'Go on,' he said. 'Have a sniff. Pure gin.'

I always felt sorry for Margaret, born to a status that might look like fun, but rather like gin, sometimes fostered a joyless dependency. Now another scion of the house of Windsor risked heading in a similar direction, from asset to liability. To keep Andrew out of trouble, the government and Palace devised a role for him: UK special envoy for trade and investment, with a remit to promote British interests globally. His heavy use of taxpayer-funded flights soon appended 'Air Miles Andy' to the 'Randy Andy' label that had stuck to him from schooldays.

When MPs requested that the National Audit Office investigate his use of travel expenses to combine business and pleasure, Buckingham Palace came out fighting. 'He is not doing anything wrong,' a spokeswoman told *The Times*. 'He is the busiest member of the royal family. That is why his costs are higher. It is all completely above board.'

A few months earlier, I had accompanied Andrew on one of his trade missions, the only journalist ever to do so. Royals are often disconnected from everyday realities, but the gaps in Andrew's understanding of the world yawned startlingly wide. I heard him reassure students at Beijing University that western imports would not dilute Chinese culture. After all, Britons had consumed American culture for years without any appreciable impact. On another occasion, he demanded to know why I was barefoot. He had apparently never noticed that his convoys set off as soon as he was seated, leaving anyone travelling at the back of the column to fling themselves at moving vehicles. I had lost a shoe in the process. He told me, for decorum, to wear the remaining one.

His royal status brought British businesspeople and Chinese officials together at a series of set-piece events. Any benefits to the UK came with a hefty price tag: intensive preparations, transport and accommodation for Andrew and his entourage, and four royal protection officers for the duration. Other costs are now being calculated as investigators sift millions of documents unearthed by criminal investigations into Jeffrey Epstein and his associate, Ghislaine Maxwell, including correspondence that suggests Andrew may have passed sensitive briefings to Epstein. On 19 February 2026, his sixty-sixth birthday, Andrew was arrested on suspicion of misconduct in public office. Whatever the outcome of the investigation – and he has consistently denied any financial or sexual improprieties – nobody in royal circles ever believed him a good fit for the trade envoy role, not even Andrew himself. One afternoon in China, he confided to me that he wished he could have been a plumber.

He stood down as envoy in 2011 after the publication of pictures showing him strolling in New York with Epstein, recently released from a jail term for sex offences with minors. Soon, another photo emerged showing Andrew with his arm around the waist of then seventeen-year-old Virginia Roberts, with Maxwell behind them, beaming. Virginia, who would later take the married name Giuffre, claimed in the accompanying article that Epstein trafficked her to Andrew three times. Meanwhile, Sarah Ferguson admitted accepting money from Epstein to meet her debts.

The next time I crossed paths with Andrew at a London book launch for Hillary Clinton, he seemed not contrite but buoyant. A new gig had been created for him, Pitch@Palace, an organisation founded with the twin purposes of fostering British entrepreneurship and the impression that its figurehead added value to public life. Andrew pushed his way over to me: 'I'm doing what you do. I'm an investigative journalist now,' he announced.

Might Andrew have been referring not to journalism but oppositional research? Epstein, Maxwell and their defenders were pumping out stories painting Giuffre as crazy, unreliable, complicit and avaricious as she continued to seek legal redress.

In July 2019, Epstein was arrested on federal sex-trafficking charges; the following month, he was found dead in his prison cell. Even then, the Palace, guided by the Queen, attempted to shield Andrew. Nobody, however, could protect him from his own folly. That November, he willingly submitted to an interview with BBC *Newsnight*, assuring interviewer Emily Maitlis that he had visited Epstein to break off contact with him in person. My 'judgement,' he said, 'was probably coloured by my tendency to be too honourable.' He denied Giuffre's allegations and cast doubt on the image of them with Maxwell.

The words kept coming, but in all the verbiage, he did not once express sympathy for Epstein's victims. Any remorse was reserved for the damage he had done the monarchy. 'We try and uphold the highest standards and practices, and I let the side down,' he said. 'Simple as that.'

In 2021, Maxwell was jailed for offences including sex trafficking and conspiracy to transport minors to participate in illegal sex acts. That August, Giuffre sued Andrew under New York's Child Victims Act for sexual assault. In February 2022, he reached an out-of-court settlement with her under which he made no admission of liability but agreed to pay her an undisclosed sum, thought to be more than ten million pounds.

I do not propose in this book to pull together all the claims and counterclaims against and by Andrew in relation to Epstein or any other areas of his life, including his finances. I would instead encourage you to explore the reams of journalism that helped to expose Epstein's abuses, some of the best reporting female-led, and the flood of material about Andrew, his ex-wife and their dealings. Above all, read Giuffre's autobiography, published in October 2025, exactly six months after her death by suicide.

The release of the Epstein files reinforced her testimony and that of other victims. Emails to Epstein from both Maxwell and

Andrew discussing the Giuffre photograph raise no questions over its authenticity. After its publication, Andrew wrote to Epstein, 'we are in this together'. He signs off: 'we'll play some more soon'. The files make clear that he kept that promise, rather than breaking contact as he claimed.

Moreover, they socialised not only in New York and on Epstein's infamous island but at Buckingham Palace and other royal residences, with Epstein also promising to bring or send women to Andrew. At time of writing, police from different forces are sifting evidence retrieved not only from the files but other sources, including searches of Andrew's former home, Royal Lodge, and interim residence on the Sandringham estate.

*

And what do you do? This was Elizabeth's standard conversational opener, though she often fell back on an alternative gambit: *Have you come far?* At the conclusion of this chapter, let us turn those questions back on her. What did she do for the monarchy, for the countries and peoples she represented?

By the end of her reign, she was widely regarded as a near-flawless queen and an icon of probity. That she responded to Diana's death with her usual reserve did not harm her in the long term. Yes, a MORI poll conducted at the time showed the monarch's popularity dip to 57 per cent. That is still a decent rating, and soon her star ascended again, ultimately rising further still.

Moreover, the obsession with that slice of history – *The Queen, The Crown* and other dramas, documentaries and biographies – performs a similar function to the UK's ongoing focus on its role in the Second World War. Both reinforce a stoical, stiff-upper-lip ideal of Britishness, connecting it to moments when the smoke cleared and still Buckingham Palace stood proud.

This particular idea of national identity came into sharp and hilarious focus at the opening ceremony for the 2012 London Olympics. Audiences saw James Bond, in the shape of Daniel Craig, prevail on his sovereign to board a helicopter to confront an unspecified emergency. The film clip merged into a live action sequence, with stunt doubles dressed as Elizabeth and 007 parachuting from the craft towards the stadium. Seconds after they landed, the real queen entered the stands, her consort two paces behind her. The cheers, even in the section reserved for journalists, were deafening. I noticed a veteran sports reporter wiping away a tear. Elizabeth may not have been a weeper, but she was quite capable of inspiring emotion in others. This is a significant part of Elizabeth's legacy, but it may not be the story that endures. As this book shows, queens are reassessed and repurposed after their deaths.

Some details of her life, though in the public domain, get little attention because they are at odds with current narratives. Take the case of Major Dick Hern, who in 1988, twenty-two years into his job as her principal racehorse trainer, suffered a coronary. He already used a wheelchair since sustaining spinal injuries in a riding accident. While recuperating from an operation to fix a leaky heart valve, he received unwelcome news. Porchie, by now the seventh Earl of Carnarvon, informed Hern's wife that his services were no longer required. Hern's replacement had already been approved by Elizabeth.

Porchie's explanation – that the Queen needed someone fitter in the post – looked increasingly silly when Hern was cheered into the winner's enclosure within weeks of leaving hospital. Eventually, a compromise allowed Hern a further year at the stables. After that, Dubai royalty snapped up his services. He continued to work for another decade, outliving Porchie by eight months.

The incident revealed a ruthless streak that Elizabeth might have better deployed towards her second son. Then again, perhaps she backed Porchie for the same reason many attribute to her leniency towards Andrew – not hardheartedness, but rather its inverse, partiality. For decades, Elizabeth permitted her second son to do things that risked, in his own terms, 'letting the side down'. Even before the Epstein scandal, Andrew's links to figures such as Timur Kulibayev, scion of Kazakhstan's dictatorial president Nursultan Nazarbayev, and Tarek Kaituni, a Libyan gunrunner, raised questions about his judgement – and hers. An email in the Epstein files describes her offering Andrew her 'full support' and labelling his visit to the convicted paedophile merely 'unwise'. Officials eye-rolled, sometimes despaired, but there was little they could do. The Queen protected Andrew, indulged him, enabled him. Most interpreted her leniency as a blind spot. He was her favourite child; she could not believe ill of him. The situation worsened after Philip retired. Andrew and Charles combined efforts to oust Elizabeth's private secretary, Christopher Geidt, then in the process of planning for a smooth succession by coordinating and rationalising the work of competing royal households. The coup cost another key adviser, Samantha Cohen, who left after overseeing the Commonwealth Heads of Government Meeting the following year, then agreed at the Queen's behest to help out with Harry and Meghan.

In late 2018, an insider offered me a striking take on the Andrew problem. We were discussing a cascade of fresh revelations about Epstein from the *Miami Herald*'s Julie Brown. 'It isn't just that the Queen loves Andrew,' this contact said. 'It's that she knows he needs protecting. He can't be trusted to look after himself.' Four years later, at the counter of a different bar in an equally fancy hotel, a different insider, with direct knowledge of anguished conversations in royal circles, expressed the same idea in near identical terms. In both cases, I pushed back. Were these sources trying to suggest that Andrew should not be held responsible for his actions? Though startlingly obtuse, he clearly meets legal definitions of capacity. They clarified. The Queen was not, as the dominant narrative suggested, blind to Andrew's fallibilities. She saw them all too clearly and, fearing their potential consequences, considered it her duty to shield him for his own sake and in the interests of the monarchy. She loved him, and the monarchy, in equal measure.

In the end, this strategy rebounded on Andrew and the institution. Curbed much sooner, he might still be one of those fading royals who appear on the balcony at state occasions. Instead Elizabeth herself removed his HRH designation, military titles and royal patronages. Even then, she invited him to escort her to Philip's memorial, a sign of solidarity made more jarring by Harry's absence. Which of the two Windsors merited exile?

Elizabeth did not live to see Andrew stripped of his princedom, his dukedom and his Windsor home, then captured in another defining photograph, slumped in the back of a car after his arrest. Nor would she have anticipated the swelling criticism of her own role in these events. Andrew's legal settlement, thought to have been funded in large part by his parents, contained a gagging clause that stopped Giuffre speaking out during the Queen's platinum jubilee. The most obvious interpretation is that Elizabeth prioritised damage limitation even as Epstein's victims pushed for justice and transparency. It is unclear how much she knew about the extent to which her family name lent a veneer of respectability to the convicted paedophile and his coterie of abusers. Perhaps she never questioned her choices, believing she acted as a mother must, a monarch should. History may have other ideas.

That, of course, will depend not only on the outcome of ongoing investigations but whether her successors succeed in regaining public trust and popularity. Ironically, the potential damage to Charles and William might ultimately burnish her memory. Comparisons between the first Elizabeth and Victoria and the less successful kings who followed them helped to cement their status as great queens.

Elizabeth II's funeral, though devoid of the disbelieving anguish that had characterised Diana's, pointed to another factor that blunts criticisms of her. The day hit people hard, so many memories – so much of our past – gone. To question her is to question ourselves.

After the ceremony at Westminster Abbey, the cortege travelled to St George's Chapel, Windsor. On the final approach, cameras captured Elizabeth's aged fell pony bending a foreleg as if to curtsey. Andrew could be spotted too, gripping the leashes of his mother's surviving corgis.

The committal service was smaller than the London

commemoration, a reminder that this most private of public figures kept the intimate core of her life hidden from view. The music came as her coffin descended into the vault, the lament of a lone bagpipe. For a time, the piper faced the congregation. Then he turned and walked away, the notes fading with him.

Chapter 5

Diana: Hunted and Haunting

'History fascinated me. Tudors and Stuarts, I adored them,' said Diana, about the education that had failed to interest her in most other subjects. 'To think that all these people lived X many years ago. I never anticipated I'd end up in the system, in the books.'[15]

This observation hints at a strange duality that helped to define her. The People's Princess would prove too modern for the Windsors and too primordial. They continued to behave like the German imports they once had been, modelling a stiff, performative Britishness. Her roots stretched back, as theirs did, to a blue-blooded, blood-spattered past, but without that constraining quality or the pressures monarchs face to maintain support, not only as individuals but for their institution.

The Spencers started as sheep farmers (all nobility begins somewhere, often with slaughter) and amassed great wealth. During the English Civil War, they sided, after more havering than you might suppose, with the Cavaliers. Aristocratic strains are as apt to breed rebels as conformists, and if that generation of Spencers leaned towards upholding the status quo, at least as many made waves. The most famous of

Diana's maverick ancestors were women. The family tree boasts Queen Anne's frenemy, Sarah Churchill, Duchess of Marlborough, played by Rachel Weisz in the 2018 movie *The Favourite*, and Georgiana Cavendish, Duchess of Devonshire – Keira Knightley in 2008's *The Duchess*. While many women of Georgiana's class contented themselves with the indirect exercise of influence, holding salons and bending the ears of powerful men, she campaigned for the Whigs. This earned her fierce censure in the media of her day. The 1784 caricature, *A certain Duchess kissing old Swelter-in-grease the Butcher for his Vote*, not only gives a flavour of such attacks but points to the unease that underpinned them. Every woman, no matter how high born, must know her place.

In the drawing, Georgiana embraces a potential voter. 'O Times! O Manners!' reads the caption. 'The Women Wear Breeches & the Men Petticoats.' Georgiana's domestic arrangements also attracted gossip. Born at Althorp, ancestral seat of the Spencers and Diana's final resting place, she married a man hailed as England's most eligible bachelor. There were three people in her marriage: the Duchess, her husband and his lover – Georgiana's best friend – and though she railed against the menage, she endured it, unlike Diana. The trio lived under the same roof, birthed children, legitimate and illegitimate, and remain, now as in their own time, the subject of speculation.

To their bones, every member of the Spencer family knows what it is to be prominent, its benefits and downsides. In 1954, Diana's parents married in front of seventeen hundred guests, Queen Elizabeth and Prince Philip among them. Fifteen years later, the audience for the Spencers' divorce and custody battle proved exponentially larger. Society weddings may be good for shifting newspapers, but nothing beats a juicy scandal.

Part-Tudor, part-Stuart, their daughter embodied history, yet whatever lessons Diana took from her schoolbooks were not the ones she needed. Those who forget the past may well be doomed to echo it.

*

'I am a free spirit – unfortunately for some,' she said, but that was much later. The Lady Diana Spencer, iconoclast and future icon, appeared, at first, a model of conformity. Early paparazzi shots catch her as a fawn in the headlights, frozen in the act of flight. During the couple's engagement interview, she palely loiters in a pussy bow, eyes downcast, her cheeks as round and smooth as a child's.

If Charles's courtship had been perfunctory, his unvarnished answers during this set piece were chilling. The same candour revealed a royal culture matter-of-fact in privileging dynastic ambitions over romance. No, he says, he did not buy his Gloucester bolthole, Highgrove, with marriage in mind. It was convenient for his Duchy of Cornwall holdings. The response will have meant nothing to viewers, but Diana knew of Highgrove's proximity to the Parker Bowles's home. When her prince declares himself 'amazed that she's been brave enough to take me on', the reporter ventures that the pair must be in love. 'Of course,' Diana replies, prompting Charles to issue his infamous equivocation, 'whatever in love means'.

Should she have broken off the engagement right then? Hindsight, and the ghosts of her ancestors, might well say yes.

Popular culture has overwhelmingly made up its mind. *The Crown*'s Diana is lumbered with a gurning, emotionally stunted prince more un-charming with each of the two successive actors in the adult role. The 2021 film *Spencer* shows Anne Boleyn haunting Diana during the royals' Christmas break at Sandringham. 'Go,' the spectre tells the Princess. 'Run.'

Ahead of Diana and Charles's nuptials, flesh-and-blood women issued similar warnings, then watched aghast as the bride dragged a train as long as her lineage up the steps of St Paul's Cathedral. Reporters bored on about fairytales, but feminism saw a darker story unfolding. Not since Victoria had the women's movement engaged so actively with a royal, and the relationship, unlike the match about to be solemnised, would only get stronger.

Monarchy deliberately fosters an illusion of timelessness, but this spectacle appeared out of its time, an anachronism. Second-wave feminism had achieved great things, not least by identifying the domestic sphere as a primary battlefield. Never mind the mountain still to climb, change oxygenated the air. The UK had recently notched up its first female prime minister, if not a feminist one, and America its first female supreme court judge. Angela Davis's groundbreaking book, *Women, Race and Class*, offered a sharp analysis of the intersections of these categories, while bell hooks articulated her own brilliant take in *Ain't I a Woman*. Yet here, in front of a global audience, all that progress seemed to be repudiated. 'Don't do it, Di', urged the magazine *Spare Rib*, and distributed its own royal wedding merchandise, a pink badge bearing the phrase.

This was sisterhood in action, and, as sisters occasionally will, they underestimated their sibling. In Diana, they saw a pawn at the heart of the pageant, the cherubic fiancée transformed, as feminist writer Beatrix Campbell put it, to 'a thin, wan, whiter-than-white woman [walking] down the aisle, propping up the aged patriarch who had got her into all this.' Diana's waist, twenty-nine inches at the first fitting of her bridal gown, measured twenty-three and a half when she wore it.

Perhaps some of these onlookers recognised the signs of the eating disorder gripping Diana, or guessed that her dramatic weight loss hinted at more than a pre-wedding diet. Women in the public eye often dwindle to skin and bone, as if the psychological pressure of having their bodies relentlessly scrutinised translates into the barometric kind. *Fat is a Feminist Issue*, a book by psychotherapist Susie Orbach published four years before Diana's unhappiest day, had identified fat-shaming as a weapon of female subjugation and weight gain as an expression of female defiance. As Diana found herself at the epicentre of media attention and preparing for a loveless future, she began, literally, to disappear. *Show not tell* – that is the royal approach to their public-facing role, and in this respect, Diana fitted in seamlessly, acting out her misery rather than vocalising it. Later, she would break that code of silence, consulting Orbach as a client and speaking openly about her bulimia, depression and self-harm.

Nobody foresaw these developments or anticipated the Amazon she would become, unapologetically taking up space and striding through minefields, metaphorical or actual. Who would have guessed that the 'very jolly and amusing' teenager Charles remembered from their first meeting had it in her to be and represent so many different things to so many different people? Seven years before Diana's induction into royal ranks, an armed revolutionary group kidnapped American heiress Patty Hearst, then nineteen, just as Diana would be at the time of her engagement. Hearst responded by embracing the ideology of her captors. Diana exhibited the opposite reflex, defining herself against the forces that sought to contain her. As the tenth anniversary of her death approached, a *TIME* magazine cover story attempted to understand her astonishing, and ongoing, metamorphosis.

By now, the women's movement had claimed Diana as one of its own, with 'many feminists read[ing] her struggle against a sclerotic system as a parable of empowerment'. *TIME*'s London bureau chief demurred from this analysis. Diana 'would never have located herself in the feminist firmament,' the journalist wrote. 'She wasn't interested in gender equality. She fought against a patriarchy because it was old-fashioned and restrictive, not because she repudiated its male values. The Princess was one of the first and most potent symbols of the "girl power" celebrated by the Spice Girls.' Their message of female solidarity rather than revolution 'was a neat fit for Diana, with her close women friends and her troubled search for a mate. What Royal Spice really, really wanted was not at all radical: to love and be loved.'

Oops. I wrote that piece and beg to differ with my younger self. 'I don't think I've been given any credit for growth. And, my goodness, I've had to grow,' Diana declared in her BBC *Panorama* interview. Given the opportunity, she would surely have continued to develop and change. People are not fixed entities. Social shifts and our own experiences alter us. Nor is it true that age pushes a majority into risk-averse conservatism.

Those at the sharp end of discrimination are just as likely to be radicalised – and Diana was never the type to go quietly. The more she came under fire, the more she resisted.

Feminism might have provided a vehicle and framework for a fightback. She, in turn, could have brought to the movement an unparalleled reach. The most marginalised women are always the hardest to engage, lacking time, resources and easy connection to the wider world, but everyone, everywhere, knew Diana. Whether her involvement would have helped or hindered feminism in confronting another of its greatest challenges – internal division – is harder to judge. While Diana aimed to be a unifying figure, 'a queen of people's hearts, in people's hearts', she would have found it tricky to avoid further co-option into culture wars. By the time of her death, she had already been pressed into service – not as a role model but a warning; a fairytale gone wrong, her openness about her mental health battles turned against her, her refusal to stay within the narrow lanes of her class and race cited as proof of her volatility, and her every achievement recast as dangerously transgressive.

It might have been easier to stand up for her – and easier for Diana to stand up for herself – if those achievements had been instantly nameable. Some of her power flowed from qualities beyond her control. Her beauty, though underpinning her appeal, was not something she owned or trusted. At heart she remained the 'fat, podgy, no-make-up, unsmart lady' who unaccountably caught the eye of a prince. Her initial transformation took a terrible toll on her physical and mental health. In those early years of marriage, 'I was on the way down fast. I just cried at every opportunity,' she told James Colthurst, a friend who was taping their conversation for her biographer, Andrew Morton. 'The public side was very different from the private side. The public side, they wanted a fairy princess to come and touch them and everything will turn into gold and their worries would be forgotten. Little did they realise that the individual was crucifying herself inside, because she didn't think she was good enough.'

Nor did the excitement she generated please her husband. He had spent years trying to inject meaning into the role of heir to the throne, hoping to showcase a palette of urgent causes alongside the traditional preoccupations of royalty, yet all the crowds wanted, or the press reported, were sightings of Diana. Had she looked good but followed the template set by her mother-in-law, remote and silent, she would have been popular, but no more so than, say, Kate, and largely uncontroversial, as Kate has tried to be. It was Diana's departure from this model that damned her in life and propelled her to mythic status in death.

Until the seventeenth century, sovereigns claimed to rule by divine right, a notion still reflected in the rituals of coronation and the royal family's odd relationship with touch. 'The state of monarchy is the supremest thing upon earth, for kings are not only God's lieutenants upon earth and sit upon God's throne, but even by God himself, they are called gods,' said James I. As gods, monarchs were untouchable, and as mortals, they remain so. Protocol dictates that royals can initiate contact with commoners but not the other way round. Donald Trump, to nobody's great surprise, fist-bumped Elizabeth II and put his arm around her waist during his 2019 state visit. Kings and queens believed in the curative powers of their touch.

Charles II laid his hands on tens of thousands of scrofula sufferers. Queen Anne, the last sovereign to invoke her supernatural powers, issued special gold pieces to the subjects who came to her for healing.

Diana tapped into this strange royal tradition purely by chance. Her instinct to hug and handhold came from a place of pain. While some people who have been hurt or abused go on to hurt or abuse others, the same experiences can build empathy, sometimes even activism.

At school, Diana and other pupils were assigned voluntary service roles in the local community. Hers was to visit an elderly woman. While many of her contemporaries did the bare minimum demanded of them, Diana put in extra hours, sometimes cutting class to see her new and lonely charge. 'She was, without doubt, one of the most compassionate and empathetic people I've ever met,' says one of her oldest friends. From her first walkabouts, Diana reached out to the strangers who reached out towards her. In 1987, she famously held the hand of an AIDS patient, at once challenging myths around the transmission of the disease and the homophobia a diagnosis often unleashed. It matters that she did this on camera and continued to be seen with AIDS patients, but she did not do it in order to *be* on camera. In private, she made many more such visits.

She was an inveterate hugger. Hundreds of images show her embracing members of the public, friends, family, spreading her arms as wide as wings to enfold her sons. It made the spaces between Diana and Charles all the more conspicuous as their marriage decayed. 'I hug my children to death,' she said. 'I get into bed with them at night, hug them and say, "Who loves them most in the whole world?" and they always say "Mummy". I always feed them love and affection – it's so important.' Her words, recorded for Morton, reveal a mix of impulses, some admirable, others messily human. Her unhappiness informed her determination to nurture her children, but her love could be transactional and, within the context of her irretrievable marriage, competitive.

Such flaws, seized on and magnified during her life, are often underplayed in post-mortem paeans, as her brother anticipated in his stirring speech at her funeral. 'There is a temptation to rush to canonise your memory,' he said. 'There is no need to do so. You stand tall enough as a human being of unique qualities not to need to be seen as a saint. Indeed, to sanctify your memory would be to miss out on the very core of your being.'

Famous men are often lionised not just in spite of their defects but because of them, obsessive behaviours recast as the sign of brilliant minds, fury as passion, detachment interpreted as nothing more than a front concealing sensitive souls and golden hearts. Women enjoy less leeway. The line between a passionate woman and a crazy one remains faint and moveable, and woe betide the female who gives vent to her anger, however righteous.

The first thing a woman in a top job or running for high office learns is that perfection is demanded of her. Any missteps will be cited as proof of her inadequacy, and any inadequacy will be held up as evidence that all women are deficient. Men are allowed to fail while women are punished for the slightest wobble.

Their media portrayals reflect and reinforce wider inequalities. In many fields, women are underrepresented at senior levels to the detriment of those industries and organisations, as well as to the people they are supposed to serve, never mind the young seeking role models. One of those fields is journalism, another is entertainment. The men who run or fund the media give prominence to stories they consider significant or marketable, defaulting to familiar stereotypes in determining whether a female warrants column inches or screen time. The few women who reach executive ranks learn to mimic male values and the male gaze (and I write as a former top editor at *TIME*).

Diana appeared to tick every box because most of these decision-makers neither understood nor cared who she really was. They defined her by her partners, while missing the significance of her choices. They analysed her body as clinically as a team of pathologists. They pressed her into service as a storybook princess, a madonna or a delinquent mother, a doting wife or a bad one, vulnerable or a vixen. And then, of course, she became a victim, and not only that but their favourite kind: pretty, white, young and blonde.

*

At times, she was all of these things. There is usually at least a shred of truth to dominant narratives. Diana entered the union with Charles unfinished, undefended and unsupported by him, his family or palace aides. She would discover and flex her agency, experiment, test boundaries, flail, fail, vamp it up. In death, she has come to resemble a secular saint.

Yet to reduce her to broad brushstrokes or single categories is to ignore what makes her so compelling: her complexity and glorious, messy humanity. Nor did it ever serve Diana's cause, or wider views of women, to caricature Camilla as the conniving Other Woman. It is an irony that even feminist framings, shorn of nuance, risk lending themselves to catfight tropes. As we have seen, when Anne Boleyn is reclaimed as a heroine, Catherine of Aragon finds herself denied the justice of her position, while Anne's successor, Jane Seymour, becomes a manipulative Eve Harrington to Boleyn's Margo Channing.

The three people in the Waleses' marriage found themselves entangled in powerful currents: love, whatever that means; an institution pushing for a virgin bride; and a media that drove narratives as well as charting them. At various times, each of them behaved dishonourably; at others, they sublimated their own interests to their perceptions of the greater good. How, then, did they get themselves into such a pickle? The answer, like the Princess herself, is complicated.

Diana was naive, but few readings of their story fully grasp the fact that this was true of Charles too. In common with his bride, he aimed to find happiness within the marriage and entered it in good faith. The problem lay in their mismatched visions of happily ever after. Charles, under pressure to find a future queen, approached the task as a recruitment process: *Wanted: silent, fruitful woman. Must be intact. GSOH appreciated but not essential.* Bride and bridegroom both belonged to a centuries-old strain of upper-crust culture in which, as biographer Julia Baird describes it, marriages served as 'comfortable contracts within which one should produce a male heir'. Such arrangements, modelled by Charles's own parents and advocated by Dickie Mountbatten, relied on mutual understanding and discretion.

Inevitably, the same unwritten rules held women to tougher standards than men. Ideally, wives were to remain faithful, at least during their childbearing years to avoid alien gene sets invading dynastic lines. Certainly they would do nothing to embarrass their husbands. When Diana's parents split, her mother, Frances, earned the condemnation of her peers (quite a few of them actual peers), not because she strayed but because she left. Aristocrats still apply a derogatory word to women like her: they are 'bolters'. In the ensuing court battle, Frances's own mother testified against her. Frances lost custody of her children, condemning them to the uncertain care of their depressive father and boarding schools. For once, the Spencer girls got the better end of the deal. In his 2024 memoir, Diana's brother Charles revealed that he had been physically and sexually abused by staff at one of these institutions.

Diana's childhood left scars too, underpinning her determination to avoid divorce while simultaneously making such a fate more likely. If you have never witnessed a loving relationship, you may lack the tools to create one. Long after her marriage failed, she resisted formalising the break, paralysed with fear that she might lose her sons.

Her parents both married again – Frances to her lover, Peter Shand Kydd, who eventually left her. Diana's father, Johnny, took up with the married Raine, Countess of Dartmouth. Restyled Countess Spencer after her remarriage to Johnny, she proved unpopular with his children, acquiring from them an additional title: Acid Raine. Much later, Diana's resentment against Raine boiled over at a family wedding. 'I remember really going for her gullet – I was so angry,' Diana recalled.

'I said: "I hate you so much, if only you knew how much we all hated you for what you've done, you've ruined the house [Althorp], you spend Daddy's money and what for?"'

Raine's mother, Barbara Cartland, showered Diana's world with something that can corrode too – pulp romance. The author dressed head to toe in shocking pink, powdered her face as white as Elizabeth I and wrote an extraordinary number of novels, each with the same, basic plot. Diana devoured them by the truckload and they were, one of her schoolfriends told me, 'the source of reading for her entire year. She literally had a whole drawer filled with these things.' Cartland's granite-faced noblemen unsheathed their swords in defence of wilting maidens, winning their hearts and virginity. (A sample sentence from Cartland's *A Shaft of Sunlight*: '"Good-Heavens!" the Duke ejaculated. "What brings you here so early in the morning?"')

If Diana failed to spot that Charles was incapable of giving her the love she craved, it cannot have helped that the love she craved was a fiction – a modern-day version of courtly love. Before she ever met her future husband, she developed a passion at a distance for one of his brothers. The schoolfriend says that every year until Diana turned fifteen or sixteen, she sent Andrew a valentine card, anonymously of course.

Charles fitted the Cartland mould in one respect: his emotional unavailability. The reticence of Cartland's heroes belies agonies of loneliness. Wounded by past trauma and hemmed in by convention, they hide their emotions – but never fear! A good woman can unlock their hearts. It is a meme that repeats throughout every one of Cartland's 723 books and across the wider romance genre, including variations of the

Cinderella story. At the end of the movie *Pretty Woman*, posh Edward scales a fire escape to offer Vivian, whom he originally hired as an escort, a more secure contract: marriage. 'So what happens after he climbs up the tower and rescues her?' he asks. Vivian responds: 'She rescues him right back.'

Unfortunately for Diana and Charles, the future king had already found salvation in the warmth and steadiness of Camilla, and like Diana, Charles didn't yet know what he needed. His early life had mirrored hers, his parents emotionally and physically distant. At school, fellow pupils cold-shouldered or bullied him rather than risk accusations of sucking up to royalty. 'It's such hell here, especially at night,' he wrote from his second school, his father's alma mater, Gordonstoun. 'The people in my dormitory are foul. Goodness they are horrid. I don't know how anyone could be so foul. They throw slippers all night long or hit me with pillows or rush across the room and hit me as hard as they can.'

Though the age gap between Charles and Diana amounted to close to thirteen years, he came to the relationship almost as ill-prepared as she was, deprived of normal formative experiences: cocooned, but never sheltered; entitled, but denied free choice by courtiers and the exigencies of his position.

He delivered his proposal with so little preamble that Diana laughed. 'I remember thinking, "this is a joke",' she revealed to Morton. At that stage she had met her future spouse, by her calculation, just twenty-seven times. At those encounters, Charles made minimal effort to get to know her and displayed not a hint of sexual interest. 'Frigid wasn't the word. Big F when it comes to that,' she said.

This behaviour makes sense within the view of marriage Mountbatten set out in correspondence with Charles. The heir to the throne must 'choose a suitable, attractive and sweet-charactered girl before she met anyone else she might fall for. After all, [your] Mummy never seriously thought of anyone else after the Dartmouth encounter [with Philip] when she was thirteen!'

He continued: 'I think it is disturbing for women to have experiences if they have to remain on a pedestal after marriage.' In other words, Charles should withhold the mystic royal touch from any female deemed potential marriage material, while 'sow[ing] his wild oats and hav[ing] as many affairs as he can'. Mountbatten's letter is dated 14 February 1974, quite the valentine.

A woman who briefly featured in gossip columns as Charles's official girlfriend told me what it was like to be assessed for potential queendom. Other people spend their first dates at pubs or the cinema. Charles first took her to lunch with his mother, then to dinners at royal residences. 'People would be having fun, relaxing, smoking out of the windows, but then before he arrived, they'd stub out cigarettes and stand to attention,' she said. Everyone called Charles 'sir'. All of them greeted him by bowing or bending the knee. She remembered an incident when he mistimed a peck on her cheek, attempting to deliver it just as she curtseyed and receiving a Glasgow kiss instead.

Older and more worldly than Diana, she shied away from the transaction on offer. Diana ran at her destiny full tilt, right up to the eve of the marriage. 'I didn't have anything to go by, because I had never had a boyfriend. I'd always kept them away, thought they were all trouble – and I couldn't handle it emotionally. I was very screwed up, I thought,' Diana confided to the Morton tapes.

At the last minute, she told her sisters that she wanted to call it off. They replied that it was too late; her face was on the tea towels. Her friends also had misgivings, as one of them recently revealed to me. Charles seemed highly strung and petulant, getting himself in a lather about the loss of a cufflink just before the pre-wedding ball at Buckingham Palace. Surely, Diana's friends thought, he had hundreds of pairs. They only later understood the significance of the item, part of a set given to him by Camilla, as Diana was well aware.

Unbeknownst to all but his innermost circle until publication of my biography of Charles, he baulked too. One of his close friends, Lucia Santa Cruz, in describing his pre-marital crisis to me, added a comment that carried a distinct whiff of the Tudors: 'I always told him afterwards that if it had been a Catholic marriage, it could have been declared null. Because he wasn't really [committed], because [Diana] started with the bulimia and everything before the wedding.' He resolved to proceed, believing it was his duty to do so.

So it was that on 29 July 1981, two damaged innocents came together with conflicting expectations and similar reservations, under the glare of world attention, to serve an institution creaking under the weight of its own history.

*

All of this made the implosion of the marriage near-inevitable, yet even so, its collapse came as a shock to the wider public.

Among Elizabeth II's many sleights of hand had been to style her dysfunctional blue-blooded family into the simulacrum of a solid, middle-class ideal: mother, father, four children and her mum in the granny flat. She benefited from surprising allies in this endeavour: journalists and editors.

The print press had expanded under Queen Victoria, with twenty-one dailies published in London by the end of her reign. Soon, cinemas carried newsreel footage, and broadcast media began to offer fresh ways for monarchs to connect with their subjects. In 1932, the BBC transmitted George V's Christmas Day message, initiating what is now an annual tradition. When, two years later, the MP Sir Stafford Cripps suggested in a speech that 'undoubtedly the Labour Party will have to overcome opposition from Buckingham Palace and other places when it comes into power', the establishment united to monster him. 'It is clear from the outrage of the press and politicians that . . . the Crown occupied a near-sacred place in national life,' as the historian Ed Owens has observed. All but one of the monarchs who ascended in the twentieth century solidified this status.

They did so partly through their own efforts, using media and personal visits to show interest in the lives of the working classes, and positioning the monarchy as both a symbol and guarantor of unity. How effectively this tamed the media became clear after Edward VIII's abdication. Newspapers had known of his affair with Wallis Simpson but suppressed the story for fear of damaging the institution.

Sixties counterculture eroded such reflexes, but this did not lead to greater scrutiny across the board. The tabloids fixated on personal rather than political doings. Elizabeth's *annus horribilis* provided plenty of fodder. Broadsheet journalism increasingly regarded the royal family as celebrities, unworthy of serious attention. Moreover, most outlets across print and broadcast remained monarchist, through a mixture of conviction and to preserve relationships and access.

In 1995, Diana travelled to Berkshire to beg Max Hastings, then editor in chief of the *Daily Telegraph*, to assist her in getting her side of the story out. According to Hastings, she 'hated' Charles and put forward the idea she would shortly volunteer in her *Panorama* interview, that the throne should pass straight to William. You might think that an editor would see in this encounter a story demanding publication in the public interest. Instead, as Hastings told a Channel Four documentary, 'I felt that my job was to help them keep a lid on this rather than to lift it off.'

It did not help that Diana sounded paranoid. She worried that a plot was afoot to 'have her put down'; felt she was being betrayed, surveilled and followed. Clearly, these were not baseless delusions. She had reason to believe people close to her had sold her out. Her conversations had been recorded and wherever she turned, paparazzi lay in wait.

*

'Don't worry,' the movie-star-turned-Princess Grace of Monaco joked to the freshly engaged Diana, 'it'll only get worse,' and it did. The problem was not that Diana failed to win public approval, but that it was immediate and overwhelming. 'She didn't like the attention, ever,' remembers one of her friends. 'Even though she became more confident, she was always a shy person.' Editors and photographers claimed that her courteous response and occasional smiles indicated the opposite. 'You have to understand the way we were brought up,' says the friend. 'We were all brought up with the idea that manners were the most important thing. Being polite was the most important thing. So even if you were mobbed by sixty-four photographers in the street, manners dictated that you couldn't just tell them to fuck off.'

In the eyes of Charles's inner circle, Diana's popularity came at his expense. 'It was like Marilyn Monroe publicity. She only had to click her heels and the whole world was at her feet,' said Diana. 'It was very odd. I'm never comfortable in it, never ever. I was absolutely mesmerised by the whole thing. I couldn't believe it. The royal family all thought, "Oh she's got lots of press, she must be doing all right."'

A whispering campaign gathered pace, as always happens when royal is pitted against royal, court against court. Sometimes anonymous speakers take it upon themselves to defend one royal by disparaging another; at other times these deep throats speak with the approval of the principals. The phrase 'sources close to' generally signals that such a game is afoot.

Diana played it too, but more rarely used proxies. She wined and dined journalists, kept Richard Kay of the *Daily Mail* on speed dial, supplied Andrew Morton with direct accounts and went to her grave denying her involvement in the biography that resulted, but not before pointing the finger at Charles in her *Panorama* interview. 'Friends, on my husband's side, were indicating that I was again unstable, sick, and should be put in a home of some sort in order to get better,' she said. 'There's no better way to dismantle a personality than to isolate it.'

Journalists, not content with picking up stories they were fed, constructed additional narratives. In Diana's last weeks alone, they produced thousands of articles disdaining her efforts to build a new life, hijacked a press conference meant to highlight her campaign against landmines with questions about her personal life, and repurposed photographs of her abdomen, now slightly and healthily rounded, to launch pregnancy rumours. How tough this must have been for someone in recovery from eating disorders.

The same misogyny that pushes women to starve themselves into unsustainable sizes punishes them for ageing, whether naturally or not. Tabloids slaver over teenaged girls, yet the sight of a mature woman, especially one who appears to be sexually active, sends thcm into conniptions.

Diana was just thirty-six when she died. Imagine if she had lived. Picture the glee with which paparazzi would have zeroed in on signs of orange-peel skin. Think with what professions of concern columnists would have rubbished her choices, especially of sexual or romantic partners. No relationship, not even a return to the type of posh white boys who comforted her as her marriage imploded, Jameses Gilbey or Hewitt, could have escaped their condemnation. The first man she fell for in this final phase of her extraordinary life suggests how little appeal such a retreat held for her.

Hasnat Khan, a cardiothoracic surgeon, represented a dramatically different form of service to the gesture-heavy, content-light incarnation of the royal job she had come to repudiate. This was someone who worked a ninety-hour week and aimed to establish a free-to-use medical centre near his birthplace in Pakistan. While publicity would benefit such a project, he feared that the media would make his life 'hell' if they married. In a statement to Diana's inquest, he described the afflictions that came merely with dating her: a stream of death threats, including 'envelopes containing cut-out pictures of me together with a noose around my neck', and his family and coworkers harassed. How could he and Diana hope to raise a family under such conditions?

The Windsors themselves have never satisfactorily answered the question of how to carve out a semblance of normality amid remorseless attention and the risks that go with it. Little girls may dream of being princesses, but princesses dream of life beyond palace gates and so do many princes. Harry's difficulty in realising the dream shows how complicated the process can be. Though royals rub shoulders with commoners, they primarily do so under controlled circumstances, interfacing with staff or presiding at events where guests arrange themselves, as if by magic, into deferential semicircles. Outside such protected environments, members of the royal family risk a rougher reception. Charles discovered this at school and again at university, where he endured another penalty of difference: alienation. Lacking the shared references and experiences that make for easy bonding, pursued by press and in danger of assaults or kidnapping, he remained largely on the fringes of student life. His ancestors built grand palaces and castles to show off their power; he stays within them because he is powerless to leave.

Still, he yearns to connect. During his decades-long apprenticeship to the throne, he seized opportunities to visit what he imagined to be the real world, even if it tidied itself up in expectation of his arrival. 'He's lived in a croft on the Outer Hebrides, he's been on hill farms, he's been on trawlers, he's been on fishing rigs down in Cornwall. He's been in the inner cities all over the country, inner cities everywhere,' an aide told me. Yet, like the rich girlfriend in Pulp's song 'Common People', all Charles ever had to do to bring his adventures in normality to an end was to place a call.

Diana, by contrast, knew the luxury of anonymity, if only fleetingly. After school, she worked as a childminder and happily shared a London flat. A poignant passage from Khan's inquest statement revealed that she later took delight in rediscovering activities from that period: ordering a drink in a pub or queuing for a concert. The couple had discussed moving to Pakistan; she also investigated alternatives, including South Africa and Australia, rejecting the latter as being too far from her sons. Might she have fled the UK, with or without Khan? The novel *Untold Story* by Monica Ali imagines an older Diana settling in suburban America. In *TIME* magazine, I tipped a different US location: Manhattan.

Wherever she went, her fame would have imprisoned her. 'The world's most photographed woman cannot simply wake up one morning and say, "Hey, I don't want to be famous any more,"' wrote paparazzi Mark Saunders and Glenn Harvey in their jaunty memoir of hounding her, *Dicing with Di*. One of her close friends recalls a party where she wanted to chat, but constant interruptions made that impossible. 'People just wanted a piece of her like she was a wedding cake; they wanted to gobble her up bite by bite. So, she said, "Look, I've got to go to the loo. Come with me, and we'll have a chat in the loo."

We just sat in the bathroom for about an hour. She wanted to escape. She needed to escape.'

*

Perhaps Dodi Fayed appeared to the harried princess not so much as a lover but a potential solution. His father Mohammed boasted his own security teams, grand homes, hotels, yachts, helicopters, and had for some years organised private, after-hours shopping trips for her to his department store Harrod's. Her divorce in August 1996 deprived Diana not only of her HRH but gave new urgency to her efforts to establish a way to live independently from her former in-laws. Royal residences might provide family members with safe, relatively private holiday destinations, but they hardly offered the break from the past she sought. She had also dispensed with close protection, uncertain whether officers were protecting her or spying on her. When Fayed invited her to bring her boys on a break aboard the *Jonikal*, his superyacht, she accepted.

Soon, the sea around the vessel churned as if marine predators were gorging on sardines. Eventually, Diana took a tender to a boatload of tabloid journalists. They might consider it her fate as a public figure to be 'abused and followed', but perhaps they would draw back for the sake of the young princes. William, she said was 'really freaked out'. Columnists promptly twisted her plea into a fresh line of attack. 'This is a woman who, from the moment she became Princess of Wales, has actively courted the attentions of the media,' wrote Ros Dodd, the women's editor of the *Birmingham Daily Post*. 'She has basked in the glow of the camera flashbulbs and has frequently manipulated the press for her own ends.'

Though most tellings of Diana's story insist that she and Khan broke up before her first stay on the *Jonikal*, his testimony provides a different timeline. 'When Diana went to St Tropez with Mr Al Fayed, everything was fine between us, I said goodbye to her the day she went as I had stayed with her the previous night at Kensington Palace . . . After a few days, I felt something was wrong. Her mobile kept going on to answerphone.'

Diana and her heart surgeon had hidden from view as best they could. After she returned for a second stint on the yacht, minus her sons and with only Dodi for company, a photographer called Mario Brenna hit paydirt. Here was Diana with another brown-skinned, Muslim boyfriend, and this time she was kissing him. Grainy images of the embrace would go on to earn Brenna, by his own estimate, £1.7 million over the next six-to-eight months alone, reflecting the sales boost news organisations anticipated from publishing his pictures. The feeding frenzy intensified until small craft outnumbered seagulls, the sunlight bouncing off the telescopic lenses of Brenna's rivals. Competition and an overheated market drove hacks and snappers to ever-riskier conduct. Editors urged them on. The images could be recycled endlessly, first as news, then for features, profiles, pieces about beachwear or beach bodies, and always and inevitably, to garnish scabrous opinion columns. As members of the media rained down harsh judgements on Diana, none of them stopped to examine their own behaviour.

Five years earlier, a recording of an intimate phone call between her and James Gilbey had also proved great business.

The Sun published transcripts of Squidgygate, named after Gilbey's endearment for Diana, and set up a telephone line so punters could pay to hear the couple's conversation. Soon another recording surfaced, this time of Charles and Camilla. The original explanation for both tapes – that amateur radio enthusiasts stumbled across the frequencies and fired up reel-to-reel recorders – stretches belief. If these were professional operations, proofs – and a motive – remain elusive. Some theories hold secret services responsible, either foreign spies or homegrown, the latter shadowing Diana either to anticipate and defuse any moves against the monarchy, or for the protection of her and her sons. While tabloids might seem the obvious culprits, editors sat on the recordings for years before publishing. Even so, Charles Spencer suspects his sister was a victim of a technique that had not yet acquired a name. 'It's my theory that before anyone even knew the term she was probably being phone-hacked,' he told journalist Andy Webb.

In 2005, members of the royal household called in the police after details, gleaned from their mobile voicemails, peppered news reports. The investigation would eventually broaden to reveal phone hacking to be widespread and indiscriminate, targeting private individuals including a schoolgirl, Milly Dowler, who had been murdered by a serial killer. Though the first phase of the scandal centred on Rupert Murdoch's Sunday tabloid, *News of the World*, further corporations and newspapers were implicated, with thousands of cases settled out of court and another publisher held to account in legal action brought by Prince Harry. In 2024, the high court ruled that there was evidence of 'extensive' hacking by three MGN titles – the *Daily Mirror, Sunday Mirror* and *Sunday People*, from

2006 to 2011. Additional lines of inquiry around the bribing of public servants, plundering of confidential records and other corrupt practices suggest that a significant swathe of the media had resorted to illegal shortcuts.

Diana's bankability contributed to this culture shift within newsrooms, also nudging them to the criminally irresponsible as well as the criminal. Dodi's arrival set journalists to honing dog-whistling skills they would deploy two decades later against Diana's biracial daughter-in-law. Again and again, reports of Dodi's relationship with the Princess harnessed the same trio of adjectives for him: 'oily', 'hairy' and 'dark'. Not infrequently, the press said the quiet part out loud. 'The biggest obstacle to Diana and Dodgy living happily ever after is that he is simply not good enough for her,' declared Tony Parsons, formerly a 'hip young gunslinger' at the *New Musical Express* (*NME*) and now writing for the *Daily Mirror*. 'What possible relationship does she imagine this selfish, sated sheikh of St Tropez could have with her children?' The *Daily Mail* posed a similar question, embedding it in one of its interminable headlines: 'Who would ever have thought that Princess Di would become the trophy of a rich Middle Eastern man?' A Dublin newspaper, attempting to denounce this piece of racism, produced one of its own: Dodi, its columnist protested, was 'a millionaire courting her, not someone trying to sell her into white slavery from a Cairo casbah'.

*

It would be easy to forget how badly journalists traduced the Princess herself, because they too forgot, within days. Among the worst offenders were other women. Female columnists are often used this way by editors, as if misogyny voiced by women were legitimate. On 27 August 1997, the *Daily Mail*'s Lynda Lee-Potter fulminated against Diana: 'Teenagers want their mother to be modest, ordinary and scandal free. They can't bear any hint of her having a sexual life. The sight of a paunchy playboy groping a scantily dressed Diana must appal and humiliate Prince William. Unfortunately, she appears determined to reveal to the world that she and Dodi are lovers and can't keep their hands off each other.'

Three days later, the *Sunday Mirror*'s Carole Malone filed a piece pegged to Diana's reported comment that, while Labour backed banning landmines, the previous Tory government had been 'hopeless' on the issue. The Princess's trip to Angola, widely derided as a publicity ploy, had in fact been personally approved by the Queen. The Princess had also denied making party-political remarks. 'It's a pity Gucci don't make designer face zips,' Malone wrote. 'Then when Diana was on the verge of opening her ill-informed mouth and causing an international incident (an increasingly frequent occurrence these days), she could just keep her trap shut.' The edition of the newspaper carrying Malone's item landed on doorsteps the following morning, 31 August, just as broadcasters interrupted programming to announce Diana's death.

Across the nation, editors and journalists performed the manoeuvre British tabloids call 'a reverse ferret'. Lee-Potter penned a sickly eulogy to Diana. The Princess had 'helped to give despairing people a sense of their own worth, self-esteem and dignity'. Diana's mothering, the target of Lee-Potter's previous broadside, had in fact been exemplary. 'Throughout their childhood she gave her sons endless loving cuddles. She gave them the freedom to show their feelings. She didn't believe in the stiff upper lip, and I hope that no one is today telling them to be brave. I hope they are allowed to cry until they have no tears left.'

Malone constructed a two-headed beast, a mea (ex)culpa that bared fangs at its readers: 'None of us could have known Diana was going to die in that terrible crash and it would be impossible for me to do my job if I had to assume everyone I wrote about might die the next day. The point now is that it doesn't matter what I or anyone else has said in the past. Because it wasn't words that killed the Princess. It was a car running out of control which did.' She added, 'But this isn't about blame. [Author's note: *yeah right*.] The real issue here is how we are ALL going to change in the face of this tragedy. Because it isn't just journalists and commentators who must change. From now on we ALL have a responsibility to be different.'

Beatification usually takes years, sometimes centuries. In Diana's case, the process was completed in the blink of a watery eye. Mounds of flowers outside royal residences grew so deep that the underlying layers turned to mulch. People wept in the streets, sobbed in the supermarket, crying for her loss and their own unhappinesses. Suicide rates in England and Wales rose by over 17 per cent in the month after her funeral, with the sharpest spike among women, while cases of self-harm among female patients surged by more than 65 per cent.[16]

Author and journalist Christopher Hitchens dismissed these reactions as 'infantile regression' in his 1998 documentary, *Diana: The Mourning After*. The public response, he argued, was not organic but manufactured: 'It was in Paris that Princess

Diana was cruelly and abruptly translated from the banal to the sublime . . . Lives that are cut off too soon, like those of James Dean or JFK make good iconic material because they can be mourned for what they never became, to say nothing of what they never were.'

His sideswipes at 'Our Lady of the Versace' reveal contempt for Diana, but these are incidental, an expression of the misogyny common among men of the left (a phenomenon deserving of a book all of its own). His sights are trained on the media that damned then canonised her, in the process stifling dissenting voices such as his.

Certainly, if hypocrisy were an Olympic sport, sections of the press would have emerged from the period garlanded in gold. News organisations that had recently queued to buy paparazzi shots – and continued to illustrate their homages to Diana with them – condemned the photographers for streaming after the Mercedes like the tail of a comet. Soon, though, they alighted on other culprits. The same journalists who praised Diana's empathy and compassion picked at the bones of Henri Paul, the driver killed in the crash alongside Dodi and the Princess. (Bodyguard Trevor Rees-Jones, though gravely injured, survived.) 'Love-Split Turned Driver into Drunk' reads the banner headline above a *Mirror* piece which mentions Paul frequented a gay bar before quoting a source saying he wasn't gay. The focus on why a man with high blood alcohol had ended up behind the wheel, while legitimate, overshadowed the question of why Paul, as acting head of security at the Ritz and not one of the hotel's chauffeurs, was driving at all. Conspiracists quickly provided baroque explanations, while ignoring an obvious possibility: that the wealthy have a habit of assuming they deserve generals rather than foot soldiers to wait on their needs.

Unanswered questions, and the cold shoulder shown to him by the royal family, helped to fuel Mohamed Al-Fayed's own imaginings. Soon he began speaking of a plot, masterminded by Prince Philip, to murder Diana and Dodi. The press encouraged his outbursts, while mocking him. Hitchens refers to Fayed in his documentary as 'a rather dubious Egyptian grocer'.

The irony, of course, is that there should have been huge concerns about Fayed, not because of his race or religion or background but the swell of allegations of sexual abuse and rape that had swirled around him for years. Like two other prolific predators, Jimmy Savile and Jeffrey Epstein, he hid in plain sight, the prejudices against 'outsiders' working in his favour. 'The devastating thing is the class system, created of people who think they are above the rest of the human race. They think they can shit just on anyone,' Fayed told *Vanity Fair* in 1995. The avidity with which he sought and tended royal connections read as a desire for acceptance in the highest social echelons. What he, Epstein and Savile really craved, of course, was the cover those connections could provide.

All of them used the law to intimidate their prey and scare off inquiries. Fayed sued *Vanity Fair* for libel over that same article, which detailed disturbing behaviours, including Fayed chasing female employees around his office and trying to stuff money down their blouses. When another female journalist and I interviewed him two years later about his crash conspiracies, he interrupted proceedings to instruct us to sit on his lap. The lack of reaction from his staff suggested that this was, for him, unremarkable behaviour, and that those around him either suffered from it or enabled it. A 2024 documentary detailing rapes, assaults and harassment confirmed that suspicion, prompting 146 complaints of historic crimes. An interviewee remembered him asking her to sit on his lap, the prelude in her case to serious sexual assault.

That Diana viewed such a man as a safe harbour makes more sense if you understand her state of mind at the time. In the early days of her marriage, a protection officer, perceived to be too close to her, had been let go, dying shortly afterwards when his motorbike hit another vehicle. She had seen her intimate conversations recorded and published. The press seemed to be able to find her no matter that she took precautions, sweeping Kensington Palace for bugs and using mobiles registered to someone else. In 1995, she informed her lawyers that she had been tipped off about plots against her, including tampering with her car brakes.

No wonder then that so many see her death as preordained. Perhaps the most extraordinary thing is that it was not. Neither the French investigation nor the operation by British police found evidence to suggest the car crash was anything other than an accident – and an avoidable one at that. A coroner's inquest lasting nearly six months reached the same conclusion: 'The crash was caused or contributed to by the speed and manner of driving of the Mercedes, the speed and manner of driving of the following vehicles [photographer's cars and motorbikes], [and] the impairment of the judgement of the driver of the Mercedes through alcohol,' said the foreman of the jury, delivering their verdict. 'In addition, the death of the deceased was caused or contributed to by the fact that the deceased was not wearing a seatbelt, [and] the fact that the Mercedes struck the pillar in the Alma Tunnel, rather than colliding with something else.'

These days, we are accustomed to a post-truth world that developed many of its defining characteristics around this time. The nineties saw the internet begin to emerge in the form we now know it, providing a vast, amorphous space less easily policed and more easily accessed than analogue platforms. The living princess became the focus of gossip sites, fan pages and chatrooms. Dead, she fed online conspiracies that nourished an offline product range. A fraction of the books published in this genre include *Diana Inquest: Corruption at Scotland Yard*; *Paris-London Connection: The Assassination of Princess Diana*; and *How They Murdered Princess Diana: The Shocking Truth*. You get the picture.

Documentaries picked up the theme. Stories claiming fresh evidence continue to surface. More poignantly, Prince Harry, who, along with his brother, had released a statement thanking the inquest jury, revealed in his memoir, *Spare*, that he and William had weighed a challenge to the verdict. 'Even if the man [Paul] had been drinking, even if he was shit-faced, he wouldn't have had any trouble navigating that short tunnel,' Harry writes. 'Unless paps had chased and blinded him. Why were those paps not more roundly blamed? Why were they not in gaol? Who had sent them? And why were *they* not in gaol?'

Nobody should be surprised that a man who saw his mother hounded to death and fears that he and his wife risk acting out the same history has taken on the tabloids. However, another British institution played a decisive and dishonourable role in Diana's last years. The BBC, like the monarchy, still commands trust, though, like the monarchy, risks testing that trust to destruction.

*

'There are lessons to be drawn from her life and from the extraordinary and moving reaction to her death,' said Elizabeth in her address to the nation five days after Diana died. But what are those lessons, and have any been learned?

The Diana industry churns on, instrumentalising and exploiting her. Together, this output forms what cultural historian Susan Bordo calls 'sedimented mythology, turned into "history" by decades of repetition'. Despite the volume of volumes, there are few books about Diana that future scholars will lean on. An obvious exception is Andrew Morton's, which transcribes her actual voice. Harry's *Spare*, though more about him than his mother, situates her loss in terms of those most directly affected by it. *Dianarama*, about Diana's BBC *Panorama* interview, will also be an essential read.

Most broadcast recordings of her enhance our understanding of Diana, not least by providing insights into the culture she inhabited. 'What do you say, ma'am, when you read in the papers that you're a determined, domineering woman?' asks ITV's Alastair Burnet, quizzing the Princess just four years into her marriage. But *Panorama* was by far her most significant foray into television.

That makes its removal from public view troubling, even though there are good reasons for it. Her eldest son has stated that it should never be shown again. After all, Martin Bashir obtained Diana's agreement by deceit. Yet this conversation, conducted without the interventions of palace press minders, also allowed her to express herself with agonising clarity. In a note to Bashir, the Princess acknowledged how important she herself felt it to be: 'There are no words adequate to express how I now feel having had my wings returned to me,' she wrote.

Instead of the direct-from-source interview, we are left to watch *The Crown*'s reconstruction with actress Elizabeth Debicki eerily mimicking Diana's dipped-chin, kohl-rimmed gaze. In this version, we see prominent viewers react to lines made more pointed and sometimes sexed up. Prime Minister John Major exchanges a glance with his wife, Norma, as the Princess discusses her fragile mental health. 'I was in a very dark place,' she says. 'I suffered alone.' In the original, Diana partially excused the royals for failing to understand that she needed help. 'Well, maybe I was the first person ever to be in this family who ever had a depression or was ever openly tearful,' she mused. 'And obviously that was daunting, because if you've never seen it before, how do you support it?'

Asked about the breakdown of her relationship with Charles, Debicki's Diana moves straight from 'well, there were three of us in this marriage' to the rhetorical 'was I devastated? Yes.' In response, screen Camilla drags deep on a cigarette, while Charles (an improbably rugged Dominic West) exhales smoke of a different kind: 'What the hell is she doing?' Diana's original answer pointed to the culpability of a fourth party: 'Well, there were three of us in this marriage, and the pressure of the media was another factor.' It was indeed. That very interview, far from being a release, represents a shocking and consequential example of this pressure.

*

The first hot day of 2024 was also its longest: the summer solstice. In an airless basement room at the Field House Tribunal Hearing Centre in central London, a listless electric fan offered little relief to the small assembly gathered for closing statements in a case seeking the truth of how the *Panorama* episode came to be filmed.

Andy Webb, himself ex-BBC and an award-winning documentary maker, had dressed not for the heat but the gravity of the occasion, in a black suit. He had come to give testimony in the case he brought against the regulatory authority, the Information Commissioner, and the BBC. His research had turned up evidence that Bashir used falsified bank statements to get close to Diana, by suggesting people working for her brother were peddling stories to the tabloids – and that was not all. Webb believed that Bashir had painted a terrifying vision of Diana's world in which nobody could be trusted, and only by speaking out could she protect herself.

None of this was news to the BBC. Matt Wiessler, a graphic artist commissioned by Bashir to create the bank statements in question, had contacted the BBC shortly after watching the *Panorama* episode to warn them about the forgeries. The corporation moved to quash Wiessler's worries, holding a secret investigation into Bashir and itself – and exonerating both. For the next two decades, the broadcaster blocked and obfuscated, managing the scandal into low-level obscurity until Webb's freedom of information requests turned up a piece of evidence that drew Charles Spencer into the fight.

Webb originally laid out these allegations in three documentaries. Forty-eight hours before the first aired in 2020, he received a dump of emails and internal memos relating to the programme. Many had been so thoroughly redacted as to be unintelligible. One claimed that the forgeries had been created with Spencer's cooperation. Webb then submitted a fresh request for information. Who, he wondered, had tried to 'blacken Spencer's name'?

The new evidence spurred the BBC board into commissioning a second inquiry, headed by former judge, Lord Dyson. The resulting report backed many of Webb's findings: Bashir had deployed trickery and then lied to both inquiries; the internal inquiry had been 'woefully ineffective' and 'the BBC covered up in its press logs such facts as it had been able to establish about how Bashir secured the interview'. However, Dyson too fell short, in Webb's view – for example, failing to quiz Bashir about a fax sent to Spencer falsely implying the then Prince of Wales had impregnated royal nanny Tiggy Legge-Bourke. Days before Diana sat down for her interview with Bashir, the Princess repeated an expanded version of this story to her lawyers. Her ex-husband intended to marry Tiggy. She and Camilla were, one way or another, for the chop.

If the BBC hoped to draw a line under these events, executives had reckoned without Webb and Spencer, by now working in concert to pinpoint responsibility for the corporation's failures and to discover what had really happened. That required access to uncensored documents. The corporation continued to fight such a release, summoning legal rather than moral arguments. Now, as Webb laid out his final argument at the tribunal, a combination of rage or exhaustion brought him to tears. After a brief break, the hearing resumed. The tribunal gave its judgment a few months later, dismissing Webb's bid for the unredacted emails, but criticising the BBC for spending public money on stonewalling his quest for the truth.

Dianarama charts Webb's battle. 'I kept a small photo of Princess Diana Blu-Tacked to the right-hand top corner of my computer screen,' Webb writes. 'It was a reminder that there was a point to all this, and a poignant one. It seemed to me that because of what Martin Bashir had done in 1995, and more importantly because it had then been covered up, Diana's life had been sent off on a terribly dangerous course, resulting in her death.' You can see his point. Until that broadcast, Diana, though separated from Charles, remained part of the Windsor family. Had she remained so, she might never have accepted Mohamed Al-Fayed's invitation or relied on his security team. Had she learned of Bashir's subterfuge, she could have reassessed relationships, repairing some and cutting off others. The miasma of misinformation left her vulnerable.

*

Twenty-three million people tuned in to *Panorama* back in 1995, Andy and I among them. Our friends, TV presenter Paula Yates and Michael Hutchence, frontman of the Australian mega-group INXS, themselves at the centre of a toxic media barrage, came to our flat to watch. Paula wore a tiara in solidarity with the Princess.

Earlier that year, Paula had left her husband to be with Michael, a decision that triggered a media backlash. Her ex, like Diana's, occupied a unique position in British life. Bob Geldof, though Irish, had become something of a national treasure, licensed to dress scruffily and swear inventively, even on telly or in the presence of royalty. Originally known for a string of hits with his band, the Boomtown Rats, his role in launching Band Aid and Live Aid in response to the Ethiopian famine earned him the embrace of the establishment. Queen Elizabeth made him an honorary Knight Commander of the Order of the British Empire; the press dubbed him 'Saint Bob'.

You might imagine that left-leaning media – and any feminist within its ranks – would have given Paula a gentler ride than their red-top colleagues. They did not, as demonstrated by this screed from an *Observer* columnist: 'Yates's biggest public relations problem is that, she is, to use the taxi driver vernacular, "a bit of a stupid cow". A consummate self-publicist, with no common sense or dignity to speak of, she has been wandering the corridors of showbiz in too-tight/too-young clothes too damn long now to merit anything like automatic respect. What after all, can one say in defence of a woman who started out as a groupie and went downhill from there? In many ways, she is a born loser. Even when she did *Penthouse*, she ended up looking as sad and badly lit as a Reader's Wife. And those "post-Bob" new breasts. Oh Paula, Paula, Paula . . .'

This, then, was the poisonous environment Diana also tried and failed to navigate. Later, I would drive Michael's jeep through an inferno of flashbulbs while he and Paula tried to shield their newborn daughter in the backseat as a photographer lay across the bonnet, firing his flash directly into my eyes. I thought about that moment when Diana died and again reading *Spare*.

Within five years of our evening watching *Panorama*, Michael and Paula would both be dead too, cracking under the pressures of the same toxic media environment that tormented

Diana. Michael hanged himself months after Diana died. Paula struggled on for a while longer before overdosing. Her death, when it came, felt inevitable. One reason for this – intrinsic to Diana's story – is that people in the eye of the media are eroded by it. Every photograph steals a piece of the soul. Each jab, each criticism, cuts and undermines. Stable personalities develop coping mechanisms – they insulate themselves, build tight friendship groups, stop reading anything about themselves, good or bad.

Fragile people often become hooked on the attention that is killing them. It cannot help that some are attracted to fame by the very thing that makes them susceptible to its comorbidities. An academic study, *Dying to Be Famous*, compared a non-famous control group with almost fifteen hundred rock and pop stars. A high proportion of the musicians had been subject to 'adverse childhood experiences' and died young. The authors observed that stars 'may seek fame as a mechanism to escape deprived and abusive childhoods [but] such factors are rarely considered when examining their premature mortality. Instead, substance use and risk-taking in stars are largely discussed in terms of hedonism, music industry culture, responses to the pressures of fame or even part of the creative process.'[17]

Paula's childhood bore striking similarities to Diana's with its combination of precarity, privilege and disruption. Both Paula and Diana reinvented themselves and pursued ideals of love and cosy domesticity. Neither made reliable witnesses – a fact amplified and weaponised by their opponents. But their single greatest point of congruence was not their backgrounds or characters or overlapping social sets but the relentlessness of the misogyny they endured.

Shortly before Diana's fateful holiday with Fayed, she happened to spot Paula out shopping. 'I am relieved whenever I see you in the papers,' she said, only half-joking, 'because it means I get the day off.'

TV companies still approach me every year with new projects promising to set the record straight about Paula. I always decline, sceptical that the industry that helped to destroy her will do her justice.

Diana's afterlife, meanwhile, has taken on a life of its own, a tapestry of myths, her reconstructed persona a series of Rorschach blots. Their interpretation often reveals more about the observer than the observed – and how closely she is observed, forever caught in the searchlights, a royal woman as hunted and haunting as any since Anne Boleyn.

Chapter 6

Camilla: Mistress of the Long Game

Sunlight bounces off the gilt-tipped gates of Buckingham Palace. The guests filing through them shine too, gussied up for a reception to celebrate International Women's Day. Just twenty-four hours a year are dedicated to acknowledging half the world's population, so the date invariably staggers under its weight of special programming, shedding some of its load into neighbouring weeks. This party is three days late, but Planet Windsor anyway operates to different schedules than the rest of us.

Edward VII decreed that every timepiece on the Sandringham estate should be set thirty minutes ahead of Greenwich Mean Time to stop the gathering gloom of winter curtailing his hunting and shooting. Edward VIII suspended the practice. Since his abdication, royal clocks typically run not fast but slow, the forward movement of their hands fighting a constant drag of calculations. If a king chooses love over duty, might his subjects come to view monarchy not as destiny but choice? How should the institution present itself as immutable, and therefore unquestionable, yet fully in step with the diverse populations under its sway?

Aides, charged with helping the royals square these impossible circles, fret over the details of every public-facing event, from finger food to guest lists. The disconnect between the theme of this particular reception and its location – a room bristling with old masters' renderings of great men – illustrates the scale of the challenge. Doing feminism at the epicentre of the patrimonarchy is bound to throw up contradictions. Most women occupy these spaces by association or invitation, or to serve crustless sandwiches.

Not that I or my sister guests show any signs of concern. We mix and mingle under the male gaze, excited to catch up with old friends, and only briefly interrupting animated conversations to gawp as Posh meets posher – Spice Girl-turned-fashionista Victoria Beckham bobbing to the actual Queen. We pause again, this time to watch two Camillas collide. The presence of Olivia Williams – Mrs Parker Bowles in *The Crown*'s final seasons – signals a consort secure enough of the glittering present to smile in the face of her turbulent past.

So she should be. Camilla, once caricatured as a latter-day Wallis Simpson; a danger to the monarchy rather than one of its pillars, has achieved a rare transformation from public enemy to press favourite. She seems more relatable than other royals, earthier too – or as her friend, actress Emma Thompson once put it to me, 'rude and raunchy'. People meeting her for the first time, their expectations set by a protracted period when picture desks deliberately chose shots of her grimacing, are surprised to discover that she is pretty. At the tail end of her seventies, she looks and sounds like someone worn not by care but its absence, her voice husky and a touch nasal, as if she has just dragged herself out of bed after a night on the tiles. She smiles easily, laughs heartily and reduces her husband to fits of giggles. Dianaists will always view her as an interloper, but to her widening fan base, Camilla represents the opposite: proof that true love triumphs. By now a seasoned royal, she has also learned to work a photo opportunity or a room, whether in a Victorian pile or a woman's refuge. It may look simple enough to exchange pleasantries and deliver speeches, but at least one of her in-laws, though born to the job, was as apt to actively offend a crowd as please it, until his enforced retreat from working royalty.

On this occasion, Camilla speaks as president of the WOW – Women of the World foundation – and festivals and in support of the organisation's goal of gender equality, a distant prospect. 'At the current rate, globally, it will take an estimated two hundred and eighty-six years to remove discriminatory laws, one hundred and forty years for women to hold half the positions of leadership in the workplace and forty-seven years to be represented equally in national parliaments,' she tells us. Those numbers are hurtling in the wrong direction with populist governments in many countries trampling on hard-won progress. This the Queen does not mention, for to do so would be branded too political, and her own views and values are a mixed bag.

She concludes on a rousing note: 'By following in the footsteps of [the] amazing women and girls who will not take "no" for an answer, we members of the WOW family fervently hope that [this goal] will be achieved in a much shorter time. Seeing you all here, I am filled with confidence that, together, we can make sure this happens.'

As improbable an activist for equality as, say, King Charles, when Camilla urges us to fight long odds and reject rejection, she nevertheless draws on lived experience. Resilience delivered her to this place and palace and continues to define her. Other women marrying into the Firm conform or flail. This queen may have entered through the gleaming gates, as we did, on sufferance, but now she determines who comes and goes. In every such instruction and interaction she remains herself, neither ditching hard-edged causes nor tying herself up in protocol. Today, as is her wont, she greets long-term acquaintances – including me and other members of WOW's founding committee – not with a regally extended hand but a peck on the cheek. I exit the palace digesting a few too many petit fours and the implications of that kiss.

*

Camilla slots seamlessly into the continuum of royal women profiled in preceding chapters. Her status exacts a high price, as theirs did. For years the focus of remorseless inquiry, criticised, reviled, attacked and widely misrepresented, she has often been used to propagate misogynistic ideas and reductive stereotypes just as they were. Dig into the better-known 'facts' about her and more than a few turn out either to be embellished or entirely fictional. However – and this is a profound distinction to those others – she still walks among us, literally if you inhabit certain circles or, like me, gain access to her through journalism and/or involvement with one of the charities in her portfolio.

Writing about any living human can be a tricky business on multiple levels and for legions of reasons. For a start, as this book aims to demonstrate, interpretations of a person continue to evolve post-mortem and in step with the changing values of each age. Attempting to pin down the meaning of a life before it ends is more problematic still. Imagine yourself a time-travelling biographer. Think how sharply your pen portraits would vary from one age and stage of Camillian existence to another.

Born on 17 July 1947, into a world that expected little more than that she make a good marriage – a union of wealth and status, capable of producing children and enduring without scandal – Camilla Rosemary Shand by her thirties appeared to have checked off every item on her limited brief. As a debutante and young woman about town, she had managed to tread the fine reputational line between being considered fun or written off as a slapper. Even so, she racked up too many life experiences – or 'history' in the teeth-sucking term applied by Mountbatten and his ilk – to be considered an appropriate partner for Charles. The 'sweet-charactered' virgin bride Mountbatten prescribed for his great-nephew might ride horses, as Camilla did. She would not, however, roar around the United States on a motorbike, in leathers, as Miss Shand also chose to do, or conduct a fevered on-again, off-again romance with an army major.

Andrew Parker Bowles, the raffish inspiration for novelist Jilly Cooper's fictional womaniser, Rupert Campbell-Black, played the field before and, reputedly, during his marriage to Camilla. Described by one of Camilla's closest friends as 'a real charmer, but he's always terribly misbehaving', his premarital amours also included the nineteen-year-old Princess Anne. Camilla, though by now herself involved with Anne's eldest brother, accepted Parker Bowles' proposal. People who knew her during these heady days variously ascribe her decision to either a-bird-in-the-hand pragmatism about securing a suitable spouse or her burning passion for Parker Bowles.

He also came from similar stock. The elevated social standing of his parents, respectively a baronet and army officer and a baronet's daughter, secured Andrew a role as a pageboy at Elizabeth's coronation. Camilla's father, Bruce Shand, was a decorated former soldier turned wine merchant, her mother, Rosalind Cubitt, the daughter of a baronet. Rosalind's grandmother, society beauty and mistress of Edward VII, Alice Keppel, is by no means Camilla's only ancestor with close royal connections. Her great-great-great-grandfather, Thomas Cubitt, master builder and property developer, not only created some of London's most famous squares, but also worked to realise Prince Albert's vision for Osborne House, and remade and extended the façade of Buckingham Palace. 'He is a real national loss,' wrote Queen Victoria in her diary on news of Cubitt's death.

In 1973, Andrew and Camilla exchanged vows at the Guard's Chapel at Wellington Barracks in Kensington – a Catholic service in keeping with the groom's faith – then headed to their reception, at St James's Palace no less and attended by Princesses Anne and Margaret, as well as the Queen Mother. This was, opined society magazine *Tatler*, the 'society wedding of the season'.

Installed first at the seventeenth-century Bolehyde Manor in Wiltshire and later twelve minutes down the road as the chatelaine of a splendid Georgian property called Middlewick House, Mrs PB – an abbreviation soon in wide usage among palace aides – had no need to work, nor any apparent urge to do so. Her husband rose through the ranks to lieutenant colonel, colonel and finally brigadier, collecting a commendation for bravery from Queen Elizabeth and acting as one of her ceremonial bodyguards. Camilla raised their son, Tom, and daughter, Laura; rode with the hunt; pottered; and socialised. If she undertook good works, these were of a small, local nature. You might have thought her the sort of well-heeled woman to read *Country Life* or gain a glancing mention in its news-in-brief columns. Nobody would have dreamt her a candidate for its cover, yet there she appeared, in September 2022, photographed by her step-daughter-in-law Kate, 'the future queen consort' in the words of the magazine, 'smiling as she sits on a wooden bench holding a basket of pelargoniums'. That same month, future became present when Elizabeth died, catapulting Camilla to queenship.

She might never have risen to this role without Diana's intervention. It was the Princess who, by telling biographer Andrew Morton about her rival, and despite libel laws that restricted Morton's first edition of the book to labelling Charles's affair with Mrs PB as nothing more than a 'secret friendship', set off the chain of events that forced everyone involved to make choices. The Parker Bowles union had appeared solid to this point, despite Andrew's reputed affairs and, as some sources claim, the hurt these caused Camilla. By these same reports, her husband showed little sign that her liaison with Charles troubled him until it became public. Meanwhile, the heir to the throne, though actively unhappy in his marriage, gave every sign of accepting the status quo, muddling on in the upper-crust tradition that prefers to break hearts rather than split up estates, much less rattle the Crown.

If Diana had an outcome in mind in identifying Camilla, it was to make her nemesis suffer. 'The rottweiler', as she nicknamed her, wanted a slice of Charles? Well, Camilla would have to share another part of Diana's life too. The Princess understood the downsides of global fame better than most: the hounding, the vilification. As Camilla transitioned from private person to international pariah, she could do nothing but keep her head down and endure. Any complaint would have raised an orchestra of tiny violins. 'It was horrid,' she admitted to the *Mail on Sunday* much later. 'It was a deeply unpleasant time, and I wouldn't want to put my worst enemy through it.'

Her situation would become more difficult still, not least with the release of the so-called Camillagate tapes. Charles also made things worse. Before he had any inkling of Morton's book, he had started work with the journalist Jonathan Dimbleby on his own biography and accompanying film to come out in 1994, the twenty-fifth anniversary of his investiture as Prince of Wales. Originally conceived as a way of showing Charles as a philosopher-king-in-waiting, the project inevitably became a counterweight to Morton's damning narrative. Dimbleby, of course, had to ask Charles about Camilla. Had he tried to be 'faithful and honourable' in his marriage to Diana?

'Yes, absolutely,' Charles replied.

'And you were?' Dimbleby inquired.

'Yes.' A pause that lengthened and seethed. There was no good answer. A denial at this point would have been futile. To dodge the question would look dodgy. Finally, he managed a response of sorts. 'Until it became irretrievably broken down, us both having tried.'

Even after the Parker Bowles' divorce, the idea that Charles might make an honest queen of Camilla stretched credulity. He would, after all, succeed his mother as the Supreme Governor of the Church of England, an institution that holds congregants to higher standards than its foundational history should warrant.

Had you profiled Camilla during her scarlet-woman era, you might well have concluded, as her earliest biographer Christopher Wilson did, that the couple should never marry. Wilson, who had worked for a time as 'William Hickey', the *Daily Express* gossip columnist, invoked Simpson and the abdication, concluding that the current heir to the throne could neither afford to sever his relationship with his lover (too brutal) nor formalise it (too risky). 'If he seeks to retain the affection and esteem of his future subjects, the only course of action left open to Charles,' Wilson wrote, 'is to remain in love with Camilla Parker Bowles – but remain single.'

When Wilson ventured this opinion, Charles was not, technically, a singleton. Though separated, he and Diana at first insisted they had no plans to formalise their breach. Establishing a civilised model of detached coexistence was another matter. Both parties, far from remaining traditionally tight-lipped, continued spilling to the media, and revelations were flowing fast and thick, with royal retainers adding to the mudslinging. Diana's *Panorama* interview proved the last straw for Elizabeth. Buckingham Palace issued an announcement: 'After considering the present situation, the Queen wrote to both the Prince and Princess earlier this week and gave them her view, supported by the Duke of Edinburgh, that an early divorce is desirable.'

The court issued a decree absolute the following August; Diana's death came a year later. Still Charles was not a free agent. Shackled to his ex-wife's dazzling ghost and concerned, to whatever degree and in whichever order, for himself, Camilla, her children and his sons, the monarchy and public opinion, he instructed a key aide to write to the Press Complaints Commission. 'There is no intention of remarrying,' the letter stated. 'We keep saying it, but it is ignored or dismissed as dissembling.'

Perhaps because it was. Certainly, Charles deemed Camilla's role in his life a 'non-negotiable', a phrase variously attributed to him or anonymous friends, and together, the couple had embarked on the painstaking programme of rehabilitation. Eventually, in February 2005, officials announced their engagement. Then the real fun started. Concerns about every aspect of their plans – from the proprieties and implications of their union to its form, location and date – forced U-turns and reversals right down to the wire.

While a civil ceremony seemed far from the ideal solution for the future head of the Church of England, it trumped other options, including the route taken by Charles's sister. After her 1992 divorce from Mark Phillips, Anne sidestepped Anglicanism's prohibition against divorcées remarrying in church by yomping to Crathie Kirk, near Balmoral, to wed second husband, Timothy Laurence, under the auspices of the Church of Scotland founded by John Knox.

Such a manoeuvre on Charles's part, though it would have permitted him and Camilla a Christian ceremony, risked further enraging Anglican traditionalists without address-ing their central objection. Three years earlier, the Lambeth

Conference of Anglican bishops worldwide had agreed, after decades of wrangling, to permit church weddings to divorced couples under 'exceptional circumstances', but distaste for the idea of rewarding adultery burned as bright as ever. 'Under no circumstances ought the guilty party, in the case of a divorce for fornication or adultery . . . be regarded, during the lifetime of the innocent party, as a fit recipient of the blessing of the church on marriage' runs a resolution agreed in 1888 and still enforced in conservative corners of the communion. Moreover, Simpson's ghost haunts not one palace, but two: Buckingham and Lambeth, residence of the Archbishop of Canterbury. The abdication caused a crisis for the Church of England as well as the monarchy, forcing it to rebuke its own Supreme Governor.

'It has happened to many a man before now to find himself beginning to fall in love with another man's wife,' wrote the then Archbishop of York. 'That is the moment of critical decision, and the right decision is that they should cease to meet before the passion is so developed as to create an agonising conflict between love and duty . . . When the power of personal attraction is reinforced by the glamour of the throne, the moral obligation is more urgent for that reason.'

Princess Margaret's love affair with Peter Townsend flipped the script – a woman in line to the throne proposing to marry a divorcée. The Queen put obstacles in her sister's way: Margaret must delay her engagement; if she subsequently proceeded with the plan, she would abjure her place in the succession and forsake the financial and organisational support her position afforded her. The intervention worked as intended. There would be no wedding.

For Charles and Camilla, securing Elizabeth's agreement to their marriage was something of a miracle. That did not resolve the ecclesiastical conundrum. A secular ceremony it must be. They consoled themselves with the prospect of staging the event in the splendour and security of Windsor Castle. Only after aides announced the plan did its glaring flaw come to light: the special licence required to turn the royal residence into a wedding venue would, for the next three years, open it to any Tom, Dick or unprincely Harry who fancied marrying there. The town's Guildhall was hastily booked instead. Elizabeth would not participate in this part of the day but agreed to attend a blessing at the castle's St George's Chapel and to host a party afterwards.

All appeared set and settled. Then, 472 years after Henry VIII's Act of Supremacy theoretically stopped the Holy See from ever again intervening in the marriage plans of English royals, Pope John Paul II died and the Vatican scheduled his funeral for 8 April, the date chosen for the royal nuptials. Palace officials, by now weary to their bones, postponed the marriage to 9 April, never mind that the horse-mad monarch would have to divide her attention between her son's second canter down the aisle and Britain's famous annual steeplechase, the Grand National.

When dawn finally broke on her happiest day, Camilla reportedly felt a little broken too, reluctant to emerge from under her duvet. When she did, it was to a service that joined her and Charles in the prayer of preparation, an admission of 'manifold sins and wickedness' written by Thomas Cranmer for Henry VIII. Still, this daughter and ex-wife of military men has never allowed adversity to rain on her parade. Photographers captured the couple laughing as they posed on the steps of the chapel after the blessing, while the wind tried to whip away the feathered confection Camilla had chosen in place of a more traditional tiara. It was a glimpse of a key dynamic between them. Alongside Diana, Charles often semaphored discomfort, turning away from her, avoiding her gaze, fiddling with his cufflinks. He and Camilla, by contrast, tend to mirror each other, engaging with a sustaining intimacy that is instantly recognisable and impossible to counterfeit.

Everyone close to Charles and Camilla appreciates the extent to which she cheers and stabilises him. This made them optimistic that the public would embrace her presence at his side. Paddy Harverson, then communications secretary to both the couple and Princes William and Harry, recalls a conversation with journalists who had converged on Windsor. Sentiment towards the wedding was positive, he told the press pack. After all, 'most people in Britain will have someone in their extended family who has been through a divorce and a second marriage; they understand that people should get a second chance at happiness'.

Contemporary polls suggest a more divided response, also captured in a news clip of a wedding-day protest outside Windsor Guildhall and shared on TikTok a quarter of a century after the event. Behind the demonstrators, a drawing of Diana is lashed to the railings like a latter-day suffragette. Charles and Camilla's behaviour has been 'despicable', a protestor complains. She appears, like most of her comrades-in-arms, to be white, of middle years and class, her 'William for King' sign urging Charles to abdicate before he has even acceded. What does she think of Camilla, an unseen reporter asks.

'She is determined to get a crown,' the protestor replies. 'She's a slut,' says a male voice off camera. 'Isn't she?' the protestor agrees. 'That's the answer to that one.'

Attitudes towards Camilla were nonetheless softening, as Harverson predicted, with media organisations leading the way. Many news outlets gave the wedding positive reviews, though two rival tabloids manufactured a negative spin, implying that the mother of the groom had telegraphed disapproval. 'One day and thirty-four years late, Charles makes his mistress Camilla his wife (and the Queen JUST managed a smile)' ran the subhead across the front page of the *Sunday Mirror*. Rupert Murdoch's *News of the World* splashed on Elizabeth frowning during the gusty photoshoot. The title, then the UK's top-selling Sunday newspaper, would be shuttered six years later amid a phone-hacking scandal that unfurled after the interception of voicemails between parties including Prince William and Harverson. Its picture desk must have worked hard to find that sour image of the Queen. Television footage shows her not only looking cheerful throughout the session, but unusually so. She would go on to toast the newlyweds with a speech as strewn with racing puns as the Grand National is with fences and ditches. 'They have overcome Becher's Brook and the Chair and all kinds of other terrible obstacles,' she told guests. Now, finally, her son was 'home and dry with the woman he loves'.

The couple and their advisers reached a different and correct judgement of Camilla's situation: that she still faced headwinds. 'The most critical debate in the period between the engagement and wedding was "what's her title going to be?" and "when he becomes king, what will happen then?"'

says Harverson. The first part proved comparatively easy. Though technically now Princess of Wales, Camilla styled herself Duchess of Cornwall. Media and the public might still refer to her as 'Mrs Parker Bowles', much as Kate and Meghan struggle to shed their maiden names, but only rarely did anyone address Camilla by her predecessor's honorific, and then only by accident. In 2014, during the couple's tour of Canada, I witnessed a Nova Scotian dignitary rehearse a speech welcoming the 'the Prince and Princess of Wales' to Halifax. The phrase, corrected by the time of their arrival, jarred, but no more so than the music that soundtracked their progress to the podium, the sea shanty, 'What Shall We Do with the Drunken Sailor?' Royal occasions often serve up portions of surreality alongside the pageantry.

Apprehensions about Camilla's rank once Charles became king proved harder to allay. While some members of the public might believe in second chances, fate had denied this opportunity to Diana, 'queen of people's hearts'. A mere 7 per cent of those polled at the time of the wedding believed Camilla deserved to be any kind of queen. However, when officials confirmed that Charles's second marriage had not been morganatic – a form of union sometimes used by blue-blooded families to prevent spouses from lower social orders from inheriting titles and estates – her rise seemed a foregone conclusion. The Palace deployed a form of words to calm tensions: Camilla aspired to ascend no higher than 'princess consort' and her designation would ultimately be 'a matter for the government of the day'. Though technically true, the phrase suggested the involvement of only one government or legislature. The reality was a little more complicated. To give any such change legal force, every commonwealth realm would have needed to pass a law adopting it.

On 5 February 2022, Elizabeth resolved the issue by releasing a statement expressing a 'sincere wish' that her daughter-in-law eventually enjoy the status to which marriage entitled her. Just over seven months later, flags hung at half-mast and Camilla, once judged to carry too much history to marry a prince, made history as the second-ever royal paramour to transition to queen consort. The first was Anne Boleyn.

These days, the word 'consort' is dusty with disuse and Queen Camilla looks unsinkable. Of course, there are choppy waters still to navigate, not least the backwash from Prince Harry's memoir, which suborned her into the fierce battle roiling the royals. For now, however, she sits on the winning side, at least as far as UK press and public opinion is concerned. When illness forced Charles and Kate to withdraw from royal duties, she took up some of the slack, gaining additional visibility and sympathy. Shortly before the 2025 International Women's Day reception, polling company YouGov revealed that she had risen to seventh most popular royal – still a divisive figure, but her ratings now in net positive territory. For Camilla, once and for years labelled the UK's 'most hated woman', in the words of biographer Robert Lacey 'the Cruella de Vil of *The Crown*'s season four', this is a triumph.

What is it that has enabled her to sustain and endure? Has she driven events or been swept along by them? Is Camilla the power behind the throne, a power in her own right, a rare example of female agency within the patrimonarchy? And if, as some allege, her route to queenship came at the expense of a princess and her sons, how does this sit with her royal work supporting women?

*

Even intimate gatherings with Elizabeth retained their protocols and formality. Camilla's is a more relaxed presence, warm, though she shivers in the frigid temperatures her husband maintains, rolling her eyes like a schoolgirl as he asks for another window to be opened and once confiding that she was wearing thermal underwear and suggesting I do the same. These touches make her seem closer to the rest of us than born royals, though this too is an illusion. Her life and yours almost certainly differ in crucial aspects. Mine and hers certainly do, our attitudes, expectations and experiences more often divergent than aligned. Initially – and much as Diana bitterly remarked – Camilla and I shared just one interest: Charles. The WOW Festival gave us another, and I soon learned of a third: we both have a passion for reading. Only recently did I recognise a fourth, more diaphanous commonality: both of us play a long game.

Charles first piqued my curiosity in 1985. Here was a man out of his element on planet earth, even in the rarified environment of our initial encounter, the St James's offices of *The Economist*, where I occupied the lowly editorial position that marked my first step into journalism. If the Prince showed no desire to connect with ordinary life, trampling over and through it as blithely as his brother Andrew, I would have dismissed him there and then as just another braying hooray, albeit a royal one. It was his obvious discomfort that fascinated me. Gaining access to him turned out to be a wearisome process, however, even after I worked out how to do it. Reaching that milestone took me almost three decades from that first meeting.

Public figures often play hard to get, but in all my years of profiling heads of state, prime ministers, tycoons and world-bestriding stars, the only person whose aides attached more onerous conditions to access was the uncharismatic French President François Hollande. Then again, my interview with Hollande coincided with the revelation of his love affair with an actress, Julie Gayet. In the UK, such a story would almost certainly pass a public interest test, the public's right to know trumping an individual's rights to privacy. The French legal system, however, criminalises non-consensual publication of information about peoples' private lives. *Closer*, the magazine that broke the story, eventually lost a privacy case to Gayet.

British privacy laws are somewhat looser, and Camilla herself has championed the right of individuals to express themselves without fear or favour. 'I believe passionately in freedom of expression. I believe freedom of expression – so long as it doesn't contravene the law, or offend others – to be at the heart of our democratic system,' she told the media-heavy audience at the 2011 London Press Awards. At a 2023 reception for the Queen's Reading Room, her online book club, she returned to the theme, urging writers to 'please remain true to your calling, unimpeded by those who may wish to curb the freedom of your expression or impose limits on your imagination'.

However, it would be foolish to assume that her patience with the exercise of this precious freedom is infinite – and should it snap, Camilla is well equipped for battle. On top of the standard mechanisms available to commoners, she has recourse to firepower reserved for the seriously wealthy plus the unique protection of special exemptions under the Freedom of Information Act. These are absolute in respect of communications relating to the sovereign and first and second in line to the throne and 'with a person who has subsequently acceded to the throne or become heir to, or second in line to, the throne'. Other family members benefit if the information in question is deemed to relate to the top royals.

The Queen might kiss me on the cheek one day and cold-shoulder me the next, embrace me or send me a writ. This of course is only fair: journalists and biographers have a duty to truth and accuracy. Moreover, she and her kith and kin have stronger reasons than most to insist on boundaries. Much of the job of royalty consists not in the doing but the being – being present, being visible, being royal. Anyone interested in royalty invariably follows the lives of its representatives because a royal's life and work can never be fully separated.

The Windsors are entitled to privacy like the rest of us, perhaps even more so because of their unique role, except when what they get up to behind closed doors potentially impacts wider society. This means that at the toughest and most personal moments of a royal's life – relationship breakdowns, deaths, births, marriages, revelations about associations with convicted paedophiles, sudden relocations to Los Angeles – the press comes knocking and is justified in doing so.

In the same way, royal aides are right to defend their charges against intrusions, though they do not always make the correct calls about how to do this or what merits action.

Biographers and journalists who tangle with the institution risk professionally damaging sanctions. Access to royal archives, hardly generous at the best of times, may suddenly be barred. Documentary projects founder because the Firm controls everything from where cameras are placed on state occasions to whether and how the footage produced may be used. Unofficial blacklists see reporters mysteriously drop off the group emails that alert members of the media to palace news and briefings. After first publication of my biography of Charles, a source told me that my name had been scored through more than once to block me from attending royal engagements. As recently as 2024, I failed to make the cut for Camilla's annual WOW International Women's Day bash. There she received a Barbie doll fashioned in her image and praised two suffragettes who hurled stones through palace windows. 'I believe they represented hope to the women who threw them, hope that, in the future, they would not be victims of their history, nor of the social and economic forces that were ranged against gender equality,' she said.

*

The most obvious first-line defence of a royal against a story they consider inaccurate or damaging is to provide an alternative narrative. Some Windsors attempt to do this directly. Diana, Charles, William, Kate, Meghan, Harry and, disastrously, Andrew, have all tried to put their own spin on events. The safer option from a public relations perspective diminishes the risk of backlash by filtering preferred messaging through unnamed palace sources, obliging reporters and friends. If challenged on this practice, everyone in the chain denies this is what happened. 'Who me, gov?'

Such counterattacks can be intimidating. When *The Times* launched a six-day serialisation of my Charles biography, the *Daily Mail* got in on the act too, publishing unofficial extracts, mysteriously obtained and imaginatively enhanced. Before anyone on Charles's team contacted me to discuss what was actually in the book or request a copy, the *Telegraph* printed a salvo against it attributed to an unnamed Clarence House source. 'She had about nine minutes with [the Prince]; to suggest she had ten minutes would be stretching it,' declared the woman or man of mystery, adding that I had been given 'the same amount of access as any other journalist.'

You had to admire the brass neck of it. My on-the-record conversation with Charles had been subject to multiple preconditions – I must not label the exchange of questions and answers in his sitting room at Birkhall on the Balmoral estate an 'interview', for example, and his aides would need to approve the text. Still, even after they edited it, removing interesting sections along with boilerplate material, there was a fair chunk left. And what of my overnight stay at Dumfries House with tours of the grounds led by Charles and dinner in the company of just twenty-three other people including him and Camilla? Most guests were wealthy donors and potential donors to his charities and initiatives whom staff, hilariously, dubbed 'Bond villains'. Then there were my second and third visits to Scotland, again to Dumfries House and for the don't-call-it-an-interview at Birkhall, when Charles and Camilla were entertaining houseguests: William, Kate and baby George. There was also an informal agreement that enabled me to interview significant numbers of Charles and Camilla's friends and aides for the book, not to mention the fact that I set out the exact terms and extent of this access in its introduction.

Of course, nobody confronted the anonymous briefer with the counterevidence, because how do you call shadows to account? Plus it made for a good story. Now-unnamed Clarence House sources threatened legal action. Still, none of them had read the actual book. The official who finally returned my calls denied the briefings came from their ranks. I might have been more inclined to believe her had William Nye, then principal private secretary to Charles and Camilla, not sent a letter to *The Times* which opened with a broadside: 'There has been ill-informed speculation recently, in your columns and elsewhere.' There had indeed, apparently from within the institution itself.

After a week or so, threats failed to materialise and book sales flourished, boosted by the furore. This, of course, is why 'never complain, never explain' is a more reliable PR strategy than outrage. My own anonymous sources ascribed the whole kerfuffle to a phenomenon I described in the book, the competition for royal favour fostering a stab first, ask later culture. 'Life at court,' I wrote, 'can be every bit as brutal as in the days when a twitching arras might signal a hidden assassin. One former householder refers to Clarence House as "Wolf Hall", in reference to the treacherous and opportunistic world depicted by Hilary Mantel in her fictionalised account of the rise of Thomas Cromwell under Henry VIII.'

A number of palace aides and interviewees, understanding the lie(s) of the land, sent messages of support and attended my book launch. Then, eleven days after the book's publication, the WOW festival brought me face to face with Camilla at a small gathering to unveil her as the organisation's president. With photographers clustering around us, she displayed the poise that is one of her defining characteristics. 'They think you're going to throw your drink over me,' I said. She laughed: 'That would be a waste.' We chatted amicably before she moved on. When, some months later, a filmmaker called on the recommendation of Clarence House to request my participation in a documentary about Charles, I asked if aides had ventured any opinions about my biography. 'Yes,' the filmmaker replied, 'that it's 98 per cent accurate.'

That cannot be said of much royal coverage, and Camilla has suffered more distortions than most. Perhaps you have heard the story about her, at the height of her unpopularity, being stoned just as Moses commanded adulteresses should be, except that the missiles were bread rolls and the venue a supermarket car park. Sources swiftly and repeatedly denied the incident, and no hard evidence of an assault with baked goods has ever emerged, whether on Camilla or the Camilla lookalike those same sources believed might have been hired to stage the drama. The tabloids themselves hinted at the latter possibility, while never admitting to such capers. Here's Emily Andrews writing in the *Sun*: 'Women would spit at her in supermarkets, her every move was trailed and although it was an actress posing for a stunt that was pelted with bread rolls in Waitrose, everyone still thinks it was Camilla.'

Some stories, such as Boleyn's sixth finger and Queen Victoria's ignorance of lesbianism too perfectly mirror our cultural prejudices to succumb easily to fact-checking. In 1998, four years after the first reports of Breadrollgate, a column-ist for the *Liverpool Echo* admitted her disappointment that the story could not be stood up. 'The picture of Mrs Parker Bowles fleeing . . . in a storm of cobs has always appealed to me,' she wrote. 'Still,' she continued, 'if Camilla ever cares to step up to the bakery department at Sainsbury's in Wootton where I shop, I'd be delighted to lob a few bread rolls at her.' Headlines from later eras demonstrate the tale's staying power. 'From a pariah pelted with bread rolls to the duchess who has won over her doubters' crowed the *Daily Mail* in 2013. 'Queen Camilla has come a long way from being pelted by bread rolls in a supermarket car park' observed *WalesOnline* in 2022.

The urban legend of Camilla's first meeting with Charles also endures despite a credible eyewitness account to the contrary. Here's how the narrative usually goes: they are both young, free-ish (no heir to the throne is ever truly free) and single, though Camilla has already dallied with Andrew Parker Bowles. The Prince wears tight jodhpurs and a light film of sweat after a vigorous game of polo. She, windswept and winsome (if, in this context, literally 'horsey'), makes the first move, issuing an invitation in that throaty voice of hers: 'My great-grandmother [Alice Keppel] was your great-great-grandfather's [Edward VII's] mistress, so how about it?'

Lucia Santa Cruz provided a different origin story when I interviewed her in 2014. She remains close to Charles since meeting him at Cambridge University, he an undergraduate, she a research assistant for the same Rab Butler whom Queen Elizabeth twice passed over as a possible prime minister. The press had assumed that Charles and Santa Cruz, daughter of the then Chilean ambassador, were an item. This was never the case, she told me, but she did propose a candidate for that role. By now living in a block of flats in Belgravia, close to Buckingham Palace, and worried that Charles 'needed more emotional life', she suggested he meet her downstairs neighbour. In her view, Camilla Shand would be just the 'human, down-to-earth, warm person' to 'appreciate him in spite of his position, and that was his greatest need,' Santa Cruz said, 'to be appreciated for what he was in spite of what he represented'. The rest is mangled history. According to Santa Cruz, it was she, not Camilla, who uttered a version of the famous line. 'I said: "Now you two watch your genes" because of Alice Keppel.'

Camilla's genes may not have predestined her to become a royal mistress, but her family background is key to understanding why she is now queen. It helped that her social set, worldviews and interests intertwined with the Windsors, but the Shand upbringing mattered more. 'People say she's tough,' Santa Cruz said to me. 'She's not tough, she's amazingly strong . . . she has the strength that people from very, very solid families tend to have.' That chimes with how her sister Lady Annabel Elliot describes their childhood to Robert Hardman in his biography of Charles: 'wonderful, really wonderful'.

Diana, battered by her formative experiences rather than tempered by them, could not provide Charles with the affirmation his alienating life left him craving. Had he recognised the common wellspring of their needs, perhaps things might have turned out differently. This, after all, is a driving force behind his charitable endeavours, the impulse to alleviate his own pain by fixing birds with broken wings. Instead he took flight, seeking refuge with the two classes of people who reliably comforted him.

From his earliest years, Charles had compensated for Philip's gruff parenting by attaching himself to father figures (Mountbatten, Laurens van der Post). That he also gravitated to women who enveloped him in affection speaks to tensions encapsulated in the phrase with which, even as an adult, he greeted his mother: 'Your Majesty Mummy'. How should a child navigate a relationship with a parent to whom one bends the knee before seeking solace for a scraped knee? In *Spare*, Harry discusses this aspect of royal culture: 'No matter how much you might love someone, you could never cross that chasm between, say, monarch and child,' he wrote. 'The older generation maintained a nearly zero-tolerance prohibition on all physical contact. No hugs, no kisses, no pats. Now and then maybe a light touching of cheeks . . . on special occasions.'

Charles's grandmother, the Queen Mother, though married into the Windsor tradition, was enough of an outsider to provide the boy prince with more substantial emotional sustenance. Santa Cruz and other platonic female friends would help fill that requirement too, as did his married paramours, most notably Lady Dale Tryon, known as Kanga. Quite a few important women in Charles's life, including aides and advisers, have been not just a little older than he, as both Santa Cruz and Camilla are, but decades his senior, and all share similar traits: outgoing, tactile and unflinchingly loyal. Nobody, however, could equal the care and devotion lavished on him over long and tumultuous years by Camilla.

Invert the sexes, and Charles and Camilla's romance might be a tale told by troubadours; Camilla the courtly hero navigating the fire-breathing dragons of the palace, public and press to rescue her prince from towering loneliness. A six-minute telephone conversation between the pair, clandestinely recorded, highlights how dearly he prized her feats of valour.

Camillagate, as this bonfire of the couple's privacy, came to be known, is even more deeply etched into our collective memory than Squidgygate, the similarly mysterious recording of Diana and James Gilbey exchanging sweet nothings. It is Charles's proposal that he live inside his lover's trousers or embed himself more deeply still, as a tampon, that makes it the stuff of folk legend. He and Camilla riff off each other's lavatorial humour before, with characteristic pessimism, the prince of wails reaches a comedic climax: 'My luck to be chucked down the lavatory and go on and on forever swirling round on the top, never going down.'

Ignore the image and their other clunking jokes, and you will notice how often Camilla offers Charles positive reinforcement, complimenting his 'awfully good brain', asking to read one of his speeches and praising his work. An exchange of *I love yous* proves so protracted that it threatens to keep the sweethearts, and whoever eavesdropped on them, awake until dawn. Charles's profusion of endearments towards Camilla are all the more striking by comparison to his famously laconic response to the idea he might love his first fiancée: 'whatever in love means.'

The most revealing exchange in Camillagate nestles among the professions of adoration, near the end of the call. Camilla expresses pride in Charles, and he returns the compliment.

'Don't be silly,' she says. 'I've never achieved anything.'

'Your great achievement,' he replies, 'is to love me.'

'Oh darling, easier than falling off a chair.'

'You suffer all these indignities and tortures and calumnies.'

Again she reassures him. 'Oh, darling, don't be so silly. I'd suffer anything for you. That's love. It's the strength of love.'

*

While some readers may recoil from the idea that loving a man might be counted a woman's crowning achievement – or that he would say such a thing out loud – Camilla is no surrendered wife. In winning, and deserving, Charles's trust, she has also gained sway within a series of systems: the patrimonarchy, the media and the more diffuse world of soft power. An accusation sometimes levelled at her is that she coveted Charles as the gateway to these things. There are obvious ripostes to that sort of thinking. The first is that sustainable love embraces the whole person. While Charles, as a personification of monarchy, needed a partner who would, in Santa Cruz's words, 'appreciate him in spite of his position', he could only build a life with someone who accepted its strictures along with the privileges. Another response to the caricature of Camilla as a gold-crown-digger is the relationship itself. It works. The third is a shrug. So what if the allegation were, at some point or to any extent, true? Women of Camilla's age and background grew up primed to secure a high-status husband as their primary vocation. If only such social prompts were confined to her generation, class and continent.

Also, it should be remembered that at least two factors prevented the path of Charles and Camilla's relationship from running smooth – her perceived unsuitability as his wife and the fact that she chose to marry Andrew Parker Bowles. In his 2018 biography of Charles, author Tom Bower apportions some blame for her decision to the pusillanimous prince. Charles, he says, rang Camilla ahead of her wedding 'sounding desperately lonely' to ask 'whether she was sure about marrying [Parker Bowles]' without offering her an alternative proposal. Bower's more damning assessment, however, is reserved for Camilla, whom he depicts reacting with cartoonish heartlessness to Charles's distress. 'After ending the call,' he writes, 'Camilla immediately repeated the conversation to her fiancé. They both laughed knowing that Charles felt isolated and depressed.' The author then summons unnamed friends to claim that, though her husband's absences and infidelities eventually pushed Camilla back into Charles's arms, she still loved Parker Bowles and was merely 'flattered by the Prince's attentions'.

While people might root for star-crossed lovers, they are less likely to sympathise with a woman who assuages the pain of betrayal by encouraging someone else's partner to stray. To what degree Camilla bears responsibility for the royal mess of Charles's first marriage is no easier to pin down than the exact timeline of Anne Boleyn's entanglement with Henry. Testimonies exist, many of them, but all are coloured by the sympathies of their narrators. In the end, all a biographer can do is zero in on what is known or can reasonably be intuited and test conclusions against the reactions of trusted sources and one's own judgement.

Blame games over affairs of the heart are anyway misconceived, except in cases where ordinary human messiness veers into abuse. My interest in revisiting these events is twofold: to determine whether anybody did overstep those boundaries, and to gain insights into Camilla's character. As consort, she may not be openly interventionist like Albert and will occupy the post for a far shorter period than Philip did, yet already she has rerouted the future of the monarchy through her relationships with, and impacts on, key royals: notably her stepsons and their wives, and, of course, Charles.

Look at any accounts of the 1980s and 1990s, whether pro-Camilla or Dianaist, and a consistent detail stands out: Camilla's affability conceals tungsten. Charles, immature for his years, kept in suspended animation by palace culture, and Diana, painfully young and vulnerable, tended to behave as people in the grips of such situations do – reflexively. In the midst of the chaos, the sole adult kept her head down and firmly on her shoulders. The debate about whether Charles, as he claimed, suspended sexual relations with Camilla before marrying Diana and maintained abstinence until that union proved, in his judgement, irretrievable, misses a bigger truth. He and Camilla never severed their emotional connection. There were always three people in the marriage, but one alone was strong.

Diana sensed Camilla's power even if she did not understand it. In a curious inversion of custom, Charles gave wedding presents as well as receiving them. Andrew Morton reported that Diana tried to break off her engagement after finding a bracelet commissioned for Camilla, its inscription 'GF' standing for the lovers' pet names for each other, Gladys and Fred. Diana failed to spot another gift destined for another of Charles's exes, jewellery for Kanga. Charles's biographer Jonathan Dimbleby confirmed the existence of the bracelet but offered a different interpretation for the initials. Charles called Camilla his 'girl Friday'. She had become indispensable to the Prince, his crutch and comfort. Diana interpreted her rival's overtures of friendship towards her during this period as intelligence gathering. Camilla seems unlikely to have taken on such a mission unilaterally. A more plausible theory, suggested by sources with some knowledge of these events, is that Charles saw Camilla as the person best placed to induct his fiancée into his life. After all, she knew him and his ways intimately. If accurate, this is the detail among all others that comes closest to crossing the line from the disordered impulses common to such situations to something colder. Even if Charles, at this stage, lacked the emotional intelligence to grasp how misguided the idea was, you might have expected Camilla to demur.

That she did not suggests both a capacity for ruthlessness and a mitigating reason for it. For years, and in all things, his girl Friday has put Charles first. This does not mean she is subservient to him, though the phrase often carries that connotation. It comes from Daniel Defoe's 1719 novel *Robinson Crusoe*, in which the hero frees a prisoner from cannibals, then trains him as a personal servant, his 'man Friday', christened for the day of his rescue. The first usage of 'girl Friday' to describe a personal assistant or female dogsbody dates to the 1920s. Howard Hawks' 1940 movie *His Girl Friday* injected the concept with more vigour. Though Rosalind Russell's character, a journalist, is professionally subordinate to her spouse, a newspaper editor played by Cary Grant, ultimately accepting him on his terms despite his foibles and follies, she retains the upper hand because he is dotingly dependent on her.

So too Charles with Camilla. This creates a balance between them that pomp and his position could otherwise permanently skew. Inevitably, Camilla's emotional and domestic sovereignty draws criticism. Originally disparaged as a homewrecker, too long in the tooth to be toothsome, once embedded in the monarchy, she began to be attacked for her agency. Always she has set rules and boundaries with a surety other immigrants to Planet Windsor struggle to achieve. She still maintains a separate home – Ray Mill, the Wiltshire house she bought after her divorce, escaping there periodically to rest and recuperate. It is her own space. Aides build downtime into her schedules rather than imposing the relentless pace favoured by Charles. She stops for food and occasional lie-downs as needed. He used to forgo food during the day, but kingship and cancer have eroded his resistance. On the eve of the coronation, he hosted a lunch for the governors-general and prime ministers of his realms. His queen chose not to attend, according to Robert Hardman 'pacing herself before the trip to the abbey'.

She shows a similar grit about court practices, observing the required etiquettes at moments of high ceremony and otherwise conducting herself much as she always did. Her family anchors her, though the ranks of its older generations are thinning. Osteoporosis shortened the lives of her mother, Rosalind, and maternal grandmother, Sonia Keppel, spurring Camilla to become patron of a charity devoted to combating the disease and eventually take on its presidency, giving the organisation, now renamed the Royal Osteoporosis Society, a prominence it might otherwise have struggled to achieve. Her father, Bruce, survived to walk her down the civil aisle at her second wedding, dying the following year. In 2014, her younger brother, Mark, an adventurer in the old-school mould, the author of travel books and founder of an elephant conservation charity, fell outside New York's Gramercy Park Hotel, sustaining fatal brain injuries.

Remaining family members assembled for her enthronement, with some occupying official roles in proceedings, her sister acting as Camilla's attendant, their grandchildren as pages of honour. After the coronation, this portion of the Shand clan reappeared to wave at the rain-sodden crowds from the balcony of Buckingham Palace. During the closing years of Elizabeth II's reign, only working royals had been invited to stand alongside the Queen.

In his biography of Charles, Tom Bower interprets Camilla's determination to do things her way not as a woman preserving health and sanity in a system capable of destroying both, but as self-indulgence. His version of Camilla – congenitally lazy and a bit of a slattern – is assumed like that other famous divorcée Wallis Simpson to be 'a skilled mistress', deploying sexual wiles to get ahead. Far from cocooning Charles, Bower's Camilla terrorises him, 'laying down the law', 'snapping' and goading him and aides in her eagerness for their relationship to be made official. Her success in this endeavour is also construed as a negative: 'The accepted view of a woman whose youth had been exclusively focused on social excitement, especially parties and hunting, making good in middle age was entirely accurate,' the author concludes.

By 2022, however, Bower had transferred his animus to Meghan, dubbing her a 'brazen hussy' during an interview with Meghan-fan-turned-scourge, Piers Morgan. Bower's book about the Sussexes, published the following month, recast Camilla as 'a practical, solid English upper-middle-class woman . . . grounded and not grand . . . a no-nonsense, self-deprecating plain speaker with a good sense of humour who, when necessary, displayed a stiff upper lip'. Unlike Charles,

Camilla 'could see through the American actress's coquettish smiles and tactile performance'. That infernal seesaw returns, but this time viewed from the opposite direction: for one royal woman to fall, another must rise. Bower refashions Camilla into a role model for royalty to make her a credible critic of his new target, Meghan.

His conversion is notable both for its speed and its tardiness. By the time of Elizabeth's platinum jubilee, just months before her death and Charles's accession, Camilla's rehabilitation was well advanced. Though the calm advice of Paddy Harverson did much to help her to reach this point, he built on the labours of an earlier aide, Mark Bolland. The former director of the Press Complaints Commission (PCC), Bolland joined Charles's staff in 1996 as assistant private secretary, winning promotion the following year to deputy PS, Camilla's de facto private secretary. The former gamekeeper to media standards quickly demonstrated his skill as a poacher, bagging favourable publicity for his charges even as some of his methods raised hackles. His ultimate goal, an anonymous insider told journalist Valentine Low, 'was to get the *Daily Mail* and the *Sun* to like Camilla'. And the way to do that? To give these newspapers 'tons of stories', not necessarily about the royals who employed him.

*

Folk wisdom holds that when a publicist becomes the story, it is time for him to go. A *Telegraph* article in December 2001 headed 'Has the puppet-master of St James's finally pulled one string too many?' marked that moment for Bolland. A month earlier he had walked to the podium to collect one of his industry's top awards: PR Professional of the Year, in recognition of how effectively he had changed the mood music around his employers. He achieved this feat in part by deploying the favoured royal trick of show-not-tell, in 1999 stage-managing the first image of Charles and Camilla's non-negotiable, post-Diana togetherness. When they emerged from her sister's birthday party at the Ritz hotel, so many flashbulbs lit the London sky that the British Epilepsy Association warned broadcasters against transmitting more than five seconds of footage. Another photo opportunity saw the couple modelling family harmony as Prince William joined them at a reception for the PCC, by then under the stewardship of Bolland's future husband, Guy Black.

There was, however, a rougher side to Bolland's playbook, or so anonymous sources alleged. The piece dubbing him a puppet master claimed that he traded unflattering stories about Prince Edward and his wife, Sophie, herself still a PR executive, for better coverage for Charles and Camilla.

'Many in royal circles now believe,' wrote journalist Peter Foster, 'that Mr Bolland is not content simply to promote the interests of his boss by whispering calculated indiscretions over lunch at fashionable restaurants like the Ivy or Le Caprice. In the minutely plotted world of spin and manipulation, it seems that if the Prince's stock is to rise, another's must fall. [Edward and Sophie] are not alone in believing that they have been the victim of an aggressive campaign to blacken their names.'

Other royals cited as collateral damage to Bolland's project were Andrew (entirely capable of trashing his own reputation, thank you), Philip and William, the last of whom, the piece revealed, nicknamed his father's employee 'Lord Blackadder' after the scheming TV-comedy character. Though Harry did not appear on the list, his memoir cites an unnamed 'spin doctor' as the source of tabloid leaks about his first meeting with Camilla, a watershed he characterises as 'just like getting an injection'. It will not have been easy for him, just a year after Diana's death, to sit down with his dad's girlfriend, but *Spare* paints Harry and his brother as initially sympathetic to Camilla. After all, Harry muses, she had 'been trapped like everyone else in the riptide of events. We didn't blame her, and in fact we'd gladly forgive her if she could make Pa happy.' Their father too is cut some slack. He 'deserved a proper companion. That was why, when asked, Willy and I promised Pa that we'd welcome Camilla into the family. The only thing we asked in return was that he not marry her.'

Charles would disappoint his sons on that score, but the book airs more serious allegations against Camilla: 'Shortly after our private summits with her, she began to play the long game, a campaign aimed at marriage and eventually the Crown,' Harry claims. How to do this? By currying favour with the media. 'Stories began to appear everywhere, in all the papers, about her private conversation with Willy, stories that contained pinpoint accurate details, none of which had come from Willy of course. They could only have been leaked by the one other person present. And the leaking had obviously been abetted by the new spin doctor Camilla had talked Pa into hiring.'

In fact, another aide, Amanda McManus, soon took responsibility for the first of those stories, falling on her sword after explaining that her then-husband, who worked within

Rupert Murdoch's empire, had told a colleague about William's parlay with Camilla. Rehired just days after her resignation, McManus went on to serve for decades as Camilla's closest aide, re-emerging from a brief retirement to become a trustee of the Queen's Reading Room. Bolland, who left royal employment in 2002, would deny that he had smeared other Windsors, instead accusing courtiers jealous of his success of tarring him with a technique they themselves used. 'It's a very medieval environment [full of] jealousies and intrigues and backstabbing and plots . . . The received wisdom at Buckingham Palace was always that provided the Prince of Wales was down the Queen would stay up.'[18]

It is impossible at this distance to draw firm conclusions about who briefed which stories and on whose instructions, if any. Certainly my own experience endorses Bolland's characterisation of the courts, but he neglects to mention how closely each reflects the character of its principals. Elizabeth always ran a tidier, less passionate ship than her eldest son, instinctively recoiling from publicity and undertaking the bare minimum. Until the closing years of her reign, the atmosphere around Charles and Camilla remained febrile and their attitudes to the media significantly more conflicted. It is easy to see why. Without the turnaround in public opinion, they might never have married, never have been able to plan a joint coronation, yet Charles, who had long relied on journalists to spotlight his causes and organisations, fiercely resented both a lack of attention to these things and any coverage that departed from his desired script.

They were also aware that staff might not always remain loyal, no matter that most sign non-disclosure agreements. In

2002, Bolland departed, apparently on good terms, still undertaking projects for Charles and Camilla until the following year. After that contract came to an end, he expanded his portfolio to encompass a stint as a gossip columnist for the *News of the World*, writing under the mischievous pen name 'Blackadder'. Remaining bridges to his erstwhile bosses went up in smoke when he provided a witness statement in support of the *Mail on Sunday* during its 2006 legal battle with Charles. Ultimately, the high court agreed with the royal plaintiff that his copyright had been infringed, and his confidentiality breached by the newspaper publishing excerpts from a diary he kept during the handover of Hong Kong. The same outlet would lose a similar case to Meghan over a letter she wrote to her father.

In the meantime, *News of the World* royal editor Clive Goodman had taken over Bolland's 'Blackadder' column – an editorial move that the newspaper's proprietors swiftly came to rue. Clarence House alerted the police after noticing that some of the stories Goodman ran could only have emerged from listening to private voicemails.

These revelations led to further, and crueller, discoveries. The parents of missing schoolgirl Milly Dowler had taken heart from the fact that she appeared to be accessing messages they left for her. In fact, she was already dead, murdered by her abductor, and the people trawling her voicemails were journalists from the *News of the World* and the private investigator contracted to them. After public outrage made the tabloid too toxic to sustain, the scandal rumbled on, embroiling other titles and organisations in claims and counterclaims.

Investigations and lawsuits have identified culprits, though not many, while laying bare a wider toll. Stories obtained by hacking not only breached the privacy of individuals but ruined friendships and destroyed trust. The subjects of articles obtained by these means naturally blamed people close to them for peddling information to the press. Moreover, hacking was merely one tool available. *What Price Privacy?*, a report issued by the Information Commissioner, detailed 'a widespread and organised undercover market in confidential personal information' stretching back years, which exploited evolving technologies and human susceptibilities to gain knowledge of everything from trivia to tragedy. Officials, including police, took bribes. Innocent parties fell victim to blagging, a practice in which perpetrators 'pretend to be someone they are not in order to wheedle out the information they are seeking'. Such scams saw reporters and private investigators pose as relatives of hospital patients or health visitors to obtain confidential medical records and even genetic material. Within this context, it seems possible that at least a few of the revelations Harry blames on his stepmother may, in fact, be the product of the dark arts he continues to challenge in the courts.

If this is not something he acknowledges, that may be because of his and Camilla's sharply divergent approaches to the media. While the Prince battles British news organisations, Camilla cultivates connections with them. The current Buckingham Palace communications director is Tobyn Andreae, a former deputy editor at the *Daily Mail* and *Mail on Sunday*. In 2022, Camilla raised eyebrows after the guest list to her private Christmas lunch included not only those queens of the stage and screen, Judi Dench and Maggie Smith, but also notorious Meghantagonists, Piers Morgan and TV-presenter and columnist Jeremy Clarkson. Two days after this cosy get-together, the *News of the World*'s surviving sibling, the *Sun* published a diatribe by Clarkson. He hated Meghan, he declared, and was 'dreaming of the day she is made to parade naked through the streets of every town in Britain while the crowds chant, "Shame!" and throw lumps of excrement at her'.

Online conspiracists accused Camilla of teeing up the piece, but Clarkson boasts a long record of supposedly comedic controversialism. A truck driver's day, he once joked, consists of 'change gear, change gear, check the mirror, murder a prostitute, change gear, change gear, murder'. Attempts to open television to wider talent pools prompted a tired complaint – 'If one presenter on a show is a blond-haired, blue-eyed heterosexual boy, the other must be a black Muslim lesbian.' His Meghan item sat within an established pattern.

That still leaves open the question of why Camilla rolls out the red carpet for people whose views appear to be at odds with the values of organisations she represents. Her defenders interpret the presence of guests from across the spectrum as an example of best practice in royal terms – the family is meant to be politically neutral. One of her admirers also ventures that she nose-holds for the sake of good media relations. That is both true and misleading. She does prize media relations, but the phrase implies discomfort with some parts of the spectrum. That overlooks a history of associations and instincts at odds with the kindly, liberal version of her showcased at WOW events or in 2024's *Her Majesty the Queen: Behind Closed Doors*, a documentary spotlighting her efforts to raise awareness of domestic and sexual violence.

Some discrepancies are easily explicable. Horizons expand, views change and few of us can claim to be relentlessly consistent. Camilla's universe includes friends of many stripes. Emma Thompson told me about an exchange over dinner the year after Diana died. As Thompson and her partner, fellow actor Greg Wise, discussed the arrest of former Chilean dictator Augusto Pinochet, whose regime deployed torture and 'disappeared' more than three thousand people, Camilla urged Charles to lend Pinochet a plane to freedom. Charles responded with amusement, knowing Thompson to be, in her words, 'a raving lefty'. 'I don't think,' he said, 'that Em would approve.'

Just as Camilla's support for feminist organisations and causes does not make her a progressive, so her failed plea on behalf of Pinochet fails to identify her as a raving righty. Her position might well have been informed by Lucia Santa Cruz, whose brother campaigned to liberate the general.

My reading of Camilla is that her personal loyalties transcend ideology; she seems pragmatic and strategic, rather than evangelistic. Given her day job, I would guess that her feminism is less of the variety that aims for systemic and structural change and instead focuses on smaller incremental gains. While a Dianaist theory holds that Camilla has invaded their heroine's territory to feminism-wash herself, she certainly sounds sincere.

Indeed, her public pronouncements often go beyond platitudinous empowerment-speak to address the tougher issues and realities of inequality. She has discussed sexual assault, female genital mutilation and coercive control with those who bear the scars. She does not wait to be asked but offers help – for example, in 2021 contacting human rights barrister and peer Helena Kennedy, then in the process of organising the evacuation of female judges, prosecutors and lawyers and their families from Afghanistan, to ask what she could do. That same year, she spoke eloquently at the launch of a project aiming to shift the blame felt by victims of violence to its perpetrators and enablers. The power of her language was striking; so too was the dissonance when she urged those present to get 'the men in our lives' engaged in the anti-violence movement. Her brother-in-law Andrew was at that moment preparing to contest Giuffre's lawsuit against him.

Even so, her willingness to speak about sexual violence is notable – and not only because royalty generally shies away from crunchier themes. Her beloved, of course, did not reliably do so, but Charles possesses none of Camilla's innate caution. While the aims of the charity he founded, originally the Prince's Trust, now the King's Trust, these days seem uncontroversial, his impulse to address the lack of opportunities for young people in 1980s Britain could easily be read as a reproof of Margaret Thatcher's pull-yourself-up-by-your-own-bootstraps monetarism. His advocacy on topics from architecture to the environment has inflamed opinion as well as uniting it, driven by a sense of urgency and his own self-assembled blend of philosophies and religious beliefs.

Camilla, a skilled player of the long game, understands the limitations of royalty. At the time she began to focus on gender equality, the move mirrored the political consensus. Now some of her friends in the media are rebranding the ideal as dangerous wokery. Will she stick to her guns as culture wars rage? I sought opinions from a wide range of sources, including former palace insiders. One replied with a question: 'You like her, don't you?'

'She seems likeable,' I deflected.

'Oh, she is,' the source concurred, 'until she isn't.' The source clarified. This was not a criticism, but rather an observation. Camilla could be 'flinty'. And her core beliefs? A shrug.

*

The source was not wrong that I am predisposed to like this queen who backs the WOW Festival, spoke to me with sensitivity after the death of my husband, and so visibly cheers up her own spouse. She is entertaining to be around, not an attribute in oversupply across the royal estate. However, the single biggest factor that inclines me to view her positively is the esteem in which she is held by women I admire.

Jude Kelly, who created WOW during her stint as artistic director of the Southbank Centre, sees Camilla as a force for good. The Queen is empathetic and driven, 'a very good woman who thinks, as many of us do, there but for the grace of god go I,' says Jude.

Camilla took on the presidency of WOW in 2015, but the idea germinated earlier, during an event for the Women's Prize for Fiction, when she and Jude fell into a debate about the award entries. Realising, to her surprise, that the royal 'had read all the books', Jude told her about WOW. 'How interesting,' said Camilla, a phrase that from Queen Elizabeth often signalled the opposite emotion. Camilla, though, followed through, inviting Jude to Clarence House for further discussions. Jude found her to be 'engaged and fun and curious. And obviously I talked about the range of subject matters that WOW covers.

We always make a point of having some snazzy titles like "I am a feminist – can I vajazzle?", for example. She was completely unfazed by the candour. In fact, I think it actually excited her.'

As president of the WOW Foundation, Camilla promotes the organisation and its aims, interacting with survivors and victims, activists and refugees and 'women trembling with fear because of their experiences'. Jude, who has travelled with her to Jordan, Gambia, Ghana, the United States, New Zealand, Australia and Rwanda, says the royal makes the effort to understand women's stories 'not as a PR exercise, but as a genuine act of equalising'.

The calculation for WOW sounds straightforward, but there will always be questions about the extent to which any royal can move the dial or merely burnishes the status quo. In 2022, these tensions sparked a debate within Southall Black Sisters (SBS), a specialist support service aimed at minoritised women and combining crisis intervention work with campaigning. The team had received an invitation to a reception at Buckingham Palace designed to spotlight violence against women and girls and the sector engaged in combatting it. SBS had a strong motive to accept: the charity always needs money. 'Increased visibility could lead to increased funding which was important for the services we run,' wrote Rahila Gupta, who has served as SBS chair and on its management committee. Her article in the *Independent* explained why SBS had nonetheless declined, worried that the event would be 'a PR exercise for Camilla and would make the Palace look good at our expense'. Moreover, 'there was no invitation to speak, only attend, which meant that we couldn't even get our message across to the great and good'.

'Thank God we didn't go,' Rahila says now. 'Thank God we didn't muddy our hands.' The reception did not make the Palace look good at attendees' expense; rather, it made the Palace look bad at the expense of two attendees. At first, it appeared to go swimmingly, attracting a high turnout. Camilla gave a brief speech about the importance of listening to survivors of violence. The first sign of trouble came later that day, when Ngozi Fulani, the founder of Sistah Space, a service for women of African and Caribbean heritage who have experienced violence and abuse, posted on social media. Fulani's account was endorsed by a witness, Mandu Reid, then leader of the Women's Equality Party, the first Black woman to helm a UK political party. As their posts went viral, Mandu emailed me, the party's co-founder. A palace aide, she explained, had persisted in asking Fulani where she was from, apparently unable to countenance the idea that she might be British. 'It made us feel like we didn't belong,' Mandu wrote.

By now, old media was picking up and cannibalising the story. While initial responses to Fulani's post had been sympathetic, the backlash swiftly gathered pace and ferocity. The aide turned out to be Lady Susan Hussey, Prince William's godmother; a former woman of the bedchamber to the late queen whom Camilla retained as a lady of the household, an honorary – unpaid – role. Within days, Hussey resigned. Soon Sistah Space announced its temporary closure over safety concerns. Meanwhile, as online allegations triggered a Charity Commission investigation, Fulani also stepped back from her role.

The organisers of the reception briefly copped criticism too: how had they thought it a good idea to mix an old-school retainer like Hussey, then eighty-three, with this particular set of guests? Prince Harry leapt to her defence. 'Meghan and I love Susan Hussey,' he told ITV News. 'And I also know that what she meant – she never meant any harm at all.' In a US interview, he contrasted Hussey's swift apology and departure to the failure of the Palace to issue a statement about Jeremy Clarkson's 'horrific and hurtful and cruel' diatribe against Meghan. 'The world is asking for some form of comment from the monarchy. But the silence is deafening. To put it mildly . . . Everything to do with my wife, after six years, they haven't said a single thing.' Only one key player was left unscathed by the turmoil: Camilla.

*

Hers has been an extraordinary arc, from hate figure to media darling, enemy of women – or one in particular – to advocate for gender equality. By the time you read this, however, the shock waves from the Epstein scandal or some other unforeseen news might have shifted the narrative again. Her husband's cancer came as an unexpected hammer blow. Yes, he was already, by some standards, old on assuming kingship, but nothing to the ages his parents and maternal grandmother attained. Camilla too has suffered health problems, including a bout of pneumonia in 2024. For now, both continue in their regal roles, sustained by each other as well as more prosaic regimens.

One thing is certain: people in the public eye, however acute their instincts or adept their PR advisers, never fully control their own stories. Social media has further weakened their grip, often in the oddest of ways. TikTok, for example, is breathing new life into the dead princess, awash with posts garlanded with heart emojis and comments such as 'Diana is strong as fuk [sic]'.

Many feeds make dark claims about Camilla. It is not always easy to work out who operates these accounts or to what purpose. While ardent Dianaists make up a growing segment – with an evident crossover between her fans and Meghan's – a proportion of activity on all social media platforms is driven by troll farms and state-sponsored actors working to destabilise countries, societies and systems. That is only getting worse.

A quick search of Camilla's name in combination with Diana's instantly turns up the real footage of the Windsor wedding day protest, plus a slew of fake news. 'Princess Anne', morphed into a ventriloquist's dummy by AI, declares she will never bow to Camilla. 'Prince William' seethes against his stepmother. Falsified TV reports make absurd claims, for instance that the Queen is planning to 'take over the Palace' to install her (adult) children there and that she has broken down in court after being found guilty of Diana's murder. Genuine film and stills of both women are interspersed with photoshopped pictures of Camilla in the dock.

Laugh if you must, but people and populations lacking the context within which to situate and dismiss such allegations may well buy into them. Social media companies are notoriously reluctant to remove hate speech or libel or to stop deleted content from being reposted. Many posts fall below the thresholds that theoretically trigger takedowns. There are few, if any, legal sanctions against general nastiness. Misogyny and sexism are not only permitted but embedded in many cultures by misogynistic and sexist laws. More countries than you might imagine still restrict women's reproductive choices; permit men to earn more for work of equal value than their female counterparts; bar women from participation in politics and whole industries and areas of working life; deny women the right to remarry; allow rapists to go unpunished if they marry their victims, and demand that a wife obeys her husband. Jeffrey Epstein did not act alone or in a vacuum but with the help of hundreds of accomplices and enablers in a culture of impunity.

This should be our focus, not reheated or confected battles between royal women. So, go ahead: compare Camilla to Diana as if they were heifers at a county fair. Nobody can stop you. But remember, if you do, that the impacts of indulging in this activity extend beyond individuals and institutions, damaging democracies and entrenching hatreds. Careless talk costs lives and causes devastation, as the subjects of my last two chapters, Kate and Meghan, know only too well.

Chapter 7

Kate: 'What Can't She Do?'

It would have been quite the high-profile death, run over not just by any royal but the unrivalled superstar among working Windsors. Listening to a recent biography on audiobook while walking to meet a rare source, I failed to hear the convoy speeding down a side street towards the Embankment. The first vehicles passed me with a whump of air, blue lights flashing, black paintwork gleaming, and then I saw her through tinted glass darkly, facing the road ahead, neither pixilated nor blurry, solid flesh, but gone in an instant like a dream.

Journalists covering the event that brought her to this part of the city sounded equally startled by her presence. She looked 'amazing', they declared. Headlines referred to her 'surprise appearance'. 'The fashion crowd in London is generally known for keeping cool,' noted the *New York Times*. But 'the editors and designers at a ceremony for one of the industry's most pres-tigious local awards became palpably excited when Catherine, Princess of Wales, emerged'.

Google her names (any of them) and newer results come back studded with the same trio of adjectives: 'beautiful', 'radiant', 'perfect'. The biography that played through my headphones that day extols her as 'a beautiful symbol of the

Crown' whose 'unwavering presence and radiant spirit serve as a beacon of hope and stability in uncertain times'. Her schoolmates recall her as 'the perfect pupil' while the book's author, veteran royal correspondent Robert Jobson, detects not a single flaw in the adult woman. To him, she exemplifies 'the quintessential image of a picture-perfect princess', always 'perfectly turned out' with her 'perfect ectomorph body type that makes her couture outfits look chic'. Not only that, but she and her husband are Britain's 'perfect envoys for the post-Brexit era'.

Most press coverage in the UK is similarly hagiographic. The question 'what can't she do?', meant rhetorically – and routinely posed by feature writers and her devoted fan base – drew an unexpected response from her husband during a 2025 tour of a community project on the Isle of Mull. After the Duchess of Rothesay – her title in Scotland – used a nail gun to fix a few tiles to a frame, an onlooker exclaimed: 'What can't she do?' William gave a theatrical sigh, the *Sun* reported, 'and admitted proudly: "That always happens."'

The visit, which also encompassed stops at an early-learning initiative, a croft restaurant and a ferry ride to the smaller island of Iona, earned the kind of rolling commentary more usually associated with peace talks or hostage negotiations. Admittedly, it marked two milestones: the couple's fourteenth anniversary, and Catherine's first overnight stay on official business since the end of cancer therapy. Yet even before her sudden absence from public life and fragile re-emergence, the princess had attained a mythic quality, her light workload, once a source of criticism, now a wellspring of her power. Elusive as the hind in Thomas Wyatt's sonnet to Anne Boleyn, her manifestations are fleeting and all the more impactful for that.

How did it happen, this transformation from sporty public-school girl to glamorous wraith; ordinary to extraordinary; fodder for spiteful columnists to immaculate press darling; from tame Kate to remote, unknowable Catherine? Luck – good and bad – offers only part of the answer. Strategy and self-preservation play a key role too. The Art History graduate has turned curator, controlling her own image with the dedication of Elizabeth I and the caution of Elizabeth II. Her constructed persona appears not of our times but outside of them, the styles and hemlines that located her firmly in this century banished from her wardrobe. Apply a retro filter and you might easily imagine her in the same frame as Wallis Simpson, if maintaining a cool distance to the American interloper, or departing the Grand Hotel like Greta Garbo.

If she wants to be alone in determining who she is and what she means, that is understandable. Jobson's biography describes her as a 'modern-day Cinderella', but this fairytale more closely resembles *The Little Mermaid* – a girl from Berkshire surrendering her voice and freedom for the love of a prince.

The transaction occurred on April Fool's Day, 2004. It was the *Sun* who broke the agreement between Palace and press to leave Diana's boys in peace during their studies by publishing a 'world exclusive': a paparazzi shot snatched on a snowy mountainside in Klosters, William to Kate's left, five words to her right, 'FINALLY . . . Wills gets a girl'.

In that instant, the old Kate Middleton, a private individual, ceased to exist, leaving the new Kate Middleton to smile and endure the priapic lenses. She did so silently. Her friends, if they spoke at all, said nothing of note, possibly because there was nothing noteworthy, in media terms, to say. Also, real friends don't blab (unless asked to do so), and she inspires loyalty. Her absence of scandalous 'history', while qualifying her as suitable royal marriage material, limited press lines of inquiry. Hacking her phone – one journalist, the *News of the World*'s Clive Goodman, would admit to doing so 155 times over a nine-month period – produced no juicy scoops. Visuals became her curse and currency.

True, her family yielded additional narratives: a sister, Pippa, objectified; a mother, Carole, accused of vaunting ambition; a brother, James, then not yet seventeen, who identified his sudden loss of anonymity as a trigger for subsequent battles with depression. There was the requisite garrulous relative too, Gary Goldsmith, Kate's 'infamous uncle' by his own description. To weave a rags-to-riches storyline, journalists resolutely overlooked the family's wealth and lofty antecedents. Her paternal grandmother came from a line of landed gentry stretching back to a man who served as provost of Eton college and chaplain to kings Henry VII and Henry VIII. No matter: the fact that Kate's maternal great-grandfather had toiled down the mines made better copy. Headlines positioned the royal squeeze not only as a commoner but a member of the proletariat: 'Kate, the coal miner's girl'.

This narrative soon mutated, with the Middleton women – and only the women – coming under attack for their imagined social aspirations. That trope gingered up the online comments sections, a boon for digital ad sales. While additional plot developments would surely follow – marriage, probably, and kids, or maybe a break-up – editors crave jam today. For more than two decades the media has feasted on Kate's body, anatomising, exposing and critiquing it.

That such attention to women and girls in the public eye is bad for all women and girls is well documented. Research shows that female populations suffer from a constant barrage of imagery that reinforces unobtainable and often unhealthy ideals. Recent research examining the use of a single telling word by UK tabloids, 'flaunt', in connection with stories about celebrities' weight loss, concluded that this coverage could 'contribute towards the pervasive unsolicited sexualisation of women, and exacerbate adverse body image and mental health issues'.[19] What is less widely acknowledged is the effect on these celebrities themselves. Many of them, far from expanding to take up space, dwindle to shadows. There are other reasons too. Caught in the machinery of celebrity, they exercise their last vestige of control by subjugating their own bodies to extreme diets or to signal distress to an oblivious world.

Nor is thinness the only attribute famous women are assumed to flaunt. To be photographed with buttocks or breasts is to be accused of flaunting curves. To be pregnant is to flaunt, in the twee terminology of mass media, a 'baby bump'. To age, as all humans do, is to flaunt wrinkles. This last example is, of course, fake news. Cellulite and eyebags do indeed please the press, but only as a pretext for mock concern: 'I sincerely hope that it was Prince William's turn to do the early childcare shift at the weekend,' wrote *Mail* columnist Sarah Vine in 2015. 'Because judging by pictures of Kate out shopping in Chelsea on Friday afternoon, she was long overdue a lie-in.'

Denizens of the entertainment industry increasingly seek refuge in cosmetic interventions that make them look different, if not always younger or prettier, cheeks round and hard as unripe apricots, mouths like air mattresses with slow punctures. If they admit to having 'work' done, that simply adds to the pressure on everyone else to do likewise, a way, as writer and critic Sarah Manavis wrote in the *Observer*, 'for the culture to say what it has always wanted to all along: now that you have all the information, you are the only thing keeping you from being hotter'.

The patrimonarchy, though no less prescriptive about how its women should look and act, diverges from the wider patriarchy on such interventions, preferring a more traditional model of growing old: fascinators traded for headscarves and any tweakments so discreet as to be undetectable. Even those royals based in Montecito, an enclave where unmodified teeth are more conspicuous than blinding veneers, remain recognisably themselves, at least for now.

This does not deter press and public from jumping to different conclusions. Speculation about Meghan's theoretical enhancements has accompanied her since the only documented one, from plain Ms Markle to HRH the Duchess of Sussex. Nor has her sister-in-law escaped this line of inquiry. The crimes against journalism contained in a January 2024 magazine article, 'Has Kate Middleton Had Plastic Surgery?', would be funny if such crimes were victimless. Published in response to the announcement that Kate had been admitted to hospital for an abdominal procedure, it contains the following lines. 'While Kate has not confirmed ever going under the knife, Dr Ryan Neinstein of Neinstein Plastic Surgery exclusively tells *In Touch* that he thinks she has had a tummy tuck. According to the doctor, who has not treated Kate, there has been a "60 per cent increase in demand in the past year for these types of procedures"'. Just say Neinstein to this sort of clickbait.

Not that we should ignore the intrusions visited on famous women. The predicament is how best to illuminate the damage they do without amplifying mendacious claims, replicating press incursions or sparking manufactured firestorms. Hilary Mantel saw her essay 'Royal Bodies' reduced from nearly six thousand thoughtful words to a clutch of screaming headlines. Her attackers wilfully misconstrued her empathy for Kate, then pregnant with her first child and in the grips of hyperemesis gravidarum – severe morning sickness – as hostility. The *Wolf Hall* author accurately observed that reporting tended to render Kate 'a shop-window mannequin'. 'These days,' Mantel added, 'she is a mother-to-be and draped in another set of threadbare attributions. Once she gets over being sick, the press will find that she is radiant. They will find that this young woman's life until now was nothing, her only point and purpose being to give birth.'

Mantel 'writes great books, but I think what she's said about Kate Middleton is completely misguided and completely wrong,' protested then prime minister David Cameron. It seems unlikely that he had read to the end of the piece. Her criticism was directed not at Kate but her portrayal in the media. 'Cheerful curiosity,' Mantel wrote, 'can easily become cruelty. It can easily become fatal. We don't cut off the heads of royal ladies these days, but we do sacrifice them, and we did memorably drive one to destruction a scant generation ago. History makes fools of us, makes puppets of us, often enough. But it doesn't have to repeat itself.'

I hope that this book helps to break the cycle that traduces royal women at the expense of all women, but the press shows little inclination to change its spots, its embrace of Kate, Meghan and other female Windsors as vampiric as ever. News organisations, locked in a toxic relationship with the online platforms that have destroyed their business models, just as often hoover up content from them as break stories themselves. Those platforms are, of course, running wild, polarised and vicious, with deep fakes and pornography but a single incautious search term away. Princess Anne, who in her youth experienced the special treatment editors lavish on nubile women, raised her concerns in a documentary marking her seventieth birthday. At least, she said, 'there was no social media in my day'; the digital insurgency, she surmised, 'has probably made it more difficult' for rising generations of royals. This most resilient of Windsors senses that she too might struggle under the combined onslaught of legacy media and evolving forms of communication.

As apps and chatbots harness generative AI, the nature of this threat shapeshifts and swells. Kate and her in-laws are being puppeteered by artificial intelligence, their eery likenesses pressed into deep fakery, their real, in-person appearances doubted. Footage of Kate at a farm shop before her return to public life was widely written off as a forgery; her presence at the Trooping of the Colour explained away as a clone, a double or 'her sister with plastic surgery'.

When prominent women speak about the cumulative effects of these phenomena on their mental health, their testimonies earn plaudits – often from the outlets and online hordes that pulled them apart in the first place. Royal women find themselves in a uniquely invidious position, expected not only to grimace and bear these affronts, but to submit themselves to additional probing. Everything that lies beneath their famous exteriors, from blood to bone and, deeper still, to cell division, whether regulated or uncontrolled, can be construed to carry implications for the monarchy. Actors act, singers sing, yet royalling is a nebulous profession. The job for all but the sovereign consists of 'support[ing] the King in his many state and national duties' and 'carry[ing] out important work in the areas of public and charitable service', according to the royals' own website.

This rubric fails to mention their other core dynastic duty: securing the institution by marrying and reproducing. Because the monarchy sustains itself through its members, any spouse a royal chooses is considered a matter of public interest, so too every aspect of the reproductive process, should the resulting union prove fertile. The *Sun*'s editorial made this explicit on the day it splashed on those first confirmatory images of Kate at Klosters: 'One of William's girlfriends could become queen one day. Her subjects will be entitled to know *all* about her.'

*

That morning, no matter how grounded Kate was, the wave of interest that crashed over her head could easily have uprooted her, and this was just the beginning of her trial by media. The couple were in their early twenties, yet soon the sniping started, its inevitable target not William but Kate, mocked for her presumed failure to march him down the aisle, a Miss Adelaide just waiting around for that plain little band of gold.

'As Prince William whispered sweet nothings to his girlfriend, the press muttered nasty somethings about her supposed ambition to wed above her station. They dubbed her Waity Katie and bracketed her with Pippa as "the wisteria sisters", determined to climb,' I noted in *TIME* magazine.

Looking back at that piece and others I wrote over that period, my discomfort is clear – but as a journalist I added to the coverage, if also critiquing it. When my editor asked me to file on Kate's first pregnancy, I described the 'prurient documentation in the British press of the growing maternal "bump" and a swirl of supposed facts that range from informed speculation to purest invention'. By now this apparently happy story had taken the bleakest of turns. 'Kate's hospitalisation in December for severe morning sickness precipitated an announcement of her pregnancy. An ill-judged prank call to the hospital by an Australian radio show triggered a tragedy when Jacintha Saldanha, the nurse who inadvertently connected the pranksters, killed herself during the ensuing flurry of publicity.'

The spotlight had proved deadly for an innocent woman touched by its beam. You might have expected these events to prompt soul-searching and the resolution to give Kate space to deal with her debilitating medical condition and the shock of her own blameless involvement in Saldanha's death. Instead, the free-for-all continued. As Kate's due date drew near, palace officials agreed a friendly compact with journalists. We would be tipped off when she arrived at the private Lindo wing of St Mary's Hospital in Paddington and given a second heads-up in time for us to inspect the mother and baby before they left.

Still, Kate could be grateful for small mercies. Up to the second Elizabethan age, officials had positioned themselves inside or at the door of the delivery room to ensure the integrity of the royal bloodline. In 1688, this tradition failed to avert the so-called warming pan scandal, named after the large copper vessels used to take the chill off bedsheets. Though witnesses observed the birth of James II's heir, his opponents spread rumours: his queen had either faked her pregnancy or swapped their sickly newborn for a healthy child smuggled into the palace in such a pan. These suspicions helped to trigger the Glorious Revolution that ousted the Catholic James in favour of the solidly Protestant William and Mary.

Perhaps institutional memories of this episode persuaded Charles and Diana of the wisdom of showing off William and Harry on the steps of St Mary's within hours of their births. Their firstborn and his wife would dutifully follow suit, parading each successive infant for banks of cameras, with Kate emerging on all three occasions miraculously camera-ready, as if the rigours of labour cost her as little effort as unveiling a portrait or pulling the trigger on a nail gun.

What can't Kate do? you might ask – and there is one answer the media prefers not to acknowledge. What Kate can't do is go about her days anonymously. Hers is a life eternally observed, and no revolutions on her part, however glorious they might feel in the moment, would restore her peace and privacy. The harder Diana kicked against the restraints of royal culture, the greater the interest in her, and the more limited the protections she enjoyed. Kate's best and only defence – and an uncommon skill at which she excels – is to hide in plain sight, on show much as Hilary Mantel described, except maybe with a twist.

Could it be that what we see is not the Little Mermaid but a royal woman drawing on Elizabeth II's playbook?

Perhaps we should hail Kate as an unalloyed royal success story. Certainly, her press management looks majestic given the headwinds she has faced, and faced down, since 'Hurricane Meghan' blew in. A counterintuitive question is where Kate might stand in public affections if there had been no such dramas and no such squalls. At the moment they first hit, she appeared to have reached a steady equilibrium, nothing like the passions she now triggers. The majority of her coverage was positive, but mildly so; the criticisms lacked bite. There were just a few complaints directed at her workload, or lack of it, and her safe wardrobe (a big tick for players of the long game). 'The Duchess of Drab', the *Daily Mail* dubbed her (columnist Sarah Vine again), complimenting a 'figure most would trade their left kidney for' before dismissing Kate as 'an incorrigible frump' and 'style kryptonite' and lamenting 'there are Carmelite nuns that look foxier'. Fashion-editor-turned-broadcaster Janet Street-Porter picked up Vine's idea and trotted with it. 'The British Monarchy has worked its usual magic, turning a vibrant commoner into an underweight thirty-something with no pizazz,' she sighed in the *Independent*. 'Princess Diana had her shortcomings, but she understood perfectly that the public expected glamour at all times.'

The other perennial complaint centred on the then Cambridges' perceived failure to do their bit for the family firm. In December 2016, the annual totting-up of royal engagements revealed that they and Harry had collectively clocked up fewer official gigs than Princess Anne, earning headlines such as 'Your royal LAZINESS: How royals TWICE their age are putting Wills, Kate and Harry to SHAME'. Harry was in fact transitioning from the military as his brother and sister-in-law enjoyed a spell of normal life (or what passes for it in royal circles) by agreement with the older Windsors. The pair lived on the Welsh island of Anglesey while William served as a search-and-rescue pilot for the Royal Air Force, then relocated to the ten-bedroom Anmer Hall in Norfolk so he could take up a post at the East Anglian Air Ambulance service. Their idyll, however, was drawing to a close in more ways than one. Soon, William would be called upon to stop playacting at being a regular person and embrace his destiny as a full-time royal. Even then, he and Kate would push back, maintaining a schedule designed to give their children something closer to Middletonian nurturing than the haphazard upbringing that scarred generations of royals.

Media sniping at 'workshy Willy' and his wife was as nothing compared to the unfriendly fire assailing the latest addition to the royal line-up. Two months earlier, the *Sunday Express* had broken news of Harry's relationship with Meghan. Coverage swiftly plumbed such depths that Harry leaned on Kensington Palace to respond. The resulting statement, since quietly removed from the website, decried the harassment of Meghan's family, friends and colleagues, 'the smear on the front page of a national newspaper; the racial undertones of comment pieces; and the outright sexism and racism of social media trolls and web article comments'.

Though more direct than the doublespeak typically deployed by palace officials, the phrase 'racial undertones' fails to capture quite how blatantly racist a chunk of that commentary was, or the extent and violence of the online abuse. Some journalists continue to insist that our profession bears no responsibility for the trolling or to claim that the worst examples were outliers. This ignores both the interplay between old and new media and the nature of dog whistling. Repeating descriptors identified Meghan as 'other'. Equally powerful were the words left unspoken. Articles drew attention to her failure to wear the 'nude' tights standard for palace women, providing columnists with an excuse to refer to Meghan's mixed heritage without actually mentioning it.

What is also true is that some quarters of the media were enthusiastic about her in this first phase, gorging on new plotlines and her glamour. It helped that Harry was popular, in public imagination still the bereft boy trailing his mother's coffin or the charming party prince, a bit rambunctious but good for a laugh. Meghan's sophistication read as maturity. Surely she offered the love and support he needed? Trailing alongside William and Kate, he had appeared not just the spare but a spare wheel. Together, the two power couples added up, as the media spun it, to the 'Fab Four', the same Beatles'-inspired epithet they had applied to the ill-starred combination of Charles and Diana, Andrew and Fergie.

Unfortunate though that resonance was, the construct did appear to offer the possibility of both Kate and Meghan enjoying similar levels of popularity at the same time. In practice, columnists frequently laced favourable takes on Meghan with disparagement of Kate, deeming the latter stuffy and stiff by comparison. The other side of the coin saw the press castigate Meghan for behaviours that in Kate earned a free pass. Consider these two headlines from the *Mail*: 'Pregnant Kate tenderly cradles her baby bump' (March 2018) and 'Why can't

Meghan Markle keep her hands off her bump?' (January 2019). Lest you doubt the double standards, here is how columnist Liz Jones answered the second headline: 'Personally, I find the cradling a bit like those signs in the back of cars: Baby on Board. Virtue signalling, as though the rest of us barren harridans deserve to burn alive in our cars.'

The bigger point is not who got the rawer deal, but that journalists reflexively pitted the women against each other. They would have done so even if the sisters-in-law had forged a close bond. Soon, however, real-life antipathies flared into view, saving the media the trouble of continuing to invent them. The virtual world, already inflamed, became an inferno. Warring fans duked and duchessed it out, #TeamCambridge versus the #SussexSquad, each side ascribing to their heroes competing value sets. In this new scenario, William and Kate came to represent duty and tradition, Harry and Meghan progressive ideals. Royalty aims to unite its peoples, but this situation demanded that everyone pick a side. The result was predictable: adherents of each pair became ever more con vinced and combative. Popularity, however, is a numbers game. After the Sussexes spoke about racism in the Palace and amid the fall-out from the Cambridges' tone-deaf 2022 tour of the Caribbean, both couples' poll ratings slipped.

William let his anger show, while Kate maintained at least a semblance of serenity. This was the wiser call. As Meghan continued to lose ground, the British media embraced Kate again and with greater fervour. Once the Sussexes had turned in their credentials as working royals, and with Andrew ditched from balcony duties, the remaining family suddenly looked thin on numbers, especially with the frail Queen Elizabeth paring back her official engagements. 'The monarchy is in desperate need of reassuringly conventional royal performers,' Diana's former private secretary Patrick Jephson told the *New York Post*. 'Catherine is just what these troubled royal times need – it's no exaggeration that the Windsors' future lies in her hands.'

The iconography of Charles's coronation reinforced this sense, the elderly king and his consort enthroned under the gaze of the next in line, their own heirs and spares in tow. Kate 'cut a stunning figure', enthused the magazine *Marie Claire*, 'the picture of regal power and grace', agreed *Tatler*. So yes, in public relations terms, Kate or Catherine, HRH the Princess of Wales, if you prefer, appears triumphant. But saviour of the monarchy? What an extraordinary burden to lay on shoulders already draped in the ermine-trimmed tyranny of projected perfection. For nobody stays perfect, as Gloriana could have told you. Time would have worked its slow destruction, if missteps or the media's desire for a change of narrative failed to demote Kate to ordinary humanity.

The first quarter of 2024 served up intimations of such a change. Her absence from royal duties sparked carping and conspiracies. A Mother's Day photograph published to allay speculation achieved the opposite effect when her clumsy edits to the image raised questions about how much of the image had been faked and why.

And then it came: news of her cancer diagnosis. Media critics retreated or retrenched. Maybe that marked a victory of a kind. Her illness put her out of range of the usual brickbats. It did not, however, shield her from view. Imagine coming to terms with your own mortality in the crosshairs of scrutiny, the body for so long claimed as public property subjected to the most intrusive lines of investigation yet; debated, even denied, a vessel for the hopes, fears and fantasies of millions of strangers. Imagine how tough it must be to stand for the future when your own is clouded.

*

A confession: when I met Kate at a Buckingham Palace reception seven months after her wedding, her physical presence made a deep and immediate impression on me. This poses one of several dilemmas about how to tackle this chapter and the next. The trickiest is the Meghan question. These women impacted each other's lives. That needs to be acknowledged and explored without falling into the trap of defining them against each other. As for assessing what the world's unblinking focus on Kate's body means for her and the rest of us, I cannot do this without repeating comments and judgements, by others, that ought never to have been made. I could – and, you might argue, should – refrain from venturing my own observations. I include them here because, as with other royal women, there may be gaps between what we think we see of Kate and the person behind the façade.

I am tall. Kate, though reportedly a fraction smaller, gazed down on me, graceful in high heels. If I am scrawny, she is willowy. Before age coarsened my hair, it earned a backhanded compliment ('just like a wig'). If so, alongside hers, it looked like the joke-shop variety, nylon not silk. This helped me to understand something about the princess-as-girl-next-door imagery that has flooded the media since the slopes of Klosters. In the flesh, she is not so much relatable as an *ideal* of relatability, like those spotless interiors created by advertisers to shift furniture or kitchen appliances. During our brief conversation, I found myself wondering about the effort entailed in maintaining those gleaming surfaces, the anxiety embedded in those rituals, and the knock-on effects on women and girls who mistake her look for an attainable goal.

These thoughts formed during awkward lulls. The paintings hung in tiers around the room seemed to offer an obvious ice-breaker – Kate has a degree in Art History – but she refused to be drawn. My queries elicited non-replies. She had not yet familiarised herself with the royal collection. What kinds of art interested her most? Again her formulation discouraged further inquiries. She had 'varied tastes'.

A few years later, at a private dinner for superrich donors to Charles's charities, my neighbour, a self-described art collector, would answer the same question with a phrase simultaneously uninformative and revealing: 'art that I like'. Kate's apparent detachment struck me much the same way, jarring with palace briefings that identified the visual arts as the pinnacle of her passions after William and her family. Even Queen Elizabeth, who defined restraint, became animated when conversation turned to horses. Might the speculation about Kate's choices in higher education have some basis in fact after all? Until this moment, I had dismissed gossip about how she came to enrol on the same course as William at the University of St Andrews in Scotland, assuming it to be part and parcel of the misogyny directed at the Middleton sisters and their mother.

Trawl sources for hints of Kate's earliest academic leanings and she comes across as a classic all-rounder, good at everything. Her preferences and dislikes are harder to detect.

Born on 9 January 1982, her childhood and adolescence seems to have run smoothly, but for one unpleasant interlude, which saw her parents remove her from an expensive private boarding school, the girls-only Downe House, and install her at another, the co-educational Marlborough College. 'She hated [Downe House], absolutely hated it,' an unnamed Marlborough contemporary told *Woman & Home* magazine. 'Some of the girls there were horrible. She was picked on because she was perfect.'

What couldn't the young Kate do? Not much according to a *Mail* profile. At Marlborough, she 'excelled at hockey', became 'co-captain of the tennis team', 'was never caught with illicit booze' and 'blossomed' into 'an absolute beauty', in her yearbook 'hailed as [the] "person most likely to be loved by everybody"'.

She had acting talent too, not merely participating in student productions but cast in leading roles. A clip shows Kate, then still at primary school, acing her performance as the titular *My Fair Lady*, Eliza Doolittle, a common-as-muck flower girl promoted to high society via lessons in elocution and etiquette. A second snippet, which surfaced only as suddenly to disappear, captures her at thirteen playing Maria Marten in *The Murder in the Red Barn*. Here she stands, a sweet country maiden. A fellow pupil, costumed as a soothsayer, stares at her palm before issuing a prophesy. 'Soon you will meet a handsome man, a rich gentleman.'

'This is all I've ever hoped for,' Kate/Maria replies. 'Will he fall in love with me?'

'Indeed he will.'

'And marry me?'

Yes, the soothsayer affirms; moreover, this suitor – a squire named William – will take her to London. When the video originally surfaced, news outlets presented it as proof that Kate's fairytale future was written in the stars. Perhaps the nature of the play itself holds a clue to the clip's disappearance. A Victorian melodrama, *The Murder in the Red Barn* fictionalises the real-life 1827 killing of Maria Marten. William Corder lured his lover to her doom with the promise of marriage. A chronicle of these events, bound, grotesquely, in Corder's own skin after his public hanging, remains on display in a museum in Suffolk.

If there are insights to be gleaned from such glimpses into Kate's evolution, they relate to the comfort of her upbringing – well-staged productions, schools with drama facilities – and her conflicted relationship with the limelight. There is a guarded quality to her star turns, fluent and free from mistakes though they are. Always, it seems, she has been able to make herself go through the motions, whether for parents seated on rickety chairs, or before vast, milling crowds. There is little sense, however, that she revels in the public gaze, much less that she actively seeks it.

You can discern that same duality in footage of a pandemic-era carol concert, as singer-songwriter Tom Walker performs his ballad 'For Those Who Can't Be Here' with Kate accompanying him on piano. Daniel Nicholls, who tutored her in the instrument when she was at school, devised the musical arrangement. She 'was absolutely lovely, a really delightful person to teach,' he commented to the *Evening Standard*. 'I don't think anyone would say she was going to be a concert pianist, but she was good at it. She always did everything she was told.'

His assessment is borne out as his erstwhile pupil hits all the right notes in the right order. When Walker grins in delight at the end of the piece, she responds with a strained half-smile. This has been an ordeal.

So, what does excite her, thrill her, move her? Her choice of A levels provides few clues. She studied Art but also Mathematics, netting top marks in both, along with English, for which she received a respectable B. William, schooled at Eton, sat A levels at the same time, lagging her scores, but easily outperforming his immediate family with a tally that included an A in Geography, B in Art and a C in Biology.

Kate's grades guaranteed her place to read Art History at the University of Edinburgh, her first choice. She had planned to start there in September 2000, reportedly liaising with friends about sharing accommodation. Then, inexplicably, she changed tack. That she decided to take a gap year, spending part of it in Chile with Raleigh International, would surely warrant less attention had she and William not enrolled with the same organisation in the same part of northern Patagonia, missing each other by weeks. In a similar vein, Kate's revisions to her universities application form, in other circumstances unremarkable, pitched her into unprecedented competition to study Art History at St Andrews. Widely considered less prestigious than the Edinburgh course, this programme was now suddenly and wildly oversubscribed, with applications spiking by 44 per cent on the news that William would be among its next intake. Holding a solo press conference for the first time in his young life, William also revealed details of his impending sojourn in Chile and commented on Patrick Jephson's then soon-to-be-published memoir about Diana.

'Our mother's trust has been betrayed and even now she is still being exploited,' he said.

It later transpired that both Jephson and Diana had been victims of Martin Bashir's machinations. She died, hunted to the last, wrongly believing that the loyal Jephson had conspired against her. Now William was being hailed by the media as a heartthrob and thus a prime target for the same sorts of attentions that afflicted his mother. It was within this context that he and Kate connected. 'There is this extraordinary pattern for these two,' said royal author Katie Nicholl in a documentary. 'It's almost as if they were destined to be together.' Though the couple claimed in their engagement interview to have first met at St Andrews and certainly did get to know each other there, Nicholl's research suggests they crossed paths years earlier, when Kate was at Marlborough. The Middleton sisters, though not core members of the so-called Glosse Posse, 'a chummy band of Prince William and Harry's best pals from Gloucestershire', intersected with it.

The Crown leans into the tabloid caricature of Carole Middleton as a schemer who thrust Kate in William's way. In his book, *Battle of Brothers*, Robert Lacey, who was also the series' historical consultant, paints the wider Middleton clan as co-conspirators. 'Throwing away a solid place at Edinburgh for the uncertainties of oversubscribed St Andrews a year later was not a risk that many would-be students would have incurred in Britain at that time,' he writes. 'But the Middletons must have discussed and supported the gamble their daughter was taking in full knowledge of the Prince William dimension. What other rationale could there have been for this last-minute swerve?'

I can think of at least one: that William and Kate really were destined to meet, not for supernatural reasons or through plotting, but simply because the lives of England's gilded youth flow along limited channels from a small number of feeder schools to a handful of colleges or other acceptable options, the less academically minded boys enrolling in the military or learning estate management, their female equivalents acquiring Cordon Bleu cookery certificates, smatterings of French or jobs at Mayfair art galleries. Eventually, quite a lot of them end up in adjacent white-fronted town houses or sprawling rural piles (or shuttling between both), married to someone from the same set, perhaps sleeping with another, and godparents to each other's children, who grow up to repeat the pattern.

Art History also attracts a specific subset. There have been efforts to broaden its appeal and syllabus but, back then, it tended to be a white, upper-middle-class enclave focused on the European visual arts. Even now, the intake skews heavily female. Maybe William, who grew up surrounded by the same old masters dominating the then-curriculum, saw the discipline as an extension of estate management; or perhaps enthusiasm for art (excluding modernism) transmitted from father to son. Whatever William's original motivation, he quickly regretted his decision, threatening to drop out of university altogether before family and palace advisers persuaded him to persevere. He switched to Geography.

Had he bailed, his friendship with Kate might never have developed into romance. Legend in the shape of biographers, journalists and, of course, *The Crown*, has William struck by a thunderbolt in March of that first year, when Kate, his quiet, reliable buddy, sashayed down a catwalk at a charity event in a see-through skirt refashioned by her into a dress. Here was a body that commanded love, even from a prince. Not that he or Kate, by their own account, shifted the basis of their relationship at this point. In their engagement interview, William insisted that their move to off-campus accommodation that September, a property shared with two other students, was platonic. 'It just sort of blossomed from there really.' The flat, on the optimistically named Hope Street, had to be fitted with bullet-proof glass.

*

William needed protection: from terrorism, unscrupulous journalists, would-be princesses and a prying, exploitative world. Already, he was constructing a vigilant inner circle, much as a Tudor king might gather privy councillors and grooms of the stool. Kate's inclusion at the core of this tight-knit community sealed my original scepticism about the notion of her as a royal groupie or fame-hunter. While Windsors can be spectacularly lacking in awareness – just think of Andrew emerging from his *Newsnight* interview congratulating himself on a job well done – William's early life made him suspicious, and his university experience compounded it.

Within days of his arrival at St Andrews, a film crew broke the agreement between Palace and media to leave him unmolested during his studies, chasing him down as he attended a lecture and refusing to desist even after warnings. They may have imagined their employer, Ardent Productions, enjoyed special dispensation through its founder, Prince Edward. 'It beggars belief when I think of the efforts we have gone to square the press . . . to allow William a normal undergraduate life,' the university's rector, Andrew Neil, told the BBC. 'We knew somebody would break it at some stage. But for it to be broken by a company owned by his own uncle, well, you just couldn't make it up.' Nor would you lightly invent a further detail of the imbroglio. Neil himself was the former editor of the *Sunday Times* who had greenlit the serialisation of Andrew Morton's biography of Diana.

The first extract landed as William prepared to celebrate his tenth birthday. It included the detail that Diana had tried to kill herself at Sandringham when pregnant with him. 'She was suffering dreadfully from morning sickness, she was haunted by Camilla Parker Bowles, and she was desperately trying to accommodate herself to her new position and new family,' Morton wrote. When she 'threatened to take her own life', Charles 'accused her of crying wolf', but 'she was as good as her word. Standing on top of the wooden staircase she hurled herself to the ground, landing in a heap at the bottom.'

Had William wished to discuss these revelations, the most significant adults in his life were fiercely partisan and he was anyway away at school, a boarder, like Charles, from the age of eight. Father and son had something else in common too, considered problem children compared to their sunnier younger siblings, with Charles judged 'sensitive', William 'spoiled'. 'No one tells me what to do! When I am King, I will have you punished,' the four-year-old William allegedly warned his nanny.

Humans are shaped by multiple factors: heredity, environment and perhaps also birth order. The oldest child, subject to the anxieties and mistakes common to new parents, picks up on stresses in family relationships, sometimes tries to shield siblings from them and may well be lumbered with additional responsibilities. Charles's seniority carried these consequences and more. William's encumbered him with greater burdens still.

In his memoir, Harry describes their childhood from the perspective of the little brother who got the smaller room; the supposedly rougher deal. 'I was the shadow, the support, the Plan B. I was brought into the world in case something happened to Willy. I was summoned to provide back-up, distraction, diversion and, if necessary, a spare part. Kidney, perhaps. Bood transfusion. Speck of bone marrow,' he declares. Certainly, nobody should envy Harry his upbringing. Like most Windsors, he was born to the deadening prospect of a supporting role within an institution that deprived its members of privacy and choice. William, then third in line to the throne, never had to wrestle with existential questions of meaning or purpose. Yet his life would always be more restricted than Harry's, the expectations on him more stifling and, until recent years, his relationship with their father trickier, complicated by their joint predicament of future kingship and the rivalry Diana helped to stoke by suggesting that 'the top job' ought to bypass her ex-husband in favour of William.

Even before the tumult of 1997, the brothers had sustained scars that would likely have coloured their adult lives and relationships. Then came the news from Paris. The loss of a parent will always leave its mark, but grief can evolve and become liveable; a bittersweet companion. Trauma is a different beast, reluctant to loosen its grip even with specialist treatment. Diana's death hit her children without warning, and its aftermath could only have compounded the damage. 'My mother had just died, and I had to walk a long way behind her coffin, surrounded by thousands of people watching me while millions more did on television,' said Harry. His brother, though describing the experience as 'one of the hardest things I've ever done', saw their participation as part of the royal role. 'There is that balance between duty and family and that's what we had to do.'

Trauma-related disorders manifest in a range of different ways. Post-traumatic stress syndrome alone can cause flashbacks, nightmares, nausea, guilt, shame, emotional numbing or its apparent opposite, hyperarousal expressed in anger, insomnia and fractured concentration.

It would be almost two decades before William and Harry finally began to acknowledge injuries invisible to the outer world. To promote Heads Together, a mental health initiative launched with Kate, they released a video. 'Harry and I, over the years, have not talked enough about our mother,' William said. 'It's very easy to run away from it . . . to avoid it the whole time.' He added that he and Harry were 'uniquely bonded because of what we've been through'. The subsequent rupturing of that bond illuminated the vulnerability of both brothers and a profound anger that may be the legacy of trauma.

Once Harry began to describe his anguish, in interviews and his memoir, he could or would not stop. William is more reticent. When he does address these issues, he tends to open the conversation, only to close it down again. His mother's death, he admitted to documentary makers, inflicted 'pain like no other pain'. He added that his work piloting air ambulances had triggered 'raw emotion . . . I could feel it brewing up inside me and I could feel it was going to take its toll and be a real problem.' He did not link this experience to his decision to work for a service dedicated to saving the lives of accident victims.

*

These then were the princes that young girls dreamed of snaring, never once imagining what such a relationship might entail. To live with someone who carries unresolved trauma, as Diana's sons well might, is to be constantly vigilant, navigating sudden moods and creating calm. That can be difficult enough in normal circumstances, and royal life is not normal. No incomer has ever found assimilation easy. Of Elizabeth II's daughters-in-law, only Sophie has avoided divorce. She also proved sufficiently robust to overcome early blunders and remake herself as a stalwart and steward of royal culture.

In this context, the lengthy 'courtship' of William and Kate, as newspapers quaintly called it, appeared sensible. They weathered break-ups, two or more, reuniting after the longest hiatus when Kate, according to media lore, haunted nightclubs, deploying that body of hers, wrote biographer Nicholl, in 'a mission to show William what he was missing'. The couple finally announced their engagement in November 2010. He had wanted to give his bride 'the chance to see what life . . . is like in the family,' William explained. 'I wanted to give her a chance to see in and to back out if she needed to before it all got too much.'

Harry later appeared to snipe at this approach. 'For so many people in the family, especially obviously the men, there can be a temptation or urge to marry someone who would fit the mould as opposed to somebody who you perhaps are destined to be with,' he told Netflix. 'It's the difference between making decisions with your head or your heart.'

Those of us who documented Charles and Diana's ill-conceived rush to the altar understand Harry's distaste for any calculation that risks privileging dynastic concerns over compatibility. However, William and Kate's eight-year run-up to marriage could be read not as an audition but rather, a deepening and strengthening. One might still wonder why any woman would willingly consign herself to the Windsor life, handsome prince or not, but the couple's longevity gave comfort. There must be respect on both sides; an acceptance of the trade-offs involved; hopefully also love, whatever they might mean by it.

It was their engagement sit-down with ITV's Tom Bradby that gave pause. The camera found Kate dressed in blue, as Diana had been for the equivalent set-piece, with what appeared to be Diana's sapphire glinting on her finger. William confirmed to Bradby that this was indeed his mother's ring. Wearing it would make his fiancée 'the envy of many', said Bradby. 'Well, I just hope I look after it,' Kate replied. 'If she loses it, she's in big trouble,' William deadpanned. The similarities with his parents' interview, both deliberate and unintentional, suggested she might be.

William deflected and joked, as his father had done, coming only marginally closer to a declaration of his feelings than Charles had managed. He did offer a stilted description of the proposal – 'I had done a little bit of planning to show my romantic side'. Still, the pair looked happy, leaning into each other and laughing. What rang alarm bells was William's answer when Bradby asked how Kate would deal with comparisons to Diana: 'There's no pressure,' William said. 'No one is trying to fill my mother's shoes. What she did was fantastic. It's about making your own future and your own destiny – and Kate will do a very good job of that.'

How could William protect his future wife from the locomotive heading her way if he chose to deny its reality? No royal woman escapes comparisons with her peers and forerunners, and Kate, the most glamorous addition to the family since the mythic Diana, would be the first since her death burdened with the Princess of Wales title. Moreover, William might think Diana's contribution 'fantastic', but the Palace struggled with it. His mother's celebrity came close to eclipsing the institution and its members rather than shining a light on them. If Kate failed to sparkle, she would be criticised. If she blazed, her in-laws would not thank her. William seemed neither to have fully understood his family history nor the media.

Though he does have friends who are journalists, Bradby for a time included, William is no more enamoured of our breed than his brother, vibrating with hostility in our company. Speaking as the twentieth anniversary of Diana's death approached, William recalled that 'most of the time she ever cried about anything was to do with press intrusion'. That shared memory prompts very different responses in the brothers, Harry by turns spilling to the media and confronting it; William seeking distance and control. 'Harry and I, you know, we lived through that and one lesson I have learned is, you never let them in too far because it's very difficult to get them back out again,' William continued. 'You've got to maintain a barrier and a boundary because if you cross it, if both sides cross it, a lot of pain and problems can come from it.'

In Kate, William found a partner as wary as he, private by instinct, despite press narratives that brand all Middleton women as attention-seekers while showering them with attention they do not seek. Coverage of Carole also betrays the media's ingrained snobbery while unblushingly accusing her of precisely that sin. How 'could a former air stewardess from Berkshire ever hope to take on the House of Windsor and win?' wondered the *Mail* during one of Kate's brief splits from William. The piece featured a quote from an unnamed palace source: '[Carole] is pushy, rather twee and incredibly middle class. She uses words such as "Pleased to meet you", "toilet" and "pardon". The irony is that Carole has been so busy pushing her daughter forward and doing her best to groom her for royalty that she's rather missed the point that she might not fit in herself.'

Another factor also coloured attitudes to Carole. 'She's a Jew, you know,' a journalist told me, except that was not the noun he used. This idea – based purely on Carole's maiden name, Goldsmith – gained prominence ahead of the birth of William and Kate's first child. The BBC's former royal correspondent, Michael Cole, by this stage a director of Harrod's and publicist for Mohamed al Fayed, confidently claimed that 'the Duchess of Cambridge is a Jew on her matriarchal side and therefore her baby will be a Jew'. Challenged by the *Times of Israel* to provide supporting evidence, Cole replied: 'Mrs Middleton, born Goldsmith, is a talented businesswoman.' The exchange fed into a wider debate, with some communities delighted by the idea of Jewish royalty and antisemites fulminating about a 'tainted' royal bloodline, the same charge later directed at

Meghan and her Ragland ancestry. As it happens, researchers who looked into five generations of the Goldsmith family found no suggestion of Jewish heritage.

Carole did not give an interview until seventeen years after William (officially) met Kate, and then it was to mark the thirtieth anniversary of Party Pieces, the company she set up. 'Over the years, it's proved wise not to say anything,' she told the *Telegraph*, going on over the course of the lengthy conversation to deliver not a single headline-grabbing nugget. She described a happy home life, with her husband, Michael, sharing the professional and domestic load and their offspring all getting involved in the business. 'I think it's really good to work,' she said. 'It was part of the children's lives – it still is.' Her husband may have brought inherited wealth to their union, but for decades her enterprise helped to provide the family with every comfort and more: private educations, country-house living and employment as and when anyone needed it. The double-whammy of the pandemic restrictions on socialising and competition from online retailers sent Party Pieces into administration. It now operates under new ownership.

Had Kate not met and married William, this development would have gone unremarked, except perhaps as a footnote in the business pages. Nor would Kate's sister have found herself catapulted to global fame only to be accused of self-promotion. The furore started when Pippa acted as bridesmaid to Kate. Cameras set to record Kate's arrival at Westminster Abbey captured a view of what the same broadsheet called Pippa's 'scandalously pert posterior . . . the derriere that launched not merely a thousand ships, but a billion internet searches, fan sites and Facebook appreciation pages'.

The excitement continued long after the wedding, with the picture editor of the *Daily Mail*, a heavy user of Pippa content, at one point estimating he received four hundred photographs of her every day. For as long as she passively enriched the ecosystem of paps, hacks and news organisations, they slavered. As soon as she attempted to channel their interest into her own projects – a short-lived health and lifestyle column; occasional inoffensive freelance pieces – she became a columnists' punchbag, recast as her mother's daughter, voracious for social advancement, eager for exposure. Her guide to party planning: *Celebrate: A Year of British Festivities for Families and Friends*, attracted industrial levels of scorn. Could it really be that bad? Leafing through a second-hand copy, I cannot help but notice how closely in tone and intention Pippa's book anticipates the Netflix show, *With Love, Meghan*. That in turn raises questions about how it is that we are so easily persuaded to attack women for endeavours that, yes, might not be our cup of sun tea, but surely do not merit the venom directed at them.

In 2014, a friend invited me to a fancy dinner for women in advertising and communications where Pippa gave a speech. If you shut your eyes, her voice was indistinguishable from her sister's, despite Kate's rumoured elocution lessons. Pippa delivered a joke about fame – 'recognition has its upside, its downside and – you may say – its backside' – and a more poignant passage in which she talked about being hurt by the accusations of cashing in. 'Most of the advertising Mufia [sic] were bored rigid,' declared a columnist describing the event. 'Then again, if a great arse gets you the speaking gig . . .' Shortly afterwards, Pippa gave an interview to US television network NBC in which she said she felt 'publicly bullied' by traditional and social media. Three years later, after her own, inevitably high-profile wedding, she disappeared from view but for occasional sightings at her sister's side.

Not so Gary Goldsmith, Carole's younger brother. A target and source for the tabloids since Kate rose to prominence, he joined the reality TV show *Celebrity Big Brother*. His eviction by public vote freed him just in time to offer his opinion on a controversy brewing around his niece. A photograph of her with her children, the first sighting since her retreat from public life, appeared to be digitally manipulated. 'Obviously the family wouldn't be the ones to do any touch-ups,' he said.

His comment did provide one useful insight: into the folly of assuming a familial relationship guarantees high-grade information. Goldsmith, as he admitted, had not at that stage spoken to Kate for a year or more, and he was wrong too about the photoshopping. Within hours, Kate had posted an apology for editing the image.

*

It was March 2024, and by now, every day fresh and unlikely rumours surfaced. Kensington Palace had kept its briefings minimalist, just the initial mid-January statement revealing her abdominal surgery and a second press release speaking of 'good progress'. Behind-the-scenes, aides also let it be known that her condition was 'non-cancerous'.

Her father-in-law's communications team had delivered news of their own: Charles, admitted to the same hospital as Kate and like her for a planned procedure, turned out to have cancer. His illness forced William to take on additional royal duties rather than stepping back from them. When the Prince cited 'personal reasons' for missing a memorial service for his godfather, King Constantine of Greece, speculation about his wife's condition cranked up. Officials, however, stuck to their guns. They intended to provide further details about Kate's health only in case of 'significant updates'.

Then, on 11 March, Kensington Palace released the first new photograph of Kate since her disappearance. News organisations published the image as a picture story, running it a second time to deconstruct it. At the heart of the group, the princess crosses her legs demurely at the ankle in the manner prescribed for royal women, though she is wearing jeans. Her eldest son, George, stands behind her, arms around her neck, while she hugs her other children, Louis and Charlotte. Everyone grins broadly. The caption reads: 'Thank you for your kind wishes and continued support over the last two months. Wishing everyone a happy Mother's Day.'

Within minutes, amateur sleuths were identifying inconsistencies: a misaligned sleeve, a zip hanging in space, a wonky skirting board, trees in full bloom though spring had yet to arrive. AI did not appear to have created the image from scratch, but some experts theorised that the technology had been used to make a composite from several similar shots. Alternatively, persons unknown had tweaked a single original. Such distinctions mattered little to picture agencies which adhere to strict codes of conduct forbidding alterations as minor as the elimination of 'red eye'. Nor did these theories satisfy conspiracists.

Obviously, the Princess had been murdered and replaced by a body double like a Stepford wife. Or she was recovering from cosmetic surgery. Oh look! No wedding ring! A royal divorce was on the cards. Then Kate held up her (ringless) hands to the changes, raising a different set of questions. Surely Kensington Palace staffers should have intervened before the picture was sent out. Did culpability rest with aides, or might the couple share a weakness common to royalty: a reluctance to listen?

The incident marked a rare own goal from a woman who has learned to balance the demands of her public-facing role with the need for privacy. Courtiers credit her with the sensible strategy of providing the media with photographs of her family on a regular basis. While this practice might appear to breach William's 'maintain a barrier and a boundary' approach to media, it feeds press the pictures they crave before they pay paparazzi to snatch them. Kate takes many of the stills herself, choosing photographers and videographers for other shoots. The resulting output mimics authenticity, simultaneously repudiating the past and evoking it. Subjects, artfully positioned to look spontaneous, appear not so much humanised as super-humanised, their eyes preternaturally bright. The group formations, full of movement, ditch the formality of royal portraiture that has predominated since Victorian times, yet the texture of the images, colour-saturated, grainy or soft-focused, harks back to bygone days of Polaroids and Super 8 home movies.

This content, brilliantly judged for the Instagram era, goes some way to answering that earlier question about Kate's passions and preoccupations. While still at university, she approached photographer Alistair Morrison and persuaded him to mentor her. Later, she would art-direct and produce product shots for Party Pieces, curate shows for Morrison and exhibit her own photographic landscapes. In a parallel universe, she might have turned her talent into a professional vocation, though then again, she has, harnessing her skills to the royal role.

Kate understands art and imagery as a tool of communication – and as a source of controversy. Her undergraduate thesis, 'Angels from Heaven', explored the representation of childhood in the photography of Charles Lutwidge Dodgson, better known under his pen name, Lewis Carroll. Many of his photographs feature Alice Liddell, the inspiration for *Alice in Wonderland* and *Alice Through the Looking Glass*, captured aged seven or eight and depicted in ways troubling to modern scholarship, apparently sexualised. Others argue that Alice's poses are unremarkable within their social and aesthetic context.

Of course, Kate was tight-lipped when I broached her degree subject with her all those years ago. There is no such thing as a safe picture, as the curious case of an old master chosen from the Royal Collection for display in her sitting room at Kensington Palace would prove. Painted by Aelbert Cuyp in the mid-seventeenth century, it is considered among the Dutch artist's finest works. It is also typical of his output: human figures set against a landscape, seemingly unposed, much like Kate's photographic subjects. Two noblemen stand to one side, deep in conversation and partially obscured by horses they will shortly mount. In the middle of this scene and foregrounded, a black attendant holds the reins.

Who selected it or why remains unclear, nor does anyone seem to have worried about the name plate affixed to its frame until Barack Obama, on the fourth and final UK visit of his US presidency, came to dine with First Lady Michelle chez the Cambridges. Minutes before their arrival, an aide reportedly manoeuvred a lamp into position to obscure the picture's title, *The Negro Page*.

Harry, the only other guest at the dinner, may have overlooked that wording too, or did not yet find it troubling. This was April 2016, three months before his first date with Meghan at London's Soho House. By his own account, it took him 'living a day or a week in my wife's shoes' to alert him to the dissonances people of colour routinely experience in societies built on historic inequality. An Art History graduate, however, might have been expected to pay closer attention.

This is certainly the view of those who, in the wake of Meghan and Harry's departure, depict Kate as an instrument and avatar of white supremacy. On the online publishing platform *Medium*, a post demands that we 'imagine how racist you have to be that there were THOUSANDS of paintings to choose from, and you choose the one with a title so racist that you had to hide it when Obama came over to your palace!' Social media is littered with similar comments.

So ought Kate's degree have sensitised her to that caption? Probably, but then again, anybody seeing it should have realised its power to offend. A better question is why the royal institution and its principals show so little curiosity about the story the painting tells. The monarch automatically serves as head of state in the remaining overseas realms and by tradition heads the Commonwealth too, fifty-six independent countries, almost all former British colonies. These facts, together with the diversity of the Crown's UK subjects surely demand of the royals a deep and constant engagement with their colonial legacy.

The Cuyp remains in the Royal Collection with a revised title, *A Page with Two Horses*. Kate too has been rechristened, dubbed KKKate by the Sussex Squad. Though prepared to forgive Harry for his pre-Meghan mistakes, they extend no such leeway to William and his wife, imputing to them a fixed and toxic ideology. The damage, serious and seemingly permanent, makes her current popularity all the more striking.

*

If there have been teaching moments for Kate, an official visit to the Caribbean, timed to support Elizabeth II's platinum jubilee, was one. Her tour of the region with William coincided with the height of the Windrush affair. In 1948, the HMT *Empire Windrush* had transported immigrants from Trinidad, Mexico, Jamaica and Bermuda to England. The UK, its workforce depleted by the Second World War, promised a welcome, but the passengers who disembarked at Tilbury, the scene of Elizabeth I's legendary speech against the Armada, would themselves be treated as invaders. Decades later, 164 members of the original contingent, their descendants and others from similar cohorts were torn from lives they had built in Britain and summarily deported, unable to produce documentation that the UK authorities had themselves destroyed. Those who remained found themselves denied access to benefits and healthcare.

The Cambridges and their aides should have been acutely aware of the anger this betrayal provoked, and alert to a wider picture of burgeoning independence movements in the realms. Add to that demands by CARICOM, the bloc of Caribbean nations, that the UK pay reparations for historic slavery and native genocide committed under the auspices of the Crown, the global ripples of the Black Lives Matter protests and, of course, the Meghan and Harry factor, and this was always going to be a royal visit that needed delicate handling.

How then to explain photographs of William and Kate in Jamaica reaching out to black children who are cooped like chickens the far side of a wire fence, an image that looked, as BBC correspondent Jonny Dymond observed, like 'some sort of white-saviour parody'? How to fathom the decision to place the couple on the back of a Land Rover last used by a youthful Elizabeth and Philip? There to showcase the monarchy's future, the pair appeared as ghosts from its colonial past with William in the white military uniform of his Blues and Royals regiment, and Kate in matching white, from oversized hat to vertiginous heels.

Their host, Prime Minister Andrew Holness, politely informed them that a parting was on the cards. Jamaica, he said, was 'very proud of its history, very proud of what we have achieved, and we are moving on, and we intend to attain, in short order, our developing goals and to fulfil our true ambitions . . . as an independent, developed, prosperous country'. They received similar messages throughout the journey. Surveys suggest that a majority of the populations in half of the remaining realms favour transitioning to republics.

While it is doubtful that the Windsors' first member of mixed heritage could have turned the tide single-handedly, Meghan's exit soured the mood against the monarchy in general, and the next-in-line to the throne and his consort in particular. The royals were already expecting to shed a realm or two, but they had not anticipated the damage to William and Kate. UK opinion polls rattled confidence still further, with two-thirds of over-sixty-fives viewing the monarchy as 'good for Britain', yet only 30 per cent of eighteen to twenty-four-year-olds concurring. A hefty 43 per cent of young Britons from ethnic minority backgrounds expressed a desire to trade the Crown for an elected head of state.

The Caribbean missteps underlined a throwaway remark Harry made to Oprah Winfrey in her primetime special with the Sussexes: A 'lack of understanding' in palace circles, he said, had influenced his and Meghan's decision to leave. In the aftermath of the rupture, Buckingham Palace and Clarence House for the first time published statistics on workforce diversity. Only around 8 per cent of staff came from 'ethic minority backgrounds'. The reports did not break down those figures to reveal how few occupied senior positions. Kensington Palace declined to release any numbers, but sources said the picture was worse. A more diverse team would likely have anticipated the optics of that jeep ride and other pitfalls.

Instead, they had to crisis-manage, and there was more to come. Meghan and Harry's Oprah interview attracted audiences of over seventeen million in the US and eleven million in the UK. Buckingham Palace issued a statement with unusual speed. In speaking of an unnamed senior royal who expressed concerns about 'how dark [baby Archie's] skin would be', the Sussexes had triggered a guessing game. *Who could the culprit be?* The response, attributed to Queen Elizabeth herself, sidestepped specific allegations, professed love for the couple and added, 'The issues raised, particularly that of race, are concerning. While some recollections may vary, they are taken very seriously and will be addressed by the family privately.'

That was a clever script, but William did not stick to it, growling 'we are very much not a racist family' at a reporter.

Kate stayed silent, even as the charge sheet against her lengthened. Meghan said Kate had made her cry during a disagreement over bridesmaids dresses and not, as universally reported, the other way round. Harry's memoir painted his sister-in-law as painfully brittle, impervious to Meghan's charm and 'on edge' over being 'compared to, and forced [by the media], to compete with' the newcomer. He describes Kate gripping her seat so tightly that her fingers turn white as she demands an apology from Meghan for ascribing a moment of forgetfulness to 'baby brain'. 'We're not close enough for you to talk about my hormones,' she admonishes. *Spare* also puts a new spin on an incident that took place long before Harry met Meghan, when the young prince provoked outrage by wearing a Nazi uniform to a 'colonials and natives' costume party. William and Kate, Harry reveals, encouraged him to choose the outfit.

Two books by Omid Scobie, a British-born correspondent for US news organisations, added to the growing sense of Kate as an ice queen. *Finding Freedom*, co-written with Carolyn Durand, started as a friendly look at the latest royal couple and ended up providing a sympathetic perspective on their turbulent withdrawal. From the beginning, Kate 'had seemingly not shown much interest in finding out who this woman was who had made her brother-in-law so happy,' the authors wrote. 'But that indifference wasn't necessarily directed toward Meghan. "[Kate] is an extremely guarded person," a friend explained.'

Endgame, Scobie's solo project published in 2023, presents a harder-edged portrait. Kate was never 'a fan' of Meghan, 'jokingly shiver[s]' at mention of her name, 'can be cold if she doesn't like someone' and 'spent more time talking *about* Meghan than talking to her'. A few words Scobie did not intend to include in the book inflicted further damage. For reasons never fully explained, the Dutch edition of *Endgame* contained a sentence purporting to identify Kate and her father-in-law as the mystery royals who had speculated about Archie's skin colour. Publishers swiftly pulped those copies, but media old and new had already broadcast the claim.

'If you love me you don't have to hate [Kate],' Meghan told Oprah Winfrey. 'And if you love her, you don't need to hate me.' In *Courtiers*, his book about the inside workings of royalty, *The Times'* former royal correspondent Valentine Low suggests that the live-and-let-live message hit stony ground. Kate, says one of Low's sources, unhappy with Buckingham Palace's first draft of the palace response to the Winfrey interview, successfully argued for tougher language and the inclusion of the famous phrase 'recollections may vary'.

However you view this reported intercession – as a mark of strength, loyalty or stone-hearted killer instinct – those three words raised doubt over Harry and Meghan's narrative far more effectively than could any direct denial. Similarly, though people unversed in the art of media management might assume Kate's best way to counter accusations against her would be to address them head on, such a course of action would spread them further and faster. To play the long game you have to bottle up your feelings and accept that quick corrections of the record work only in limited circumstances. You might encourage friends and aides to defend you, but you must not be implicated in this activity. Above all, you must look serene, no matter what troubles you.

'She never gives much away,' says Simon Perry, *People* magazine's veteran correspondent in the UK. For decades he has observed Kate, listened as she interacts with the public, chatted to her on the margins of events. 'You think, oh my gosh, she's just told us something fresh. Then you look it up and realise she's actually said it before. She's smart.'

*

Leaf through the cuttings about Kate and you will find thousands upon thousands that promise piping-hot revelations but deliver reheated gruel. For example, a piece in the *Mirror* teases a big revelation in its title: 'Kate Middleton puts on brave face to hide secret heartache at huge royal event'. Yet all the first several hundred words tell us is that Kate is good at smiling through public appearances.

Smile though your heart is breaking. The lyric might have been written for royalty, especially the women and the compromises they make in their patrimonarchal marriages. Think of Katherine of Aragon presiding at a masque as Henry VIII romanced her successor, or that successor watching his growing infatuation with Jane Seymour. Think of Catherine of Braganza enduring years of public hostility and the private grief of multiple miscarriages to serve as dutiful consort to Charles II, a king not only famous for his sexual incontinence but celebrated in popular culture for it. Think of Queen Alexandra tolerating Bertie's serial mistresses, including Camilla's ancestor, Alice Keppel. Think of that footage of Diana on a visit to Melbourne, by now miserably aware of the third party in her marriage and a shadow of her former self, beaming at Charles as they danced for onlookers.

So, was the *Mirror* about to reveal turbulences in Kate's life? Not on your Nell Gwyn. The piece hinges on an old observation by Katie Nicholl that 'as a dedicated parent' Kate finds it 'tricky' to be away from her children on royal tours. There was no peg. The article belongs to a genre of royal coverage that takes a quote from an old book or documentary and repurposes it as news for clicks and to fill space.

On the surface such pieces are easy to confuse with another journalistic staple, the 'blind item'. To the untrained eye, the latter look just as pointless: snippets in gossip columns or brief, stand-alone reports that hint at purported scandals but withhold the details. The purpose of the exercise is twofold: to make readers curious enough to return for updates, and to nudge a story closer to the point where it can no longer be suppressed by legal means. Once allegations are in the public domain, the only redress for subjects is to sue, a path many are reluctant to take even if innocent of the derelictions attributed to them. The downsides to individuals of lawsuits are substantial, potentially eye-watering costs and reputational damage arising from the disclosure process and renewed press attention. To push back against a story risks spreading it, much as operations to excise cancers can distribute diseased cells to other parts of the body.

In March 2019, the *Sun* carried a classic blind item. Written by a journalist called Dan Wootton, later dubbed 'sad little man' by Harry in *Spare*, it quoted an anonymous source claiming that Kate and her Norfolk neighbour, the Marchioness of Cholmondeley Rose Hanbury, had fallen out for reasons unspecified. Hanbury and her husband, David Rocksavage, the Marquess of Cholmondeley, 'used to be close [to William and Kate] but that is not the case anymore,' Wootton reported. 'William wants to play peacemaker so the two couples can remain friends, given they live so close to each other and share many mutual friends. But Kate has been clear that she doesn't want to see them anymore and wants William to phase them out, despite their social status.'

Though the newspaper quickly deleted Wootton's exclusive from its website, rival outlets, including the *Mail*, followed up with similarly vague stories. Then the *Mail*'s Richard Kay, who had numbered among Diana's closest media confidantes, weighed in with a new take. 'Both sides have considered legal action,' he wrote, 'but, because none of the reports have been able to offer any evidence about what the so-called dispute is about, they have chosen to ignore it.'

The 'gossip' – which Kay still declines to share – 'started doing the rounds at smart dinner parties late last year . . . There has been talk that the rumours were got up to damage Kate. So what is going on?' The answers the journalist proposes are as open to colourful interpretations as Wootton's original piece. 'Aesthete and former filmmaker' Rocksavage who 'had a string of glamorous girlfriends without showing any sign of wanting to settle down' had married Hanbury, 'a willowy ex-model, twenty-three years his junior . . . to the surprise of friends'. This unlikely couple are close to William and Kate only in geographical terms, part of the aristocratic set dubbed the Turnip Toffs who live on or close to the Sandringham estate in Norfolk.

Kate's targeting is both inexplicable and unjust, according to Kay. 'No friends of Kate have gone chatting to gossipy magazines as Meghan's have done. As a royal wife and mother, Kate has never put a foot wrong, her family are loyal and discreet. She carries out her official duties with enthusiasm. She and William have not been photographed exchanging so much as a cross word in public. If,' he concludes, 'this whole sorry episode turns out to be some cack-handed attempt to dent Kate's unshakeable standing with the public, it has almost certainly backfired.'

In other words, move on, nothing to see here, except the ill-matched Cholmondeleys, the uxorious heir to the throne and the perfect Kate – unless, of course, you were plugged into social media conspiracies or happened to travel to France during this period, where press carried headlines such as '*Rose Hanbury, la prétendue maîtresse du prince William, en route vers le divorce*': Rose Hanbury, the alleged mistress of Prince William, heading for divorce. When *Spare* came out, you might also have wondered which press reports prompted William, by Harry's account, to call him in April 2019. 'Something had happened between him and Pa and Camilla,' Harry writes. 'I couldn't get the whole story, he was talking too fast, and was way too upset. He was seething actually. I gathered that Pa and Camilla's people had planted a story or stories about him and Kate and the kids, and he wasn't going to take it any more.'

Given the timing, this could conceivably refer to Wootton's piece and follow-up articles, if by no means proving the notion of Charles and Camilla's involvement. Whatever the case, lacking publishable details about the supposed rift between Kate and Hanbury to sustain coverage, the British media backed off. Perhaps lawyers or spin doctors played a part too. Often, it takes a mix of threats and blandishments to kill a story. It helped too that Kate and other royals were spotted amicably mingling at events where Hanbury was also present. So things might have remained. It was Kate's disappearance and the lack of information explaining it that combined to explosive effect. The doctored Mother's Day photo lit the fuse.

Had Kate even been present for a shoot? people asked. And why was the Princess minus her wedding ring? Hanbury instantly trended on social media, along with hashtags such as #KateGate, #WhereisKate, #PrinceWilliamAffair and one that directs the unwary to hardcore content. Millions more learned who Hanbury was and what the gossips were saying when US TV host Stephen Colbert devoted the opening monologue of his talk show to the subject: 'Internet sleuths are guessing that Kate's absence may be related to her husband, and the future king of England, William, having an affair,' he said. 'Oh no, my heart goes out to poor Kate.' He paused, rang a bell. 'Now let's dish the hot goss.'

'So, I think we all know who the alleged other woman is, say it with me, the Marchioness of Cholmondeley . . . Now there have been rumours of an affair between William and the Marching Band of Chicanery [guffaws from the studio audience] since 2019. According to tabloids, back then, when Kate supposedly confronted him about it, he "laughed it off, saying there was nothing to it". Aha, always a good response when your wife accuses you of cheating.'

Hanbury's lawyers wrote to Colbert's network, CBS, and 'other reputable media organisations to confirm that the allegation is false'. It is not clear that this alone would have prompted an apology. Television executives are used to receiving legal letters and in a country with freedom of speech written into the constitution, tend only to respond to specific threats of action. It was a video released on 22 March that forced a retreat, not just by Colbert but legions of people who had treated the question, 'Where is Kate?', like he did, as a joke.

That day, I received two calls in quick succession, from a royal source and a journalist. We already knew of an announcement coming later, but my contacts had the scoop on what it was. I messaged a top editor at one of the major UK broadcasters. She had not yet heard. While it speaks to the loyalty of the Kensington Palace team and the Waleses' friends that the news did the rounds hours rather than weeks before its release, the sequence of events also laid bare the powerlessness of traditional news management in the transformed media environment. Kate had faced a cruel choice: allow speculation to continue unchecked, or reveal her cancer diagnosis.

The next and final chapter of this book cannot hope to glimpse the real Meghan without an awareness that this same environment shapes, and distorts, perceptions of her. Disinformation is a toxin in public life. The less we trust what we are told, the more easily we swallow lies. This has always been the case, but social media changed the speed and scale at which the process occurs while hollowing out legacy media until much of it has become a vessel for a similar befuddling brew of real information, angry opinion and fake news. The originators of such material 'often don't care about the underlying issues,' says Gina Neff, Professor of Responsible AI at St Mary's University and executive director of Cambridge University's Minderoo Centre for Technology and Democracy. 'Their whole playbook is to sow the seeds of doubt and mistrust.'

Real people started the clamour around Kate, initiating or reposting the accusations of body doubles and other trickery, but bots and troll farms leapt onto it, while old media fed the beast with storylines or, in Colbert's case, handed it a foghorn. In his first show after Kate revealed the reason for her convalescence, he issued something resembling an apology – to Kate, rather than to Hanbury. 'A lot of my jokes have upset people in the past, and I'm sure some of my jokes will upset people in the future,' he said. 'But there's a standard that I try to hold myself to, and that is I do not make light of somebody else's tragedy . . . I know that any cancer diagnosis of any kind is harrowing for the patient and for their family.'

*

The single camera trains on her, its gaze unblinking. Thought or instinct have gone into this film. At just two minutes, seventeen seconds, it is concise without feeling hurried, pared to the basics and more powerful for that. She faces the lens head on, though the bench on which she sits angles away from it. A weak sun emphasises her pallor. She allows herself just two sentences before reaching this headline: 'In January, I underwent major abdominal surgery in London and at the time, it was thought that my condition was non-cancerous. The surgery was successful. However, tests after the operation found cancer had been present. My medical team therefore advised that I should undergo a course of preventative chemotherapy, and I am now in the early stages of that treatment.'

Kate does not name any of the allegations about her and her family, which would give them status. Instead, she presents an alternative narrative: William and she had hoped to keep her diagnosis under wraps to give them time to prepare their children for it. She is 'well and getting stronger every day by focusing on the things that will help me heal, in my mind, body and spirits. Having William by my side is a great source of comfort and reassurance too.'

Aides will consistently refuse to elaborate on her condition, just as her father-in-law's communications team keeps mum on the exact nature of his. All this reflects the difficulty of balancing privacy with the royal role. Unless the medical status of an individual can have serious consequences for the wider world, then that individual should be able to choose whether to disclose it. For Charles, consigned by birth to constant scrutiny, and Kate, relentlessly anatomised, this interest in their bodily dysfunctions adds insult to longstanding injury. Yet their attempts to turn their joint misfortune to useful public-health messaging are inevitably hamstrung by the lack of detail. The NHS already has huge waiting lists for diagnostic tests. Encouraging everyone to get themselves checked without naming specific cancers and symptoms could lengthen those queues.

Still, what else should they do? As for quietening the rumours, the effect of Kate's announcement is limited. Lots of people do step back from online conspiracies about her, but others are already fully captured, primed to disbelieve what institutions such as monarchy or the 'MSM' (Mainstream Media) tell them and confirmed in their scepticism by networks of websites and content creators that deploy generative AI to plagiarise or invent news. A French researcher recently identified four thousand such websites, describing them as the 'tip of the iceberg'.[20]

Because of this context, I do not immediately understand the curatorial choices Kate makes with a second video, released on 9 September 2024, to announce the end of her chemotherapy. This is everything her first film is not, almost a minute longer, lush and self-conscious in its counterfeit authenticity. At times, the picture is grainy, edges sputtering as if we are watching a misalignment of celluloid. The rest of the camerawork is retro in a different way; soft focus, an Athena poster come to life.

That she wishes to convey two core messages simultaneously is clear from the tenth second, which unlike the rest of the action is set neither in woodland or meadow nor on a beach, but with Kate on her own, in the driving seat. As she changes gear, we see her wedding ring and, lest we miss it, there are further shots of it as the film nears its conclusion. By then, we have already witnessed her husband kissing her, sharing a blanket with her, putting his arm around her.

The confection boasts a voiceover by Kate delivering the other strand of messaging, that life has been tough for her family, 'the cancer journey is complex, scary and unpredictable', she is not yet recovered, and any return to royal duties will be gradual. Her last sentence implies that she now also considers it part of her role to speak about and for cancer patients. 'To all those who are continuing their own cancer journey – I remain with you, side by side, hand in hand. Out of darkness, can come light so let that light shine bright.'

The language, art direction and swelling music confuse me, and I wonder if the film will attract pushback for such obvious artifice, perhaps even launch additional conspiracies. I am wrong. 'Who knew that something so short could pack such a punch?' asks *The Times*. 'The Princess of Wales's update on her health . . . is probably the most consequential change to royal comms since the invention of the printing press.'

In fact, the video is not of itself transformative, nor will it rock the status quo the way Gutenberg's invention did. It is, however, innovative, a clever response to technology-driven transformation. Kate, the Art History graduate, watched analogue shots fired by palace press teams glance off the incoming barrage of digital deception like arrows hitting a tank and has brought updated weapons to the fray, fighting fakery not with dry facts but hyper-emotive content.

What can't Kate do? Stop the onslaught or regain full control over her life and body. The effects of cancer rarely end with the treatment. 'You have to find your new normal and that takes time,' she said, talking to fellow survivors during an official visit to a wellbeing garden in the summer of 2025. 'It's a rollercoaster.' Or, as she might have said, a seesaw.

She is mortal, subject to the same physical laws as the rest of us, prey to anxieties, capable of error, vulnerable, human and all the more impressive for that than those who insist on her perfection acknowledge.

Chapter 8

Meghan: 'It's Not Enough to Just Survive'

Hers is a fairytale that feminists yearn to believe. Some of us warned, 'Don't do it, Di', yet dare to imagine a better outcome for Meghan Markle. She is different, we tell ourselves, nor are we wrong, though, that difference will count against her. Today, we see only the mirage. Deceptively traditional in silk cady and tulle, she pauses on the steps to St George's Chapel, waves to cheering crowds, then proceeds along her chosen path. Inside, royalty lines the pews or rests in peace. The Tudor Henrys are buried here, so too Jane Seymour, Edward VII, the ever-tolerant Alexandra, George V, his consort Mary, and, in an annex, George VI and Princess Margaret. Over bones and dust Meghan glides, escorted by one prince to two who wait: the best man, and her groom, Harry, from this day forth the Duke of Sussex.

Her mother, Doria, watches from the quire, a prime position opposite the Queen of England. Both matriarchs sport green dresses, matching hats and surnames imposed on earlier generations of their families. Now Meghan seems to promise another reinvention. On 19 May 2018, it is still just about possible to imagine that peace and progress, like the Queen, will reign for ever. Humanity, learning from its past mistakes, might be inching towards enacting the precept that all men are created equal, though the founding father who wrote it into America's Declaration of Independence did not. Perhaps even women will rise. A hereditary monarchy appears an unlikely engine of change, but the family's first biracial member, first declared feminist and, in a sign of institutional shift, the first divorcée permitted to marry a Windsor in the Church of England, offers a glimpse of how she might use her status for good.

The run-up to the wedding has proved her mettle. Paparazzi photographs of her father getting ready for her big day turn out to have been staged with his connivance. Hospitalised with heart trouble and amid confusion over his intentions, Thomas Markle has stayed home in Mexico. The breach between father and daughter is by no means the only behind-the-scenes drama, yet the bride betrays not a hint of stress. As a gospel choir launches into an old standard, the familiar words acquire new meaning. *No, Harry won't be afraid, oh he won't be afraid, just as long as she stands by him.* Does she take Harry for better, for worse, for richer, for poorer? He turns pink with happiness. Already, the vows depart from tradition, dispensing with his full burden of names, Henry Charles Albert David Mountbatten-Windsor. 'Those whom God has joined together', the Archbishop of Canterbury intones, 'let no one put asunder.'

I click on the screen, scroll back, study the footage again.

To revisit these scenes is to peer down the wrong end of a telescope, the optimism of that day as distant as the moon, or at least California, where the Sussexes have lived in exile since 2020. Scarcely a week passes without the press quoting anonymous sources to suggest that their union is fraying. Palace insiders talk of a plan to 'rehabilitate' Harry if the marriage fails. Media executives circle, scenting blood and calculating how to secure coveted post-split exclusives.

I ask someone who has closely observed the couple whether he has directly witnessed signs of tension. No, he replies, but 'the thing that raises my suspicions is that they say too much about each other publicly. If you're in love with your husband or your wife, you don't need to be saying that every five minutes to the outside world.' Perhaps. A few days before this conversation, Meghan has raved about Harry on a podcast hosted by her friend, entrepreneur Jamie Kern Lima. 'That man loves me so much. I mean, look what we've built, we've built a beautiful life, and we have two healthy, beautiful children, and you know, I always think about it like the end of Super Mario Brothers, and you get to the final, final level with the golden Super Mario and they're like "slay the dragon!", "save the princess!" – that's my husband.' To suspicious ears, this tribute could sound performative rather than sincere. Then again, most of us are never forced to navigate the outside world calling doubt and digging dirt on our relationships.

Despite these pressures, the Sussex marriage has so far confounded the sceptics, but this is far from the joyous scenario we were promised. How on earth did so many of us fall for the princess myth yet again? Why did Meghan? The teachings of the past should send any female unlucky enough to catch a princely eye running not towards him but for the hills. Search continents and centuries, and you will be hard pressed to identify more than a handful of royal women whose lives look tolerable, much less enviable. Even those who glister from a distance turn out on closer inspection to have sacrificed great chunks of themselves: their desires, opinions, bodies. Those jewels winking in the light might just be their tears.

One answer, of course, is that love conquers all misgivings. Another is that each successive generation hoodwinks the next into imagining princessdom to be a golden ticket. Most such narratives end at the wedding, the future swathed in a shimmering haze. Princesses, like portraits of Elizabeth Tudor, exist outside the ordinary rules of time and mortality.

For the best part of a century, two global corporations have done more than any others to sustain this idea, especially via the medium of film. In 1937, Disney released its first full-length animation, *Snow White and the Seven Dwarfs*. As its heroine sings to a rapt audience – someday her prince will come to make her 'happy forever' – a voice from the corner mutters 'mush'. I stumbled across a film clip in which company founder Walt Disney airily labels the dissident dwarf 'Grumpy, the woman hater', yet in modern terms, the character's hard-edged realism could actually be construed a kindness. After all, Snow White will be poisoned and her stepmother killed before the prince breaks the spell by kissing her when she is out cold and thus unable to consent.

As the company expanded its princess franchises, Windsors Inc did its bit by serving up gorgeous real-life wedding sequences – never mind that the 'ever after' part kept coming unstuck. At least the OGs, Elizabeth and Philip, stayed together. Their marriage brightened postwar Britain, attracted acres of print coverage and broke new ground. Radio broadcast the whole caboodle live, and TV cameras captured highlights. In 1960, some twenty million viewers enjoyed the first fully televised royal wedding, the toxic union of Princess Margaret and Antony Armstrong-Jones. Astonishing numbers tuned in to witness the vows of Margaret's eldest nephews: 750 million globally transfixed by Charles and Diana's ceremony, and 500 million to see Sarah Ferguson promise to obey Andrew.

In 2011, I sat glued to my computer terminal for another blockbuster, Kate and William's nuptials. Across the world, many of us watched this way. By now, broadcasters were jostling for market share with digital platforms. Legacy print media, including my employer, *TIME*, got in on the act too. From early that morning, I flexed our new technological capacities, live-blogging the build-up and ceremony, embedding video and stills in the feed, and interacting with commenters. As the newly created Duke and Duchess of Cambridge exited Westminster Abbey, I handed over the reins to a colleague and started writing a cover story for the commemorative magazine we would send to press the same night.

During my eleven years at *TIME*, New York editors deemed only three events sufficiently newsworthy to merit global standalone issues: the 2009 death of Michael Jackson, the Cambridges' wedding and, later that same weekend, the raid on Osama bin Laden's compound. This unexpected juxtaposition of confetti and killing raised questions about whether William and Kate had warranted their special edition, especially given lower-than-predicted viewing figures. Interest in the Windsors appeared to be waning, if not as rapidly as audiences for live TV. Even so, around 300 million people witnessed this royal pageant by one means or another, enough to activate the phenomenon I described in the cover story as 'the mysterious alchemy that turns spectators into participants in their own history'.

Every moment of the ceremony had been choreographed to showcase the future of the monarchy while emphasising its continuity with the past. Central to that iconography was Kate's dress. Fact-checking site Snopes debunked an internet meme juxtaposing photographs from the ceremony with stills from Disney's 1950 *Cinderella* to suggest that William and Kate had modelled their wedding outfits on those worn by the Prince Charming and his love; the original animated frames had been, as Kate's Mother's Day photo would be, digitally altered. Yet the only fakery required to match the Cambridges to the Charmings was a tweak to the colour scheme to give the cartoon prince fair hair and a red tunic and make Cinderella a brunette.

The real-life marriage was a marketing triumph for the Windsors and, as a popular US blogger noted, for the princess myth. 'Little girls dream of being princesses,' she wrote. 'Grown women seem to retain this childhood fantasy. Just look at the pomp and circumstance surrounding the royal wedding and endless conversation about Princess Kate.' The blogger confessed that she identified with a princess too, but one with agency, 'She-Ra, Princess of Power', the eponymous heroine of a 1985 animated series spun off from *He-Man and the Masters of the Universe*.

This was Meghan writing on the *Tig*, a website she named for her favourite Tuscan wine, Tignanello. She used her platform to opine on everything from fine food and fashion to gentle activism. While She-Ra wields a sword, saves He-Man, defects to the rebels and in some later iterations of the story possesses a malignant alter-ego, Despara, Meghan's feminism owed less to fighting and dismantling than building and boosting. 'It is said that girls with dreams become women with vision,' she declared in a 2015 speech reproduced on the site. 'May we empower each other to carry out such vision.'

Two years later, she shuttered the *Tig* and prepared to put her career on ice, filming her seventh and last series of the legal drama *Suits*. That November, she and Harry announced their engagement. Would She-Ra really surrender her voice and liberty to marry a prince? 'I don't see it as giving anything up. I just see it as a change. It's a new chapter, right?' Meghan told the BBC's Mishal Hussain. She was proud of her professional achievements, but now it was time to work with Harry as a team to promote 'causes that are really important to me'. To those unfamiliar with Windsor ways – and to some of us who really should have known better – her words raised a tantalising possibility. Everybody looked set to win: the Windsors finally edging towards the diversity of the populations they are meant to represent; a contented Harry saved from a downwards spiral; and Meghan, Princess of Power, handed not a sword but a global platform for those causes.

How and why did that dream crumble? Before we delve into the forces and factors that derailed her hopes and ours, please humour me by examining your own attitudes to her. My agenda is not to persuade you of one position or another, but rather to reveal the mechanisms that shaped your views.

Unless you paid keen attention to the briefcase-wielding assistants on US gameshow *Deal or No Deal* or noticed the unnamed 'hot girl' in a forgettable Ashton Kutcher romcom, Meghan is unlikely to have troubled your consciousness before

2011, when she landed the role of Rachel Zane on *Suits*. If you missed the series in its original run, you probably became aware of Meghan's existence when Camilla Tominey, at that stage royal editor of the *Sunday Express*, scooped the rest of Fleet Street: 'Prince Harry', Tominey revealed, 'is secretly dating a stunning US actress, model and human rights campaigner.' Her piece triggered a first and revealing burst of coverage.

'Harry's girl is (almost) straight outta Compton: Gang-scarred home of her mother revealed – so will he be dropping by for tea?' asked the *Mail Online*, though the house in question sits in a middle-class suburb. In the *Mail on Sunday*, Rachel Johnson, sister to Boris Johnson, wrote that Meghan would 'thicken [the Windsors'] watery, thin blue blood and Spencer pale skin and ginger hair with some rich and exotic DNA'. However egregious these examples, there were enthusiastic write-ups too – optimistic takes about progress, plus a huge volume of the kinds of pulp reporting inflicted on every royal bride that can numb interest as well as driving it. Even by the time of the wedding, Meghan neither divided most crowds, nor could she necessarily rely on their recognition. Some 62 per cent of respondents to an Ipsos poll conducted in twenty-eight countries declared that they either lacked strong emotions about Meghan or were unaware of her, with 29 per cent positive towards her and just 10 per cent harbouring negative feelings.

Royals and other public figures tend to envy the upper echelons of popularity, failing to realise that the comfortable middle of the table is the place to be. Harry and Meghan's marriage raised the groom to an all-time peak, fleetingly above Elizabeth II; the bride charted as high as sixth place. Soon enough, she learned the difference between manageable celebrity and her new level of fame: one opens doors, the other imprisons you. Also, for all but a lucky few, what goes up must come down. A 2025 survey of UK public opinion found respondents split on the question of whether it would be a good thing for former favourite Harry to return home. Reactions to the idea of Meghan moving back revealed a bleaker picture, with just 12 per cent in favour, with 41 per cent insisting she should stay the hell away.

A third of respondents still professed to be devoid of any leanings pro- or anti-Meghan. Perhaps this is a claim you would make too. Forgive my scepticism, but scores of interviews and background conversations for this book made clear to me that declarations of neutrality often conceal an element of contempt, the sense that the royals in general or Meghan in particular are unworthy of serious attention.

The monarchy survives not only because of positive feelings towards it, but also the widespread misapprehension that it is little more than a tourist attraction. In fact, the institution possesses considerable soft powers, constitutional and economic heft, and extraordinary geographical and cultural reach. As for Meghan, there is no need to connect with her, watch her shows or consume news about her. However, to dismiss her as unimportant is to miss the problem she embodies. Meghan matters, quite simply, because she is one of the most prominent women in the world. Her popularity rankings may have tanked, but her name recognition charts at 100 per cent in recent multi-country polls, an astonishing level of fame. That she is a woman of colour and, rightly or wrongly, associated in the public imagination with particular value sets, adds to her significance.

This argument is of course redundant for the Sussex Squad, her devoted fans. That does not mean that their position – and actions – are beyond challenge. If, for example, they discount reports about Meghan clashing with palace staff as malicious slander, how does this square with her own position that it is vital to listen to women, to minorities, to the disempowered when they speak about their experiences? How should her fans defend Meghan without undermining the values she espouses, including sisterhood? What if attacking other women in her name not only betrays what she stands for but energises her opponents, and possibly even serves the agendas of regimes and political movements and profit-hungry corporations that care not a jot about Meghan or any women?

As for those who clamour for Meghan to be expunged from public life like a latter-day Anne Boleyn, there is really only one question they should answer: what exactly has she done to earn such hostility? The Sussex Squad suspects her critics of misogyny, racism or an admixture of the two, misogynoir.

Not so, say these detractors. Meghan has earned their contempt, for example by inflicting reputational damage on the monarchy. Yet compared to Andrew's actions, anything Meghan has said or done are bagatelles. His ex-wife Sarah Ferguson's misjudgements include accepting money from Jeffrey Epstein to settle her debts and, after her public apology for doing so, emailing Epstein to apologise for her apology: 'I know you feel hellaciously let down by me,' she wrote. 'You have always been a steadfast, generous and supreme friend to me and my family.'

Nor are Meghan and Harry more talkative than many other royals. Fergie's literary works alone could fill a sad bookshelf:

novels that owe a debt to Barbara Cartland; not one but two memoirs; plus a self-help manual, *What I Know Now: Simple Lessons Learned the Hard Way*. Her multiple 'candid' broadcast interviews spilling the beans on the royal family include a pair of sit-downs with Oprah Winfrey and a six-part series in which Winfrey is filmed calling the then-duchess to give her advice about building a new career as a media personality. 'All you've got to do, and trust me with this,' says Winfrey, 'is get really real.'

The current king got real many times before his accession, confessing to adultery on national television and launching vigorous interventions on issues from architecture to wellness. He also riskily fundraised for charitable initiatives from donors, at least a few subsequently involved in scandals and one who reportedly arrived with a bag of cash.

His court as Prince of Wales was simultaneously hierarchical and dysfunctional, its historical substructure visible through the gloss of modern HR practices. Over the decades complaints from staff ranged from racism to rape, all denied and unproven. One of few Black staffers, Elaine Day, alleged sex discrimination and unfair dismissal. She lost her case, but not before the tribunal got sight of a memo, apparently annotated by Charles in response to her query about possible career paths to a higher-ranking role. 'What is wrong with everyone nowadays? Why do they all seem to think they are qualified to do things far beyond their technical capabilities?' the perplexed Prince scrawled on the document. 'People think they can all be pop stars, high court judges, brilliant TV personalities or infinitely more competent heads of state without ever putting in the necessary work or having natural ability.' It was a bold question from a man whose job was inherited rather than earned.

Though his household appeared more combustible than others, nobody takes a job in a palace for the money or the conditions. Royal employees – typically paid less than they could earn elsewhere and on call day and night – also seem peculiarly vulnerable to bullying and other forms of workplace abuse. Those who successfully cultivate favour with their bosses may in turn misuse it. The Queen Mother's most powerful servant, William Tallon, aka 'Backstairs Billy', once mythologised as a jovial exemplar of royal service, emerged in accounts after his death as a serial harasser and a bully.

Nobody without experience of palace life anticipates quite how intricate the internal politics can be, or how tough it is to make change in systems creaking with tradition. In pre-Meghan days, an American friend, headhunted for a significant position at Kensington Palace, sought my advice about whether to put in an application. I duly quizzed insiders about the perils and potential of the role. Here is the message they gave me to pass back to him: 'Do it for the experience but keep your New York apartment.'

None of these examples are intended to minimise the seriousness of the bullying allegations against Meghan, but rather to ask critics whether, in light of the wider context of Windsor foibles and failings, what we know – or think we know – about Meghan explains the strength of the animosity towards her.

Might other factors be at play? Does her voice grate? Is she simply too Californian, too politically correct, too new-age-y for British tastes? A persistent criticism relates to her perceived lack of authenticity. A Venn diagram consisting of three circles, the first holding people who consider Meghan phony, the second containing anyone who uses 'woke' as a pejorative and a third filled with the legions who appreciated Prince Philip *for* his 'gaffes', not in spite of them, would probably see the Philip circle swallow the other two whole. Nothing bellows 'what you see is what you get' quite like unvarnished racism and sexism.

Perhaps resentment towards Meghan stems from her snagging a prince and then forgetting to be grateful, or from those who went to bat for her only for her to disappoint their initial hopes. Meghan does not think of herself as rebellious, says a well-informed source. In 2018, she cheered the #MeToo movement, not to wage politics or force her husband and William and Kate, alongside her on the platform, into endorsing the campaign, but on the reasonable assumption that ending sexual harassment was a mainstream goal – and therefore uncontentious.

More than a few of her feminist supporters from those early days have fallen silent. They wanted her to go further; to do more to walk her talk of equality. Some tell me they have been put off by the sun-drenched lifestyle showcased in *With Love, Meghan*, which can appear, in the words of the *Telegraph*, a tad 'Montecito Marie Antoinette'. Then again, the uber-privileged Marie Antoinette of popular mythology bears little resemblance to the historical figure, a child bride like many other royal women, sent at fourteen from her native Austria to marry the French dauphin and still in her teens when he acceded. She would face her final reckoning at the guillotine on the Place de la Revolution, now the Place de la Concorde, the place of peace. As she mounted the scaffold, the deposed queen accidentally trod on the foot of her executioner. 'I'm sorry,' she said. 'I didn't mean to do it.'

Two centuries later, another royal woman would die in the city, observed not by crowds but by paparazzi and medics. These days, Diana is regarded in some quarters as a secular saint. To her younger son, she is also an inspiration and a warning. Harry has equated her unhappiness with Meghan's and spoken of his fears that the pursuit of Meghan by the media might lead to tragedy. Meghan studiously avoids such direct parallels, at least in public. That protects her neither from allegations that she angles to position herself as a new Diana, nor from constant, belittling comparisons with her. An Instagram post in which Meghan wears a Northwestern University sweatshirt provoked howls of rage because Diana had been photographed in the same sweatshirt. 'That may be [Meghan's] most pathetic attempt yet at cosplaying Harry's mother,' snarled one commenter. 'She is completely psychotic now,' fumed another. Thousands of similar posts ignored the fact that Meghan, unlike Diana, was a Northwestern alumna, with a degree in International Relations and Theatre Studies.

'Meghan is no Diana,' a palace insider muttered to me recently. If this sentiment chimes with you, think about the venom directed at Diana. Remember the *Sunday Mirror* column about Diana that hit newsstands on the morning of her death. 'It's a pity Gucci don't make designer face zips.' Diana was no Diana either – until she could no longer speak for herself.

*

While many of us ignored the lessons of history, Yasmin Alibhai-Brown refused to buy into the mush her profession churned out in response to Harry and Meghan's engagement. The veteran journalist, who had breached barriers herself as the first person of colour to get her own UK newspaper column, responded with sound advice: 'This is not a dreamy fairytale,' she wrote in the *i-Paper*. 'Most crowns are made of thorns as well as diamonds.' Invited to defend her views on ITV's *Good Morning Britain*, Alibhai-Brown came under attack from the programme's then co-host, Piers Morgan, who had not yet transcribed his arc from an oleaginous admirer of Meghan to one of her more vituperative critics. 'The truth is,' he bellowed at Alibhai-Brown, 'you don't like any of them.'

That was not a million miles wide of the mark. Alibhai-Brown is certainly not a fan, referring to the Windsors collectively as 'this ghastly family'. However, as a republican and author of books that intelligently explore British multiculturalism, colonial heritage and attitudes to race, she tends to focus less on individuals than the meaning and impact of the monarchy. Such distinctions do little to quench the anger directed at her. 'My Muslimness actually sets them on fire,' she says wryly of the hordes that come after her online. Strains in British society inflamed by the mere existence of Alibhai-Brown and already smouldering at rumours that Carole Middleton might have Jewish roots were never going to accept the idea of Meghan contributing to the Windsor bloodline. Around the same time that Alibhai-Brown urged 'don't do it, Meg', the girlfriend of the then-leader of the anti-immigration UKIP party sent texts to friends complaining that Meghan's 'seed' would be a 'taint'.

Foam-flecked racism is easy to spot, but Alibhai-Brown worried Meghan might be wrong-footed by the paternalistic kind that artlessly asks a British-born Black woman at a palace reception where she comes from or uses racialised slurs as supposed endearments. In a clip of Harry recorded during his time at the military academy Sandhurst, he can be heard jokingly calling a fellow cadet a 'paki'. He 'used the term without any malice and as a nickname about a highly popular member of his platoon,' said a spokesman. After it emerged that property developer Kuldip Singh Dhillon had been dubbed 'Sooty' by fellow members of the Cirencester Polo Club, including the then Prince Charles, Dhillon himself defended the practice in a statement. 'You know you have arrived when you acquire a nickname,' he said. 'I enjoy being called Sooty by my friends, who I am sure universally use the name as a term of affection with no offence meant or felt. The Prince of Wales is a man of zero prejudice, and both his sons have always been most respectful.'

Ahead of Meghan's induction into the royal family, journalist and writer Aatish Taseer wrote a piece for *Vanity Fair* drawing on his direct experience of its culture. For a while, he had dated Gabriella Windsor, daughter to Queen Elizabeth's first cousin, Prince Michael of Kent. Gabriella's mother, Princess Michael, kept a pair of black sheep named Venus and Serena after the Williams sisters and also complained that she 'daren't even say I want my coffee black anymore. I say, "Without milk."' Born Baroness Marie Christine von Reibnitz and dubbed 'Princess Pushy' by the British press, she arrived for Meghan's first pre-Christmas lunch at Buckingham Palace sporting a blackamoor brooch. When a close-up of the jewellery did the rounds, her spokesman issued a statement: 'The brooch was a gift and has been worn many times before. Princess Michael is very sorry and distressed that it has caused offence.'

Racism in the UK is 'more casual than its American coeval but more insidious, because its animating prejudice is class,' Taseer observes in his *Vanity Fair* piece. 'The British are perfectly happy to deal with people of colour who know their place'. It is those 'uppity' types 'who arouse in them an animal hatred'.

Seen through this prism, did Meghan ever stand a chance? The very qualities that appeared to give her an edge – her confidence, intelligence, education and experience – put her squarely in that 'uppity' bracket. Moreover, the only female incomers to royalty who have made the transition successfully in the modern age have done so by emulating not She-Ra but Hans Christian Andersen's Little Mermaid. For years, Camilla bit her tongue, Sophie learned to pipe down, Kate always kept mum. Meghan understood the transaction: 'Oh my God, she falls in love with the prince and because of that she loses her voice,' she told Oprah Winfrey.

Perhaps if Meghan had shut up, closed down, worn nude tights and deferred as if her life depended on it, she might have made a go of things. Reboots can work. Disney's 1989 animation changed Andersen's story to let the milk-skinned, red-haired Ariel win back her powers of speech – and audiences loved it. On the other hand, the company's 2023 live-action remake, casting the actress and singer Halle Bailey in the title role, unleashed a cartoonish tidal wave of protest under the hashtag #NotMyAriel. How utterly unrealistic, these critics wailed, to imagine that a mermaid could be Black.

What really defies belief, of course, is the idea that someone used to the wide-open seas would easily adapt to the royal fishbowl. Both Disney films skirt this consideration by ending as the prince and the mergirl unite. The original fairytale takes a darker turn, the heroine vaporised, becoming, like Diana, a saintly presence.

'Meghan must have known what she was getting into,' a friend insists. He refuses to accept Meghan's denial to Oprah that she Googled Harry before their first date. I tell my friend that he is missing the point. No matter how many hours, days, weeks or years Meghan spent trawling the internet, nothing her search turned up could convey the weirdness and complexity of palace culture.

'How do you explain that you bow to your grandmother?' Harry muses in the 2022 Netflix six-parter, *Harry & Meghan*. 'And that [Meghan] would need to curtsey.' Meghan picks up the story, describing her first encounter with the Queen. 'Americans will understand this. I mean, we have "Medieval Times: Dinner and Tournament". It was like that.' She then mimes a deep curtsey. Tabloids and trolls alike seized on the gesture to accuse her of disrespecting royalty.

If so, then such disrespect is rife. Curtseying is funny, like much else that goes on in palaces – and the royals themselves know it. In the suppressed fly-on-the-wall documentary, *Royal Family*, the Windsors chortle about the difficulty of maintaining a straight face on ceremonial occasions. Elizabeth tells a story about Queen Victoria managing to contain her laughter after an ambassador takes a tumble in front of her. ('Afterwards, of course, the tears poured down her cheeks.') Elizabeth says that she herself was nearly undone after the home secretary told her '"there's a gorilla coming in" . . . so I stood in the middle of the room, pressed the bell, the door opened and there was a gorilla, and I had the most terrible trouble in keeping . . . you know he had a short body, long arms'. 'Oh,' responds Charles, 'if that happened to me, I would absolutely dissolve.' It is unclear who the diplomat was and whether the description was merely 'unkind', by Elizabeth's own admission, or also racially charged.

Years ago, I coined the term 'Planet Windsor' to try to convey not only the absurdity of palace culture but also its alien qualities. It is life, but not as we commoners know it. A member of Charles's household tipped me off about a competition among female staff to see who could curtsey lowest without falling over. Like Meghan, I too learned to make this obeisance, if without a flourish. Like her, I would have expected the Windsors to shed such formalities in private, kicking them off with their shiny shoes and sighs of relief. Instead, they police them.

Sophie's promotion from Countess of Wessex to Duchess of Edinburgh put her on a par with Meghan, finally absolving her, a source told the *Mail*, of the requirement 'to curtsey to someone in the family who has not only left Royal duties but has spent the past three years criticising the institution that Sophie works so hard to support'. Many people would find it surprising that Sophie kept curtseying in the first place. Passive-aggressive curtseying. Who knew it was a thing?

The rules deciding who bends the knee to whom are carefully codified, to be revised as necessary to reflect the changing female line-up among the Windsors, as well as the feelings of the rule-setters. Camilla's marriage to Charles, for example, should have catapulted her up the order of precedence. Her new mother-in-law, never fully at peace with the circumstances of the marriage, ordered that Camilla continue to rank below Princesses Anne, Beatrice and Eugenie, though not poor Sophie. In a similar vein, Meghan found herself required to curtsey to most royals if alone, but only to the most senior when Harry accompanied her. Inevitably, she sometimes defaulted to real-world behaviours, and just as predictably the press documented these breaches with glee. Listicles such as 'Seventy-Two Times Meghan Markle Broke Royal Protocol' enumerate heinous acts including crossing her legs, shutting a car door (that's what servants are for) and being spotted with a manicure that diverged from the approved baby pink palette and 'squoval' shape.

Even born royals chafe at the thickets of customs and restrictions that separate them from the rest of us. Before his accession, Charles often yearned, like the Little Mermaid, to explore the land on his own two legs. 'I try to put myself in other people's position and because I drive about the country endlessly, I've often thought about the lives of people in the places I pass, the streets,' he told me back in 2013. During Andrew's post-military, pre-scandal years, he too acknowledged the invisible pane of glass between royals and the rest of the world, if only to dismiss its importance. To reach his Buckingham Palace apartment, we passed along corridors cluttered with unwanted gifts, sentimental sculptures, rolled carpets and monogrammed trinkets. 'People say to me: "Would you like to swap your life with me for twenty-four hours? Your life must be very strange,"' he remarked, once we were seated to his liking and sipping tea delivered by a liveried footman.

'But of course, I have not experienced any other life. It's not strange to me.'

I remembered that statement when he admitted on *Newsnight* that he pays no attention to people paid to dance attendance on him. 'I live in an institution at Buckingham Palace which has members of staff walking around all the time and I don't wish to appear grand, but there were a lot of people who were walking around Jeffrey Epstein's house,' he said.

Now picture Meghan plunged into this life, servants and aides around her all the time, zero privacy. Should she regard staff as potential friends or emulate the indifference of a born prince? Would they serve her or spy on her or, as in Tudor times so often the case, both? Harry has described the royal existence as 'this surreal state, this unending *Truman Show*'. He 'almost never carried money, never owned a car, never carried a house key, never once ordered anything online, never received a single box from Amazon, *almost* never travelled on the Underground'.

Everything he and his wife said to Winfrey has been picked apart line by line, but one comment by Meghan, largely overlooked, not only rings true but points to a key factor in the tensions that quickly blew up. 'I think,' she said, that 'there was no way to understand what the day-to-day was going to be like . . . It's easy to have an image of it that is so far from reality . . . That is what was really tricky over the past several years [because] you're being judged by the perception but you're living the reality.'

'Hardly anybody in America knows this country or the ins and outs of this family or its history. They think it's all cream teas and crowns,' says Alibhai-Brown. 'I was quite scared for

Meghan. There were so many things she was representing without even knowing it. It was almost like she was being led into a horror film where she could be easily destroyed because she knew so little.'

The ignorance is mutual. As a citizen of both the US and the UK, it has long struck me how poorly my compatriots either side of the Atlantic understand each other. Just as we Americans are apt to conflate the histories and cultures of, say, England and Scotland, and fully overlook distinctions between English regions, so too we British talk about the States as an amorphous blob but for locations familiar from films and TV shows.

In order to comprehend Meghan, and what went wrong, we need to take a trip to the Golden State, not to the gang-scarred hoods of the *Mail*'s imagination, but to places and ideas that actually shaped her.

*

In 1850, California became America's thirty-first state as part of a package of laws that briefly reduced tensions between Northern abolitionists and Southern slavers but could not head off civil war. Situated on the San Andreas fault and at least six other major rifts, it had already experienced more than its fair share of turbulences. Spanish colonialists dispossessed indigenous populations while importing missionaries and diseases. Francis Drake is said to have made landfall here, claimed this part of the new world for Elizabeth I and sailed off again. Modern research points to him more likely anchoring in Oregon or never coming ashore at all.

Whatever the case, there would be many invasions of one kind or another. When a sawmill operator reported finding flakes of gold in a Californian streambed, the resulting rush brought some hundreds of thousands of prospectors to the state, to disastrous effect for the indigenous peoples who had survived earlier incursions. The California genocide killed tens of thousands, with many more starved out or forced into labour.

Towards the end of this period and then with gathering speed, Los Angeles metastasised from a small town to an urban sprawl. Black gold turned up alongside the shinier kind, with oil production taking off in the early twentieth century. The depression sent yet more people to California in search of work. By now a new industry had planted a flag: the Hollywood dream factory.

To foreigners, the state's palm-fringed boulevards appear the epitome of Americana, but Californians pride themselves on doing things differently to the rest of the nation. Democrats and Republicans dominate Californian gubernatorial and mayoral races just as they do elsewhere, but the winning candidates tend to be social liberals and distinctive in other ways too. California's best-known Republican governors, Ronald Reagan and Arnold Schwarzenegger, entered their campaigns as movie stars. Kamala Harris broke one ceiling after another in her home state. Los Angeles' longest-serving mayor, Democrat Tom Bradley, was the first African American to head a white-majority conurbation.

Hard-nosed entrepreneurialism not only coexists with multiple strands of spiritualism, defined in one study as 'nature religion, esotericism (including Theosophy and the occult), counterculture (including psychedelic use), East-west Hybridity, and the human potential movement', but inter-mingles with them.[21]

All of this, the good, the bad and the harmless-but-cringey, inflects the way Californians speak. To outsiders, West Coast variants of the English language often sound inauthentic – which is ironic given the frequent references to authenticity. Here's Meghan in a 2025 Bloomberg interview discussing the expectation that royal women wear nude tights: 'Let's be honest, that was not very myself. I hadn't seen pantyhose since movies in the eighties. That felt a little bit inauthentic. That's a silly example but it is an example of when you want to dress the way you want to dress and say the things that are true and you're able to show up in that space really organically and authentically – that's being comfortable in your own skin.'

Positivity is considered, well, a positive. So are career choices and behaviours the British media disdainfully labels 'attention-seeking'. The entertainment industry is one of the main employers in the state; contracts include clauses requiring performers to publicise their work, and a significant social media footprint is not an option but a necessity for those who hope to rise. Meghan's creation of the *Tig* fits into that pattern, as does her brand ambassadorship for the designer Ralph Lauren and cultivation of press contacts in the pre-Harry period, all now routinely cited as proof of her insatiable ambition. In the summer of 2016, she drank dirty vodka martinis with Piers Morgan, at that stage host of *Good Morning Britain* and a columnist for the *Daily Mail*. That she blanked him afterwards, he wrote, was 'perfectly understandable under the circumstances . . . All will be forgiven though if I get an invite to the wedding of the year.' He did not and it was not.

Emotions and feelings – topics to rattle the teacups in the drawing rooms of British people posh enough to have drawing rooms – are not merely up for discussion among Californians, but central to conversation. There is a perception that Californians hug more than other Americans. In *Harry & Meghan*, its eponymous heroine gives it a boost, describing William and Kate recoiling from her embrace. 'They came over for dinner, I remember I was in ripped jeans, and I was barefoot,' she says. 'I was a hugger. I've always been a hugger. I didn't realise that is really jarring for a lot of Brits.'

Another sign that Meghan might not mesh smoothly with the buttoned-up Windsors could be detected during the Sussexes' official visit to South Africa. When Tom Bradby inquired how she was coping with the pressures of royal life, she replied, 'Thank you for asking, because not many people have asked if I'm OK.' Back home, such an oversight would be unthinkable. She went on to muse that 'it's not enough to just survive something, right? Like, that's not the point of life. You've got to thrive, you've got to feel happy.'

This simple, seemingly uncontroversial idea would shake the monarchy, dislodge Harry and send both of the Sussexes to the place that nurtured it.

*

On 4 August 1981, Doria née Ragland and Thomas Markle, who met on the set of the medical soap *General Hospital*, welcomed their only child. They named the baby Rachel Meghan.

From the moment the Markles' princess was linked to Harry, it was clear that some British journalists struggled to understand her origin story. For one thing, they saw her biracial heritage as 'exotic' in Rachel Johnson's revealing phrase, assuming the union of 'a dreadlocked African American lady from the wrong side of the tracks' (Johnson, again) and a white, middle-class man to be a rarity. That is based on not one mistake but several. Doria, the daughter of a nurse and an antiques dealer, followed a degree in Psychology with a master's in Social Work, met Thomas during a stint as a trainee make-up artist, has run small businesses and taught yoga. Moreover, the US, notably diverse compared to the UK, is becoming more so. The white population, currently below 60 per cent of the total, is projected to be a minority by 2042. California is ahead of the curve. Its Hispanic and white populations achieved parity around the start of this century.

Meghan's biographer Tom Bower calls her parents' relationship 'unusual', citing a US-wide statistic for the period of one white American man in a thousand marrying a Black woman. In fact, the marriage, like the baby it produced, sat within local trends. Thomas, a divorcé with two children by his previous wife, reflected California's standing as the state with the highest rate of divorces and legal separations.[22] As for interracial marriages, the 1967 Supreme Court judgment on Loving vs Virginia, which ended America's restrictions on such matches, cited a groundbreaking Californian case nineteen years earlier. By the time Meghan celebrated her tenth birthday, over 13 per cent of households in Los Angeles described themselves as mixed race.

This is not to depict California as an oasis of equality. Protests in Los Angeles after the 2020 death of George Floyd tapped into the sense that little had changed over the nearly three decades since a court in the city failed to convict four white policemen filmed beating a Black man called Rodney King. Their acquittal triggered days of rioting. In an address to high school students after Floyd's murder, Meghan talked about those earlier events. 'I remember the curfew, and I remember rushing back home and seeing ash fall from the sky and smelling the smoke,' she said. She regretted that Floyd's killing would leave pupils with similar memories. 'That's something you should have an understanding of, but an understanding of it as a history lesson, not as your reality.'

Meghan worried about making this statement, she said. 'I wanted to say the right thing, and I was really nervous that I wouldn't, or that it would get picked apart, and I realised the only wrong thing to say is to say nothing.' Saying nothing, of course, would be the preferred Windsor approach. On Floyd's death, as so often, her in-laws kept quiet. Nor was she wrong to fear a backlash. Because she appears, in her own words, 'ethnically ambiguous', some detractors, typically themselves white, caricature her as a freeloader at a pity party; a kind of Rachel Dolezal, the civil rights campaigner unmasked as a white woman pretending to be Black, and thus ill-qualified to pronounce on matters of race, much less to do so from a position of empathy. Google the phrase 'I didn't know Meghan Markle was Black' and you will find that it frequently precedes this sentiment.

Those same words also surface pieces by Black or Brown authors criticising Meghan for saying too little, or else the wrong thing entirely. In a 2012 anti-racism film and again in *Harry & Meghan*, she appeared to suggest that her appearance made her a bystander to racism rather than its target. 'I'm biracial,' she said in the campaign video. 'Most people can't tell what I'm mixed with and so much of my life has felt like being a fly on the wall.' In conversation with her mother for the Netflix series, she recalled as a child seeing Doria subjected to racial abuse and mistaken for her nanny. Doria in turn revealed that she had warned her daughter that the media's fascination with her dating Harry was 'about race'. 'Mommy,' Meghan replied, 'I don't want to hear that.'

'Meghan presents passing for white – or the fact that "people didn't know what I was mixed with" – as a passive act, as something that just happened to her. But while many light-skinned people have the *ability* to pass, passing as an *act* is intentional,' wrote journalist Nylah Iqbal Muhammad after watching the episode. Long after the US abolished slavery, rafts of prohibitions and repressive laws continued to enforce white supremacy. Light-skinned people of colour sometimes 'passed' as white to circumvent these barriers, cutting themselves off from family and community, enduring lives of precarity and the risk of reprisals if discovered. Fear of unseen 'others' inspired fresh restrictions well into the twentieth century, including the one-drop rule, which defined anybody with a Black ancestor as Black, no matter how many generations removed.

Economic and cultural disparities remain entrenched, even in those regions and industries considered bastions of liberalism. In 2015, no actors of colour received nominations for the Academy Awards, an omission highlighted by the hashtag #OscarsSoWhite. It took until 2018's *Black Panther* for Hollywood to produce a mega-budget movie with a Black director and largely Black cast positioned not just for Black audiences but everyone. Both the film and its sequel were hits. Even so, a recent study of Black representation in the industry highlighted continuing problems such as the limited narratives told – a relentless focus on trauma, for example – as well as the exclusion of talent on screen and off.[23] Casting directors also still privilege Black actors with lighter skin.

Meghan embarked on her career with an advantage over darker-skinned counterparts, though her ambiguity could count against her too. She was, she wrote in *Elle* magazine, neither 'Black enough for the Black roles' nor 'white enough for the white ones'. Rachel Zane, her mixed heritage character in *Suits*, marked, she said, a breakthrough, 'the Goldilocks of my acting career – where finally I was just right'.

The series promoted her to a level of success enjoyed by only a small number of actors and fewer of Black or mixed heritage, guaranteeing her significant earnings and creating further opportunities within the field and for commercial endorsements. It also meant a move to Toronto for filming, while her first husband, movie producer Trevor Engelson, remained in Los Angeles. Their divorce and her split from a subsequent boyfriend, Canadian chef and restaurateur Cory Vitiello, would be repurposed by hostile commentators to fit a narrative of overweening ambition. In these versions of her story, Meghan traded in Engelson and Vitiello to snag a greater prize, though she did not yet know Harry.

The idea of princes and kings as the ultimate catches and common women scrambling over shattered hearts to reach them has long antecedents. Even Kate became 'Waity Katie'. The archetype, of course, is Anne Boleyn. Meghan named her product line As Ever, echoing Boleyn's motto, *semper eadem*.

Might Meghan feel a kinship with the Tudor royal? The source to whom I posed this question replied obliquely: whether people glorify Boleyn or vilify her, they do so without reference to the real woman. Nor do the parallels end there. Not since Nicholas Sander's sulphurous depiction of Boleyn and George Wyatt's hagiography of the 'Virtuous, Christian and Renowned Queen' have two accounts of the same person diverged more sharply than Tom Bower's *Revenge* and Omid Scobie and Carolyn Durand's *Finding Freedom*.

If Bower's book resembles a fairytale, it is *Goldilocks*, his Meghan temperamentally too cold, sexually too hot but never ever just right. Bower's Meghan does not ask, she 'demands'. The text includes thirty-seven references to her exerting control. A few examples: 'Meghan needed to be in total control'; 'Total control was essential'; 'When [during phone conversations] Harry is in the room, she is sweet, but when he steps out of the room she is a different person – mean and controlling'; 'My daughter is very controlling'; 'Meghan's a liar and very controlling'. The last three quotes are attributed to her father.

As a young actress, Bower writes, Meghan attended all-night Hollywood parties 'conservatively dressed and known to pose as an innocent. Yet she was usually among the last to leave as dawn broke.' How does he know her innocence was a pose? Because, Bower informs us, she soon 'lost her coyness. Dressed in hot pants and little else, she starred in the lifestyle magazine *Men's Health* making burgers on a grill.' His wording suggests a skimpy top or none. In fact, Meghan wore a shirt. 'The champion of women's empowerment later described those experiences as being objectified,' sneers Bower. Well, yes. Just like being a briefcase girl on *Deal or No*

Deal, the gig involved acting out a male fantasy as directed by a male-dominated media organisation within the context of a male-dominated industry and wider world.

Bower's understanding of racism is similarly literal. He takes Thomas Markle's testimony that he whisked his daughter to Palm Springs during the Rodney King riots to mean that the unrest made no impression on her. Meghan has been inconsistent in her descriptions of these events, but always characterised them as formative. Even at a physical remove, something which speaks to your own identity, your own vulnerability, can have a profound impact. In 2021, despite pandemic-era restrictions on public gatherings, the otherwise cautious Kate attended a vigil for Sarah Everard, who had been abducted and murdered by a serving policeman. In the US, up to twenty-six million people are thought to have participated in protests over George Floyd's death, with many more taking to the streets in other countries. Bower grants that Meghan once witnessed a motorist hurling racist insults at Doria but states that otherwise 'race was not deemed to be an issue' for Meghan during her school years. 'Until recently,' he writes, 'she never suggested suffering any sense of exclusion.'

*

If something bad really happened, she would have spoken up right away. This is a charge designed to undermine the credibility of any complainants who do not immediately report physical or verbal abuse or harassment. Yet whistleblowing carries the risk of retaliation and reputational damage. Early coverage of Virginia Giuffre referred to her as a 'masseuse' and in more explicitly sexualised terms, though she had been trafficked to Jeffrey Epstein as a minor. Later, her reliability as a witness came under attack and her fragility was weaponised against her.

#MeToo grew into a movement because so many women feared the consequences of revealing their experiences and, once the dam was breached, the stories flowed. So did retribution. The penalties were often more severe for targets already on the receiving end of discrimination but take a look at high-profile cases and you will see how swiftly initial sympathy turned to victim-blaming, even for established stars. In Hollywood, it is easy to acquire a reputation as a troublemaker, harder by far to shake it; and stories of women harassed and then blacklisted abound across other industries and sectors too.

As a rising actress, Meghan sometimes used her platform to protest against sexism and racism, but she also played the game. Yet denying or downplaying sustained or repeating aggressions, whatever their form or trigger, also takes its toll. As anyone who has been on the receiving end can testify, these experiences are exhausting. A meta-study identified some of the mechanisms those targeted deploy, from blaming themselves to self-medicating with drugs and alcohol or spinning alternative realities.[24] If these responses remind you of the behaviours of trauma victims, that is no coincidence. Research suggests that the experience of non-life-threatening 'prejudice events' puts victims at risk of a 'PTSD-like disorder'.[25]

Whatever the difficulties of Meghan's life before Harry, her new existence served up prejudice events in more generous portions by far, and at least a few of them existential. Soon after she moved to Kensington Palace, she received a letter filled with racist hatred and a white powder. The former head of counter-terrorism policing in England, Metropolitan Police assistant commissioner Neil Basu, later said that the force had investigated 'disgusting and very real' threats to Meghan during her time in England, some from the far right. He added that he would understand if she had felt 'under threat all the time'.

A theory spread by Bower and others, including the *Sun*'s veteran photographer Arthur Edwards, promotes the idea that she duped Harry into believing she would settle for the royal role, while always intending to tear him from the bosom of his family. A 'ruthless adventuress', in Bower's judgement, her eyes were fixed on Hollywood. 'She had no intention of staying here,' said Edwards. 'She is dragging Harry along and, unfortunately, he's gone along with it.' He added, plaintively, 'He didn't talk to me for a year. I've been photographing him since he was born, and it was down to her.'

My own research, which included conversations with deeply informed sources, produced a different picture, of two people naively optimistic that they could develop their own interpretations of the royal job, thrown off balance as they hit resistance and swiftly developing a siege mentality. Where some couples moderate each other's responses, the one more inclined to conciliation, the other to confrontation, Harry and Meghan share similar reflexes: he the product of a culture that valorises the masking of pain and at that stage only just addressing his scars, she, for all that she deploys the Californian language of self-exploration, outwardly directed and driven.

Amid rising tensions with other principals, and with Harry ever more fearful for his family's safety, he and Meghan did not surrender the idea of royal service but began to reimagine it. Perhaps they could base themselves on another continent 'still doing work for the Queen, but beyond the reach of the press'. Meghan had proved a natural at royalling. Her in-laws might recoil from her hugs, but strangers on the street leaned into them.

It severely hampered their search for solutions that they batted away good advice with the bad, reading interventions as the product of dusty palace thinking or inter-household rivalries. On the other hand, you can see why they might. Often the first reflex of officials, confronted with an innovative proposal, is to squash or temper it. In his twenties, Charles tangled with courtiers who tried to block his first substantial initiative, the Prince's Trust. It would be too political, they argued, plus it infringed on territory staked out by his father. He prevailed and the organisation, now the King's Trust, claims to have helped more than a million young people into training and employment. Anne offers an object lesson too, combining her sporting career and equestrian businesses with service as a working royal. A hybrid model can succeed, and not all ideas that bend or break with tradition destabilise the monarchy.

'Yes,' said an insider when I pointed this out, 'but that depends on the royal in question.' Anne is staunch and sensible, Harry his mother's son. Meghan would not have respected boundaries. Left to their own devices, they risked becoming more Andrew-and-Sarah than Anne-and-Timothy. That analysis, widely shared by family and officials, meant the institution spent less energy on helping the Sussexes expand their role, more on containing them. Harry and Meghan, in turn, continued to misread their situation, assuming that courtiers were misrepresenting them to the top decision-makers – the

Queen, Charles, even William – who would surely see the merit of their case if given the chance. After all, the Sussexes connected with younger and diverse populations across the realms, demographics left cold by other Windsors. The monarchy needed them.

There were, however, other issues at play. The prospect of change loomed large, with Elizabeth soon to pass the crown to Charles, already in his seventies and expected to reign for, at most, a couple of decades. The paramount concern of these principals and their officials was to smooth the way for the next two kings and their consorts. In this context, the volatile, limelight-stealing Harry and Meghan appeared not jewels in the crown but risks.

They were not the only people blindsided by this assessment. The authors of *Finding Freedom*, who had signed up to chart a Disney fairytale, found themselves confronted with the Grimm version instead. Their book opens with a description by Omid Scobie of the Sussexes' last royal engagement, on 9 March 2020. 'As Megan gave me a final hug goodbye, she said, "It didn't have to be this way."'

Meghan and Harry had returned to England at the beginning of that year after a six-week break on Vancouver Island spent developing their proposals. At first, they considered basing themselves in New Zealand or South Africa, but now leaned towards North America, where they felt they could continue with their royal duties while developing outside ventures compatible with their public role. Harry distilled these thoughts into a series of emails to Charles and officials, receiving a non-committal reply from his father: everything needed to be discussed in person. The earliest possible date for such a summit would be in a few weeks. Eager to speed the process, Harry rang his grandmother, explained his 'plan to create a different working arrangement' and secured her agreement to meet. As he and Meghan boarded their flight for London, word came through that the audience had been cancelled.

For most people, the first news of 'Megxit', a term Harry rejects precisely because of its implication that his wife engineered their departure, came on 7 January. *Sun* journalist Dan Wootton, who seven months earlier had published the story about the alleged falling out between Kate and her friend Rose Hanbury, dropped a new and curiously well-sourced bombshell. Its banner headline contained the main thrust of the piece: 'WE'RE ORF AGAIN: Prince Harry and Meghan could move to Canada for 2020 and ditch HRH titles after "feeling sidelined" by royals'. The scoop set in motion a chain reaction.

Arguments about where Wootton got his information raised temperatures already running high, with everyone blaming each other. In *Spare*, Harry writes of a 'telling detail . . . that we'd offered to relinquish our Sussex titles. There was only one document on earth in which that detail was mentioned – my private and confidential letter to my father. To which a shockingly, damningly small number of people had access.'

The Sussexes rushed to get out their own spin on events, publishing the following announcement: 'After many months of reflection and internal discussions, we have chosen to make a transition this year in starting to carve out a progressive new role within this institution. We intend to step back as "senior" members of the royal family and work to become financially independent, while continuing to fully support Her Majesty the Queen . . . We now plan to balance our time between the

United Kingdom and North America, continuing to honour our duty to the Queen, the Commonwealth and our patronages.'

Five days later – and just after Meghan flew back to Canada – the meeting Harry had requested finally took place, arousing suspicions that the organisers deliberately excluded his assertive wife. There was to be little discussion anyway. The decision laid out by Elizabeth in her subsequent statement was reached before Harry arrived at Sandringham, though officials made a show of laying out other models before rejecting them. 'My family and I are entirely supportive of Harry and Meghan's desire to create a new life as a young family,' her statement read. 'Although we would have preferred them to remain full-time working members of the royal family, we respect and understand their wish to live a more independent life as a family while remaining a valued part of my family.

'Harry and Meghan have made clear that they do not want to be reliant on public funds in their new lives. It has therefore been agreed that there will be a period of transition in which the Sussexes will spend time in Canada and the UK. These are complex matters for my family to resolve, and there is some more work to be done, but I have asked for final decisions to be reached in the coming days.'

The drama dominated headlines, giving brief respite from chilling news coming out of Wuhan. The Sussexes, racing to leave before national lockdowns stopped flights, completed a last round of official engagements, departing not for Canada but California. There they took temporary refuge in a house owned by Tyler Perry, an actor and filmmaker they had never met. In July, they bought their own home, a nine-bedroom mansion in Montecito, Santa Barbara County, north of Los

Angeles. Though they might appear to be putting down roots, the Sandringham agreement designated this as a transitional period. They could yet return to the Windsor fold.

*

These events barely registered with me. Widowed as the Sussexes prepared to depart the UK, I had sadder preoccupations. A trawl through old emails reveals that my only reference to Meghan during the whole of 2020 relates to a photograph published by the *Sunday Sport* in which the tabloid claims to discern an image of my Women's Equality Party co-founder Sandi Toksvig on the Duchess's left knee. In the email, I mention laughing about this with one of the Sussexes' former employees. We had talked about more serious matters too. Despite no longer reporting on the royals – or precisely because I did not – quite a few former royal contacts had become friends. It was on this basis that they had been confiding their concerns to me for more than two years.

In June 2018, I arrived at a lunch expecting to feast on gossip about the Sussexes' recent wedding and thinking I might ask for a steer on the extent to which Meghan could espouse feminist causes. While Meghan's position obviously ruled out her backing the Women's Equality Party, perhaps she might use her platform for nonpartisan women's sector organisations, as Camilla did. Many were and are in desperate need of money and profile. What I heard that day banished such notions. The frictions Yasmin Alibhai-Brown predicted had materialised – with a twist. In this account and others shared with me over the coming months, Meghan was not the victim but the aggressor.

Soon, I noticed hints of trouble filtering through to the public domain, with reports suggesting Meghan and Harry's move from Kensington Palace to Frogmore Cottage signalled a chill between them and their neighbours, Kate and William. Another item claimed the Sussexes had offended Princess Eugenie by skipping her wedding reception. Camilla Tominey wrote that a clash between Meghan and Kate over bridesmaids dresses for the Sussex wedding had reduced the latter to tears. Meghan, an unnamed source told the *Mail*, was 'an acquired taste' and 'quite opinionated'.

There were news items too about staff departures and a contemptuous nickname applied to Meghan, 'Duchess Difficult'. One of those to leave the Sussexes' employ was Samantha Cohen, the Queen's former senior aide, who had agreed at the monarch's urging to help Meghan settle in. Smoke was hanging in the air, but the public would not get sight of the fire for quite a while. Even after the Sussexes left for the US, the main focus of press interest was their rapid, sometimes chaotic construction of a new life. Meghan would liken the period to flying a plane before it has been built.

Though she still had money from her acting days, and Harry could cover their current expenses with a chunk of his inheritance from his mother, their pockets were not deep enough indefinitely to sustain a large mortgage, staff and other ongoing costs. Apart from his military service, Harry had never earned a salary, dependent on monies funnelled to him by Charles, who in turn lived off income from ancient trusts and estates and the public purse. Reports differ as to why his father cut off Harry's allowance months after the Sussexes arrived in California rather than waiting for them to establish steady income streams. One theory is that Charles aimed to bring his errant son slinking back, with or without Meghan. Another holds that he sought to stem Harry's appetite for seeking redress from the UK courts.

From 2019, the Sussexes together or individually had launched a series of legal actions against British media organisations. In Harry's sights were Rupert Murdoch's News UK, publisher of two key tabloids, the *Sun* and the now-defunct *News of the World*; MGN, which owns the *Mirror*; and Associated Newspapers, rechristened DMG Media, owners of the *Mail* and *Mail on Sunday* and other titles. Actions centred on the use of hacking, bugging, deception and other forms of illegal intrusion to gather information. Each case risked forcing disclosures uncomfortable not only for the corporations targeted but the royals themselves, simultaneously resurfacing stories about them and revealing the workings of their relationships with media. Meghan's own suit against Associated Newspapers for the *Mail on Sunday*'s publication of a letter she wrote to her father illustrated these dangers. Though she eventually won, she also had to row back on denials that she had assisted in the preparation of *Finding Freedom*. The Sussexes' former communications secretary Jason Knauf testified he had passed information to its authors after first discussing their requests with his employers.

Legal fees added to the pressures on the couple's finances, and there was another big-ticket item to fund: security. Harry's anxiety, no doubt amplified by flashbacks to his mother's fate and his own experiences of being chased on busy roads by paparazzi, were far from unreasonable. Even before his deployment in Afghanistan, he represented an obvious target for terrorism. As senior policeman Neil Basu made clear, the dangers to Meghan were real too. Harry mounted a challenge to the Home Office over its decision to withdraw from his family the automatic protection granted to core royals in the UK. The case would rumble on, expensively, until its dismissal in 2025 and a decision by the Home Office to review arrangements anyway.

The Sussexes' only option was to start earning at scale and pace. By the end of the year, they had set up the Archewell Foundation, rebranded Archewell Philanthropies in 2025, the for-profits Archewell Audio and Archewell Productions, and struck deals with Netflix and Spotify. They also suffered the sadness of a miscarriage. On Valentine's Day 2021, they announced that Meghan was again pregnant. Within days, the Palace made its own announcement: Harry and Meghan had chosen permanently to relinquish their roles as working royals. The statement added that 'in stepping away from the work of the royal family, it is not possible to continue with the responsibilities and duties that come with a life of public service'. Stung, the Sussexes issued a riposte: 'We can all live a life of service. Service is universal.' And then, on 2 March, five days before the couple's much-trailed conversation with Oprah Winfrey, the bullying story finally broke.

*

Under the headline, 'Royal aides reveal bullying claim before Meghan's Oprah interview', *The Times*' Valentine Low wrote that 'sources had approached the newspaper because they felt that only a partial version had emerged of Meghan's two years as a working member of the royal family and they wished to tell their side, concerned about how such matters are handled by the Palace'. The gist of the article had been shared with me almost three years earlier because I could be trusted not to pass it on. Now it looked as if somebody wanted the allegations circulated to pre-empt the Sussexes' primetime confessional.

Low quoted an email, sent five months after their wedding by Jason Knauf to the human resources director of Buckingham Palace. 'I am very concerned that the Duchess was able to bully two PAs out of the household in the past year. The treatment of X was totally unacceptable. . . The Duchess seems intent on always having someone in her sights. She is bullying Y and seeking to undermine her confidence. We have had report after report from people who have witnessed unacceptable behaviour towards Y.' Knauf also mentioned concerns about Samantha Cohen's wellbeing.

The article included this rebuttal too: 'A spokesman for the Sussexes said they were the victims of a calculated smear campaign based on misleading and harmful misinformation. They said the Duchess was "saddened by this latest attack on her character, particularly as someone who has been the target of bullying herself and is deeply committed to supporting those who have experienced pain and trauma".'

As an attempt to discredit Meghan's charges to Winfrey – which famously turned out to range from racism in the Palace, including concerns by an unnamed royal over the colour of her unborn son to a failure to respond appropriately when she confessed to suicidal thoughts – the timing of the leak made sense. If the intention of those who approached Low was to force the Palace to strengthen protections for staff or to ensure their complaints against Meghan would be investigated, it had the opposite effect. One source told Low that the Palace had done too little to respond to Knauf's original email: 'I think the problem is not much happened with it. It was, "How can we make this go away?" rather than addressing it.' The weaponisation of the bullying claims raised suspicions among those inclined to defend Meghan that they had been confected. ('If something bad really happened, palace staff would have spoken up right away.') The publicity generated by the coverage further dented the chances that the allegations would be properly investigated.

The Palace did order a probe into its handling of the situation, briefing at its conclusion that there would be changes in 'policies and procedures . . . known to all members of staff [and] all members of the royal family' but that the details of these and of the process that led to them would remain private. Such discretion, though it smacked of a cover-up, was by now unavoidable. At this stage, to reveal the names and testimonies of complainants and witnesses would be to expose them to relentless media pursuit and the worst excesses of online harassment. The Sussex Squad knows no more mercy than Meghan's detractors. Yet the decision also denied Meghan the opportunity to answer the charges. Later, her UK lawyer Jenny Afia would take issue with the word 'bullying'. It 'is used very freely and it's a very, very damaging term as we know, particularly, I think, for career women. What bullying actually means is improperly using power repeatedly and deliberately to hurt someone, physically or emotionally. The Duchess of Sussex absolutely denies ever doing that.' Afia added a coda: 'That said, [Meghan] wouldn't want to negate anyone's personal experiences.'

For many of us, Afia's suggestion that we discount the allegations against Meghan while respecting the integrity of her accusers challenges the way we are trained to think – that if testimonies diverge, somebody must be lying. Winfrey's invitation to Meghan to tell 'her truth' attracted mockery because of its implication that facts are friable. Meghan's assertion during that interview that she had married Harry three days before their formal wedding provided a clear example of how unforgiving facts can be. Although Justin Welby, then Archbishop of Canterbury, conducted a private blessing in advance, the couple did not exchange legally binding vows until the ceremony at Windsor. Sift through Meghan's interviews looking for inconsistencies and you will find them.

Journalists have cast doubt on elements of a story about her early feminist leanings. As a schoolgirl, she wrote to Procter & Gamble to protest the sexism of a commercial for washing-up liquid. The company then proceeded to exchange the word 'women' in the phrase 'women are fighting greasy pots and pans' to 'people'. *Vanity Fair* omitted the tale from a profile piece, Bower writes in *Revenge*, because its 'fact-checkers had adamantly decided that her story was possibly false [sic]'. The profile's author, Sam Kashner, wrote to *The Times* protesting Bower's interpretation of events, which the newspaper had included in a serialisation. 'Tom Bower didn't convey my admiration and respect for Meghan Markle in the excerpt from his new book . . . I found Ms Markle to be exceptionally warm and gracious and admired her intelligence and her remarkable courage, as I still do. I regretted the oft-published account of challenging Proctor & Gamble being edited out of my *Vanity Fair* article, because I'd wanted to highlight her lifelong activism.'

In a 2025 interview, Meghan for the first time described seeing the commercial during the Los Angeles riots. She and other children were kept in school for their own safety, watching TV while they waited for their parents to collect them. 'I remember the boys in the classroom saying, "Yeah, that's where women belong – in the kitchen." And that's really what upset me . . . It was a very turbulent time in our city and a lot of uncertainty . . . But the one thing I was certain on in all of this was, that's wrong. Let's do something about it. And it was just so empowering to know that at a really young age, your voice could be heard.'

Two or more narratives from the same person or different witnesses are not invariably a signal of untruths, even if details appear to contradict each other. Think back to the story of the bridesmaids' dresses. Camilla Tominey's article blamed Meghan for the contretemps with Kate; Meghan told Winfrey that it was not she who upset Kate but the other way round: the dispute 'made me cry and it really hurt my feelings. But she owned it, and she apologised, and she brought me flowers'. My contacts describe distress on both sides.

When Piers Morgan appeared flatly to reject another part of Meghan's testimony to Winfrey – that she felt suicidal while pregnant with Archie – he angered mental health charities and ended up resigning as co-anchor of *Good Morning Britain*. 'I wouldn't believe her if she read me a weather report,' he said. Later, he stated that he had not intended to dispute her feelings but to challenge her account of the Palace's failure to help.

One detail of Meghan's story, her conversation with the human resources director, certainly sounded, on the face of it, barely credible: 'They said "my heart goes out to you because

I see how bad it is, but there's nothing we can do to protect you because you're not a paid employee of the institution".' In fact, the HR department deals with staff, not principals, so that answer makes sense. It is not clear, however, why Meghan looked for support there and not, for example, via Harry's network established through the Heads Together campaign. Sources propose a range of explanations: that both Meghan and Harry were too distressed to think clearly; that he feared her anguish would be used against her if the story got out; that the institution tried to keep a lid on things for the same reason or, as she alleged, to protect itself; that officials refused to take her pain seriously or that they did (as a palace insider insists), but that for whatever reason, she read their response as inadequate.

Perceptions may vary, and recollections too, especially as memory fades. Some people do more than fill in the blanks, of course, spicing up reminiscences or, as my friend Paula Yates did, making stuff up for no obvious reason. A woman who survived a wretchedly precarious childhood only to endure a barrage of press abuse, Paula had a flexible relationship with reality that sometimes made her friends doubt what she told us. After her beloved Michael Hutchence killed himself, her calls sometimes prompted me to dash across London only to find her lying on velvet cushions, eating violet creams. That did not make her suicidal ideation a figment. The coroner blamed a 'foolish and incautious' drug overdose for her eventual death, but those closest to her more than once saw her act on threats, whether to signal distress or with intent. Scabrous press coverage and ceaseless harassment by reporters and paparazzi played a significant part in her unravelling. Again and again, she would pose the same question Harry remembers Meghan asking him.

In *Spare*, he describes the moment he returned home to find his wife sobbing that she 'didn't want to do this anymore.

'*Do what?*

'*Live . . .*

'It's all so painful, she was saying.

'*What is?*

'*To be hated like this – for what?*'

For what indeed. The media portrayals of Meghan, some of them nasty enough, even in the early days, to prompt a letter of solidarity from seventy-two female MPs, could have pushed anyone to the brink. Even now, few reports pass the public interest test. Instead, as columnist Catherine Bennett observed, 'tormenting the Duchess of Sussex has become a national sport'.

Low's scoop about bullying does not fall into this category. This was a legitimate news story and in key respects matched what insiders told me: that Meghan's interactions with some staff from their perspectives matched Afia's definition of bullying, the improper use of power. No doubt Meghan was bullied. Did she also bully?

*

Full disclosure: I would dearly love to overlook or minimise these allegations. After all, if Meghan were beyond criticism, her story, with its echoes of Boleyn and Diana would serve as this book's strongest case study and an ideal conclusion. She has indeed come to resemble Diana, the iteration of 1997: the crown jewel turned pariah, the benchmark against whom other prominent women are measured and found, by comparison, to pass muster.

Any relief this affords the supposed beneficiaries comes at a cost. Vanishingly few humans fit neatly into saint or sinner categories. The drive to push females into one box or the other renders them caricatures, shorn of the substance granted to their male equivalents. To insist on their complexity, to paint Meghan or Kate as anything other than the unalloyed heroines or irremediable villainesses of popular imagination, feels in equal parts foolhardy and necessary. Aligning myself unequivocally with one side would at least mollify that constituency and thereby diminish the volume of backlash this book is likely to generate, if not its intensity. However, that would also betray its core aim – and my own understanding of the events and people involved.

Press reporting about Meghan's alleged bullying is abundant, but primary sources are in short supply, and neither the original claims nor the responses to them have been tested in an open process. This much we know: a number of Meghan's staff felt bruised by their dealings with her, some of their former colleagues have spoken in her defence and denials of bullying have been issued on her behalf. Not even the Palace is in a position to provide clarity, given its tardy and secretive investigation and the absence of the person at its centre: Meghan.

Critics are aligned in describing certain behaviours: Meghan's initial warmth turning to froideur or anger, her friendly gestures undermined by demands made irrespective of the hour or the viability of her asks. 'Might there be mitigations?' I asked a former member of a different royal household. 'No,' came the reply, she is a 'nightmare'. Another contact used the term 'narcissist'. Someone who worked for the couple during the period referred to in complaints expressed concern for ex-colleagues, saying their confidence had been undermined. Others spoke with understanding – if little sympathy – of the fraught context in which Meghan had been forced to operate.

If Planet Windsor can be tricky, the breakdown in relations between Harry and his brother created additional tensions that affected everyone close to them, and especially their wives. This was a fraternal love built on as many fault lines as Los Angeles. From childhood, 'Willy' and 'Harold', as they call each other, were bound by shared understandings and then, more closely, by loss. At the same time, unresolved resentments over their contrasting roles – heir versus spare, the one hemmed in by destiny, the other denied purpose – sparked small eruptions long before Meghan's arrival. So too did their contrasting approaches to the balancing act between private desires and public service.

The full-scale explosion, when it came, related to two areas of extreme sensitivity: Meghan, and media management. Harry, already bristling at William's initial caution towards his love ('she's an American actress after all, Harold'), expected royal backing for a suit against the *Mail* after it published extracts from her letter to Thomas Markle. There were precedents for the Windsors taking legal action against breaches of copyright and invasion of privacy. In 1993, the *Sun* apologised to the Queen for printing the text of her Christmas speech before its broadcast. In 2012, *Closer* magazine accepted fines for publishing photographs of Kate sunbathing topless, an infringement likened by a palace official to 'the worst excesses of the press and paparazzi during the life of Diana, Princess of Wales'. Instead, Harry writes, Charles and William 'hummed and hahed. The only answer I could get out of them was that it simply wasn't advisable . . . I told Meg: *You'd think we were suing a dear friend of theirs.'*

When William requested a meeting with Harry to talk about 'the whole rolling catastrophe', the latter hoped for a breakthrough, only for his brother to raise the complaints against Meghan.

'*Meg's difficult,* he said.

'*Oh, really?*

'*She's rude. She's abrasive. She's alienated half the staff.'*

To Harry, this was 'a press narrative . . . tabloid rubbish'. Within minutes, the brothers' shouting match became a scuffle, with William grabbing Harry by his collar, ripping his necklace and shoving him to the floor, where he landed on a dog's bowl. That, at any rate, is the version in *Spare*. William has not responded to the allegations.

Insiders pointed to another source of neuralgia. Weaknesses in the provisioning and running of the palaces meant a small, shared team serviced both the Sussexes and the then Cambridges until they divided their households and charitable work in the summer of 2019. Harry and Meghan might be the hottest story in town, but aides assigned them a lower priority and less time than the more senior couple.

There were also profound gaps in understanding of Meghan and about what she might need to help her acclimate. Lady Susan Hussey, who brought a wealth of institutional knowledge to the task of showing her the ropes, later failed to appreciate the implications of repeatedly asking British-born Ngozi Fulani where she came from. It is hard to think of many palace officials who would immediately 'get' Meghan or grasp the scale of the cultural divide, not just between commoner and royal or Americans and their former overlords, but Angelenos and the British aristocracy. Nor would Meghan have been wrong to suspect that some courtiers looked down aquiline noses at her. A source quoted by journalist Tom Quinn in his book about royal servants said: 'At times it got so bad that I heard one of the senior staff mumble that Meghan should really have been employed in the palace kitchens.'

Complicating the picture still further, Meghan's understanding of media, formed by Hollywood, stood at odds with the long horizons of successful royals, who care less about a headline here or a puff piece there than the accretion of coverage and its sentiment over time. Moreover, US and UK press cultures are as different as chalk and that Gloucestershire delicacy, Stinking Bishop. Though American television commentators, for good and for great ill, exercise the right to free speech enshrined in the US constitution, the country's broadsheet journalism can appear strangely deferential, speaking truth to power after first putting its hand up and waiting to be called. US celebrity journalism, policed by fierce PRs and powerful studios, is much kinder to its subjects. *People*, America's largest celebrity title with a print circulation of more than two million and a combined reach across all platforms of over ninety-eight million, makes a virtue of avoiding offence, benefiting from good access as a result. Regional tabloids like the *New York Post* and supermarket magazines such as the *National Enquirer*, though closer to the UK's scrappy tabloid culture, have little traction with the establishment.

Meghan's tormentors carry real clout. In Africa, she told Tom Bradby that she had brushed aside warnings from friends. They 'said to me, "I'm sure [Harry's] great but you shouldn't [marry him] because the British tabloids will destroy your life". I didn't get it.' Perhaps this was an issue she could have googled, but the frenemyships and interdependencies between UK tabloid media and other arms of the establishment are truly befuddling.

Everyone from British prime ministers to top royals continues to court tabloid favour despite the corruption and criminality revealed by the hacking scandal, a subsequent judicial inquiry into the culture, practices and ethics of the British press, and, latterly, the legal actions launched by Harry and other complainants. Prime Minister David Cameron appointed Andy Coulson, former editor of the *News of the World*, as his director of communications. Even before Coulson's arrest and conviction for conspiracy to hack, this seemed a crazy risk. For Cameron, a posh politician looking for ways to connect with common folk, however, the idea of an aide hardwired into tabloid culture outweighed other concerns.

Similar impulses underpin the Palace's cultivation of mass-market titles. As Harry had already discovered and Meghan swiftly and painfully learned, those relationships often trump the wellbeing of individual family members. This can be a dog-eat-dog world. While in theory, royal households work together for the benefit of the institution, in practice officials sometimes promote their own principals at the expense of others by leaking selectively. Dan Evans and Tom Latchem, a pair of former *News of the World* journalists – Evans received a ten-month suspended sentence for two counts of phone hacking while at the tabloid – have published a series of articles alleging that the Sussexes' plans reached Dan Wootton by this means.

Evans identifies an additonal factor that he believes 'unleashed absolute hell against Meghan': the fear that she could become 'another Diana', disruptive and beyond control. Officials encouraged negative coverage of her, he says, and the press took the ball and ran with it. Already angered by Harry's legal moves against the media, editors enjoyed the double benefit of generating income from their attacks on the couple and tasting vengeance. Evans terms the result 'an economy of hate around Meghan and Harry'.

By then, of course, social media had got in on the act too, feeding off newspaper reports or hallucinating new content and engaging millions in debates based on false premises and algorithmically boosted hostilities. With old media of all kinds struggling to survive, often becoming more sensationalist in the attempt, Harry's battles for justice appear strangely archaic, a prince in search of a grail that, if it still exists, has been spirited away for the citizens of some distant future to rediscover.

*

Meghan, meanwhile, is deliberately tapping into nostalgia, much as Kate does with her fashion choices. As I write, the world is on fire, wracked by wars, genocides, sexual violence and devastating climate change. For people seeking a break from bleak news, things that appear old-fashioned hold a special appeal, and *With Love, Meghan* does its best to serve televisual comfort food, as soft-edged and soothing as ASMR videos or *Zenimation*, 'a mindfulness soundscape experience' that splices together the most calming clips from *Snow White* and the rest of Disney's cartoon back catalogue.

The opening series of Meghan's lifestyle show gained sufficient numbers to be recommissioned for a second eight-parter, plus a seasonal special. Coverage of this development took a predictable turn in the UK: '"Vicious" Meg is trying to one-up Kate with money-grabbing Netflix deal, but it WON'T work' read a headline in the *Sun* above a story claiming that the special would 'clash with Princess Kate's beloved holiday concert', *Together at Christmas*. Since neither programme had been given a release date, and both would be available to view at any time after initial broadcast date, this stretched a point. Meanwhile, the announcement that Netflix's original multi-project contract with the Sussexes was to be replaced by a first-look deal strengthened a press narrative that the couple brings only one real asset to their media ventures: the story of their breach with the rest of the Windsors.

You can see why this particular seed germinated. Their Oprah Winfrey interview was a worldwide hit. *Spare* shattered records to become the fastest-selling non-fiction book of all time. *Harry & Meghan* attracted more viewing hours than any previous Netflix documentary title in its premiere week, watched by more than twenty-eight million households.

By contrast, Spotify discontinued Meghan's podcast *Archetypes* after a single series. 'You live in fucking Montecito, and you just sell documentaries and podcasts, and nobody cares what you have to say about anything unless you talk about the royal family and you just complain about them,' said Bill Simmonds, a Spotify executive speaking on his own podcast. This was before the termination of their deal. The announcement prompted him to a second outburst: 'I wish I had been involved in the "Meghan and Harry leave Spotify" negotiation. "The Fucking Grifters". That's the podcast we should have launched with them.'

A senior Los Angeles TV executive disagrees with this take. The middling reception for non-royal Archewell output might be as much a sign of normalisation within the market as of failure, the executive tells me. Of course the couple trades on their celebrity – and Netflix's efforts to keep them onside shows that they retain positive capital, rather than being merely notorious. In some ways, that feels like a miracle. For decades, broadcasters refused to devote primetime slots to women's football on the basis that interest in the women's game was too marginal, a logic loop that deprived women's teams of the means to grow audiences. These days, the press demonises Meghan, willing her TV and podcasting work to falter in the knowledge that the success of her ventures depends on enough of the media and wider population liking her to keep tuning in.

Even without such pressures, it is hard to predict whether Archewell, currently working on several projects, will turn out more hits. Its first docuseries for Netflix, *Live to Lead* and *Heart of Invictus*, were never tipped as ratings-grabbers. Unless Jilly Cooper had scripted *Polo* for the streamer, nobody would have expected it to gallop to the top of the charts. By contrast, if rumours that the Sussexes plan a documentary about Diana prove correct, that could fly high.

Listening to Meghan's podcasts, now lodged with Lemonada Media, reminded me of her image of building a plane while flying. *Archetypes*, though potentially a strong concept, lacked clarity in its execution and would have benefited from the more polished interviewing technique Meghan brings to bear in her second attempt, *Confessions of a Female Founder*. The latter suffers from a different problem, leaving her to prospect for entrepreneurial ideas and common ground with women whose businesses are long established. Her As Ever product range is still limited, small scale and going through teething troubles.

The *Sun*'s November 2025 headline heralding Meghan's 'shock return to acting in a huge film' turned out to refer to the Duchess making a brief appearance as herself in a movie. 'For Markle to play herself now feels more than a little overly safe and misguided,' complained a columnist in the *Independent*. 'There's always something decidedly cringe about an A-lister who cameos as their own famous face in a film.'

A continued turnover in staff has been cited as further evidence that Meghan is overbearing, with a piece in the *Hollywood Reporter* quoting a source who called her, in a revealingly gendered phrase, 'a dictator in high heels'. Leaving aside the churn common with any start-ups and the fact that other businesses and royal households would seem to lose staff at high-ish rates, let us return to the questions posed at the beginning of the chapter.

Say you dislike Meghan and are prepared to argue that your response is reasoned, not visceral – that you are not part of a pack stirred up to feel this way. Say you believe that she bullied staff. Bullying is hateful and her lawyer is quite right: personal experiences should not be negated. Does this principle justify the relentless hatred meted out to Meghan or instead replicate, at scale, the behaviour you condemn?

If we accept her hounding – whether by applauding her daily abuse as a form of natural justice or treating it as entertainment – we become part of the problem. So too do those who seek to defend her by similar means.

Divided They Fall – and So Might We

Queen Elizabeth II grips the wheel of a car as a policeman leans in to ask her a question. Does she know that she has run a red light? 'I do, officer, terribly sorry. I dropped my blunt' – she waves a marijuana-filled cigar – 'and it rolled under the pedals. I couldn't very well leave it there.' Now we see her fleeing from the law, firing defiant shots from a handgun to shouts of: 'Drop the weapon, ma'am!' 'I'd sooner drop the monarchy,' says a voiceover.

In the autumn of 2025, Sam Altman's tech company OpenAI launched the text-to-video app Sora 2 in the US and Canada. Within a week, TikTok and Instagram were awash with Sora-generated 'slop', as this sort of content is known. Much of it depicts real people and fictional characters acting out improbable scenarios. The deepfake Elizabeth appears in many of them. You can find her squealing her way down a water slide; flipping the bird at the viewer; spinning the tables as a DJ; starring in TV shows *The Bachelorette* and *Love Island*; ordering a kebab; running amok on a mobility scooter; and, time and time again, resisting arrest for crimes from shoplifting to murder.

Few are explicitly anti-monarchist, made purely for fun by people without malice or ulterior motive, and at surface level might even add to Elizabeth's legend, the monarch reimagined as Ma Baker. Some content creators appear to be reproducing their own dreamscapes: 'Never thought I'd be sharing tea in a bowling alley with the Queen,' says a TikToker called Jon who has placed his own likeness at a table with Elizabeth. She thanks him for inviting her ('very pleasant indeed') and they chink cups. The visuals are all scarily realistic, apart from a bowling ball that rolls away from the pins rather than towards them.

While OpenAI theoretically prohibits the inclusion of images of living people without their permission, the company initially considered the dead fair game. Complaints from the daughters of Martin Luther King Jr and Robin Williams prompted a tightening of the rules on this point too, but only in certain cases, and Reddit and other sites were anyway already sharing tips on how to get round Sora 2's guardrails. The *New York Times* declared 'the end of visual fact', adding this prediction: 'Sora signifies an inflection point in the era of AI fakery. Consumers can expect copycats to emerge . . . including from bad actors offering AI video generators that can be used with no restrictions.'

That bad actors seek to use royalty for their machinations is nothing new, whether inveigling the Duke and Duchess of Windsor to Nazi Germany or hobnobbing in parks and palaces with princes to burnish tarnished reputations. However, digitised ways of harnessing the royals to disinformation – the #WhereIsKate imbroglio, the instrumentalisation of online battles between her supporters and the Sussex Squad, the deepfakery – represent a step change, harder to recognise than older forms and, because they do not require the participation of actual royals, infinitely more scalable.

These campaigns, says Gina Neff, the leading AI and disinformation expert quoted earlier, often lack narrowly drawn goals, instead aiming 'to sow the seeds of doubt in government and society'. A 'news report' about Camilla standing trial for murdering Diana is more obviously damaging than deepfaked Elizabeth breakdancing, but both clips chip away at reality and our grasp on it. The Windsors, though globally recognisable, remain, with some exceptions, more remote than ordinary celebrities. Much of the royal job consists not of speaking but rather of being on show. If family members have to be seen to be believed, where does this leave them in a world that cannot trust the evidence of its own eyes?

The virality of all these memes also makes them ripe for exploitation by foreign governments, underground organisations and private companies serving political and corporate clients, who piggyback on to the posts, creating large numbers of social media accounts to augment, amplify and steer online sentiment.

Much of this activity can be automated thanks to AI. Disinformation spreaders direct armies of bots and trolls to issues 'that capture people's emotional, affective response,' Neff explains. 'Whether you're furious that the government or the monarchy is hiding a big secret, whether you are thrilled to get a bit of information about your favorite royal, whether you are devastated to get a bit of information about your most hated royal, that kind of information really builds on those powerful emotions that people have. And there are powerful emotions around the British monarchy.' Those emotions are running at unprecedented highs amid a cascade of revelations about Andrew Mountbatten-Windsor's relationship with

Jeffrey Epstein that, in turn, raise questions about what other royals knew – and when.

The real Elizabeth waymarked the digital revolution that would eventually generate her criminally-minded AI doppelgangers precisely at the moment the monarchy faced allegations of enabling criminality. Media recorded her sending her first and possibly only email in 1976, launching the royal website in 1997, tweeting in 2014 and, in 2019, posting a letter to Instagram written by Charles Babbage to Victoria and Albert about his 'analytical engine', the forerunner of the computer. It was Babbage's collaborator, Ada Lovelace, who pointed out that such a machine could potentially do much more than crunch numbers.

Technologists still overlook the uses and misuses to which their inventions might lend themselves. Mark Zuckerberg wrote in the early days of Facebook that it 'was built to accomplish a social mission – to make the world more open and connected'. It has indeed allowed strangers to connect, but the rise of social media could hardly be described as uniformly beneficial. Sites such as 4chan and 8chan, later 8kun, became early springboards for movements such as the conspiracist QAnon and the viciously misogynistic incel subculture. Facebook and another Zuckerberg product, WhatsApp, have been weaponised to skew democratic processes. There are similar concerns around the Chinese-owned TikTok and X (formerly Twitter), especially since its 2022 purchase by Elon Musk. Algorithms to increase engagement on all of these platforms tend to boost divisive content, performing a kind of automated radicalisation by detecting people's susceptibilities and serving them ever more extreme material on those subjects. Those same algorithms foster a smartphone dependency that sees us doomscrolling and slurping slop when we might be interacting with actual humans. 'We're physically present but mentally absent, unable to fully engage with the people right in front of us,' warned an essay published by the Centre for Early Childhood. Its lead author was Kate.

She and her family have other, powerful reasons to fear the online sphere as its impact on legal wrangles between divorced actors Amber Heard and Johnny Depp demonstrated. During two separate cases, multiple accounts in countries as far flung as Thailand, Spain, Chile and Saudi Arabia acted in apparent concert to demonise Heard and praise Depp. There is no suggestion that either party was involved in these campaigns, but the findings raised questions about the interplay between social media and the administration of justice, and give a more granular sense of the media environment in which Buckingham Palace and the other royal courts now operate.

The saga started in 2018, when Depp brought a defamation lawsuit in the UK against the publishers of the *Sun* newspaper and its then executive editor, Dan Wootton – yes, *that* Dan Wootton – for a piece headlined 'Gone Potty: How can JK Rowling be "genuinely happy" casting wife beater Johnny Depp in the new *Fantastic Beasts* film?'. If you doubted that the matrix of British media and lawyers is tight knit, know also that Depp was represented in this matter by a team headed by Jenny Afia, later Meghan's lawyer, and David Sherborne, lead barrister in Harry's various suits against the media.

Depp refuted his characterisation as a wife beater and countered that Heard was the violent partner in the relationship, which Heard also denied. Another prominent lawyer,

Mark Stephens, provided independent commentary on the case to some media outlets and on his own social feeds. Heard would win, he suggested. She did. The judge accepted twelve of her fourteen claims of domestic abuse against Depp. By then, Stephens found himself the target of such intense online vilification by accounts backing Depp that he sought the advice of the Oxford Internet Institute. They confirmed that he was suffering 'an attack of inauthentic accounts,' he says. Further analysis of Twitter revealed five hundred accounts that, once flagged to moderators, were immediately taken down 'so they clearly thought they were inauthentic too. These were the same accounts that were seeding hashtags like #AmberTurd,' says Stephens. 'And they also obviously had access to the transcript pretty much in real time, because they were picking out quotes faster than you could run to the court door to phone them in. A lot of the accounts were similar, and they were also coming from, apparently, different places in the world.'

Meanwhile, across the Atlantic, Depp lodged a defamation suit against Heard, claiming damages for an opinion piece she authored for the *Washington Post*. Heard countersued and, this time round, Depp won. It is impossible to say if the earlier onslaught against Heard played a part in Depp's victory, though Stephens suspects it might have. Factors such as differences between British and American legal systems will have affected the outcome too, while the televising of the US trial made for compulsive viewing and enabled the online sphere to litigate the whole thing in parallel. By the conclusion of the US trial, the hashtag #justiceforjohnnydepp had received nineteen billion views on TikTok.

Research by Alexi Mostrous, who made a podcast series called *Who Trolled Amber?*, highlighted 'a small network of pro-Depp accounts which were particularly suspicious. When we found them, the accounts were tweeting about the actor in English. But using the Wayback Machine, which saves deleted webpages, we found the same profiles had posted hundreds of now-deleted tweets in Arabic. None of these posts mentioned Depp. Instead, most praised the Saudi regime. Depp has visited Saudi on several occasions and is a personal friend of Mohammed bin Salman, the country's ruler. Saudi has also financed the actor's two most recent films – *Jeanne du Barry* and *Modi*. And Saudi Arabia has a long history of using bots to manipulate social discourse.'

Mostrous emphasised that 'Depp and his team denied wrongdoing. There is no evidence that any of them were involved in setting up any fake accounts targeting Heard. And the number of Saudi accounts we found was relatively small.' But, the journalist added, what happened to Heard is only the start. Generative AI is a gamechanger and not in the rosy way its proponents like to claim.

Depictions of Heard from this period trigger a strong sense of déjà vu. Online commentary and traditional press profiles paint a picture of a successful American actress who married royalty – of the Hollywood variety – not for love, but ambition. Denounced as a fake, a narcissist and 'a manipulative gold-digger', Heard found herself reviled by 'otherwise generally perfectly reasonable people who call themselves "feminists"', according to a rare defence of the actress in *The Times*. Its author, Polly Vernon, described how Heard's detractors damned 'the way she cried on the witness stand as not merely unconvincing, but further proof of her inferior acting skills' and concluded that 'far from being a victim of domestic abuse' she was 'clearly a perpetrator of it'.

Substitute the words 'Meghan' for 'Amber', 'Harry' for 'Depp' and 'bullying' for 'domestic abuse' and this could be a press portrayal of the Duchess of Sussex. Some of the criticisms against Meghan might be justified, some allegations credible, but the attacks on her, as on Heard, go far beyond that, aiming not merely to call her out but to tie her to the stake in the public square.

In an interview with Bloomberg TV, Meghan talked about the coping strategies she has adopted to try to deal with this: compartmentalisation and an acknowledgment that the drivers of this coverage are commercial as well as personal. The press, she said, 'are incentivised to churn out as many stories false or damaging or whatnot to feed the beast, because that's paying them'. A source told me this is bravado. She is worn down by it all, yearns for respite yet also fears it, because if the media left her in peace 'that would mean they had shifted gears to another woman'. It is exactly the same thought Diana expressed to Paula Yates: 'I am relieved whenever I see you in the papers because it means I get the day off.'

For two brief weeks in September 2025, it was possible to glimpse this phenomenon in action, signalled by a flurry of seemingly inconsequential stories about a change of hairstyle: 'Kate Middleton debuts drastic new hair colour during first outing since summer break' trumpeted a piece in *Cosmopolitan*. Hundreds of similar articles identified the shade as 'bronde', a midpoint between brunette and blonde, commenting also on the volume and length of her locks. This was nothing to the volume and length of the ensuing online debate, with positive responses and reasonable suppositions swiftly submerged in criticism and conspiracy. The Princess of Wales was wearing a wig 'atop [her] very obvious healthy hair underneath,' posted an X account called Karma. 'Is this part of her #CancerProtocol PR?'

The user, who joined the platform in June 2024, by the date of this salvo had churned out almost twenty-seven thousand posts, a rate of more than fifty-two a day, most about Israel and Palestine. It was one of many accounts, some real, others potentially bots, that pivoted straight from Kate's coiffeur to the allegation that she had never suffered from cancer.

Conspiracies about the royals are nothing new, from babies smuggled into palaces in bedpans to the notion that the Windsors are shape-shifting lizards, nor have online supporters of the Sussexes, their numbers boosted, like their opponents', by bots and trolls, ever stopped attacking Kate. The notion that Kate faked her illness for sympathy had circulated since she announced her diagnosis, receiving additional impetus when a Sky News correspondent referred in a report not to cancer but 'precancerous cells'. Kensington Palace privately steered journalists away from the phrase but chose not to issue a corrective statement. Now Kate's lightened hair reignited social media. Either she was wearing, as per Karma, a wig, or, if that plentiful mane was real, surely this proved she had not undergone chemotherapy.

What signalled a gear change this time was that old media joined in, expressing doubts about the hairstyle and its wearer. It looked as if attitudes to the Sussexes could be softening. Harry had just seen his father for the first time in over a year, a reunion that royal reporters encouraged, given the King's increasing fragility and their need for fresh data points and storylines. The visit delivered a wonderfully marketable twist: Harry not only back in London but receiving the warmest of public responses before capping this success with a surprise trip to Ukraine. Perhaps it might be time to change the record.

As colleagues tested the water with subtle digs, one *Mail* columnist took the idea much further. Under the headline, 'William and Kate have become the Prince and Princess of Boring. This is why they need to stop skulking around and take a leaf out of Harry's book – or risk Charles's wrath', Amanda Platell wrote: 'There have been fantastic pictures of Harry larking around with children in need, images like those of the cheeky Harry of old. Dare I say, the kind of pictures that Princess Diana generated during her short life, even after she lost her HRH title.' Platell went on to cite a recent opinion poll showing support for the monarchy at 'its lowest level since records began' before returning to her titular theme: 'The only images we ever see of William smiling is in the home videos he and Kate reluctantly release of them and the children frolicking around one of their many homes, not on royal duties seen by the public,' she complained.

Four days later, Platell came out with a new take, its gist again summarised in her headline. 'I'm so disgusted with myself for the cruel thing I said about Kate . . . I'm choking on my words now I know the truth. Kate, I'm just so sorry.' Platell's grovel-fest begins with a pop at Harry's 'pseudo-royal' jaunt to Ukraine and ends with a last right hook: 'Harry said that after his whirlwind tour "he now feels a lot of support from the British public". That made me laugh out loud. It's now clear his four-day trip was nothing more than a desperate attempt to improve his approval ratings.' As for her previous piece, Platell now regrets having 'overlooked what a valuable asset Kate is to the royal family'. The reason for this damascene conversion, the columnist explains, is that she has learned Kate will carry out five royal engagements during Donald Trump's imminent state visit.

Soon, any experimentation with a Sussex-friendly narrative had been abandoned. Still, a story must move forward. Another *Mail* journalist, Richard Eden, penned a series of pieces claiming knowledge of 'a sinister establishment "plot" to undermine the Prince and Princess of Wales and bring back the Duke and Duchess of Sussex'. 'It is worrying,' Eden wrote, that 'King Charles has been drawn into this, aided by some key figures of the establishment behind the scenes . . . I have heard claims senior government figures are also keen for Harry and Meghan to reconcile with the royal family. Many on the left hailed the mixed-race American actress as a symbol of change in the monarchy when she married Harry in 2018 – and still yearn for her return.'

Andrew's arrest called for another recalibration, but this time the anger directed at the front ranks of royalty also extended to the Sussexes, typically attacked for saying too much but now disparaged for their discretion. Charles's statement about his brother, carefully worded to avoid prejudicing any potential legal process, promised the police 'full and wholehearted support and cooperation', adding that 'the law must take its course'. Meanwhile, the King and the other working royals tried to maintain business as usual, feigning not to notice hecklers or the discomfort of advocating for their causes from their bespattered platform. Photographs of Camilla with Gisèle Pelicot, whose ex-husband drugged and raped her and invited other men to participate, prompted accusations of double standards. How dare the Queen claim to support survivors yet dodge reporters' questions about Epstein's victims?

Subjects of the Crown began to do something that rarely goes well for the monarchy: to look at the institution closely. Why had it sheltered and showcased Andrew and his ex-wife long after their links to Epstein came to light? And what of their daughters, until recently treated as candidates to fill gaps in the rosters of working royals? How could it be possible that Andrew, despite his disgrace, remained in the line of succession? Legislation could resolve that problem but not the fundamental issue: that heredity is hardly a reliable mechanism for selecting the head of state for one country, much less a string of them. Even those sections of the legacy media usually staunch in defence of the monarchy began not only to criticise it but to foretell its downfall. It was a significant moment, all the more so because of the convulsive changes transforming the political and media landscapes everywhere.

Rapid evolutions in digital media and AI have not rendered old news organisations irrelevant – yet. Instead, they are hollowing them out. As the economic models that used to sustain journalism crumble, legacy titles and broadcasters slash their workforces, pad them with ChatGPT-generated output and rely ever more heavily on social media as a source of stories and a marketing vehicle for them. While this might look like a symbiotic relationship, it is new media that comes away from the embrace smacking its bloodied lips.

Long-form reporting, based on deep and expensive research and reflecting the complexity of its subject matter, is endangered, though dedicated journalists everywhere continue to expose corruption and speak truth to power. Not that they can rely on their proprietors to back such work rather than shutting it down. There has been a scramble by news organisations to demonstrate fealty to ascendant populists by installing editors, columnists and commentators to carry hard-right lines and prosecute their culture wars, recasting public figures as combatants irrespective of their actual views. Coverage of Kate and Meghan is constantly distorted by the impulse to push them into opposing corners and caricatures, the trad wifely heroine facing off against the dangerous radical villainess. Their fate, like Amber Heard's, offers a glimpse of the future already engulfing us.

Fear and optimism spurred me to write this book. Progress for women is being rolled back with extraordinary speed. Technologies only partially comprehended by their own makers, much less regulators, are elbowing humanity aside. Futurists predicted the rise of smart machines but only a handful anticipated the consequences of stupid ones taking charge. AI learns by hoovering up vast amounts of published material, everything from copyrighted books and studies to social media feeds. This is a diet rich in prejudice and falsehoods. Recently, a Google alert turned up a sprawling profile of me on a site purporting to cover global news. The piece is not nasty; merely littered with errors and weird hallucinations. The whole thing will have been written by a large language model. People and institutions, including governments, are using these models not only to write their pitches and applications and research submissions, but to assess them. Recent research also highlighted the danger of 'data poisoning', in which bad actors deliberately seed the internet with material that when imbibed by large language models means they can be manipulated. What could possibly go wrong?

Writing a book may seem like a peculiarly analogue response to this emergency, yet if books had lost their power, populists would not now be burning and banning them. I hope, with this one, to have revealed the women profiled in its pages more clearly and clarified the role of communications technologies and social structures in transmitting myths about them. The first step to making positive change in the world is to understand the mechanisms that shape it. Moreover, these queens, princesses and duchesses are not just among the most visible women in history: they are fascinating, far more so than their caricatured versions lead us to believe. These were stories bursting to be told.

And I would also like to believe that at least a few readers will come away from *Divide and Rule* resolved to stop pitting royal women – or any women – against each other. You do not have to decide whether Victoria or the Elizabeths should top the best-monarch rankings. You can appreciate Katherine of Aragon *and* Anne Boleyn, Elizabeth I *and* either or both Marys, Diana *and* Camilla, Kate *and* Meghan and you certainly do not have to hate any of them.

Here is something else that makes me optimistic: the work being done to clear the 'sedimented mythology' that clogs our perceptions. Many of the best and brightest historians and curators of today are women, alert to the wider systems and structures that drive and distort history. A great pleasure of researching this book has been to familiarise myself with their research, lean on it, interview some of them and attend their lectures.

*

One autumnal evening, I listen, rapt, as Tracy Borman talks about her book, *The Stolen Crown*, which details the intrigues that swirled as Elizabeth I neared the end of her reign. Borman's account of double-dealing, murder plots and the rewriting of history would be gripping enough, but it adds to the excitement that we are gathered at the Charterhouse, in the room where the Tudor monarch held her first privy council. During the Q&A, a woman asks Borman why so many of Elizabeth's subjects celebrated James's accession. 'They'd had enough of queens,' says Borman, 'but quickly realised their mistake.'

The Windsors have no queens regnant in prospect to boost their popularity and just two consorts one current and one waiting: Camilla, who survived vilification to face the fresh trial of her husband's incurable cancer, and Kate, whose own survival has been under question. This compounds the vulnerability of an institution gripped by scandal and division while struggling to adjust its communications strategy to an age that manages to be simultaneously deeply sceptical and wildly credulous. Why should anyone put faith in what it says when its own members and press managers cannot be trusted?

'The difficulty now is trying to convince you, the press, that what you are being told is the truth,' complained one royal to the *Sun* back in 1988. 'You cannot believe you are being told the truth because for the last twenty years you haven't been. It's like the Russians.' Buckingham Palace rushed out this rebuttal: 'Further to certain articles that have appeared in this morning's press, the Duke of York wishes to make clear that the inference that palace officials had lied to the media in the past is incorrect.'

The statement was not strictly true then – officials had been economical with the truth about the state of various royal marriages and would continue to lie by omission on many other topics, not least in response to questions about the man formerly known as Prince. The ever-spreading scandals around Andrew offer seemingly iron-clad arguments for republicanism. It is a debate that is long overdue – and laden with risk.

Though by instinct no monarchist, I for years warned against ditching the institution without first addressing the weaknesses of the political systems in which it is embedded. Those concerns remain. Put bluntly: if the royals in any way act as a bulwark against tech-propelled populism, this might be a bad time to experiment with alternatives. However, the Crown's ability to unify and stabilise – never a given – looks more questionable than ever. It remains to be seen whether the current King and his heirs are able to rebuild public trust.

Charles is conflict-averse and given to agonising over decisions. We know less about the abilities and instincts of his successor, William, and next to nothing about the third in line, George. It falls to this all-male trio to rescue the monarchy. History suggests that a queen might make a better job of it.

Acknowledgements

'Let's go for a walk on the way to lunch,' she said, steering me towards a destination she had in mind from the moment we met years earlier. Lisa Milton may be a queen among publishers, but her softening-up technique comes straight from the Earl of Essex's playbook, *saepe cadendo*, slowly eroding my resolve never to write another book about the royals until suddenly I heard myself lay out the idea for this one. By the time we reached the restaurant that day, we had agreed a basic outline.

Of course she wanted me to deliver the book speedily, even though I was finishing a novel. Just as inevitably, I said yes. *Divide and Rule* marks the first time I have ever missed a publishing deadline, if only by a couple of months, so props to Lisa not only for her persistence but her forbearance. Plus, I would not have consented if I were not passionate about the subject. I enjoyed every moment of the research and the writing. I would also like to express my gratitude to everyone who helped me through the process, my wonderful editor Marleigh Price and the team at HQ Stories, my wise agent Eleanor Birne, my friends, sisters Cassie and Lise, stepmother Helen, stepsister Catherine, nephew Isaac, cousins, in-laws and godchildren.

My eldest sister, Cassie Mayer, is a brilliant researcher

and thinker, whose knowledge of history and horses proved exceptionally helpful on this project. Special thanks too to my dear friend, art historian Dr Nicola Jennings, who with every conversation casually pointed me to a connection or approach I might have missed. A host of curators, historians and authors generously offered advice, support and contacts, and sometimes consented to on-the-record interviews. Two magnificent women, Polly Putnam at Historic Royal Palaces and the author Sarah Gristwood, went further still, not only acting as sounding boards but reading key historical chapters and offering useful feedback.

I could not have written this book without the help of current and former palace insiders and other people connected to recent and current royalty. Thank you for your input and your trust.

Finally, it feels important to talk about the main reason I ran late with this book. My father, Professor David Mayer, was a distinguished (and extraordinary and funny and hyper-intelligent) theatre historian. If anyone inspired me to see history not as something dry and fixed and disconnected from the present but part of our world and changing with it, it was he. That understanding in turn influenced my approach to journalism as a first draft of history.

His death in 2023 hit hard, and while I was writing *Divide and Rule*, I found it useful to imagine conversations with him. Meanwhile I was lucky enough to be able to spend most Sundays with my surviving parent, my mother, Anne Mayer Bird, co-author with me of an earlier book for HQ Stories, our memoir, *Good Grief*, about losing our beloved husbands at the start of the pandemic. Her death in April 2025 knocked me off course for a while.

I am not sure I would have finished this book without the support of all those mentioned above and others, with special thanks to Santi Arribas, Joanna Baker, Josephine Fairley, Jeremy Gaines, Tess Glover, Joanne Mason, Elisha May, Aaron Moore, Daniel Slade, Sandi and Debbie Toksvig, all the Jenningses, the Pilates posse, the Women's Equality Party massive and the Primadonnas – who also include Lisa. Everything starts and ends with her.

Endnotes

Introduction

1   *The Diana Chronicles*; by Tina Brown; Chapter 4: The Super
Sloane; Century; 2007

Chapter 1

2   'Marquis or Marchioness? Analysing BL, Harley MS 303
and Other Previously Unpublished Sources about Anne
Boleyn's Elevation to the Marquisate of Pembroke'; by
Barbara Soberton; *The Court Historian*, Volume 29, Issue 3;
November 2024

3   'Latin Poems: To a Courtier'; by Sir Thomas More; from
A Thomas More Source Book; edited by Gerard B. Wegemer
and Stephen W. Smith; Catholic University of America
Press; 2004

4   'Was Henry VIII Infertile? Miscarriages and Male
Infertility in Tudor England'; by Valerie Shrimplin and
Chana N. Jayasena; *The Journal of Interdisciplinary History*;
September 2021

5   'Whoso List to Hunt, I Know where is an Hind'; by Sir
Thomas Wyatt; Poetry Foundation

Chapter 2

6   'The Myth of Elizabeth at Tilbury'; by Susan Frye; *The Sixteenth Century Journal*, Volume 23, Number 1; Spring 1992; The University of Chicago Press

7   'Written with a Diamond on her Window at Woodstock'; by the future Elizabeth I; 1554 or 1555; *Poetry Foundation*

Chapter 3

8   'The Labour Party and British Republicanism'; by Kenneth O. Morgan; *Laboratoire d'Etudes et de Recherches sur le Monde Anglophone (LERMA)*; February 2003

9   'The pox in Boswell's London: an estimate of the extent of syphilis infection in the metropolis in the 1770s'; by Simon Szreter and Kevin Siena; *The Economic History Review*; 1 July 2020

10   'Medicine and the 1851 Exhibition'; by C D T James; *Journal of the Royal Society of Medicine*; 1 December 1971

Chapter 4

11   'Liz Truss says in book queen told her to 'pace yourself', admits she didn't listen'; by Martin Pengelly; *Guardian*; 9 April 2024

12   'How the Queen was still gripped by racing and mating plans in her final days'; by Lee Mottershead; *Racing Post*; 19 September 2022

13   Penny Romsey's name changed as her husband inherited titles, eventually becoming Penny Knatchbull, Countess Mountbatten of Burma

14   'This Be the Verse'; by Philip Larkin; first published in *The New Humanist* magazine; 1971

Chapter 5

15   *Diana: Her True Story – In Her Own Words;* by Andrew
     Morton; transcripts of taped interviews; Michael O'Mara;
     2017

16   'Effect of death of Diana, Princess of Wales on suicide and
     deliberate self-harm'; *British Journal of Psychiatry;* Volume
     177, Issue 5; November 2000

17   'Dying to be famous: retrospective cohort study of rock
     and pop star mortality and its association with adverse
     childhood experiences'; by MA Bellis, K Hughes, O
     Sharples et al; *BMJ* Open; 2012

Chapter 6

18   'Prince is very, very weak, says his former top aide'; by
     Ian Katz; *Guardian;* 25 October 2003

Chapter 7

19   'Sexualising weight loss in British tabloids: celebrities
     "flaunting" their bodies during a pandemic'; by T.
     Coltman-Patel and D. Wright; *Journal of Language and
     Discrimination;* 2023

20   'Nous avons découvert des milliers de sites d'info générés
     par IA'; by Jean-Marc Manach; Société numérique; 8
     March 2025

Chapter 8

21   'Golden States of Mind: A Geography of California
     Consciousness'; by Erik Davis and Jonathan Taylor; *The
     Changing World Religion Map;* Springer; 20 November 2014

22   National Center for Health Statistics, 1980

23 'Black representation in film and TV: The challenges and impact of increasing diversity'; by Jonathan Dunn, Sheldon Lyn, Nony Onyeador, and Ammanuel Zegeye; McKinsey & Co; 11 March 2021

24 'A Systematic Review of Black People Coping With Racism: Approaches, Analysis, and Empowerment'; by Grace Jacob, Sonia C. Faber, Naomi Faber, Amy Bartlett, Allison J. Ouimet and Monnica T Williams; *Perspectives on Psychological Science*; Volume 18, Issue 2; March 2023

25 'Prejudice Events and Traumatic Stress among Heterosexuals and Lesbians, Gay Men, and Bisexuals'; by Edward J. Alessi; James I. Martin; Akua Gyamerah and Ilan H. Meyer; *Journal of Aggression, Maltreatment and Trauma*; Volume 22; 2023

Bibliography

The Life and Death of Anne Boleyn: 'The Most Happy'; by Eric Ives; Blackwell; 2004

Hunting the Falcon: Henry VIII, Anne Boleyn and the Marriage That Shook Europe; By John Guy and Julia Fox; Bloomsbury Publishing; 2023

Letters and Papers, Foreign and Domestic, Henry VIII; Her Majesty's Stationery Office, London; 1891

Love Letters of Henry VIII to Anne Boleyn; this edition originally published in Boston, 1906; Digital Text Publishing Company; 2009

Calendar of State Papers, Spain, 1536-1538; Her Majesty's Stationery Office, London; 1888

Henry VIII and the Court: Art, Politics and Performance; edited by Thomas Betteridge and Suzannah Lipscomb; Routledge; 2013

Lancelot de Carle's 1536 Letter; translated and edited by Christopher Smith; TwentyTrees; 2023

The Anne Boleyn Collection: The Real Truth about the Tudors; by Claire Ridgway; MadeGlobal Publishing; 2015

The Creation of Anne Boleyn; by Susan Bordo; Simon and Schuster; 2014

Anne of France: Lessons for my Daughter; translated and edited by Sharon L. Jansen; D.S. Brewer; 2004

The King's Painter: The Life and Times of Hans Holbein; by Franny Moyle; Head of Zeus; 2021

Anne Boleyn & Elizabeth I: The Mother and Daughter Who Changed History; by Tracy Borman; Hodder; 2024

Game of Queens: The Women Who Made Sixteenth-Century Europe, by Sarah Gristwood; Simon and Schuster; 2016

The Tudors in Love: The Courtly Code behind the Last Medieval Dynasty; by Sarah Gristwood; Oneworld Publications; 2021

Blood, Fire and Gold: The Story of Elizabeth I and Catherine de Medici; by Estelle Paranque; Ebury; 2022

Hall's chronicle: containing the history of England, during the reign of Henry the Fourth, and the succeeding monarchs, to the end of the reign of Henry the Eighth, in which are particularly described the manners and customs of those periods; by Edward Hall; first published in 1548

Lives of the Queens of England: From the Norman Conquest, with Anecdotes of Their Courts, Now First Published from Official Records, and Other Authentic Documents, Private as Well as Public; by Agnes Strickland; Blanchard and Lea; 1852

Elizabeth Tudor: The Lonely Queen; by Sir Arthur S. MacNalty; Christopher Johnson Ltd; 1954

Elizabeth I: Collected Works; edited by L. S. Marcus, J. Mueller, and M. B. Rose; Chicago University Press; 2000

Elizabeth's Bedfellows: An Intimate History of the Queen's Court; by Anna Whitelock; Bloomsbury; 2013

Elizabeth and her Circle; by Susan Doran; Oxford University Press; 2015

Elizabeth: The Forgotten Years; by John Guy; Viking; 2016

Rival Queens: The Betrayal of Mary, Queen of Scots; by Kate Williams; Hutchinson; 2018

Elizabeth and Essex: A Tragic History; by Lytton Strachey; Harcourt, Brace and Company; 1928

Sartorial Politics in Early Modern Europe: Fashioning Women; edited by Erin Griffey; Amsterdam University Press; 2019

The practyse of prelates. Compyled by the faythfull and godly learned man, Wyllyam Tyndale; imprinted at London by Anthony Scoloker and Willyam Seres; Dwellynge wythout Temple barre in the Sauoy rentes; 1548

The History of the Reformation of the Church of England in Six Volumes; by Gilbert Burnet; W Baynes; 1825

Selected Writings of John Knox: Public Epistles, Treatises, and Expositions to the Year 1559; Presbyterian Heritage Publications; 1995

Works of Martin Luther; A. J. Holman Company; 1915

Martinus Lutherus contra Henricum Regem Angliae (Martin Luther against Henry King of England); translated by the Rev. E. S. Buchanan; Charles A. Swift; 1928

A Thomas More Source Book; edited by Gerard B. Wegemer and Stephen W. Smith; Catholic University of America Press; 2004

Treason in Tudor England: Politics and Paranoia; by Lacey Baldwin Smith; Princeton University Press; 1986

The Printing Revolution in Early Modern Europe; by Elizabeth L. Eisenstein; Cambridge University Press; 1983; 2005

Elizabeth's England: An Afterlife in Fame and Fantasy; by Michael Dobson and Nicola J. Watson; Oxford University Press; 2002

The Queen's Slave Trader: John Hawkyns, Elizabeth I and the Trafficking in Human Souls; by Nick Hazlewood; William Morrow; 2004

In Search of a Kingdom: Francis Drake, Elizabeth I and the Perilous

Birth of the British Empire; by Laurence Bergreen; Mariner; 2022

The Stolen Crown: Treachery, Deceit and the Death of the Tudor Dynasty; by Tracy Borman; Hodder & Stoughton; 2025

Queen Anne: The Politics of Passion; by Anne Somerset; HarperPress; 2012

The Strangest Family: The Private Lives of George III, Queen Charlotte and the Hanoverians; by Janice Hadlow; William Collins; 2014

Queen Victoria's Journals; Royal Archives

The letters of Queen Victoria; edited by George Earle Buckle; Cambridge University Press; 2014; first published 1926

The Letters of Queen Victoria 1837-1861; edited by AC Benson and Viscount Esher; John Murray Publishers Ltd; 1908

Mrs Beeton's Book of Household Management; by Isabella Beeton; S.O. Beeton Publishing; 1861

The Woman Question: Society and Literature in Britain and America, 1837-1883; by Elizabeth K. Helsinger, Robin Lauterbach Sheets, William Veeder; Manchester University Press; 1983

Empress: Queen Victoria and India; by Miles Taylor; Yale University Press; 2018

Queen Victoria; by Lytton Strachey; Harcourt, Brace and Company; 1921

Queen Victoria: A Biographical Companion; by Helen Rappaport; Bloomsbury Academic; 2003

Prince Albert: The Man Who Saved the Monarchy; by A.N. Wilson; Harper; 2019

Victoria: A Life; by A.N. Wilson; Atlantic Books; 2014

Victoria: The Queen: An Intimate Biography; by Julia Baird; Random House; 2016

The Empress Brown. The Story of a Royal Friendship; by Tom Cullen;
The Bodley Head; 1969

Victoria's Secret: The Private Passion of a Queen; by Fern Riddell;
Ebury Press; 2025

*Victoria and Abdul: The Extraordinary True Story of the Queen's Closest
Confidant*; by Shrabani Basu; Rupa Publications India Pvt
Ltd; 2010

*Dearest Child: Letters between Queen Victoria and the Princess Royal
1858-1861*; edited by Roger Fulford; Evans Brothers Ltd; 1964

The Mystery of Princess Louise: Queen Victoria's Rebellious Daughter;
by Lucinda Hawksley; Chatto & Windus; 2013

The English Constitution; by Walter Bagehot; Chapman & Hall;
1867

The Soul of a Bishop; by H.G. Wells; Cassell; 1917

*Experiment in Autobiography. Discoveries and Conclusions of a Very
Ordinary Brain (Since 1866)*; by H.G. Wells; first published 1934;
J. B. Lippincott; 1967

Henry & Mary Ponsonby: Life at the Court of Queen Victoria; by
William M. Kuhn; Duckbacks; 2003

*The Little Princesses: The extraordinary story of the Queen's childhood
by her nanny*; by Marion Crawford; Cassell & Co Ltd; 1950

The Story of the Princess Elizabeth, told with the sanction of her parents;
by Anne Ring; John Murray; 1930

The Windsors at War: The Nazi Threat to the Crown; by Alexander
Larman; Weidenfeld & Nicolson; 2023

Traitor King: The Scandalous Exile of the Duke and Duchess of Windsor;
by Andrew Lownie; Blink Publishing; 2021

The Heart has its Reasons; by the Duchess of Windsor; The
Companion Book Club; 1958

That Woman: The Life of Wallis Simpson, Duchess of Windsor; by Anne Sebba; Weidenfeld & Nicolson; 2011

Winston S. Churchill: The Wilderness Years, 1929-1935; by Martin Gilbert; Houghton Mifflin; 1981

The Queen: A Biography of Elizabeth II; by Ben Pimlott; John Wiley & Sons; 1996

Elizabeth: An intimate portrait; by Gyles Brandreth; Michael Joseph; 2022

Queen Elizabeth II: Her Life in Our Times; by Sarah Bradford; Penguin; 2012

Diamond Queen: Elizabeth II and her People; by Andrew Marr; Macmillan; 2011

Prince Philip: Wise Words and Golden Gaffes; by Phil Dampier and Ashley Walton; Barzipan Publishing; 2012

Philip: The Final Portrait, first published as *Philip & Elizabeth: Portrait of a Marriage*; by Gyles Brandreth; Hodder & Stoughton; 2004, 2021

The Mountbattens: Their Lives and Loves; by Andrew Lownie; Blink Publishing; 2020

Mountbatten: The Official Biography; by Philip Ziegler; HarperCollins; 1985

The Palace Papers: Inside the House of Windsor – the Truth and the Turmoil; by Tina Brown; Penguin; 2022

Lady in Waiting: My Extraordinary Life in the Shadow of the Crown; by Anne Glenconner; Hodder & Stoughton; 2019

Dreams about H.M. The Queen and Other Members of the Royal Family; by Brian Masters; Blond and Briggs; 1972

Entitled: The Rise and Fall of the House of York; by Andrew Lownie; William Collins; 2025

Nobody's Girl: A Memoir of Surviving Abuse and Fighting for Justice; by Virginia Roberts Giuffre; Penguin; 2025

Yes Ma'am: The Secret Life of Royal Servants; by Tom Quinn; Biteback Publishing; 2025

All the Queen's Corgis: Corgis, dorgis and gundogs – the story of Elizabeth II and her most faithful companions; by Penny Junor; Hodder & Stoughton; 2018

Courtiers: The Hidden Power behind the Crown; by Valentine Low; Headline Press; 2022

Power and the Palace: The inside story of the monarchy and 10 Downing Street; by Valentine Low; Headline Press; 2025

The Rise and Fall of the House of Windsor; by A.N. Wilson; Sinclair-Stevenson; 1993

The Family Firm: Monarchy, Mass Media and the British Public, 1932–1953; by Dr Ed Owens; London University Press; 2019

The Diana Chronicles; by Tina Brown; Century; 2007

Diana: How Sexual Politics Shook the Monarchy; by Beatrix Campbell; The Women's Press; 1998

A Very Private School; by Charles Spencer; William Collins; 2024

Dicing with Di: The Amazing Adventures of Britain's Royal Chasers; by Mark Saunders and Glenn Harvey; Blake Publishing; 1996

Dianarama: The Betrayal of Princess Diana; by Andy Webb; Penguin; 2025

The Prince of Wales: A Biography; by Jonathan Dimbleby; Little, Brown & Company; 1994

Charles: The Heart of a King; by Catherine Mayer; WH Allen; Penguin Random House; 2015, 2022

Charles & Camilla: Portrait of a Love Affair; by Gyles Brandreth; 2006

Queen Consort: The Life of Queen Camilla, first published as *The Duchess: The Untold Story*; by Penny Junor; William Collins; 2017, 2023

A Greater Love: Charles and Camilla, the Inside Story of their Twenty-Three Year Relationship; by Christopher Wilson; Headline Book Publishing; 1995

Charles III: New King. New Court. The Inside Story; by Robert Hardman; Pan Macmillan; 2024

Rebel King: The Making of a Monarch; by Tom Bower; William Collins; 2018

Catherine: The Princess of Wales; by Robert Jobson; John Blake Publishing; 2024

Kate: The Future Queen; by Katie Nicholl; Hachette; 2013

Kate: The Making of a Princess; by Claudia Joseph; Mainstream; 2009

Kate: A biography; by Marcia Moody; Michael O'Mara; 2013

The New Royals: Elizabeth's Legacy and the Future of the Crown; by Katie Nicholl; Hachette; 2022

Battle of Brothers: William, Harry and the Inside Story of a Family in Tumult; by Robert Lacey; William Collins; 2020

Spare; by Prince Harry; Penguin; 2023

Revenge: Meghan, Harry and the war between the Windsors; by Tom Bower; Blink Publishing; 2022

Finding Freedom: Harry and Meghan and the Making of a Modern Royal Family; by Omid Scobie and Carolyn Durand; HQ Stories; 2020

Endgame: Inside the Royal Family and the Monarchy's Fight for Survival; by Omid Scobie; HQ Stories; 2023

Opinion Polls: History, Theory and Practice; by Nick Moon; Manchester University Press; 1999

ONE PLACE. MANY STORIES

Bold, innovative and
empowering publishing.

FOLLOW US ON:

@HQStories

If you're into it, read into it.

Reading expands worlds, sharpens minds, and fuels creativity. But fewer of us are making time for it.

The National Year of Reading is a campaign designed to inspire more people to make reading a regular part of their lives.

Find out how HarperCollins is supporting the campaign and get free resources at **harpercollins.co.uk/go-all-in**

Proud to support